AF412428

Light of Liberation

Light of Liberation

A History of Buddhism in India

Crystal Mirror Series

Volume VIII

Library of Congress Cataloging-in-Publication Data

Light of Liberation: a history of Buddhism in India.
   (Crystal mirror series: v. 8)
   Compiled by the Yeshe De Research Project and edited
   by Elizabeth Cook.
   Includes bibliographical references and index.
   1. Buddhism--India--History.   I. Cook, Elizabeth.
   II. Yeshe De Project.   III. Series.

BQ286.L54 1992   294.3'0954-dc20   92-16436
ISBN 0–89800-242-7 (pbk)   ISSN: 0097-7209

Frontispiece: Śākyamuni Buddha and scenes from his life.
Illustrations on pp. 2, 36, 76, 148, and 294 courtesy of
John C. and Susan L. Huntington.
Maps courtesy of the Yeshe De Research Project.

Series editor: Tarthang Tulku. Manuscript for *Light of Liberation*
prepared and edited by Elizabeth Cook.

Typeset in Adobe New Aster with New Aster Outline titles and initials.
Printed and bound by Dharma Press, U.S.A.

08 06 04 02 00 98 96 95 10 9 8 7 6 5 4 3 2

Contents

Charts, Illustrations and Maps

Charts and Illustrations

Maps

Introduction

*Although I showed you the means of liberation,
you must know that it depends on you alone.*
　　　　　　　　　　　—*Śākyamuni Buddha*

Before the Parinirvāṇa, the Buddha Śākyamuni urged his disciples to study the Dharma with diligence and evaluate his teachings in the light of reason. Verifying the truth of his teachings in direct experience, the Sangha, the community of the Buddha's disciples, came to comprehend the possibility of enlightenment and awakened confidence in the path. Continued by successive generations of enlightened masters, the Sangha has perpetuated the Buddha's example and teachings to the present day. These Three Jewels—the Buddha, Dharma, and Sangha—are the very heart of the Buddhist tradition. They point out the way things are, illumine the path to enlightenment, and provide the refuge and support of all Buddhist practitioners.

For more than a millennium, as the Dharma has entered new cultures, ways have been found to present the Buddha,

Dharma, and Sangha that instill a deep understanding of the compassion and wisdom communicated in the Buddha's life and teachings. Rooted in knowledge and appreciation of the Three Jewels, the Dharma has grown like a great tree, branching into numerous traditions, each bearing a rich array of flowers and fruits.

In recent years the branches of all Buddhist traditions have offered their spiritual riches to the West. There is now available a wealth of books on specific traditions and lineages, on the philosophies, psychology, logic, art, and poetry generated over millennia of Dharma study and realization. But the very abundance of teachings at hand may obscure an important issue: The roots that sustain all manifestations of the Dharma have not yet fully formed in the West; they need to penetrate deep enough into the Western consciousness to nourish the growth of new branches, bring forth new leaves and flowers, and become capable of fully manifesting enlightened knowledge.

The Buddha, Dharma, and Sangha—the foundation of all Buddhist traditions—are in themselves vast and profound teachings of enormous value. But there are many serious students of Buddhism in the West who have not had sufficient opportunity to study these teachings deeply enough to appreciate their full significance.

Since 1969, the Crystal Mirror Series has attempted to present such basic Buddhist teachings as the nature of the Buddha, the meaning of his life and enlightenment, and the importance of the Sangha as an inspiration and support. The earliest volumes, published when Tibetan Buddhism was nearly unknown in the West, lay the groundwork for a more complete understanding of Buddhist psychology, philosophy, practices, and history. They provided a basic orientation to the continuity of the Buddha, Dharma, and Sangha from their first manifestation to their transmission to Tibet, and the lineages of enlightened masters who established the roots of the Dharma in that land. More recent volumes have given a traditional unfolding of the meaning of Buddha, Dharma, and Sangha and presented the Three Jewels within the perspective of world history.

This volume emphasizes the life of the Buddha and the early history of the Sangha based on the Buddha's direct teachings: the Sūtras, Avadānas, and Vinaya. Although the Buddhist traditions hold differing views on the nature of the Buddha, the dates of the Parinirvāṇa, and the specific content of significant events, the information in this book provides students of all schools a general background for reading the Sūtras and reflecting on the Buddha's direct teachings. Reading the Sūtras opens the heart to the Buddha's wisdom and compassion; from this rapport with the view and scope of the Dharma teachings, one can more clearly discern the shape and flow of more than 2,500 years of Dharma transmission.

A special focus is the history of Buddhism in India from the time of the Buddha until the end of the twelfth century. This subject has a special importance to Dharma students: Where Buddhism figures prominently in the histories of Śrī Laṅkā, Southeast Asia, China, Japan, and other Buddhist cultures, India lost this important part of its heritage for many centuries. In the culture where the Buddha lived and became enlightened, where the Sangha flourished for more than sixteen centuries, memory of its existence virtually vanished from the historical record.

In the nineteenth century, the discovery of Nālandā, the Ajaṇṭā caves, and other magnificent Buddhist monuments by British archaeologists focused world attention on India as the homeland of Buddhism. European historians delved into the chronicles preserved in Śrī Laṅkā, Tibet, and other lands to piece together what was known of the Dharma in India. As foreigners to the culture, they worked without an inside knowledge of India or the Buddhist traditions, and their conclusions were vulnerable to distortion and misunderstanding. While this work has recently been taken up by

Indian historians and archaeologists, the historical and spiritual importance of Buddhism still tends to be distorted, minimized, or even overlooked. Many Indian accounts make little mention of Buddhism or regard it as simply one of many outgrowths of Hinduism. The centuries of disconnection with the Buddhist traditions have left their mark; although in Asian lands Buddhism was largely responsible for India's reputation as a spiritual center, India does not seem quite comfortable with Buddhism and tends to view it as somehow separate, as a curiosity rather than as an integral part of the Indian heritage. However well the works of European and Indian scholars communicate specific facts, their interpretations of these facts are not always accurate or helpful to students of the Dharma traditions.

As far as possible, this volume attempts to present to students of the Dharma an inside view of Buddhist history in clear, simple terms, leaving to scholars the work of detailed analysis and commentary. The travel guides of fifth- and seventh-century Chinese pilgrims—Fa-hien, Hsüan-tsang, and I-tsing—provide interesting first-hand descriptions of Buddhism in India, and Bu-ston's and Tāranātha's histories of the Dharma give extensive information on many otherwise blank historical periods. Modern historical and archaeological research has greatly enhanced knowledge of Buddhist history, and information from these sources has been selectively included. The suggested readings following most chapters encourage readers to investigate their topics further in the texts of all Buddhist traditions, as well as in modern sources. Full bibliographical information for books listed in the suggested readings is given on pp. 414–419.

Maps and Abbreviations

More than fifty charts and maps summarize information for easy reference. The maps in this volume are slightly modified versions of maps originally prepared in 1980 for the *Nyingma Edition of the Tibetan Buddhist Canon*. While the text of this book uses the abbreviations B.C.E. (before common era) and C.E. (common era) rather than the more common Western abbreviations B.C. and A.D., the maps were prepared with dates referenced as B.C. or A.D. Since there is no actual difference between the two dating systems, we have printed the maps without changing these abbreviations. The maps also refer to Kaśmīr, whereas the body of the book employs the more familiar modern spelling of Kashmir.

Wherever possible, the names of canonical texts, on first mention, are followed by indications of their position in the Nyingma Edition of the Tibetan Canon (NE + number). Similarly, texts in the Pāli Canon are referenced by DN (Dīgha-nikāya) or MN (Majjhima-nikāya), and texts in the Taishō edition of the Chinese Canon, where noted, are referenced by T followed by their number in that edition.

The Sanskrit forms of names are used throughout this volume, except in the chapter on Śrī Laṅkā and for citations or accounts deriving directly from Pāli texts.

Date of the Buddha: A Chronological Note

Morality, samādhi, insight, and freedom—
these are the glorious Truths,
unsurpassed, seen by Gautama.
Knowing the Truths, he declared them to bhikṣus.
Putting an end to pain, the Teacher with Vision
passes into nirvāṇa. —*Mahāparinibbāna-sutta*

Buddhist cultures usually base their calendars and chronology on the date of the Buddha's Parinirvāṇa, a primary point of reference in the traditional histories of the Buddha, Dharma, and Sangha. Although the traditions agree on the length of the Buddha's life and the major events that took place at that time, there is no clear consensus concerning the actual dates of the Buddha's birth and Parinirvāṇa. While all traditions agree that the Buddha was contemporaneous with Bimbisāra and Ajātaśatru, kings of Magadha known to many sources, the chronology of ancient India is far from reliable. Only in the sixth century B.C.E. did the records of kingdoms and their rulers begin to emerge from the realm of legend and take on historical substance.

Still, great gaps exist in our knowledge of India's pre-modern history. What we view as one country today has historically been a kaleidoscope of shifting principalities, kingdoms, and empires. As a result, Indian culture accommodates a wide range of diversity but has difficulty in recovering its history. Dynastic records were often partially or completely lost in the shifts of empire or foreign invasions. The pre-thirteenth-century chronologies that remain were based on the reigns of kings referred to by a bewildering array of titles and epithets, and the profusion of similar or identical titles of rulers complicates comparisons of dynastic records to ascertain exact dates. Whole periods of history—including the time of Aśoka, ruler of India's most extensive empire—vanished from the secular records for centuries and have only been recently partially recovered through the efforts of modern archaeologists and historians. The centuries prior to the Gupta Empire are nearly unknown, and the rise of that empire is still obscure.

Buddhism developed in this historical context, and in some cases, such as Aśoka and his reign, Buddhist records contribute significantly to the historical record. Yet the same factors affecting the dating of Indian history also complicate dating of Buddhist history. Traditional Buddhist historians and modern Buddhologists alike have attempted to address these problems with varying degrees of success.

For the most part, the Buddhist traditions rely in their calculations on genealogies, chronologies, or statements in teachings spoken by the Buddha, and the results vary depending on source and calculation techniques. The earliest date for the Buddha's Parinirvāṇa, calculated by the paṇḍita Sureśamati, is 2420 B.C.E. Atīśa, the Indian paṇḍita who worked for the Dharma in Tibet during the eleventh century, arrived at the date 2136 B.C.E. However, Kamalaśīla, disciple of the eighth century paṇḍita Śāntarakṣita, determined the date as 718 B.C.E.

Three Tibetan sources place the date of the Parinirvāṇa in the third millennium B.C.E.: the rGya-bod-yig-tshang gives 2150 B.C.E., dBus-pa-blo-gsal gives 2146, and Sa-skya Paṇḍita calculated the date as 2133 B.C.E. The Tibetan calculist 'Phags-pa-lhun-grub, who compiled an astrological treatise in the sixteenth century, arrived at 961 B.C.E. as the Buddha's birthdate, placing the Parinirvāṇa in 881 B.C.E. These are the dates preferred by Bu-ston and followed by the late Dudjom Rinpoche, an outstanding modern Nyingma scholar. This date for the Parinirvāṇa is very close to the 876 B.C.E. that Bu-ston calculated from the Kālacakra-tantra. Scholars of the Jo-nang-pa school calculated 835 B.C.E.

Basing his calculations on the history of the sandalwood Buddha, the Tibetan master 'Tshal-pa Kun-dga'-rdo-rje calculated the date of the Parinirvāṇa at 750 B.C.E. O-rgyan-pa arrived at a date of 651 B.C.E. The latest date related for the Parinirvāṇa in the Tibetan tradition is 544/543 B.C.E., calculated by Śākyaśrī, last abbot of Vikramaśīla, who took refuge in Tibet in the fourteenth century.

The *Blue Annals* refers to an early Chinese tradition that traces to Fo-lin (Horin) (572–640), which gives the date of the Parinirvāṇa as 949 B.C.E. This tradition, recorded in an inscription noted by 'Gos Lo-tsā-ba, author of the *Blue Annals,* was accepted by the Japanese masters Honen, Shinran, and Nichiren; it is followed today in the schools they founded: Jodo, Jodo-Shinshu, and Nichirenshu, respectively.

The Southern, or Theravādin tradition, uniformly places the Parinirvāṇa in 544 B.C.E. This dating relies in part on the "dotted record," the tradition of placing a dot in the Vinaya scriptures at the conclusion of the early rainy season retreat. Modern Japanese scholars have pointed out that this tradition cannot be traced with confidence before the eleventh century, and it is incompatible with what is known about the chronology of the kings of Magadha. A similar tradition came to China in 489 C.E. through Saṃghabhadra, who had counted 975 dots in the Vinaya as of that date.

This "dotted record" is said to have been started by Upāli, the Arhat who recited the Vinaya a year after the Buddha's Parinirvāṇa. This places the Parinirvāṇa in 486 B.C.E. and the Buddha's birthdate in 566 B.C.E. Some modern scholars have adjusted this "dotted record" date to 483 B.C.E., which coincides with W. Geiger's calculations based on the Pāli chronicles. Some historians find this calculation very persuasive; others reject it for lack of evidence that there was a written Vinaya that traces back to the first year after the Parinirvāṇa. (The first mention of "writing down" the texts of the southern tradition dates to 58 B.C.E. in Śrī Laṅkā).

A more recent date proposed for the Buddha is 466–386 B.C.E., calculated by modern Japanese scholars from stories in Sanskrit, Tibetan, and Chinese versions of texts such as the Samayabhedoparacana-cakra. It has recently been proposed that these dates be altered to 463–383 B.C.E. to accord with recent research on the date of Aśoka's reign.

Another approach to the date of the Buddha is to ascertain the correct dates for Aśoka, since various Buddhist accounts place the Aśoka's reign at specific times after the Buddha's Parinirvāṇa. The Mahāvaṃsa, a Theravādin text in Pāli, records that Aśoka came to the throne 218 years after the Parinirvāṇa. The Mañjuśrī-mūlakalpa and other Sanskrit Buddhist texts place Aśoka one hundred or 110 years after the Parinirvāṇa. In Indian chronology, Aśoka's date primarily depends on the dates of his grandfather, Candragupta Maurya, whom many scholars consider the same person as Plutarch's Sandrocottus, an Indian who counseled Alexander the Great to attack the Nanda Emperor. This places Candragupta Maurya around 324 B.C.E., although exactly when he became king is uncertain.

Sources for Mauryan chronology include the Arthaśāstra of Kauṭilya Candragupta's minister, and the records of Megasthenes, ambassador of the Greek general Seleucus

Nicator. (Megasthenes' records no longer exist, but his descriptions are preserved in the writings of many Greek and Latin writers.) Even so, at least one Indian scholar has expressed concern that Candragupta Maurya has been confused with Candragupta I of the Gupta Dynasty, and that Candragupta Maurya actually lived much earlier than is generally supposed.

One of the strongest confirmations of Aśoka's dates is from one of Aśoka's own edicts early in his reign, where he mentions Antiochus II Theos of Syria, Ptolemy II Philadelphus of Egypt, Antigonus Gonatas of Macedonia, Magas of Cyreme and Alexander of Epirus (*Rock Edict XIII*, in Kaliṅga). From this, Aśoka's reign appears to have been around 271 B.C.E. This would give a date for the Buddha's Parinirvāṇa around 371 or 489 B.C.E., depending on whether one places Aśoka's rule one hundred or 218 years after the Parinirvāṇa.

Still another approach is to look at the dating of other traditions which can be linked to the life of the Buddha, Dharma, and Sangha. From accounts of the Buddha's life, it is quite probable that Mahāvīra, founder of the Jain tradition, was a contemporary of the Buddha, as was Gosāla Maskarīputra, founder of the Ājīvikas. Although Mahāvīra is generally considered to have lived around 540–468 B.C.E., this is not completely unanimous, nor do we know if the Buddha entered Parinirvāṇa before or after Mahāvīra. Jain sources relate that Mahāvīra was patronized by the same kings as was the Buddha; Jain authorities place the death of Mahāvīra after the Buddha's Parinirvāṇa, whereas the Pāli Suttas (Dīgha-nikāya 29 and Majjhima-nikāya 104) relate the Buddha's reaction to the death of Nātaputta (Sanskrit Jñātaputra, son of the Jñātas, one of the Vrjian tribes; a common referent for Mahāvīra).

While attempts to piece together an exact chronological record for early Buddhist history will and must continue, the task is much like assembling a three-dimensional puzzle whose pieces are subject to reshuffling at any moment in light of new information. In the last century, archaeological excavations have illuminated many dark periods and provided a wealth of important information. Fragments of history take form that can be compared to the records and dated coin artifacts of Persians, Greeks, Parthians, Kuṣāṇas and other peoples who sequentially maintained a presence northwest of the Indus River from the time of Darius I. The works of Indian and Western scholars who have made extensive studies of Indian and Buddhist chronology are generally available and need not be repeated here. Interested readers will find that the dates of many important rulers, masters, and events still remain controversial.

Until we are certain we have complete knowledge, it seems best to keep an open mind to all the chronologies preserved within the Buddhist tradition. For this reason, all dates mentioned in this volume are conditional, useful for a general orientation to historical time and place, but not to be taken as definitive.

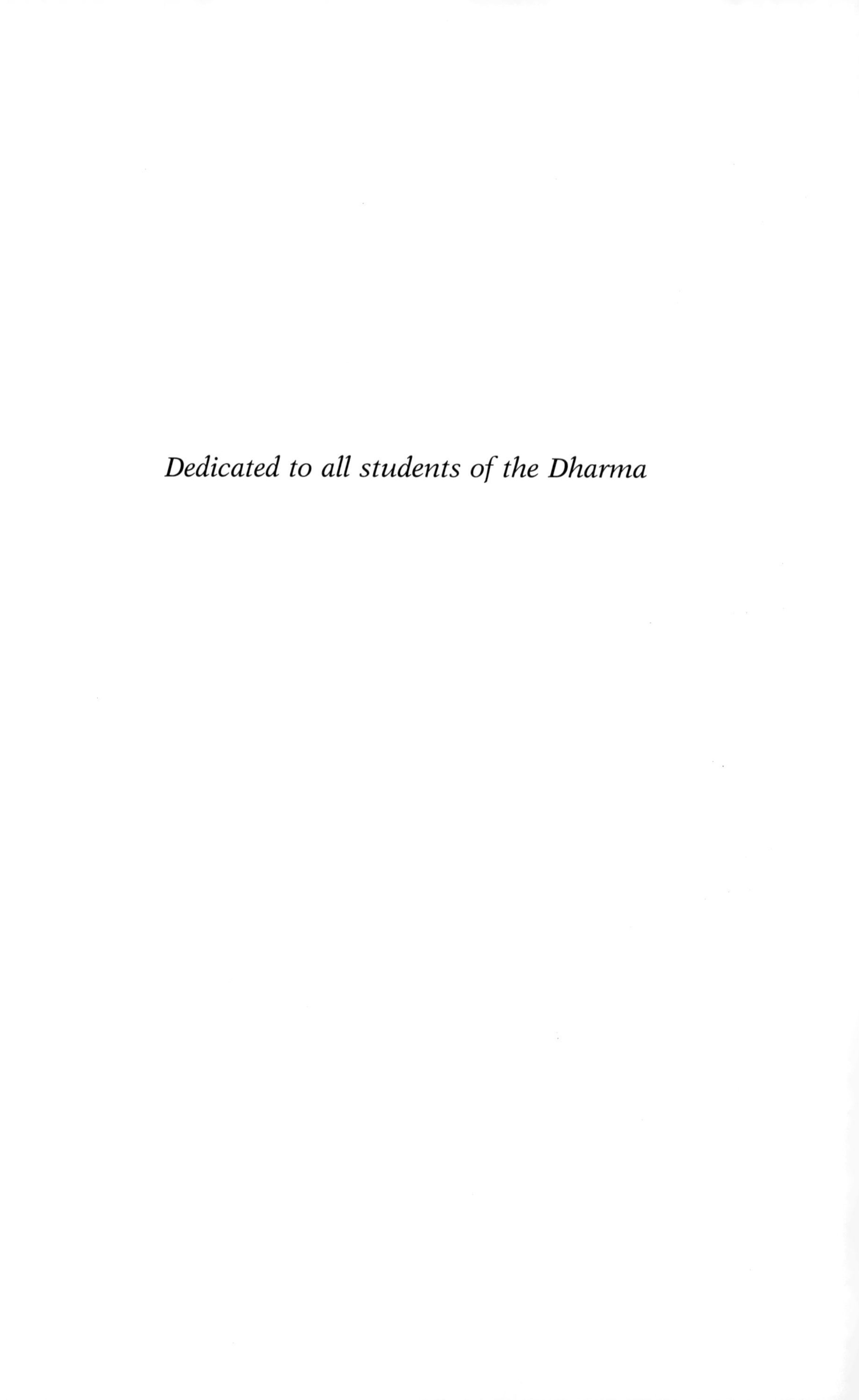

Dedicated to all students of the Dharma

Light of Liberation

Part One

The Historical Context

The Cosmological Setting

*You will become, O young Brahmin, in the future,
after an immeasurable, incalculable kalpa, in
Kapilavastu, the city of the Śākyas, a Tathāgata
named Śākyamuni, an Arhat, a perfect Buddha . . .
an unsurpassed knower of the world.*

—*Buddha Dīpaṁkara*

From ancient times to the present day, the Indian historical perspective has been shaped by concepts of cyclical
time and multidimensional space. Meaning emerged from
relationship of events and patterns, with chronology and
random events assuming a secondary role. History was
viewed as dynamic and flexible, continually forming and
transforming within the context of a vast cosmology vibrant
with the interplay of space and time. Such a cosmology encompasses vast universes that are born, develop, and disintegrate in tune with great pulses in time that define the
beginning and end of kalpas—aeons so vast that they encom-

pass the life cycles of countless world-systems and innumerable beings.

There is no beginning to this progression of kalpas, nor is there a final end. Buddhist history establishes the Buddha Śākyamuni within this inconceivable range of time. In the Bhadrakalpika-sūtra (NE 94), Śākyamuni Buddha speaks of events countless kalpas past, in a vision that also illumines events far in the future. Another text, the Mahāvastu, describes a time span of one hundred thousand kalpas, which is considered too short for a being to develop the roots of virtue and attain the condition of a Buddha.

Each kalpa has unique characteristics: Some are filled with light, and many Buddhas appear to show beings the way to enlightenment. Other kalpas are dark; though the Dharma persists, no Buddhas appear to illuminate the way. According to the Mahāvastu, it was possible for one hundred thousand dark kalpas to pass between the appearance of one Buddha and the next. Śākyamuni himself matured the roots of virtue for immeasurable, incalculable kalpas, venerating countless Buddhas and advancing through the stages of the Bodhisattva path in innumerable lifetimes. In the kalpa previous to this one, a kalpa of exceedingly long duration, he was Megha, the young Brahmin who vowed in the presence of the Buddha Dīpaṁkara to become a perfectly enlightened being. Dīpaṁkara then foretold the time, place, and circumstances when Megha would become a Buddha.

"You will become, O young Brahmin, in the future, after an immeasurable, incalculable kalpa, in Kapilavastu, the city of the Śākyas, a Tathāgata named Śākyamuni, an Arhat, a perfect Buddha, gifted with knowledge and conduct, a Sugata, an unsurpassed knower of the world, a driver of tameable beings, a teacher of gods and men, as I now am. You will become gifted with the eighteen special attributes of a Buddha, strong with a Tathāgata's ten powers, and confident with the four grounds of self-confidence. Having yourself crossed over, you will lead others across; emancipated, you

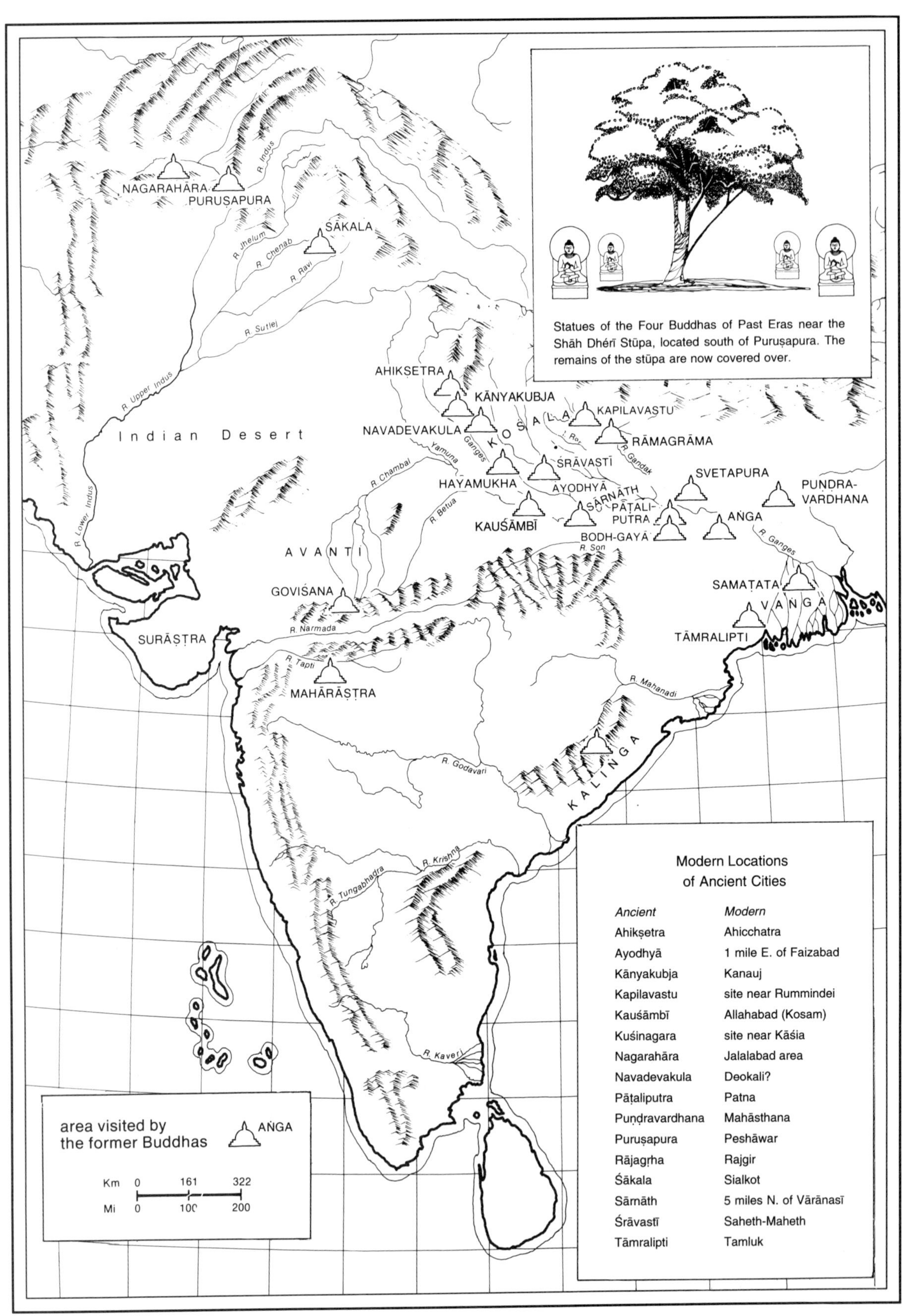

Sites of visits of four Buddhas of past eras were described by the pilgrim Hsüan-tsang.

will emancipate others; comforted, you will comfort others; having won final release you will give final release to others, as I now do. So will you set rolling the incomparable Wheel of Dharma. So will you preserve a body of disciples in harmony. So will devas and humans deem you worthy to be heard and believed. And as I now am, you will become a Buddha for the welfare and happiness of mankind, out of compassion for the world, for the sake of the great multitude, and for the welfare and happiness of gods and men." (*Mahāvastu* I, p. 195)

Our Present Aeon

According to the Mahākaruṇāpuṇḍarīka (NE 111), a great flood ended the previous kalpa. From the great ocean that engulfed the world, one thousand golden lotuses arose, an auspicious sign that one thousand Buddhas would brighten the coming aeon. The kalpa in which we now live thus became known as the Bhadrakalpa, the Fortunate Aeon, the kalpa to be blessed by the birth, enlightenment, and teachings of a thousand great beings.

The Bhadrakalpika-sūtra celebrates the great procession of these thousand Buddhas. After describing the teaching of the ten strengths, the samādhi that develops these strengths, and the perfections that open the door to this most profound and transforming of all samādhis, the Bhadrakalpika-sūtra names each of the thousand Buddhas of our aeon, detailing the circumstances of each Buddha's birth, the extent of his life, his disciples, and the duration of his teaching. Śākyamuni, the Buddha of our time, is the fourth Buddha of the Bhadrakalpa, following the Buddhas Krakucchanda, Kanakamuni, and Kāśyapa. Other sources, including the Kālacakratantra (NE 362), name seven Buddhas before Śākyamuni, beginning with the Tathāgata Vipaśyin. As the Tibetan scholar Bu-ston points out, there is no error in this, for since the seven are Buddhas that have arisen in this world (in previous kalpas as well as our own), they can be counted as precursors to Śākyamuni. All sources agree that the next Buddha will be Maitreya, who will once again set the wheel of the Dharma in motion.

Future Aeons

The Bhadrakalpika-sūtra teaches that following this Bhadrakalpa will be sixty dark aeons of great extent, in which the lifetime of beings will be extremely short, and no Buddhas will appear to teach the Dharma. Then will come the Bright Aeon, brilliant with ten thousand Buddhas, in which many of those predicted to attain enlightenment in past aeons will realize the fruit of their efforts and inspire similar efforts in others. After the Bright Aeon will come ten thousand dark aeons, followed by the Starlike Aeon, when eighty thousand Buddhas will appear to teach the Dharma. Then, after three hundred long dark aeons, the kalpa named Guṇavyūha will come, when eighty-four thousand Buddhas will appear. Beings who awaken the aspiration for enlightenment continue to mature into Buddhas throughout all time. The light and energy generated by each Buddha's enlightenment counters the forces of entropy and human lethargy, ensuring blessings of the Dharma for all living beings.

Structure of the Physical World

Buddhist cosmology sets forth a picture of a threefold universe (traidhātuka) where beings have five possible destinies (gati): that of the hells, animals, hungry ghosts, humans, and gods. A sixth classification is often included to make up six forms of existence: hell-beings, animals, hungry ghosts, humans, asuras, and gods. The traidhātuka comprises the Kāmadhātu, or realm of desire, home of beings of all destinies, including the lower ranks of the gods; the Rūpadhātu, or realm of form; and the Arūpadhātu, or the formless realm. These realms are further subdivided into levels that reflect the consciousness of the beings that inhabit them: one level each for hell-beings, animals, hungry ghosts, and humans, and twenty-seven heavens for different classes of gods.[1]

The Kāmadhātu, or realm of desire, as all the three basic divisions, comes into being through the operation of karma. Within its purview is the world as we know it, as well as the hell realms and six of the heavens. The physical world (bhājanaloka, also called the "receptacle world") is essentially circular; at its base is a thick and dense circle of wind, supporting a thick circle of water. The water, agitated by the wind of karmic actions, forms a circular layer of gold on its surface. From this circle of gold arise nine great mountain systems, with Mt. Meru (also known as Mt. Sumeru) at the center, towering over all.

Mt. Meru, broad at its base, narrowing at its middle, and broadening at its peak, forms the very axis of our physical world. Mt. Meru is formed of four jewel-substances: gold, silver, lapis, and crystal, with each substance facing one of the four directions (gold on the north, silver on the east, lapis on the south, and crystal on the west). Arranged around Mt. Meru in concentric circles are seven great mountain systems made of gold: Yugandhara, Īṣādhara, Khadiraka, Sudarśana, Aśvakarṇa, Vinataka, and Nimindhara. These mountains form unbroken great walls that diminish in height from the center outward: each range is half the height of the range it encircles. Mt. Meru (80,000 yojanas tall)[2] is the highest, and Nimindhara, the exterior rim that envelops Meru and the six inner wall-mountains, is the lowest. Between each of these wall-mountains is a great sea as wide as the bordering mountain is tall; all of the mountains are immersed eight thousand yojanas below the seas and rest on the golden circle. The outermost sea is the great ocean formed of salt-water,

---

1. The following information is based on chapter three of the Abhidharmakoṣabhāṣya, a text by Vasubandhu (late fourth or early fifth century C.E.) which is essentially a compilation of earlier teachings with Vasubandhu's explications.

2. One yojana equals eight kilometers or about five miles.

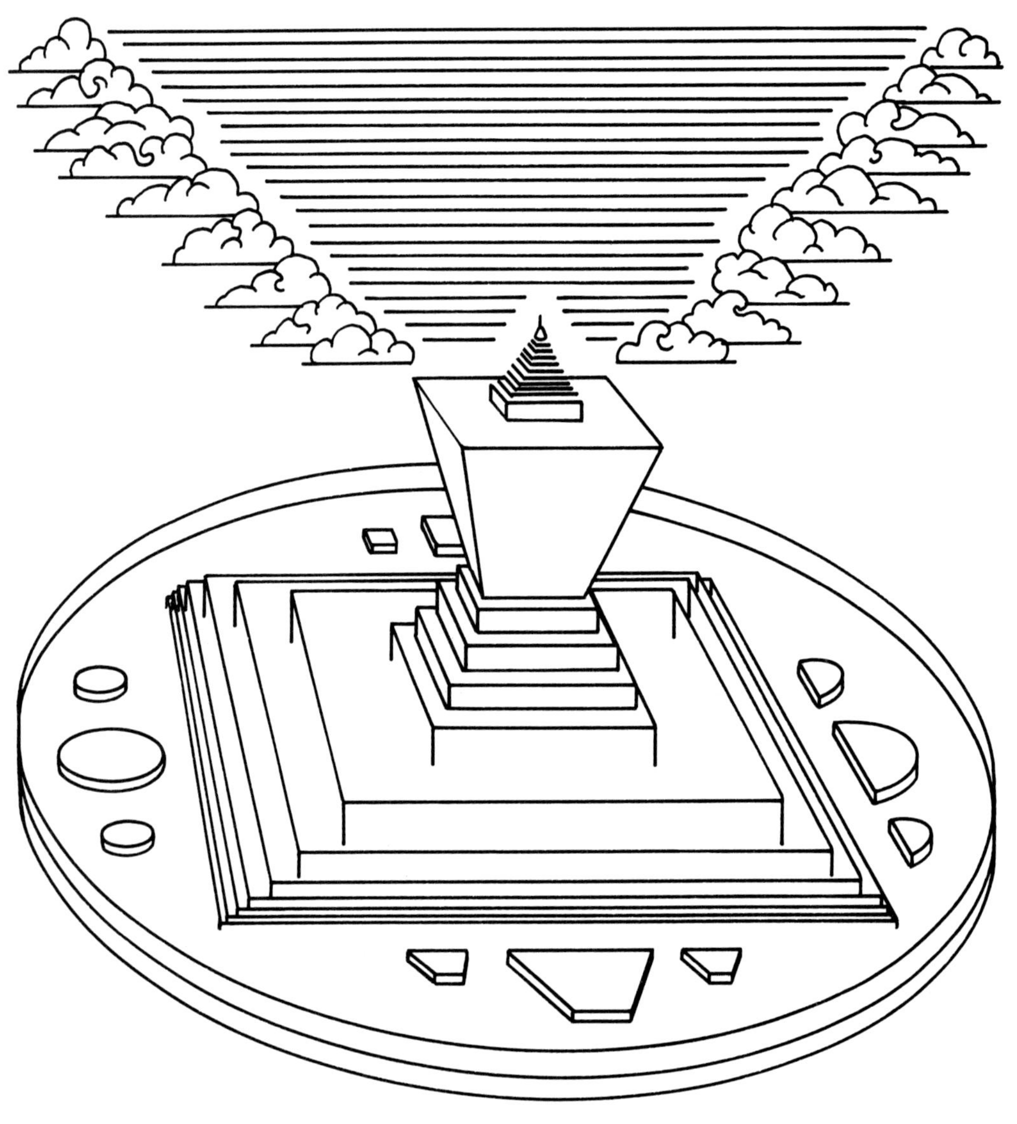

The World: A Mandalic Representation

322,000 yojanas wide, in which reside innumerable sea-creatures. Under the great ocean north of Mt. Meru is the palace of Sāgara, the nāga king, where the Buddha taught the Dharma to great assemblies of nāgas, as recorded in such Sūtras as the Sāgaranāgarāja-paripṛcchā (NE 153), Anavataptanāgarāja-paripṛcchā (NE 156), and Mahāmeghavāyumaṇḍala-sūtra (NE 234).

In this ocean are four great continents. South from Mt. Meru is Jambudvīpa, the "rose-apple island," shaped like a carriage, broad at the north and narrow at the south end. Jambudvīpa, the continent where the Buddha was born, is often used as a synonym for the world itself. Pūrvavideha, facing Meru's eastern side, is shaped like a half-moon; Godānīya, facing Meru's western side, is round like the full moon, and Kuru, a square continent, faces Meru's northern side. There are also eight smaller continents evenly spaced between the larger ones and named for the people that inhabit them. Encircling this entire world-system are the Cakra mountains composed of iron that form the ninth great mountain system. With the four major and eight smaller continents appearing like spokes in its embrace, this outermost circle of mountains resembles the rim of a great wheel.

Since Jambudvīpa faces the side of Mt. Meru formed from lapis, its atmosphere and the surrounding ocean is blue in color. Below Jambudvīpa lie the sixteen major hell realms, consisting of eight hot hells and eight cold. Of the hot hells, the lowest one is Avīci, twenty thousand yojanas below Jambudvīpa, where suffering is intense and unbroken by even an instant of relief. The highest is the Saṁjīva hell, where there are periods of recovery. The cold hells correspond to the hot hells; the lowest, Arbuda, is the metaphysical equivalent of absolute zero, and the highest is the Mahāpadma hell.

Above the world rise the heaven realms. The lowest of these encompass the six heavens of the devas (gods) of the Kāmadhātu. Beyond the Kāmadhātu are sixteen additional heavens belonging to the Rūpadhātu, or form realm, the very highest of these heavens being the Akaniṣṭha Heaven. Above the Rūpadhātu are the five divisions of the Arūpadhātu, the formless realm.

Since the Kāmadhātu realms are all perpetuated and bound by desire, the devas of the Kāmadhātu come under the power of Māra, Lord of Illusion, and do not perceive the true nature of existence. Thus, even the devas benefit from the Dharma taught by a Buddha, a fully enlightened being. The Sūtras record that the Buddha taught extensively in the heaven realms, and devas and non-human beings of all kinds would also come to Jambudvīpa to hear the Buddha teach the Dharma to human beings.

The most numerous of the devas in the Kāmadhātu realm are the Caturmahārājakāyikas—yakṣas and demigods of the realm of the Four Great Kings, who live on the four terraces on the sides of Mt. Meru and thus inhabit the physical world. Above them are the devas of the Trāyastriṁśa, the abode of the Thirty-three Devas, who live on the summit of Mt. Meru. The inhabitants of this realm are similar to the Olympians of the classical world. At the center of their city is the palace of Indra (Śakra), lord of the Trāyastriṁśa Heaven, who frequently attends the Buddha's teachings and questions the Enlightened One on points of doctrine. This is the realm where the mothers of the Buddhas are reborn seven days after they give birth, and where each Buddha, after his enlightenment, ascends to teach the Abhidharma to his mother and other beings residing here.

The other devas of the Kāmadhātu all have aerial dwellings; from lowest to highest, these devas are the Yāmas, the Tuṣitas, the Nirmāṇaratis, and the Paranirmitavaśavartins. Of these four realms, the Tuṣita Heaven is the one most often mentioned in Buddhist texts. This is where the next Bodhisattva about to become a Buddha teaches the Dharma as he awaits the time for his final birth in Jambudvīpa.

The Six Forms of Existence

All beings are subject to endless cycles of birth and death. Throughout innumerable lifetimes sentient beings reenact patterns of thought and action that subject them to the inexorable law of cause and effect. Unaware of the illusory nature of ego and the pitfalls of dualistic views, they cannot comprehend how the three poisons—desire, hatred, and ignorance—create the conditions for suffering; since they cannot perceive how the law of karma operates, they cannot foresee the outcome of their actions. Unable to stop the production of karma, or even to benefit from it, living beings increase the flow of karma with every action. Caught up in the stream of karma generated by their actions, beings are impelled into existence after existence. Depending on the accumulation of good or bad karma,[3] beings are reborn into either a favorable or an ill-favored existence. While rebirth may have a positive connotation to some people in the West, to the Buddhist, wearied of endless repetitions of patterns that produce suffering, the goal is to "stop the wheel" and bring the cycle of rebirth to an end.

Devas As a result of good actions in previous lives, beings may be born in one of the heaven realms. According to the Karaṇa-prajñapti, an Abhidharma text (NE 4087), the devas live exceeding long lives, many times that of human beings. During their heavenly existence, the devas enjoy perfect health, their desires are satisfied as they arise, they have no occasion for frustration or pain, their ornaments never deteriorate, their garments remain perfectly clean, and no dust ever settles on their bodies. Although the devas of the Kāmadhātu possess all that beings know how to wish for, they are still not free of the influence of desire and its consequences. Experiencing unbroken pleasure, they desire to perpetuate their pleasure; they have no motivation to ques-

---

3. The terms *good* and *bad* are not meant as personal value judgments. *Good* refers to actions that diminish suffering in the long run; *bad* refers to actions that tend to increase suffering.

tion their existence and awaken the aspiration for enlightenment. When the merit that earned them birth in the godrealms is finally exhausted, they too pass away and are reborn, usually in inferior realms of existence. It is said that the devas become aware of death twelve years before it occurs, and the suffering they endure in contemplating the loss of their blissful condition is exceedingly great. This is illustrated in the Alpadevatā-sūtra (NE 330), where a deva, terrified of falling into inferior realms of existence, seeks the Buddha's guidance and protection.

Asuras   Asuras are neither god nor human, although they are often called "demigods" or "jealous gods." Their realm, ruled by a king called Vemācitra, lies to the east of Mt. Meru, where they live under the earth and ocean. According to the Saddharma-prakāsa-sāsana, the asuras are hate-filled enemies of the devas. Although the asuras are gigantic in size, have long life-spans, and are nearly god-like in their power, they lack the superior merit that characterizes beings who are born in the god realms, and they are subject to violent passions. Obsession with power and competition characterizes their realm; envious of those who enjoy the bliss of the heavenly realms, they are perpetually at war with the devas and are never content. Fully occupied with various emotional fixations, their minds allow them no peace or opportunity for discernment or reflection.

Human Beings   Human beings, although born into one of the favorable forms of existence, are always vulnerable to many types of pain and fear and are often preoccupied with material well-being. However, by virtue of this vulnerability and the tendency to analyze experience, they are also able to comprehend the implications of old age, sickness, and death. While this knowledge burdens human beings with the agony of existential pain, it provides the strongest (and perhaps the only effective) incentive to strive for enlightenment. Only as a human being can one become a Buddha. This is why the great Bodhisattvas take their final birth in the human realm, where they demonstrate the reflections, actions, and resolve necessary to attain enlightenment.

Animals Animals, pretas, and hell-beings traditionally comprise the lower forms of existence. Animals have less control over their environment and biological drives than humans, and hence less choice about the quality of their lives. Vulnerable to predators, hunters, and enslavement, they suffer continually from emotionality and fear. Their consciousness, limited by preoccupations with survival and bondage to patterned responses, is not likely to perceive the connection between cause and effect or to recognize the possibility for enlightenment.

Pretas Pretas, the "hungry ghosts" with great bellies and mouths the size of a needle's eye, suffer continually from the anguish of needing and wanting. Though food may be plentiful, they lack the means of deriving nourishment from it; no matter how much they eat, they can never attain satisfaction. As a result of their failure to perform meritorious actions in the past, they are repulsive in appearance and indiscriminate in their choice of food and drink. Continually torn between hope that their desires will be satisfied and utter despair when such hopes vanish, the pretas are never at rest.

Hell-Beings The hell-beings are in a continual state of agony, whether burning in the hot hells or frozen in the cold. For exceedingly long lifetimes they abide in extreme suffering, which they have no choice but to endure until they exhaust the karma that precipitated their birth in the hells. This condition, like all else, will eventually come to an end, and the hell-beings will be reborn in one of the other destinies.

Emancipation from the Six Forms of Existence

The Buddha's teaching was the first to reveal the possibility of complete emancipation from the sufferings inherent in all six forms of existence. Within the Dharma, birth as a human was the "right juncture" and the "most excellent opportunity," for only as a human being would one have all the requirements for enlightenment: the capacity, the opportunity, and the incentive. While gods and asuras have greater physical and mental capacities than human beings, and the gods surely have opportunity, the very comfort and bliss of their existence dulls their perception of reality and their ability to comprehend the truth of suffering. Lacking this awareness, they are not able to awaken incentive powerful enough to escape the net of Māra, Lord of Illusion. Māra's influence clouds the minds of the gods and thoroughly enslaves all beings of the Kāmadhātu, the realm dominated by desire.

A Note on Buddhist Cosmology

It is important to bear in mind that Buddhist teachings present cosmology in different ways for purposes of instruction, so that everyone can comprehend according to their level of understanding. The discussion in this chapter is based on the Abhidharmakoṣa-bhāṣya, which provides a fundamental context for understanding terms and references used in traditional texts. The Buddha described far more visionary and expansive cosmologies in such teachings as the Avataṁsaka-sūtra and the Kālacakra-tantra.

Further Readings

Bhadrakalpika-sūtra. *The Fortunate Aeon: How the Thousand Buddhas Become Enlightened*, volume I, pp. 1–95.

Vasubandhu. *The Abhidharmakosabhāṣyam*, translated from the French translation of Louis de la Vallé Poussin by Leo M. Pruden, volume II, pp. 365–550.

The Mahāvastu, translated by J. J. Jones. volume I, pp. 6–29, 152–203.

Beal, Samuel. *A Catena of Buddhist Scriptures from the Chinese*, pp. 35ff.

The Śākyas
of Kapilavastu

Establishing an egalitarian form of self-government, the children of Virūḍhaka flourished in Kapilavastu. When word of their success reached their father, he praised them with love and joy, referring to them as Śākyas, the Brave and Daring Ones.

—*Vinaya-vastu*

The Mūlasarvāstivādin Vinaya (Tibetan: 'Dul-ba) preserves an account of the formation of our present sahaloka, the enduring or environing world, as well as the history of the Śākyas, the family in which the Buddha chooses to be born. The information in this chapter is based on accounts in the 'Dul-ba and in the *Blue Annals*.

Emergence of the Saha World

At the end of the previous kalpa, when the world was destroyed, many of its inhabitants were reborn in the heaven of the Rūpadhātu called Ābhāsvara, Clear Light. Their bodies were ethereal, free from every impurity; their faculties were unimpaired, they were perfect in all parts, handsome, and pleasing to behold. Light emanated from their bodies; they moved through space and fed on joy. They lived to great ages in that state. Meanwhile, the great earth churned about and mingled with the water of the deep oceans. Then a wind arose and blew across the great expanse of the blended earth and water. Just as a breeze concentrates the cream collecting on the surface of milk cooling after boiling, so the wind blowing over the surface of the earth solidified and coagulated the waters into an exquisitely-colored, delicious and fragrant essence. Its color was like butter, its taste like that of uncooked honey.

While the world was forming anew, some of the beings in the Ābhāsvara Heaven, having exhausted their merit, departed that life. Although they were reborn as humans, they retained the quality of radiant light they had possessed in the deva-realm. There was then no sun or moon, there were no stars, no night or day, no minutes, seconds, or fractions of seconds. There were no weeks, no months, no years. Neither were there males nor females; there were only these animated beings of light. Then one of the beings tasted the earth-essence, conceived a liking for it, and began taking it as food, as did others following his example. In time, their formerly clear and shining bodies became coarse and gross; they lost their brilliance, and darkness covered the face of the earth.

Then the sun, moon, and stars came into existence, as did night and day, minutes, seconds, fractions of seconds, weeks, months, and years. All the beings feeding on the earth-essence continued to live to a great age, but while the complexion of those who ate but little of this food was clear, that of those who ate much of it became more opaque and dark. Eventually the beings noticed these differences and began to make distinctions between the clearer and darker beings. When those whose complexion was clear became proud and arrogant, the earth-essence vanished.

When the essence vanished, in its place appeared a substance of exquisite color and savor, of delicious fragrance; eating this substance, the beings lived for nearly as long a time as they did before. But those who ate much of this food became darker, while those who ate less of it remained clearer. Again distinctions arose; the clearer beings became proud and quarrelsome, and this delicious substance also vanished, as had the earth-essence.

Then there appeared bunches of reeds of exquisite color, fragrance, and taste. Taking the reeds as their food, the beings lived for nearly as long as they did before. But those who ate much of this food became still darker, while those who ate less of it remained clearer. Again, when distinctions arose, and the clearer ones became arrogant and proud, the reeds also vanished.

When the bunches of reeds had vanished from the earth, there appeared a spontaneously growing rice, finely-textured, clean, with huge kernels. The rice was plentiful: If it was cut down in the evening, it grew up in the morning; if it was cut down in the morning, it re-grew by evening. Whatever was cut down replenished itself, so there was never any lack of rice. On this food the beings lived very long lives. But from eating this rice the beings developed into males and females. Some became attracted to each other and responded to lustful desires, to the great consternation of those who controlled such desires. Separating themselves, those possessed of desires began to build houses, so they might do in private what the others would not allow. In time some of these householders became lazy and began to store supplies of rice in their homes. Because of this, the rice became coarse; a husk enveloped the grain, and it ceased growing spontaneously after it had been cut.

Overcome by sorrow, these beings lamented the loss of their ethereal bodies and recalled how this had come to pass. Then they agreed to create boundary lines and establish the right of property. But eventually one person took another's rice without his consent and would not cease this behavior. The people quarreled, and questions arose among themselves over what was right and what was wrong. They decided to choose the largest and strongest amongst them to be Master of the Fields, to decide between right and wrong, and to mete out punishment and rewards. They agreed to support this chosen lord by giving him a portion of the produce of their fields.

Gathering together, they selected such a man and called him Mahāsaṃmata, He Who is Honored by Many. As he was lord over the fields and kept them from harm, he received the title of Kṣatriya, Protector of the Fields. And, as he was righteous and wise, one who brought happiness to mankind with the law, he was called Rāja, or King.

After the time of Mahāsaṃmata, the beings of earth, who had now become truly human, continued to became more distinct as individuals, and tendencies towards separation and division grew even greater. As individuals, the beings began to choose how they wished to live and work; these choices gave rise to the different classes of people. Some of the ill and infirm left their villages to seek spiritual perfection in seclusion, study, and meditation; they lived on alms and food donated by the villagers, who respected the knowledge they gained through their practice. Others built huts in the forest and sought perfection in compiling the sacred texts. The forest dwellers intent on meditation and religious activities were called Brahmins, while those who lived together in settlements became known as villagers. The villagers who became farmers or craftsmen and sold their wares were called Vaiśyas; those who protected the land and people and maintained the laws were known as Kṣatriyas. In this way three classes of beings came into existence.

Among these three classes, there were also beings who renounced worldly life, cut their hair and beards, wore saffron robes, and assumed the mendicant's homeless life. These beings became known as śramaṇas. Regardless of their class of birth, śramaṇas were treated with great respect by Brahmin, Kṣatriya, and Vaiśya alike.

The Mūlasarvāstivādin Vinaya extends this history by describing the lineage of the Śākyas from the time of King Mahāsaṁmata to Prince Gautama, who became the Buddha. This history continues the particularizing and concretizing that characterizes the Buddhist view of the evolutionary process. The lifetime of human beings grows ever shorter and more difficult as the eras progress from the bright expansiveness of the golden age to the darkness and confusion of our present time, the kāliyuga, the black age.

During the time of Mahāsaṁmata, the lifespan of human beings was more than one million times one million years. In each generation, the operation of entropy shortened the lifetime of human beings. The reigns of the first six kings mark six stages in the evolution of living beings. The seventh to tenth kings were known as the Cakravartin Kings of the Continents. For the complete lineage linking the Rulers of the Four Continents to the sage Gautama, father of the lineage of Ikṣvāku, see pp. 22–24.

The Lineage of Ikṣvāku

Gautama, Karṇika's eldest son, not wishing to rule, obtained his father's consent to renounce worldly life and became the disciple of the powerful ṛṣi Kṛṣṇavarṇa. Upon the death of the king, Bharadvāja became king of Potala, and Gautama resided in a small hermitage near the city. When the courtesan Bhadrā was slain by her lover, Gautama was wrongfully accused of the crime and impaled outside the city. As he lay dying, his teacher Kṛṣṇavarṇa came to see him. Gautama told his teacher of his innocence and spoke of his concern for the people of Potala, for his brother had no heir and Potala would soon lack a protector. Kṛṣṇavarṇa then caused a great rain to fall to relieve Gautama's pain. Two drops of sperm and blood then emerged from Gautama's body and blended. Two eggs formed from this

The Six Early Kings

Vinaya-vastu	Mahāvastu	Pali
Mahāsaṁmata	Mahāsaṁmata	Mahāsaṁmata
Roca		Roja/Vararoja
Kalyāṇa	Kalyāṇa	Kalyāṇa
Varakalyāṇa	Rava	Varakalyāṇa
Upoṣadha	Upoṣadha	Uposatha
Māndhātṛ	Māndhātar	Mandhātā

Rulers of the Four Continents

King	Extent of Realm
Cāru	4 continents
Upacāru	3 continents
Cārumant	2 continents
Upacārumant	1 continent

Descendants of Upacarumant

Bhadra, son of Upacārumant
30 Kings until: Samantaprabha

THE KINGS OF POTALA
100 kings until Śatrujit
In Śatrujit's lineage:

THE KINGS OF AYODHYĀ
54,000 kings until Vijaya
In Vijaya's lineage:

THE KINGS OF VĀRĀṆASĪ
63,000 kings until Duṣyanta
In Duṣyanta's lineage:

THE KINGS OF KAPILAVASTU
84,000 kings until Brahmadatta
In Brahmadatta's lineage:

THE KINGS OF HASTINĀPURA
32,000 kings until Nāgadatta
In Nāgadatta's lineage:

THE KINGS OF TAKṢAŚILĀ
5,000 kings until Romaputrin
In Romaputrin's lineage:

THE KINGS OF URĀŚA
32,000 kings until Nagnajit
In Nagnajit's lineage:

THE KINGS OF AJITA
32,000 kings until Kauśika
In Kauśika's lineage:

THE KINGS OF KĀNYAKUBJA
32,000 kings until Jayasena
In Jayasena's lineage:

THE KINGS OF CAMPĀ
18,000 kings until Nāgadeva
In Nāgadeva's lineage:

THE KINGS OF TĀLAMĀLA
25,000 kings until Naradeva
In Naradeva's lineage:

THE KINGS OF RĀMALI
12,000 kings until Samudradeva
In Samudradeva's lineage:

THE KINGS OF DANTAPURA
18,000 kings until Sumati
In Sumati's lineage:

THE KINGS OF RĀJAGṚHA
25,000 kings until Marīci
In Marīci's lineage:

THE KINGS OF VĀRĀṆASĪ
20,000 kings until Maheśvarasena
In Maheśvarasena's lineage:

THE KINGS OF KUŚINAGARA
84,000 kings until Samudrasena
In Samudrasena's lineage:

THE KINGS OF POTALA
1,000 kings until Tapaskara
In Tapaskara's lineage:

THE KINGS OF KUŚINAGARA
84,000 kings until Dhāraṇīmukha
In Dhāraṇīmukha's lineage:

THE KINGS OF VĀRĀṆASĪ
100,000 kings until Mahādeva
In Mahādeva's lineage:

THE KINGS OF MITHILĀ
84,000 kings until Nemi
49 kings until Rathasāra
In Rathasāra's lineage:

THE KINGS OF SAMANTĀLOKA
77,000 kings until Gaganapati
In the lineage of his son Nāgapāla:

THE KINGS OF VĀRĀṆASĪ
100 kings until Kṛkin, who made the creative effort towards enlightenment at the time of the Buddha Kāśyapa
In the lineage of Kṛkin's son Sujāta:

100 KINGS IN POTALA
until Karṇika: his two sons were Gautama and
Bharadvāja. The lineage of Ikṣvāku began with the sons
of Gautama.

This list is derived from the *Blue Annals*, pp. 3–7.

union; ripening in the sun, they burst open and two boys emerged. Those two children then hid in the sugar-cane grove nearby.

After Gautama died, his teacher found the boys and cared for them, knowing them to be Gautama's sons. Because the sun assisted in the boys' birth, they were known as the progenitors of the solar race. They were also known as Gautamas, the descendants of Gautama, and as Ikṣvāku, since they were found in a sugar-cane grove. Eventually they both ruled as kings of Potala, the elder first, and when he had no son, the younger ruled upon his brother's death.

Lineage of the Śākyas

According to the Vinaya texts, Ikṣvāku had one hundred descendants until Ikṣvāku Virūḍhaka, whom the Mahāvastu equates with Sujāta, King of Sāketa. Virūḍhaka had four sons by his first wife and another son by a second wife. He offered the second wife a boon; she asked that he send his sons by his first wife into exile, so that her son would become Virūḍhaka's heir. Although this caused Virūḍhaka great grief, he was obliged by honor to keep his word. He exiled Ulkāmukha, Karakarṇaka, Hastiniyaṁsa, and Nūpura, his four oldest sons, and was succeeded by his fifth son, Rājyānanda. The half-sisters of the exiled princes accompanied them into exile. Hearing of the banishment of the princes, the people of Sāketa were sorrowful and wished to follow them into exile. King Virūḍhaka gave them all they wished from his granary and treasury, and several thousands of Sāketa's people left with the princes. They arrived in the kingdom of Kosala, where the king of Kosala and Kāśī at first extended them a royal welcome. But this king later became jealous of their popularity among his people and asked them to leave. (*Mahāvastu* I: 296ff)

The exiled sons, accompanied by their half-sisters, traveled to the land of the ṛṣi Kapila and requested a parcel of his land on which to build a city. After Kapila granted the land, Virūdhaka's sons and daughters built huts of leaves and hunted for their food. Following Kapila's advice, the princes married their half-sisters and had many children. The ṛṣi guided them in building a town, which they named Kapilavastu in his honor. When the inhabitants grew in number, a deva pointed out a place for a new town, which they named Devadaha, meaning Shown by a Deva.

In their general assembly, the townspeople all agreed that they should marry only one wife, and that she must be of their own clan. They established an egalitarian form of self-government and flourished in Kapilavastu. One day King Virūdhaka, reflecting on his exiled sons, asked his courtiers what had become of them. Told of their adventures, he praised them, calling them Śākyas, the Daring Ones.

The Mūlasarvāstivādin Vinaya gives the Śākya lineage to the time of Śākyamuni: It continues through Nūpura, Vaisiṣṭha, and Guha, followed by 55,000 kings, ending with Dhanusthira.

Immediate Precursors of Śākyamuni

Dhanusthira had two sons, Siṃhahanu and Siṃhanāda. Siṃhahanu, who won reknown as the best archer in Jambudvīpa, became king had four sons and four daughters. His four sons were Śuddhodana, Śuklodana, Droṇodana, and Amṛtodana; his four daughters were Śuddhā, Śuklā, Droṇā, and Amṛtā.

According to the Mūlasarvāstivādin Vinaya, during King Siṃhahanu's reign the city of Kapilavastu and its environs enjoyed peace and prosperity. The neighboring Śākyan city of Devadaha, governed by Suprabuddha, also prospered. Suprabuddha married Lumbinī, renowned for her beauty, and built a fine garden for her enjoyment, which became known thereafter as the Lumbinī Grove. Lumbinī bore Suprabuddha two daughters; the elder, whose beauty was extraordinary, was named Māyā, and the younger, more beautiful still, was named Mahāmāyā. When it came time for them to marry, Suprabuddha offered both to King Siṁhahanu as wives for his son Śuddhodana. Since the Śākyan law allowed each man only one wife, Siṁhahanu had to choose between the two daughters. Aware of the prophecy that Mahāmāyā would bear a son with all the signs of a world emperor, Siṁhahanu accepted the younger to be the wife of his son.

At that time the Śākyas, troubled by raiding hill tribes (Paṇḍavas), implored the king to send Prince Śuddhodana to protect their lands. The king consented and Śuddhodana drove the Paṇḍavas out of the kingdom. In recompense for this favor, the king requested that the law be amended to allow Śuddhodana to take two wives. The Śākyas agreed to this request, and so Śuddhodana married both sisters: Mahāmāyā, who became the mother of the Buddha, and Māyā, also known as Mahāprajāpatī, who cared for the Buddha after his mother's death.

Further Readings

'Gos Lo-tsā-ba. *The Blue Annals,* translated by George N. Roerich, second edition, pp. 1–17.

The Mahāvastu, translated by J. J. Jones, volume I, pp. 285–301.

Rockhill, W. Woodville. *The Life of the Buddha and the Early History of His Order,* pp. 1–13.

Indian Kingdoms in the Buddha's Time

At the dawn of the sixth century B.C.E., the subcontinent of India embraced many different kingdoms.

The names of sixteen Mahājanapadas, or Great Communities, appear frequently in Buddhist Sūtras, either as places where the Buddha taught the Dharma or where he perfected virtues in previous existences as a Bodhisattva. While the names vary somewhat according to sources, the following kingdoms are known from texts of the Buddhist Āgamas and Vinaya: Aṅga, Magadha, Kāśī, Kosala, Vṛji, Malla, Ceḍi, Vatsa, Kuru, Pañcāla, Matsya, Śūrasena, Aśmaka, Avanti, Gandhāra, and Kāmboja. There were also autonomous republics governed by consensus of the people, such as the land of the Śākyas.

These kingdoms were located in four major regions of ancient India: Madhyadeśa, the Middle Country of the Ganges basin; Uttarāpatha, the Upper Region comprising the Punjab and Central India; Aparānta, the Western Region, and Dakṣiṇāpatha, the Southern Region, which refers to all of India south of the Vindhya Mountains. A fifth area, Prācya, the Eastern Region, referred to lands less influenced by brahmanic traditions: Puṇḍra, Vaṅga, Samataṭa, Orissa, and Kaliṅga. Since the Eastern Region rose to prominence several centuries after the Parinirvāṇa, it is omitted from this discussion.

Madhyadeśa

In the Madhyadeśa, the Ganges River formed a natural dividing line between kingdoms. To its south lay Aṅga, Magadha, and Kāśī, with Kosala, Malla, and Vṛji to its north.

Aṅga The Campā River formed the boundary separating Aṅga from Magadha. At the time of the Buddha, Aṅga had recently come under the rule of Magadha, which ended a long rivalry between the two kingdoms. Aṅga's capital city was Campā, one of India's six major cities in the Buddha's time and a place where the Buddha taught the Dharma. Although far from the ocean, Campā was a thriving seaport where merchants embarked for Tāmralipti on the Indian Ocean and engaged in profitable trade with Suvarṇabhūmi, the Golden Land (probably Burma).

Magadha Magadha, directly west of Aṅga, occupied a territory roughly equivalent to modern Bihār. In the time of the Buddha, under the strong leadership of Bimbisāra and his son Ajātaśatru, Magadha was prospering commercially and agriculturally, rapidly rising to prominence and developing a vision of empire that would eventually encompass most of the South Asian subcontinent. Magadha's capital was Rājagṛha, a major home of the Sangha and the site of many of the Buddha's teachings.

Vṛji Directly north across the Ganges from Magadha and Aṅga was Vṛji. Vṛji was actually a confederacy, formed by the alliance of Kṣatriya families that included the Videhas, the Licchavis, the Jñātrikas, and the Vṛjis. Its capital was Vaiśālī, a rich city with high walls and towers, where the

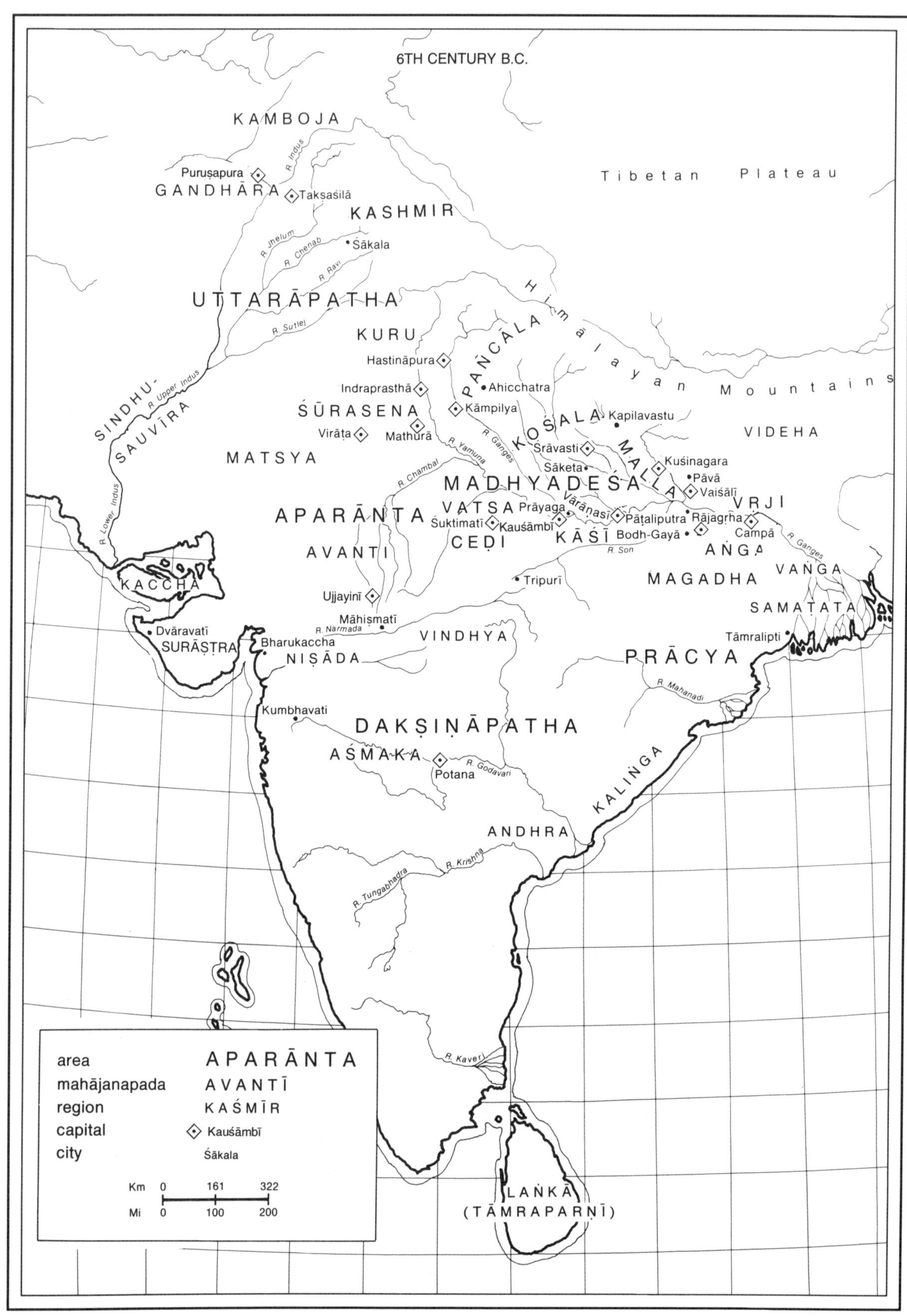

Mahājanapādas governed by ancient ruling clans formed the major divisions of India.

Buddha gave many teachings. The lands of the Vṛjis were nestled between the Ganges on the south and the Himalayas on the north; the site of Mithilā, the capital of Videha, is thought to lie within the borders of modern Nepal. In ancient times Videha was a powerful monarchy, but by the sixth century B.C.E. it had a republican form of government, as did its partners in the Vṛji confederacy.

Malla   The Mallas inhabited the region between Vṛji and Kosala, bounded by the Gandak and Gogra rivers. Neighbors of the Śākyas, the Mallas are often mentioned in accounts of the Buddha's life. Like the Vṛjis, the Mallas appear to have been a confederacy of Kṣatriya clans, friendly to the Vṛjis and allied with them for protection against the larger kingdoms. Their cities included Pāvā and Kuśinagara, the site of the Buddha's last meal and Parinirvāṇa. Although the Mallas were described as a separate state in the Mahāparinirvāṇa-sūtra, they, like the other republics of ancient India, eventually became part of Magadha.

Kosala   The kingdom of Kosala occupied a major portion of the northern Ganges basin. Roughly corresponding to modern Oudh, it spanned the region between the Sadānīrā (Gandak) and the Yamunā rivers. Located directly south of the hills of Nepal, Kosala conquered Kāśī shortly before the birth of the Buddha and became, along with Magadha and Avanti, one of India's three major powers. Kosala's borders encompassed two important cities, which both figure prominently in the Buddha's life: Śrāvastī, where the Buddha lived for many years, and Sāketa, near Ayodhyā, also a major home of the Sangha. At the time of the Buddha, Kosala was ruled by King Prasenajit, who was succeeded by his son Virūḍhaka toward the end of the Buddha's life.

Kāśī   The Jātakas describe the ancient land of Kāśī, powerful and wealthy during the eighth to sixth centuries B.C.E., as "having an abundance of the seven gems." The people of this kingdom, located on the main caravan routes, prospered greatly from trade and were famous for the production of fine cloth. The Jātakas tell the story of the Buddha's previous life as Viṣaya, a wealthy merchant, who established places in Kāśī's capital where mendicants could come and receive generous allotments of alms. The Bhojājānīya-jātaka mentions that all the neighboring kings coveted this kingdom; many Jātakas relate accounts of Brahmadatta, king of Kāśī, and describe Kāśī's conflicts with Kosala, its neighbor to the north. Shortly before the Buddha's birth, Kāśī finally became part of Kosala. Kāśī's capital city was Vārāṇasī (= Benares), located between the Varuṇā and Asi rivers.

Autonomous Republics   In addition to these Mahājana-padas, the Madhyadeśa accommodated republican clans ruled by popular assemblies. In the sixth century, the country to the east of Kosala between the Himalayas and the Ganges was the home of the Śākyas, Bhaggas, Kalamas, Bulis, Koliyas, Mallas, Videhas, and Licchavis. Although the Videhas were mentioned in Vedic sources, and Buddhist sources count Vṛji and Malla among the sixteen Mahā-janapadas, the origins of the Vṛjian tribes is uncertain. It is quite possible that at least some of these tribes were neither descended from Vedic tribes nor indigenous to India. Some theories link them to Himalayan tribes who migrated to India from the north.

Śākya   The land of the Śākyas extended north to the Hi-malayas and east to the Rohiṇī River, with the Rāpti River on the west and south. The Śākyan capital was Kapilavastu, said to have been populated by eighty thousand families, and Buddhist texts mention other Śākyan towns as well. The Śākyas were essentially one family; with the exception of the Koliyas, to whom they were related, they did not marry out-side their clan, and all Śākyas had the surname of Gautama. Before the Śākyas became followers of the Buddha, they had the reputation of being aggressive and powerful in battle. Still, the presence of the large and powerful kingdom of Kosala on their western border rendered their existence in-secure, although there were friendly relations and mutual respect between the two countries.

Uttarāpatha

West of Kosala lay Pañcāla, bounded by the northern turn of the Yamunā River. Śūrasena, Matsya, and Kuru, the other major countries of the upper region, were located west of the Yamunā.

Pañcāla The Pañcālas, closely allied with the Kurus, were strongly brahmanic tribes prominent in northern India from early Vedic times. In the sixth century B.C.E., they occupied the land from the Himalayan foothills to the Chambal River. The Ganges River divided their kingdom into north and south. The capital of northern Pañcāla was Ahicchatra (modern Ramnagar); the capital of southern Pañcāla was Kāmpilya. The city of Kānyakubja (Kanauj) also lay within Pañcāla's borders.

Śūrasena The Śūrasenas, known to Greek writers as Sourasenoi, may have had a republican form of government, since the fourth century political master Kauṭilya describes one of their tribes as a sangha. The Śūrasena's capital of their country was Mathurā (Greek, Methora), an early center for the Buddhist Sangha located on the Yamunā River. A Śūrasena king, Avantiputra, is said to have promoted the teaching of the Dharma in Mathurā. Śūrasena's borders also encompassed the prosperous city of Saṁkāśya, where the Buddha descended from the Trāyastriṁśa Heaven.

Matsya The Matsya country (modern Jaipur) lay to the west of the Yamunā River. Its capital was Virāṭanagara, named after its founder King Virāṭa. The Matsya people are often associated with the Śūrasenas. During the Buddha's lifetime the Cedi king Sahaja united Matsya and Cedi under one rule.

Cedi The Cedis, one of India's most ancient tribes, lived west of the Yamunā, west of Vatsa and south of the Kurus. Their capital city was Śuktimatī.

Kuru The Kurus occupied the upper Yamunā basin in Brahmāvarta, the homeland of the Vedic peoples. The

Kurukṣetra, the Plain of the Kurus, figures prominently in the ancient Bhārata epics. The Kuru capital was the city of Indraprasthā, near modern Delhi, with another major city, Hastināpura, to the northeast. While the Kurus were widely respected for their vigor and wisdom, they had little political importance in sixth century India.

Gandhāra Gandhāra referred to the northern region of the upper Punjab, south of the Hindu Kush range. The Gandhāra region included the cities of Puruṣapura (modern Peshāwar) and Rāwalpindi; at certain times in history it also included the valley of Kashmir. The city of Takṣaśilā (Taxila), long a center of trade and learning, was often within Gandhāra's shifting boundaries. By the sixth century B.C.E., Gandhāra was annexed to the Persian empire of King Darius, which consisted of twenty satrapies. As a Persian satrapy, Gandhāra probably encompassed the Indus Valley and parts of the Punjab. Gandhāra's ruler during the time of the Buddha was King Puṣkarasārin.

Kāmboja Although there are different accounts concerning Kāmboja, this kingdom probably was located far to the north and outside the main subcontinent of South Asia. Most historians locate Kāmboja north of Gandhāra and north of the uppermost reaches of the Indus River, on the modern border of Pakistan and Afghanistan. In ancient times, around 1,000 B.C.E., Kāmboja was inhabited by Vedic Indo-European-speaking tribes, but by the sixth century B.C.E., it appears to have been occupied by people speaking languages incomprehensible to the people of northern India.

Aparānta

Vatsa Vatsa was a rich and populous country. Its capital was Kauśāmbī, a large city with extensive fortifications located on the Yamunā River. At the time of the Buddha, King Udayana ruled this land. He was succeeded by his son Bodhi, who was a strong supporter of the Buddha and his teaching.

Avanti In the Buddha's time Avanti was a powerful kingdom ruled by King Pradyota, known as "the Cruel" from Buddhist sources. During his twenty-three-year reign, he was in continual rivalry with Bimbisāra, king of Magadha, for control of the eastern end of the trans-India trade route. Avanti's major cities, Ujjayinī and Māhiṣmatī, both lay on this prosperous caravan route. Pradyota was followed by four kings, Pālaka, Viśākhayūpa, Ajaka, and Nandivardhana, who together ruled a total of 115 years, during which time Avanti became an important Buddhist center. Avanti's last king was defeated by Śiśunāga, king of Magadha, who annexed Avanti into his kingdom.

Dakṣiṇāpatha

Aśmaka Aśmaka, also known as Assaka or Aśvaka, is more difficult to locate. Aśmaka was mentioned by the grammarian Pāṇini as a country in the Indus basin. But the Assaka of Buddhist literature appears to refer to a land in southern India between the Narmadā and Godāvarī rivers. Assaka is elsewhere identified with Mahārāṣṭra, which is located south of the Narmadā River.

Further Readings

Majumdar, R. C., ed. *History and Culture of the Indian People.* Volume II, *The Age of Imperial Unity,* pp. 1–17.

Law, Bimala Churn. *Tribes of Ancient India.*

Part Two

Life of the Buddha

The Awakening
of Prince Gautama

What you describe is good, well said, and desirable.
Entering into spiritual practice has always been
praised by the wise, for there one finds
what is useful to oneself and to other beings;
one finds a happy life, the sweet nectar
and the fruit of immortality.

—Śākyamuni Buddha

While there is no text that contains the complete life of the Buddha Śākyamuni, the Lalitavistara-sūtra (NE 92) presents the Buddha's own account of his early life from his sojourn as a Bodhisattva in the Tuṣita Heaven to his enlightenment and first teaching. A model for study and emulation that approaches epic proportions, the Lalitavistara-sūtra serves as a basic testament within the Mahāyāna traditions. Another account of this period in the Buddha's life appears in the Vinaya teachings where it forms the foundation of the history of the Sangha. A life of the Buddha is also given in the Mahāvastu, the Great Collection, a text drawn from the

Vinaya of the early Lokottaravadin school. A shorter account of the Buddha's early life is found in the Abhiniṣkramaṇa-sūtra, which also describes the Buddha Dīpaṁkara's prediction, spoken many aeons ago, of Śākyamuni's attainment of Buddhahood. Additional retellings of the Buddha's early years appear in the Nidāna-kathā, the introduction to the ancient Pāli commentary on the Jātakas, accounts of the Buddha's previous lives. Essential parts of the Buddha's life also appear in histories compiled in Śrī Laṅkā in the fourth and fifth centuries, specifically in the Dīpavaṁsa, the Island Chronicle, and the Mahāvaṁsa, the Great Chronicle. A commentary on the Buddhavaṁsa provides a chronology for the first twenty years of the Buddha's teaching.

Although there is no definitive history of the Buddha's life after his enlightenment, information on Śākyamuni's forty-five years of teaching can be gleaned from a study of his collected teachings preserved in the Canons compiled in Śrī Laṅkā, China, and Tibet. Nearly all the Buddha's teachings begin by stating the place and circumstances of a teaching and describing the assembly gathered to receive it. Often the Buddha refers to specific events, places, royal patrons, or individuals, which contributes to our historical perspective.

Many Sūtras enrich understanding of the significance of the Buddha's exemplary life by focusing on the nature of Buddhas, Bodhisattvas, Arhats, monks, or the virtues to be perfected by laymen and women. In the record provided us in the Buddha's teachings, the gardens of Śrāvastī bloom anew, the Nairañjanā River still nourishes the great trees of Bodh Gayā, and King Bimbisāra, accompanied by drums, cymbals, and full royal regalia, still leads the great procession to welcome the Buddha to Rājagṛha.

Events and teachings leading up to the Buddha's Parinirvāṇa have a special significance in the Buddhist traditions. The last months of the Buddha's life and his last journey are detailed in the Mahāparinibbana-sutta of the

Theravādin tradition and in the much more extensive Mahāyāna Mahāparinirvāṇa-sūtras.

Down through the centuries, writers inspired by the
Buddha's life have retold the great story in poetry, drama,
and historical compilations. The master and poet Aśvaghoṣa
(c. 1st century C.E.) may have been the first to retell the
Buddha's life in the Buddhacarita, a Sanskrit kāvya (dra-
matic poem) of great power and beauty.

In the chronicles of the Pāli tradition, the Buddha's path
to enlightenment involved a steady accumulation of merit in
successively higher rebirths, in which he practiced meritorious actions in countless lives before he entered his final existence and attained the enlightenment of a Buddha. In the
Vaibhāṣika tradition cited by Dudjom Rinpoche, the Bodhisattva in his last lifetime is viewed as "worthy beyond
measure," but not enlightened. After his birth as Prince
Gautama, the Bodhisattva is still an ordinary individual
bound by worldly views, who is able to penetrate illusion and
attain enlightenment by virtue of his great store of accumulated merit.

In the Bhadrakalpika-sūtra, a Mahāyāna teaching, the
Buddha Śākyamuni is considered one of an endless procession of Buddhas, an embodiment of the principle of enlightenment that appears periodically on the cosmic stage to
awaken beings to their true nature. The Laṅkāvatāra-sūtra
states that the Buddha first attained enlightenment in the
Akaniṣṭha Heaven, and then, in the physical realm of our
human world, manifested the attainment of Buddhahood.
The Lalitavistara-sūtra presents the Bodhisattva as already
enlightened, resolving to take birth solely for the purpose of
demonstrating the way to enlightenment and making the
Dharma accessible to other beings. In the Saddharmapuṇḍarīka-sūtra, the Buddha proclaims:

"For hundreds and thousands of aeons,
the duration of which cannot be measured,

I have attained supreme enlightenment (again and again) and have constantly preached the Dharma."

Twelve Acts of the Buddha

Traditionally, the life of Śākyamuni focuses on twelve acts performed by all Buddhas, through which the Enlightened Ones rekindle the light of the Dharma in the world and set the example for those who follow in their footsteps. While these acts may be listed in different ways, the texts of all traditions agree on the major events of the Buddha's life. The following list of twelve acts is as given by Bu-ston:

1. Existence in the Tuṣita Heaven
2. Descent from the realm of Tuṣita
3. Entering the womb of a mother
4. Birth
5. Accomplishment in worldly arts
6. Life in the palace
7. Departure from home
8. Practice of hardships
9. Victory over Māra, Lord of Illusion
10. Enlightenment
11. Turning the Wheel of the Doctrine
12. Parinirvāṇa

The following retelling of the twelve deeds of the Buddha is based on the Lalitavistara-sūtra and the account in the Mūlasarvāstivādin Vinaya, with additional sources noted.

First Great Action:
The Great Resolve in Tuṣita Heaven

Having perfected selfless generosity in his previous existence as Viśvāntara, Prince of the Śibis, the Bodhisattva was

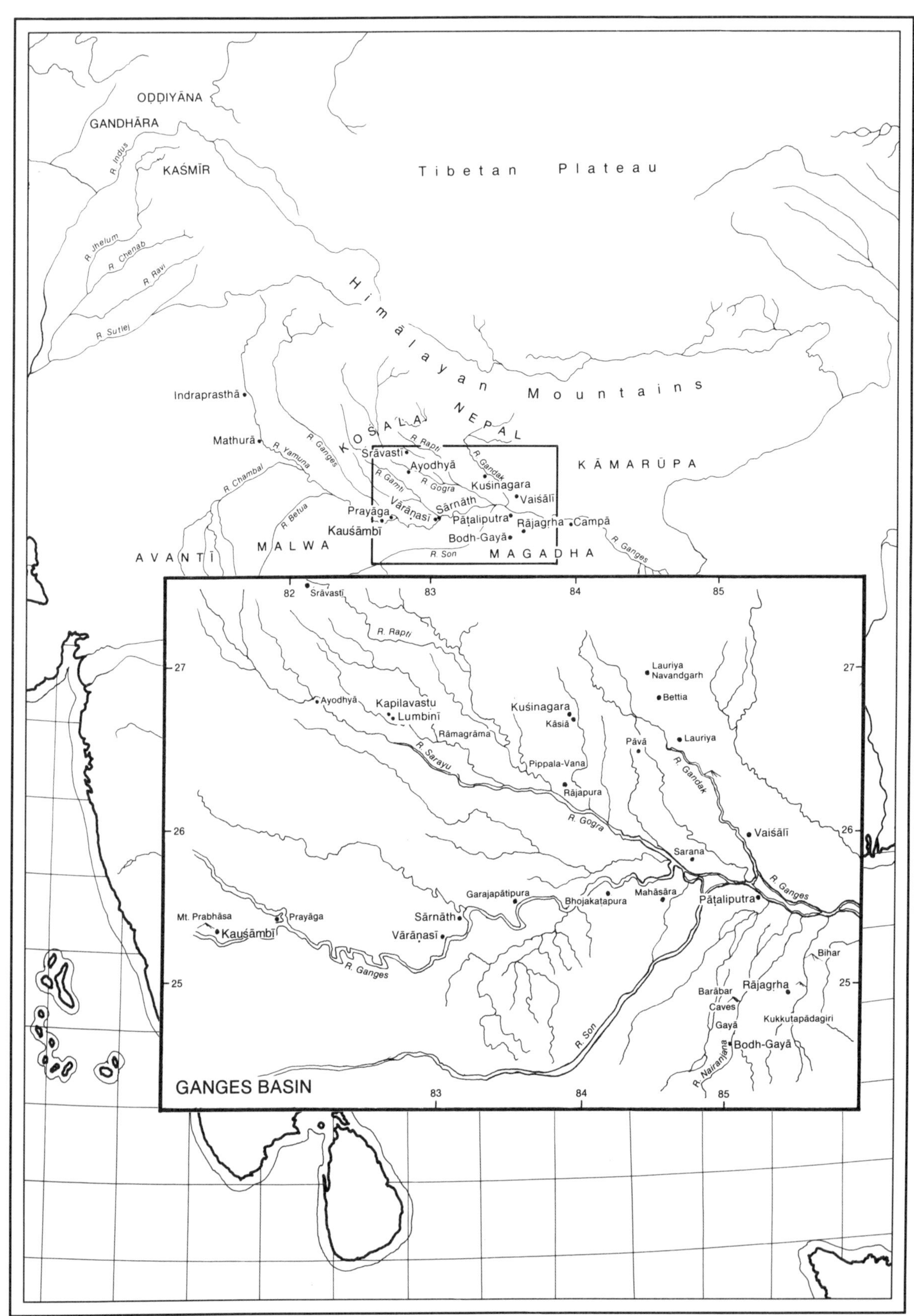

Sites important to the life of the Buddha

reborn in the Tuṣita Heaven as the Bodhisattva Śvetaketu. In that realm where all future Buddhas await the time for their final birth, Śvetaketu lived a full Tuṣita lifespan of 576,000,000 years[1] and taught the Dharma to the gods. When the time for his birth drew near, the devas of the Tuṣita Heaven exhorted him to fulfill his great purpose.

"You who have generated the light
of infinite knowledge, memory, and judgment,
keep in mind your treasure of abundant merit.
With your matchless strength and great energy,
reflect upon the prediction of Dīpaṁkara!

"You who have wiped out the sin of pride,
who have a heart full of virtue,
hold fast to the developed, spotless mind,
rid of the three defilements.
Bring to fruition your former practice of giving!

"Bear in mind the strengths
of your tranquility and morality,
your austerities and patience,
your restraint and effort,
meditation, power, and wisdom.
Reflect upon all you have done
during hundreds of millions of kalpas!

"Remember, remember, you whose renown is boundless,
the hundreds of millions of Buddhas you have honored.
Reflect upon your compassion for all;
remember your great actions.
Now is the time! Do not let it slip away!"
—*Voice of the Buddha* I:23–24

The Bodhisattva then proceeded to the great palace Dharmoccaya, where he was accustomed to teaching the gods of the Tuṣita Heaven. Seating himself on the lion

---

1. As calculated in the Karaṇaprajñapti, an Abhidharma teaching.

throne, the Bodhisattva told the gods of his intention to be born twelve years from that time. The gods, descending to the land of Jambu, in turn informed the great ṛṣis and Pratyekabuddhas of the Bodhisattva's impending birth. Hearing this, and knowing that the voice of a Buddha would soon proclaim the Dharma, the Pratyekabuddha Mataṅga rose into the air and entered nirvāṇa in a blaze of light. Elsewhere, near Vārāṇasī, five hundred other great ṛṣis also entered nirvāṇa, and their relics fell to the earth, marking their passing. To this day, the field where they attained nirvāṇa is known as Ṛṣipatana, the Place Where the Ṛṣis Fell. This place became so peaceful that it attracted herds of deer; it then received the name Mṛgadāva, the Deer Park, where the Buddha would later turn the Wheel of the Dharma.

The time and circumstances of the Bodhisattva's birth unfolded for him in a series of four visions. The place would be Jambudvīpa, the southernmost of the four great continents. He would take birth in the central country (Madhyadeśa), a land of culture and peace; he would be born into a Kṣatriya family, for the Kṣatriyas were then the most respected. The family of his birth would be endowed with the sixty-four kinds of perfections; it would possess pure morals and wisdom and be supported by a retinue which none could surpass in loyalty and virtue.

Of all the kingdoms of the Madhyadeśa, the one with no imperfections was the kingdom of the Śākyas, where there lived the descendants of the ancient sage Gautama, progenitor of the line of Ikṣvāku kings of the solar lineage. The city of his birth would be Kapilavastu; Śuddhodana, king of the Śākyas, would be his father, and Māyādevī, the daughter of Suprabuddha, would be his mother.

"The city of the Śākyas is large and prosperous; its people are flourishing and abide in happiness. Śuddhodana, the king, is of pure descent through both his mother and father, and has a pure wife. His duty is never swayed by his emotions. His body is strong and well-formed; he has brilliant merits . . ."

Of his future mother, the Bodhisattva mused: "Her beauty is like that described in fables, or like that of a goddess adorned with jewels. Free from all possible feminine faults, she always speaks truth, her words never harsh or rough, never crude or scattered. . . . Sweet and agreeable are her words, for she has truly put aside envy and arrogance, anger, pride, jealousy, haughtiness, and violence. She is generous, moral, contented, devoted to her husband, and free from desire for any other." (*Voice of the Buddha* I:43–44)

Second Great Action:
Descent from Tuṣita Heaven

Knowing the time of his departure from the Tuṣita Heaven was at hand, the Bodhisattva invited the gods to assemble to hear his last teaching, known as Cyutyākāra-prayoga, The Breath of Life. Here the Bodhisattva describes, as does each future Buddha just before his final birth, the one hundred and eight luminous doors to the Dharma. At the conclusion of this teaching, flower petals rained down on the realm of Tuṣita. Through the Bodhisattva's power, 84,000 gods generated the thought of enlightenment:

"True joy is found in listening to the Dharma,
in giving, moral conduct, patience, and firm conviction.
These are your best friends.
So always keep the Buddha, the Dharma,
and the Sangha in mind . . .

"Search zealously for the most excellent path.
With the lamp of wisdom,
clear away the darkness of ignorance.
With the lightning bolt of knowledge,
tear open the net of error.
What more is there to say?"

—*Voice of the Buddha* I:67–68

The Bodhisattva Śvetaketu then placed his jeweled crown on the head of Maitreya and empowered Maitreya to teach the Dharma in Tuṣita in his stead. He then predicted that the Great Bodhisattva Maitreya would become the next perfectly enlightened Buddha after Śākyamuni.

Third Great Action:
Entering the Womb of a Mother

The Bodhisattva caused eight auspicious signs to occur in the land of the Śākyas. Then, on the fifteenth day of the month of Vaiśākha, when the moon was full, the Bodhisattva descended from the Tuṣita realm accompanied by a great retinue of gods. Māyādevī was then resting alone in her room. Asleep, the queen dreamed that an elephant, white as snow or silver, with six perfect tusks and a body immutable as a diamond, had entered her womb. She saw also a great assembly of gods praising her and felt her mind growing calm and content. Sharing this vision with her husband, Māyādevī asked that the Brahmins be summoned to interpret this omen. After she had repeated her dream, the Brahmins predicted that this vision foretold that she would bear a most gifted son. They added,

"If he abandons love, royalty, and home,
departing to wander as a monk,
free from attachment,
out of compassion for all the worlds,
he will become a Buddha,
worthy of the offerings of the three worlds.
With the excellent nectar of immortality,
he will satisfy all beings."
—Voice of the Buddha I:99

Fourth Great Action: Birth

All of Kapilavastu rejoiced to hear of the impending birth, and the land of the Śākyas enjoyed great happiness and prosperity while the Bodhisattva awaited the moment of birth. After ten lunar months had passed, thirty-two signs heralded that the time was near. During a visit to the Lumbinī Garden, Māyādevī reached up to grasp a branch of a plākṣa tree, and the Bodhisattva emerged from her right side.

Śakra, lord of the Trāyastriṁśa Heaven, and Brahmā, lord of the Saha worlds, received the Bodhisattva in their arms, and a great lotus arose from the earth to cushion his feet. Standing without assistance, the Bodhisattva took seven steps in each of the four directions, then called out with a voice like Brahmā's: "The destroyer of old age and death has come forth, the Greatest of Physicians." Looking in all directions, he continued, "I am the Leader of the World; I am the Guide of the World. This is my final birth." (*Voice of the Buddha* I:141)

Lotuses sprang up where his feet touched the ground. A great earthquake resounded; a brilliant light shone forth, trees burst into bloom, and music flowed spontaneously from a host of instruments in the realm of gods and humans alike. Many other miraculous signs attended the Bodhisattva's birth. Great pleasure filled all beings, who for a moment were freed from the sources of misery.

The Vinaya account adds that at the instant of the Buddha's birth, four neighboring kingdoms were simultaneously illuminated with a bright light and sons were born to their kings: Prasenajit, son of Brahmadatta, king of Kosala; Bimbisāra, son of Mahāpadma, king of Magadha; Udayana, son of Śatanika, king of Kausāmbī; Pradyota, son of Anantanemi, king of Ujjayinī. All four sons would later become kings upon the deaths of their fathers and would play a role in the growth of the Buddha's Sangha.[2]

---

2. According to the *Blue Annals* (p. 17), the Buddha was born on the fifteenth day of the month Uttaraphalgunī when the constellation Tiṣya was rising, in the wood-male-tiger year. Traditions concerning the year of the Buddha's birth vary widely. See "Date of the Buddha," pp. xx.

The *Blue Annals* records that in far distant China, Chao-wang, the fourth Chou emperor, saw all four quarters of the world enveloped by a brilliant golden light. When the emperor asked his astrologers the meaning of this light, they informed him that a golden son had been born to a great king of the western quarter, and this must be the cause of the light. The emperor then understood that a Buddha had been born and asked when China would receive his blessing. The astrologers predicted the date when four monks would bring the Dharma to China, and the emperor ordered these words to be inscribed on a temple pillar.

Seven days after the Bodhisattva's birth, the time came for Māyādevī to pass from this life; upon her death she was reborn in the Trāyastriṁśa Heaven as are the mothers of all Buddhas seven days after giving birth. The Bodhisattva was then carried to Kapilavastu, where his father welcomed him with great joy. Śuddhodana named the child Sarvārtha-siddha, He Who Accomplishes All Purposes, for upon his birth all the king's wishes for his kingdom had come true. The young prince was also known as Siddhārtha, a shorter form of this name, and as Gautama, since he was descended from Gautama's ancient lineage. Śuddhodana entrusted the prince to the care of Mahāprajāpatī, the sister of Māyādevī, and provided a great retinue of attendants to assist her in taking care of the prince.

Soon after, the great ṛṣi Asita, having perceived the many auspicious omens surrounding the Bodhisattva's birth, arrived at the palace accompanied by his nephew Naradatta. Upon viewing the child, Asita saw clearly the thirty-two major and eighty minor marks of a great being and knew that one who possessed such characteristics would surely be a Cakravartin King, an omnipotent ruler of a vast empire. There was one other possibility, and no other: Should such a one leave home and become a monk, he would become a Tathāgata, a completely enlightened Buddha, a guide unparalleled in all the world. Then Asita sighed, and tears flowed from his eyes, for he foresaw the Bodhisattva's awakening, his home-departure, and his success: The prince would indeed become a Buddha and lead innumerable beings out of the cycle of old age, sickness, and death.

"And I, I will not see this jewel of a Buddha.
This is why,
Great King, I am weeping,
I am distressed, and I utter deep sighs,
for I will not become free
from sickness and attachment."
—*Voice of the Buddha* I:154–55

Then, setting aside his personal sorrow, Asita thought of how many would benefit from the Buddha's teaching and returned home with his heart filled with joy. Although Asita passed away as he had foreseen, he instructed his nephew to enter the Buddha's order as soon as possible after the enlightenment. The Vinaya verifies that this nephew did as Asita requested; since his family name was Kātya, he became known as the great Arhat Mahākātyāyana.

When the prince was several years old, King Śuddhodana took him to the temple to pay homage to the gods, following the custom of his people. But when the Bodhisattva entered the temple, the statues of the gods, including Śakra, Brahmā, and the Four World Guardians, rose up from their places and bowed at his feet. The Śākyas cried out with joy and delight; flowers fell like rain from the heavens, and the great city of Kapilavastu trembled in six ways.

Fifth Great Action:
Accomplishment in Worldly Arts

Various sources for the life of the Buddha describe the shining radiance of Siddhārtha's body, his great strength, and his accomplishment in the worldly arts. Even as a youth he astonished his nurses with his capabilities. Attending school with the Śākyan children, he demonstrated complete knowledge of the sixty-four scripts and opened the minds of the other children to the Dharma by reciting the syllables of the Sanskrit alphabet. As he spoke, the syllables all became mantra, and the meanings of each sound rang out clearly. His teacher Viśvamitra acknowledged that the prince already knew everything he could teach.

Whatever the young prince did inspired awe and praise from all observers. Once, on an outing to the countryside, the prince spontaneously entered samādhi in the shade of a Jambu tree. The Lalitavistara-sūtra describes that ṛṣis traveling through the skies felt their progress impeded by a greater power than theirs. Looking down, they beheld the young prince deep in meditation. Amazed, the ṛṣis paid him homage. Seeing the young prince surrounded with brilliant light, even his father King Śuddhodana bowed before the Bodhisattva, acknowledging that this child would indeed leave home for supreme enlightenment. While Śuddhodana's concern for the material well-being of his realm soon obscured this insight, the path remained clear for the Bodhisattva. Although Siddhārtha returned to Kapilavastu and conformed with the customs of his people, his mind was increasingly occupied with thoughts of home-departure.

As the prince grew to maturity, King Śuddhodana, sensing his son's growing tendencies to introspection, was deeply disturbed, for he feared that his son would abandon worldly life and leave the Śākyas bereft of a strong protector. The king took council with his ministers-of-state, who advised him that the prince must now marry. "Once he is married and surrounded by beautiful women, he will know such pleasure that he will not leave his family, and in this way the succession of Cakravartin Kings will surely be maintained. The Śākyas will be respected and not subject to the scorn of the frontier kings." (*Voice of the Buddha* I:212)

Reluctantly and thoughtfully, the Bodhisattva acceded to their wishes. "I know the evils of desire are endless; they are the root of sorrow, accompanied by regrets, struggles, and hostility. . . . For the qualities of desire, I have neither taste nor inclination." So the prince listed the qualities he would wish for in a wife: She must be generous, well-educated, and devoted to virtue, free from the faults of laziness, avarice, and pride. "If such a woman exists, Master of Men, choose her for me." (*Voice of the Buddha* I:212–14)

King Śuddhodana immediately sent forth a proclamation, asking that all the Śākyan women of marriageable age convene at the palace, in the hope that one maiden would stand out and be noticed by Prince Siddhārtha. Of all the women in the kingdom, Gopā, daughter of the Śākya Daṇḍapāṇi, was the only one able to engage the prince's attention. Śuddhodana then asked Daṇḍapāṇi to permit his daughter to marry the prince, but Daṇḍapāṇi, knowing the prince was accustomed to the luxury of palace life, doubted that Siddhārtha had the required skills of a Kṣatriya. To resolve this question, a tournament was proclaimed: All who wished could demonstrate their prowess; the winner of this contest would have Gopā as his wife.

The prince had, indeed, gained mastery of all worldly arts, a mastery that had come effortlessly. The Vinaya states how the prince's uncle Matulasulabha had shown him to manage elephants, and Sahādeva had taught him the art of archery. Although he excelled in physical as well as in such mental skills as knowledge of languages and scripts and mathematical calculations, so humble was the prince's demeanor that only one person, his cousin Devadatta, envied him his abilities. Devadatta's jealousy became so great that, as the years passed, he became obsessed with a single thought: to discredit Prince Siddhārtha and do him harm whenever possible.

Devadatta was exceedingly strong and proud. At the time appointed for the contest, Devadatta saw a great white elephant being led into the city. Hearing that it was meant as a gift for Prince Siddhārtha, Devadatta, overcome with envy, killed the elephant with a single blow. Although the young Śākya Sundarānanda attempted to move the body of the elephant outside the city, he was not able to get it through the gates. When Siddhārtha passed by, he took the elephant by the tail and cast the massive body past the seven ramparts and seven moats that surrounded Kapilavastu. All onlookers cheered this feat in wonder and admiration as the five hundred Śākyas went out of the city to participate in the great contest.

According to the Lalitavistara, the skills tested included language and mathematics, as well as feats of physical skill and strength in the sports of archery and wrestling. In all of these contests the Bodhisattva prevailed over the most accomplished scholars and athletes in the kingdom. In the archery contest no bow could withstand his strength, until Śuddhodana sent for the great bow of his father, the previous king Siṁhahanu, which no one since him had been able to lift or bend. With this bow the Bodhisattva shot an arrow that split in two the arrow of the warrior Daṇḍapāṇi, passed through the target, and continued onward. Finally it penetrated the ground, creating a spring known thereafter as Śarajūpa, Spring of the Arrow.

Sixth Great Action: Life in the Palace

Prince Siddhārtha's demonstration of worldly skills vanquished all Daṇḍapāṇi's doubts, and he gladly gave the prince his daughter's hand in marriage. The marriage of Siddhārtha and Gopā greatly relieved King Śuddhodana's fears, for who would leave such a gracious and virtuous woman, such a loving family, or such a life of privilege and ease? Who could abandon those who loved him and depended upon him for protection and wise counsel? Who, raised as a prince and groomed to become a king, could lightly take leave of his duty and responsibility?

While Śuddhodana was relieved, the gods became concerned, for it seemed that the prince remained too long in the palace. "Too late will the Bodhisattva withdraw from the world, and too late will he attain perfect and complete Enlightenment." The gods exhorted the Bodhisattva, speaking through the songs of the palace musicians: "Go quickly from this excellent city, remembering your great vow of former times, that when you obtained the dignity of an immortal Buddha, free from suffering, you would quench the thirst of sentient beings with the nectar of immortality. . . . For hundreds of lives you have practiced great love, taking pleasure in compassion and detachment. Share with the world this excellent conduct, which has been your practice." (*Voice of the Buddha* I:247–48)

Reciting the Bodhisattva's aspirations and vows of former lifetimes, the gods evoked the power of memory and fully awakened the Bodhisattva to his purpose. Knowing that prosperity changes and ceases, that all happiness ends in sorrow and all love in separation, the Bodhisattva cast off the net of illusion and applied himself entirely to seeking an end to sorrow.

That night King Śuddhodana had a dream that his son was wearing the garments of a pravrājaka, a wandering monk. For a moment he was overcome by sorrow; then his mind grew resolute: He would build a pleasure-palace that none could resist, so that the prince would be so distracted with pleasures that he would have no thought of even visiting the gardens outside the gate. So the king built three palaces, one for each season—summer, winter, and the time of rains. To prevent the prince from leaving the grounds, he assigned one hundred of his attendants to patrol continuously the entrances of each palace.

One day, however, Siddhārtha requested permission to visit the gardens outside the city. The king could not refuse, so he arranged for a charioteer to drive the prince. He commanded that the route to the garden be cleared of anything old or unpleasant, and that the way should be beautifully decorated. Although this was done, the prince saw on the road an old man, walking painfully, his body bent and shaking. "What affliction is this?" asked the prince of his charioteer, who spoke to him of the inevitability of old age.

"Old age takes youth from everyone,
Your mother, your father, your relatives, and allies—
all will end in old age.
For living beings there is no other way."
> —*Voice of the Buddha* I:286

Absorbed in thought, the prince returned to the palace. Three more times he traveled this route; each time a new apparition heightened awareness of what his father had sought to conceal: the reality of illness, in the form of a man suffering from disease, and the inevitability of death, in the form of a corpse being carried to the cremation ground. The final vision was that of a mendicant monk, traveling the road in serene contemplation. Deeply moved by all he had witnessed, the Bodhisattva saw clearly the magnitude of suffering and awakened the motivation to break the bonds of obligation and attachment.

In the quiet of the night, the Bodhisattva went to his father's rooms.

"Lord, the time has come for me to leave home.
Please, create no obstacles. Do not be distressed.
O King, I pray that my family
and the people of the kingdom will restrain their grief."
> —*Voice of the Buddha* I:302

Śuddhodana told his son to ask anything else, and he would give it. But when the prince asked to be forever free from old age, sickness, and death, the father stood helpless, for he knew that he was powerless to grant such wishes. Then the king controlled his sorrow and blessed his son, saying, "May you do great good in the world. May you rejoice in liberating beings, and may all you intend come to pass." (*Voice of the Buddha* I:303)

The next day the king, having taken council with his advisors, changed his mind once again; together they decided to restrain the prince from leaving. King Śuddhodana now strengthened the guards and fortified the city gates. The Śākyas were agitated with fear:

"May the Pure Being not leave home!
May the descendant of the Śākyas not depart!
May the lineage of kings not be broken!"
—*Voice of the Buddha* I:292

Guards lined the corridors and the courtyard, as well as the roads leading out of the city. The women hung lights in the palace and adorned the rooms with garlands of pearls. All agreed to help each other ward off sleep. They resolved that music would sound through the night, and the prince would have no opportunity to escape.

Yet listening to the sound of the music, the Bodhisattva recalled realizations attained in previous lifetimes:

"Alas for the world which is not at peace, whose fabric is a mass of tangled threads! Beings are always coming and going from this world to the world beyond, running around from that place to this place, unable to free themselves from the round of rebirth that turns like the illusory wheel of fire made by spinning a torch. May I make the light of the Dharma shine, bringing peace and producing the contentment of wisdom!" (*Voice of the Buddha* I:309)

Seventh Great Action: Departure from Home

During the night, despite their vows to stay awake, all the women and guards of the palace fell into a deep sleep. Walking through rooms where the women lay in disarray, as if dead or stupefied with drink, the Bodhisattva saw no beauty, but rather a charnel ground of broken bodies and distorted features. Seeing clearly that ignorance of one's destiny does not prevent suffering, he called to his charioteer Chandaka to bring his horse without delay.

Unable to dissuade the Bodhisattva from his purpose, Chandaka prepared the great horse Kanthaka for the journey. The Bodhisattva mounted, and the horse leaped toward the locked gates of the city wall. The gods cushioned the horses' hooves in their hands so that there would be so sound. As they rushed toward the wall, the massive doors swung wide of their own accord; followed by Chandaka, the Bodhisattva passed through the eastern gate, leaving his former life behind.

Looking again at the palace, the Wise One softly pronounced these words:

"I will not return to the city of Kapilavastu
without obtaining that which puts an end
to birth and death.

"I will not stand, sleep, or walk
toward the city of Kapilavastu
until I have obtained supreme Enlightenment,
in which old age and death are no more!"
                    —*Voice of the Buddha* I:335

Following the road south from Kapilavastu, the Bodhisattva crossed the land of the Śākyas and the Mallas and stopped at a place named Anumaineya (Maneya), near the town of Rāmagrāma. Dismounting, he sent Chandaka home with his horse; this place is still known as Chandaka-nirvartana, the Place of Chandaka's Return.

The Bodhisattva then cut his hair with his sword and exchanged his princely clothing for the clothing of a huntsman he met on the road. Continuing south, the Bodhisattva stopped at the hermitages of the Brahmin Padma, the great sage Raivata, and Rājaka, the son of Datrmadandika, where he was welcomed and given refreshment.

Traveling in stages, he came to Vaiśālī, where he sought out the great master Ārāḍa Kālāma and quickly mastered his entire teaching; but this teaching offered no solution to old age, sickness, and death. After dwelling some time in Vaiśālī, the Bodhisattva went toward Rājagṛha, capital city of Magadha and the residence of King Bimbisāra. For a time he resided on the slope of Mt. Pāṇḍava, where he engaged in solitary meditation.

When the Bodhisattva entered the town for alms, his radiant appearance greatly impressed all who saw him, including King Bimbisāra. Early the next morning, the king, accompanied by a great entourage, went to Mt. Pāṇḍava to meet the Bodhisattva. So joyful did the king feel in the Bodhisattva's presence, that he bowed before him and offered him half the kingdom if he would remain in Magadha.

But for one who had already abandoned a kingdom, such an offer had no appeal. Instead, the Bodhisattva spoke to the king of desires and their addictive natures, and of the more satisfying virtue of wisdom:

"O King, even if one satisfies all desires—
be they human or divine,
even those desires worthy of praise,
complete satisfaction is not obtained,
for still one seeks for more.

"But those, O King, who are calm and restrained,
content because they are instructed by wisdom,
their perceptions filled with the venerable
and faultless Dharma,
such beings are truly fulfilled.
None of the qualities of desire
give them the slightest satisfaction.

"O King and protector of the land,
the more one serves desire,
the more things to desire immediately appear.

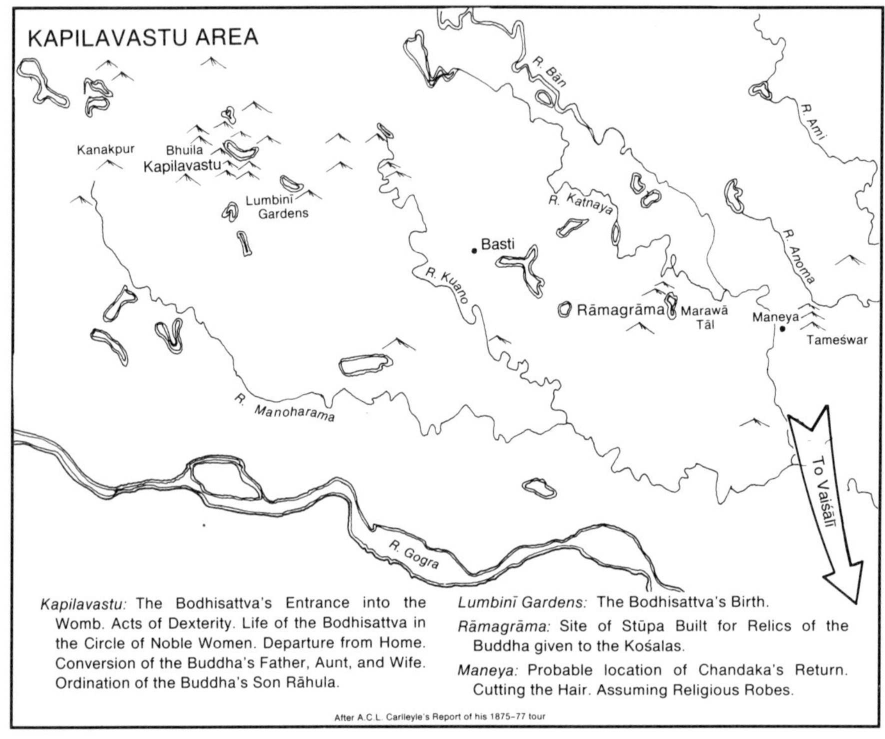

Kapilavastu: The Bodhisattva's Entrance into the Womb. Acts of Dexterity. Life of the Bodhisattva in the Circle of Noble Women. Departure from Home. Conversion of the Buddha's Father, Aunt, and Wife. Ordination of the Buddha's Son Rāhula.

Lumbinī Gardens: The Bodhisattva's Birth.

Rāmagrāma: Site of Stūpa Built for Relics of the Buddha given to the Kośalas.

Maneya: Probable location of Chandaka's Return. Cutting the Hair. Assuming Religious Robes.

After A.C.L. Carlleyle's Report of his 1875–77 tour

Sites of the Bodhisattva's early life

Just as drinking salt water increases thirst,
so he who serves his desires increases those desires."
—Voice of the Buddha II:367

Paying homage to the Bodhisattva, Bimbisāra responded,

"Pray, be patient in your heart with one
who desires to be free from all desire
and thus invites you here.

"When you have attained Enlightenment,
may you share your teachings with me,
O Master of the Dharma.
I have gained already the greatest benefit
since you have lived here in my kingdom,
O Naturally-realized Being."
—Voice of the Buddha II:368

King Bimbisāra then returned to Rājagṛha with his entourage, and the Bodhisattva left the mountain to seek out the master Rudraka, who dwelled in Rājagṛha with his seven hundred disciples. Rudraka excelled in ascetic practices and his teachings were held in great esteem. The Bodhisattva readily mastered all of Rudraka's practices, and Rudraka, greatly impressed, asked him to share leadership of his community. But the Bodhisattva declined; while he attained the samādhis promised, these practices were too transitory and limited to free beings from old age, illness, and death.

Eighth Great Action: Practice of Hardships

When the Bodhisattva left Rudraka, five of Rudraka's senior disciples followed him, impressed by his confidence in a greater realization. They traveled southwest to Mt. Gayā, where they engaged for a time in ascetic practices, considered by people of that time to be the royal road to power and rebirth in the heaven realms. At Mt. Gayā the Bodhisattva had profound insight into the nature of desire: Although there were many who kept their bodies and minds isolated from desire, they still experienced its torments and so were incapable of seeing or manifesting the highest wisdom. To liberate the mind, it would be necessary to completely calm all attachment to desire.

After some time the Bodhisattva and his five companions went on to Uruvilvā on the banks of the Nairañjanā River. Seeing the pure water and beautiful waterfalls, the banks lined with branching trees and pleasant woods, surrounded by pasture lands and villages, the Bodhisattva chose this as an auspicious site for ascetic practices.

Sustaining himself on very little food, the Bodhisattva applied himself to Āsphānaka contemplation for six years. Surviving on one juniper berry per day, then a grain of rice, and finally a sesame seed, sitting immobile through heat and cold, wind and rain, his body lost its radiance; his skin took on a leathery black hue and stretched over his emaciated frame so that every bone stood out clearly.

Finally, at the point of death, he could easily have passed into the highest of the heaven realms. But compassion for all beings impelled him to live on and strive for the perfect enlightenment of a Buddha.

"On a path where one becomes exhausted and weak, one cannot manifest complete enlightenment. And if I were to approach Bodhimaṇḍa, Seat of Wisdom, with the strength of knowledge but with a weakened body, I could not devote my last existence to compassion. Truly such is not the path to enlightenment. Therefore, only after taking nourishment and regaining strength in my body will I approach Bodhimaṇḍa." (*Voice of the Buddha* II:403)

Then the Bodhisattva made a garment from a shroud he found in a nearby cemetery and accepted food from Sujātā, daughter of Nandika, headman of the neighboring village. After bathing in the Nairañjanā River, eating the food, and regaining his strength and vitality, he walked with great deliberation toward the Bodhi Tree. A grasscutter gave him kuśa grass for his seat, a traditional offering to a holy man. Preparing a meditation mat from the grass, the Bodhisattva seated himself under the Bodhi Tree; facing east, concentrating his mind on enlightenment, he made a solemn vow: He would not arise from this place until he had accomplished his purpose.

Victory of Enlightenment

"Here on this seat my body may shrivel up,
my skin, my bones, my flesh may dissolve,
but my body will not move from this very seat
until I have obtained Enlightenment,
so difficult to obtain in the course of many kalpas."
                                            —*Śākyamuni Buddha*

Ninth Great Action:
Conquest of Māra, Lord of Illusion

As the Bodhisattva entered meditation, rays of light came forth from his body, spreading out in all directions and illuminating all of the Buddha-fields of boundless space in the vast open sphere of the Dharma. Perceiving this light, Great Bodhisattvas assembled from the Buddha-fields of the ten directions to pay homage to the Bodhisattva. Then the Bodhisattva extended this light to the abode of Māra, Lord of Illusion, whom not even the gods had the power to challenge. Knowing the meaning of this light, Māra assembled his sons and the generals of his demon warriors.

"When the Bodhisattva awakens,
he will awaken hundreds of millions of others.
When he obtains Immortality
and enters the cool of nirvāṇa,
he will empty my abode of every being.

"With a vast army we must go forth.
We will strike the śramaṇa who sits alone
at the foot of the King of Trees.
Quickly assemble the four divisions of troops.
If you want to please me, act quickly!

"Though the world is full of Pratyekabuddhas and Arhats,
my strength is not diminished when they enter nirvāṇa.
But if he becomes a Jina, King of the Dharma,
there will be countless Buddhas,
their numbers immeasurable."

—*Voice of the Buddha* II:461–62

Māra's power over the minds of living beings was formidable; with a gesture he could shape reality to suit his purpose. He was skilled in using illusion to conceal the true nature of reality and to dull the senses of beings, enslaving them through greed, lust, and fear. Now he called his demon army, shape changers all, to converge by the hundreds of millions on the Bodhisattva. Taking the most hideous and repulsive of forms, the army of demons advanced, hurling swords, lightning bolts, clubs, hammers, uprooted trees, boulders, chains and iron balls. But when they threw these fearsome implements, the weapons changed into garlands and canopies of flowers. Soon flowers covered the ground and hung as ornaments on the Bodhi Tree. So magnificent were these displays that Māra was devoured by anger and envy. The Lord of Illusion then challenged the nature of the Bodhisattva's merit, demanding that he call a witness to support his claim to enlightenment.

The Bodhisattva recalled his previous lifetimes devoted to the steadfast practice of virtue, all for the purpose of freeing beings from Māra's power. Touching the ground with his right hand, he called upon the earth to witness this truth, and the earth shook in six ways. The goddess of the earth, Sthāvarā, rose halfway from the ground to affirm what the Bodhisattva had said. Angered and humiliated, Māra hesitated, but, dominated by pride, did not yield. Then Māra sent his beautiful young daughters to seduce the Bodhisattva. But under the Bodhisattva's gaze, their beauty fell away, and they stood revealed in the ugliness of their true nature. Realizing their ignorance and ashamed for having attempted to lure the Bodhisattva with their wiles, they bowed to him and then returned to their father to implore him to cease his attack.

"O father, it would be best to turn your back
on him today.
No one who has not gone completely beyond
could ever wear him down;
no one who has not cut off the root of passion
could ever uproot him.
He is always patient and never disturbed;
no way can be found to upset him!"
—Voice of the Buddha II:497

Seeing the Bodhisattva equally unmoved by the most terrifying powers of darkness and the most seductive of heavenly maidens, Māra still could not bring himself to halt his attack. Going up to the Buddha, he proclaimed,

"What you seek is not easy to attain.
Bhṛgu, Aṅgiras, and other great ṛṣis,
even after great efforts in austerities,
did not obtain this supreme dignity.
How could you, a mere man, obtain it?"

The Bodhisattva replied:

"The austerities practiced by the ṛṣis
were not preceded by knowledge of the truth.
Their practices were meaningless;
the ṛṣis' minds were dominated by anger

and desire for the realm of the gods;
they persisted in the idea
that the self is both permanent and impermanent;
they persisted in the idea that liberation
is a place where beings go.

"Some say that life lacks a genuine purpose.
Some have no definite beliefs;
others believe in narrow dogma, and others in eternalism.
Some say that one who has a body is without a body.
Some believe in virtue, some in non-virtue.
Some believe in a creator, others believe there is
no creator.

"Here today, upon this seat,
having vanquished you,
conquered you, your pride, and your army,
I will obtain pure Enlightenment.
Then, to all beings now and in the future,
I will show nirvāṇa,
the cool nature of peace and tranquility,
free from all suffering."

—Voice of the Buddha II:503–04

In rage and frustration Māra again rallied his demon army, and they attacked with even greater ferocity than before. Again the Bodhisattva called as witness the earth, the elements, the sun and moon, and all good qualities developed through lifetimes. Again he touched the earth, and a great sound rose from within it.

Then Māra knew that his power was about to be broken; he felt himself cast down on the ground; he knew the horror of approaching old age and death, with no opportunity of regaining his former glory. His thoughts whirled in circles, and madness touched his mind, spinning off images that threw his defeated army into total disarray. Throwing down their weapons, they fled in terror and did not return.

Tenth Great Action: Enlightenment

Having overcome Māra, Lord of Illusion, the Bodhisattva remained in meditation under the Bodhi Tree. As night deepened, he successively entered the four profound levels of meditation. For a time he remained steady on the first level, which is free from all desire and non-virtue and endowed with the joy of perfect tranquility. Letting go of observation and reflection, he attained the second level of meditation; releasing all attachment to pleasure, he abided for a time in the third meditation, known as the equanimity that dwells in great joy and mindfulness. Then, releasing all hold on joy, all pleasant and unpleasant feelings ceased, and he entered into the fourth level of meditation where there is neither suffering nor pleasure, and equanimity and mindfulness are perfectly pure.

During the first watch of the night, the Bodhisattva perceived with the clear light of awareness the arising, passing away, and rebirth of living beings, each according to his actions, and fully comprehended the operation of karma. At this time he awakened the three abhijñās, or special powers of a Buddha: the power of miracles, the power of supersensitive hearing, and the power of reading the thoughts of others. During the second watch, the Bodhisattva concentrated on his previous births and knew all that had passed in each lifetime, in hundreds of births encompassing great aeons of time. In the third watch, he turned his mind toward the alleviation of suffering; with the divine eye of wisdom he knew without doubt the enormity of suffering and the hopeless condition of all beings subject to old age, sickness, and death. Nowhere could he see an end to hopelessness, frustration, and suffering.

In a supreme instant of great compassion, the Bodhisattva saw that if suffering exists, there must be a cause. Examining the cause of old age, illness, and death, he perceived that the conditioning cause for these sufferings is birth. Where birth exists, there is also old age, sickness, and death. Further, he saw that the cause of birth is existence: Where there is existence, there will inevitably be birth. He then perceived that suffering comes about in a causal chain of twelve events, or links, each dependent on what comes before. Thus the cause of existence is grasping, the cause of grasping is craving, the cause of craving is feeling, the cause of feeling is contact, and the cause of contact is the six senses. The six senses depend upon name and form; name and form depend upon consciousness; consciousness depends upon karmic dispositions, and the existence of karmic dispositions depends upon ignorance.

Then, looking from the reverse direction, it became clear that ignorance is the conditioning cause of karmic dispositions; because of karmic dispositions, there is consciousness; because of consciousness, there is name and form; and because of name and form there are the six senses. The activity of the six senses gives rise to feeling; feeling gives rise to craving, craving gives rise to grasping, and grasping produces existence. Existence gives rise to birth, and birth to old age, sickness, and death. The momentum produced through this twelve-fold chain of events impels beings from death into ignorance; the cycle repeats itself endlessly, gathering momentum with every repetition. These twelve dependent causal links became known as the twelve nidānas, and the doctrine describing their interconnection became known as pratītyasamutpāda, dependent origination.

Perceiving the cause of suffering, the Bodhisattva knew also the cure: Beings could learn to break the chain of causation and end the cycle that perpetuates misery. As the Buddha relates in the Lalitavistara-sūtra:

"So, O monks, again and again, the Bodhisattva fixed his mind on teachings previously unknown, generating wisdom and vision, generating realization, great knowledge, prudence, and understanding. And light came forth. At this time, O monks, I recognized in accord with the truth the suffering of affliction; I recognized the source of affliction, the cessation of affliction, the way which leads to the cessation of affliction. In accord with the truth, I recognized: This is the affliction of desire, this is the affliction of ignorance, this is the affliction of contact, this is the affliction of view. It is here that afflictions cease and disappear without leaving a trace." (*Voice of the Buddha* II:522)

Seeing how suffering comes into being, its cause and its cure, the Bodhisattva identified the nature of each link of the chain of pratītyasamutpāda separately; for each, there was a beginning, an end, and a path to this end. Then, during the last watch of the night, the Bodhisattva, at the age of thirty-five, attained complete, perfect enlightenment. At dawn, the first rays of the sun touched the transformed Bodhisattva, illuminating the radiant golden body of a Buddha, a fully awakened being.[1]

"Rays of light by the hundreds of thousands
escape from his body; they spread
throughout the great fields of the Jinas,
bringing peace to those in the three lower realms.

"At this instant, at this very moment,
all worries are set aside;
suffering, pride, and hatred
torment no one any longer."

—Voice of the Buddha II:533

The Vinaya relates that on that night the demon Rāhu seized the moon (indicating a lunar eclipse), and Rāhula and Ānanda were born. Rāhula was the Buddha's son, who had remained six years in the womb while his father was practicing hardships;[2] Ānanda was the Buddha's cousin, who would become his attendant and constant companion.

---

1. According to the *Blue Annals*, the Buddha's enlightenment occurred on the full-moon day of Vaiśākha, in the fire female-hog year.

2. According to the Theravādin tradition, the Buddha's son Rāhula was born before the Buddha left Kapilavastu.

The Twelve Links of Dependent Origination

1. *Ignorance* (avidyā, ma-rig-pa) A blind man groping his way with a stick

2. *Karmic dispositions* (saṁskāra, 'du-byed) A man making pots

3. *Consciousness* (vijñāna, rnam-par-shes-pa) A monkey in a house

4. *Name and form* (nāmarūpa, ming-dang-gzugs) Two people in a boat

5. *Six senses* (ṣaḍāyatanāni, skye-mched-drug) Houses with windows and doors

6. *Contact* (sparśa, reg-pa) A couple in intimate embrace

7. *Feeling* (vedanā, tshor-ba) A man with an arrow penetrating his eye

8. *Thirst/Craving* (tṛṣṇā, sred-pa) A man eating food

9. *Grasping* (upādāna, nye-bar-len-pa) A monkey climbing a tree for fruit

10. *Existence* (bhava, srid-pa) A pregnant woman

11. *Conception/Birth* (jāti, skye-ba) A physical birth

12. *Old age and death* (jarāmaraṇa, rga-shi) A man carrying a corpse

Bound to the Wheel of Becoming, sentient beings wander endlessly through the states of existence, now in the heavens, then in the hells; now torn with passions, then open and receptive. Holding the wheel firmly in his grasp is Yama, lord of death, the end of all beings. Only the Buddha stands completely outside the wheel, pointing the way to liberation.

The Wheel of Becoming (Bhavacakra)

Decision to Teach the Dharma

For a week the Blessed One remained motionless at Bodhimaṇḍa on the plain of the Nairañjana River, experiencing the profound meditation known as Prityāhāravyūha, Assimilating the Food of Joy. Deities from the various heavenly realms joyfully came to praise him, knowing the significance of this great event. Even those sons of Māra who had sided with virtue exulted in his victory, as did Śakra, king of the gods, and the deities of the earth.

During the second week, while seated in meditation, the Tathāgata, the Thus-gone One, visited the regions of the three thousand great thousands of worlds, and the third week he gazed steadfastly upon Bodhimaṇḍa. During the fourth week the Buddha walked from the Eastern Sea to the Western Sea.

Then Māra again approached the Buddha. Attempting to sway the Blessed One from his purpose, Māra praised the Buddha's attainment, declaring that having accomplished the great goal of enlightenment, the Tathāgata should reap the rewards of his efforts and enter Parinirvāṇa. But the Buddha was unmoved by Māra's flattering words. He would not enter Parinirvāṇa until knowledge of the Buddha, the Dharma, and the Sangha was solidly established in the world, and until he had affirmed the efforts of countless Bodhisattvas by giving them predictions of their complete and perfect enlightenment.

A great tempest arose during the fifth week; Mucilinda, supreme lord of the nāgas, together with the nāga kings of the four directions, wrapped the Buddha in his coils for protection from the elements. The sixth week the Tathāgata spent at the foot of the nyagrodha tree, on the banks of the Nairañjana River. To passers-by asking after his welfare during the great storm, the Buddha said:

"Sweet is solitude for the one well-satisfied
who has seen and heard the Dharma;

sweet is gentleness in the world
and care for living creatures!

"Sweet is the absence of desire,
and sweet the victory over the defilements.
Control of conceit and pride—
these are the supreme happiness!"
—*Voice of the Buddha* II:575

During the seventh week, the Tathāgata remained at the foot of the Bodhi Tree. A caravan passed by; two merchants, Trapuṣa and Bhallika, realizing he must be a holy man, offered the Buddha honey and cakes. For this meritorious action, Śākyamuni predicted that, in a future existence, both merchants would become Buddhas named Madhusambhava.

Then the Tathāgata withdrew into solitude and pondered how it might be possible to communicate the Dharma to living beings. He considered that the Dharma is profound, subtle, and ultimately clear; yet it is difficult to understand and to investigate analytically. Inexpressible, surpassing all imagining, how could the Dharma be made known? How many lifetimes had he himself worked toward this realization! Would there now be beings capable of understanding?

"My compassion for the world is boundless,
and I do not hesitate to satisfy the requests of others.
This multitude has faith in Brahmā—
if he requests it, I will teach the Dharma."

Then Brahmā, knowing the Buddha's thoughts, petitioned the Buddha to teach the view and path to liberation:

"Point out clearly the path
of peace, happiness, and prosperity,
free of sickness and far from sorrow.
Without a protector, beings stray
from the path of nirvāṇa.
O Guide, have pity upon them."
—*Voice of the Buddha* II:597

Three times Brahmā called upon the Buddha to teach the Dharma for the sake of all beings. Perceiving the diverse aptitude of beings, the Tathāgata saw that while many would not comprehend the profound meaning of the Dharma, there would be others for whom his effort would make the difference between enlightenment and misery. For them, he would teach the Dharma. The Blessed One then resolved to go to Sārnāth, dwelling place of the great ṛṣis. There innumerable Buddhas before him had set the wheel of the Dharma in motion; there Śākyamuni, the perfectly enlightened one, would cause the voice of a Buddha to resound once more in the world.

"In Vārāṇāsī I previously made
sixty thousand niyutas of koṭis of offerings.
There I have honored
sixty thousand niyutas of koṭis of Buddhas.
There in the great city of Vārāṇāsī
the ṛṣis of old have dwelt.
It is a place always praised by the gods and the nāgas,
where people are always striving for the Dharma.

I remember this most beautiful wood, named by the ṛṣis,
where ninety-one thousand koṭis of Buddhas
formerly turned the Wheel.
This place is matchless, calm, perfectly calm,
contemplative, always frequented by deer.
In this most beautiful of parks,
whose name was given by the ṛṣis,
I will turn the holy Wheel."

—Voice of the Buddha II:608

Teaching The Dharma

—Śākyamuni Buddha

After much reflection on how to offer enlightened knowledge to the world, the Buddha resolved to first teach beings unencumbered with desire, hatred, or ignorance. He thought of Rudraka and Arāḍa Kālāma, his former teachers, but through his power of omniscience, the fruit of his enlightenment, he saw that both of these masters had already passed away. Then the Buddha's thoughts turned toward his five former companions; he saw that they were meditating in the Deer Park at Sārnāth, near Vārāṇasī, in the very grove where five hundred ṛṣis had entered nirvāṇa upon hearing of the Buddha's impending birth.

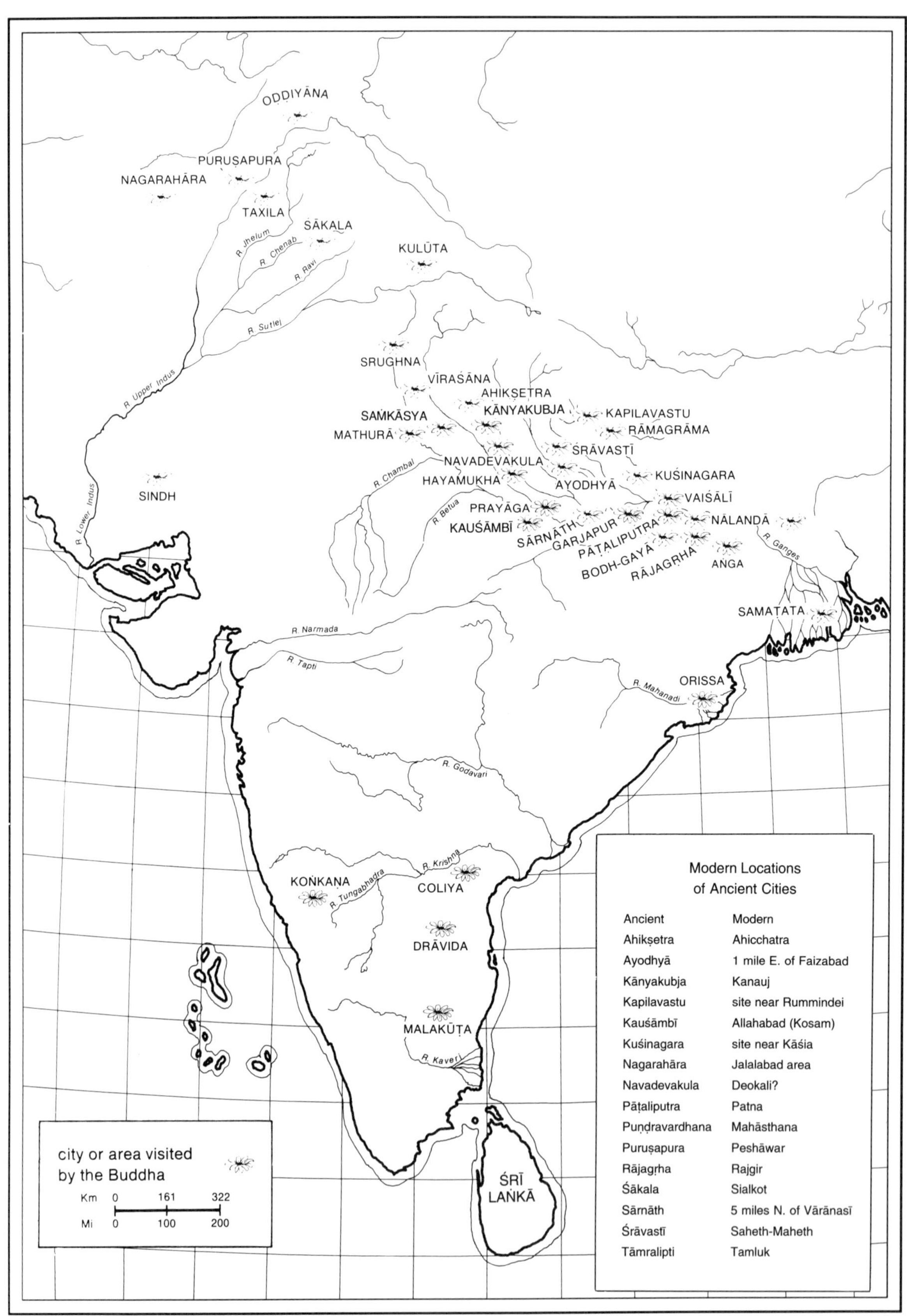

Sites of the Buddha's teaching, as described by the 7th-century pilgrim Hsüan-tsang

On his way to Sārnāth, on a road leading north and west across Magadha, the Buddha met a mendicant monk who commented upon the Buddha's radiant presence and asked who his teacher might be. The Buddha responded, "In truth, I have no teacher, and there is no one like me. I alone am the perfect Buddha." Affirming that he was a Jina, victorious over all defilements and conqueror of all wrong teachings, the Buddha proclaimed his intention to turn the wheel of the Dharma at Sārnāth. "So be it, Gautama, may it be so," the mendicant replied, then continued on his way. (*Voice of the Buddha* II:615–16)

The townspeople along the route offered him hospitality as he passed through the settlements of Rohitavastu, Uruvilvākalpa, Aṇāla, and Sārathi. Reaching the Ganges River, the Tathāgata, lacking the fare for the toll, asked a ferryman for free passage. When the ferryman refused, the Buddha crossed over through the air. Filled with regret, the ferryman reported this happening to his king, Bimbisāra, who immediately abolished the toll for all mendicant monks.

The Buddha entered Vārāṇasī early in the morning, then left the city through the eastern gate and walked north to the grove of Ṛṣipatana in the Deer Park of Sārnāth. Here, in a former life, Śākyamuni had lived as the leader of a herd of deer. The king of that time had been so impressed by the deer-king's offering his life to save another, that he had proclaimed that animals within that park would be forever safe from hunters.

As the Buddha approached the Deer Park, his five former companions saw him from afar. Considering the Buddha to be weak for abandoning his ascetic practices, four of the ascetics resolved among themselves to have nothing to do with him, while the fifth, Kauṇḍinya, held his peace. But so irresistible was the Tathāgata's radiance that they could not refrain from rising to meet him. Overwhelmed by his transformation, they requested him to teach the Dharma.

The Dhamekh Stūpa of Sārnāth

Eleventh Great Action:
Turning the Wheel of the Dharma

During the first watch of the night, the Buddha was silent; during the second watch, at midnight, he spoke on various topics. During the last watch, the Buddha prepared to teach the Dharma for the first time. One thousand thrones appeared, honoring the Buddhas of the Bhadrakalpa. After circumambulating the thrones of the three previous Buddhas of this aeon, Śākyamuni took his place on the fourth. The earth shook in six ways, and a great light shone forth, bringing harmony to all beings throughout the universe. Bodhisattvas gathered about Śākyamuni and his five companions, now his first disciples; a great number of gods joined them, together with the guardians of the four directions.

The Buddha began by speaking to his disciples of the Middle Way that avoids the extremes of indulgence and of asceticism:

"O monks, having abandoned these two extremes of laxity and ascetic discipline, the Tathāgata will teach the Dharma by means of the path of the Middle Way: right view, right intention, right speech, right action, right livelihood, right effort, right mindfulness, and right meditative concentration." (*Voice of the Buddha* II:629)

The Buddha related the teaching of the four noble truths, pointing out the pervasiveness of suffering, its cause, its antidote, and the eightfold path that ensures liberation. This first teaching of the Buddha, which explains the four truths from three perspectives, is known as the twelve-fold teaching of the Dharmacakra-pravartana, Turning the Wheel of the Dharma. (For the full text, see *Voice of the Buddha* I:630–32.)

"The eye is impermanent and non-enduring;
likewise, the ear and nose;
also the tongue, the body, and the mind.
They are by nature suffering, self-less, empty, and hollow;
they are like grass or a wall, non-independent.
They do not have a true self, a name, or life.

"All these dharmas come forth
in dependence on causes;
they are free from the two extremes
of existence and non-existence.
They are like the sky.
There is neither a creator nor that which is created;
only the karma of virtuous and nonvirtuous actions
carries on.

"In this way, suffering arises
in dependence on the aggregates;
watered by desire, it increases greatly.
By means of the path, one sees all dharmas as equal,
and by means of the Dharma, which cleanses and purifies,
one puts an end to suffering.

"When delusive mental activity is understood,
this complex of production is no more.
The ignorance which brings it forth does not arise;
there is nothing for it to come from.
When the cause of karmic dispositions is removed,
there is no driving influence
drawing one thing after another.
It is in dependence on this driving influence
that consciousness comes forth. . . .

"Through causes and circumstances all things come about.
There is no self or person that is moving from life to life—

"There is no conceptual activity, no conceptualization;
there is only the expression of the way things are.
Knowing the way things are,
there is no more ignorance.
When there is no more ignorance,
all the branches of existence are extinguished;
they do not arise.

"This succession of connected circumstances
the Tathāgata has understood;
therefore, self-arising, he taught himself.
This heap of senses and aggregates
is not 'the Buddha';
Buddha is the understanding of causes, only that. . . .

"Thus the Wheel of the Dharma
with twelve aspects has been turned.
It has been understood by Kauṇḍinya,
and so the Three Jewels—

the Buddha, the Dharma, and the Sangha—
have been made manifest."
—Voice of the Buddha II:633-35

The Sangha of Arhats

Kaundinya was the first to understand these teachings
and the first to become an Arhat, a completely dispassionate
being no longer afflicted with desire, ignorance, and wrong
views. As the Buddha continued to explain the four noble
truths, the other four listeners also became Arhats. With this
teaching to the first disciples, the Three Jewels—the Buddha,
Dharma, and Sangha—came into being.

The Sangha, the community that followed the Buddha's
teachings and example, grew steadily from that moment,
attracting people from all walks of life: rich and poor,
Brahmins, warriors, merchants, townspeople, and villagers.
Yaśas, a wealthy youth from Vārāṇasī, crossed the river in
the dark of night to become the first upāsaka, or lay follower.
Next was his father, who came searching for his son and
found peace within the Sangha. The wife and mother of
Yaśas met the Buddha, and both became lay disciples. Then
came Pūrṇa, Vimala, Gavāṁpati, and Subāhu, all friends of
Yaśas who requested full ordination into the Sangha. All
became Arhats after listening to the Dharma. Hearing of the
Buddha, fifty more young men from the leading families of
Vārāṇasī entered the order. They also soon became Arhats,
bringing the number of Arhats to sixty.

According to most traditions, the Buddha Śākyamuni
passed the first rainy season after the enlightenment in
Sārnāth with these sixty disciples. When the rains ceased,
the Buddha sent his sixty disciples to transmit the Dharma
to peoples in distant locations. From Vārāṇasī, bhikṣus could
travel established roads leading north to Ayodhyā and Śrāvastī, the major cities of the kingdom of Kosala; west to
Prayāga and Kauśāmbī, and from there to Ujjayinī; and east
to Rājagṛha and Vaiśālī, the capitals of Magadha and the Vṛji

confederacy. Some sources say the bhikṣus were asked to travel in pairs, others say that the Buddha told them to go separately, so the Dharma might be propagated more widely.

In the Theravādin Vinaya, and in a similar account in the Mahāvastu, the Buddha Śākyamuni instructs his five former companions:

"O monks, I am liberated from all the human and divine bonds, and you, also, are liberated from them. Go forth, and walk for the welfare of many, for the happiness of many, out of compassion for the world, for the profit, for the welfare, for the happiness of gods and mankind. Let not two of you go by the same path. Expound the Dharma which is good in the beginning, good in the middle, good at the end; teach it in its spirit and its letter; explain the practice of the religious life in the fullness of its purity. There exist beings who, by nature, are not blinded by passion; but if they do not hear the Dharma expounded, they are lost. These beings will be won over to the Dharma."

Then the Buddha traveled east to Uruvilvā, where he had practiced austerities before his enlightenment. Reaching the Senāni village at Uruvilvā, the Tathāgata went into a cotton-tree forest where he conversed with sixty young men who became lay disciples. Deva, a rich Brahmin, and his wife from Kapilavastu heard of the preaching of their country-man Śākyamuni and went to the forest to meet him. They both became disciples, as did two girls from the village, Nandā and Nandabalā.

At that time, Uruvilvā Kāśyapa, the most venerated as-cetic in Magadha, was staying nearby on the bank of the Nairañjana River, accompanied by his five hundred disci-ples. Not far away were his two brothers, also ascetics, each with 250 followers. Knowing that Uruvilvā Kāśyapa was capable of understanding the Dharma, the Buddha went to his encampment to teach him. But Kāśyapa, considering himself already fully enlightened, would not request teachings from the Buddha. Only when the Buddha demonstrated his greater powers did the venerable Kāśyapa accept him as his master.

The great ascetic requested ordination and entered the Sangha together with his five hundred followers, who threw the accoutrements of their old way of life into the river and clothed themselves as bhikṣus. Shortly afterward, Kāśyapa's two brothers, seeing the cast-away staffs and implements floating down the river, came with their disciples to see what disaster might have befallen their brother. Upon meeting the Buddha, they also joined the order together with their followers, bringing the number of disciples to one thousand.

These thousand disciples accompanied the Buddha as he traveled back toward Magadha. For a time they stopped at a small shrine on the summit of Gayāśīrṣa (Mt. Gayā), a short distance north of Bodh Gayā. In this holy place, the Buddha gave the teaching known as the Gayāśīrṣa-sūtra (NE 109), which touches on the nature of enlightenment, to the thousand disciples as well as to many great Bodhisattvas who joined the assembly. Gazing at the firelight from the distant hearths of the city of Rājagṛha, he also gave the fire Sermon (Pāli: Aditta-pariyaya) to the thousand bhikṣus. In this Sūtra he explained how everything—consciousness, senses, and sensations—is on fire, aflame with the fire of greed, the fire of anger, the fire of ignorance. In seeing how these fires consume life and happiness, beings can sever attachments to that which perpetuates suffering and attain liberating wisdom.

Word of the Buddha's presence at Gayāśīrṣa reached King Bimbisāra, who received the news with great joy and sent a messenger to offer the Buddha and his disciples his hospitality at Rājagṛha. Years before, this king had made five wishes that were now fulfilled: that a Buddha would appear during his reign; that he would see him; that he would hear him speak the Dharma; that he would understand it; and that he would follow the Buddha's guidance.

Rājagṛha

The Tathāgata proceeded with his disciples to the vicinity of Rājagṛha, stopping at a pleasant grove outside the city. As related in the texts and depicted in art, the king went to greet the Buddha, riding in his royal chariot accompanied by hundreds of attendants and musicians playing cymbals and drums, and followed by a great crowd of townspeople eager to view the Buddha and pay their respects. The crowd at once noticed the famous ascetic Kāśyapa near the Buddha, and all wondered if the Buddha had become Kāśyapa's disciple, or if the Buddha were so great a master that even Kāśyapa had become his student. Kāśyapa, seeing that the people were confused, at once declared himself the Buddha's disciple in front of the king and the whole multitude.

To the whole assembly, which included the thousand bhikṣus, King Bimbisāra, and thousands of townspeople, the Buddha spoke of the transitoriness of all that exists, how suffering arises, and the view and path that ensures happiness. This teaching and the description of Bimbisāra's welcoming of the Buddha is preserved in the Bimbisāra-pratyudgamana-sūtra (NE 289). The king became a lay disciple and vowed to refrain from violence from that day forward. He asked that the Buddha bless Rājagṛha with his presence and invited him to a feast.

The next day, all the people of Rājagṛha came out to meet the Buddha; according to the Nidāna-kathā, the road to Bimbisāra's palace, six miles long, could not contain all those who traveled it that day. So great was the delight of the people that the place where they viewed the Buddha became known as Vaṇṇabhū, the Place of Praise. Then, from the Trāyastriṁśa Heaven, Śakra, king of the gods, appeared to the assembly in the form of a young Brahmin; he opened a path in the multitude for the Buddha and led the way as the Buddha and the people walked to the city of Rājagṛha.

Bimbisāra welcomed the whole Sangha with a generous donation of alms. After the feast ended, the king poured water over the Buddha's hand and asked that the Buddha accept for the Sangha his favorite pleasure garden: the Kalantakanivāsa Bamboo Grove, where Kalantaka birds had once saved the king's life. This grove was the site of the Sangha's first vihāra (residence) and the site of many of the Buddha's teachings. Here the Buddha gave teachings on the four truths, impermanence, the nature of conditioned existence, and teachings on morality and conduct that provided the foundation of the Sangha's daily life. Members of the royal family, ministers, and laymen came to the Bamboo Grove to hear the Buddha's words. Even the devas descended from the heavenly realms to question the Buddha on points of the Dharma. According to the *Blue Annals,* in Rājagṛha alone the Buddha established the king, several hundred thousand of his subjects, and eighty thousand inhabitants of the heaven realms in the Dharma.

Among the Buddha's most devoted female disciples was Bimbisāra's wife Queen Kṣema, renowned for her great beauty. Although the king wanted her to visit the Buddha, at first she had no inclination to do so. But after a time, hearing so many at the palace speak highly of the Enlightened One, she decided to see him. As she approached, the Buddha showed the proud queen a vision of a heavenly maiden far more beautiful than herself. Humbled, the queen turned away, feeling her beauty inadequate in such company. Then she saw the features of the maiden changing, growing older and wrinkling with age until, as an ancient crone, she fell lifeless at the queen's feet. Understanding by this the transience of beauty and all values based on appearances, the queen awakened faith in the Buddha's teaching. Eventually she became known as the foremost in wisdom among all the female disciples of the Buddha.

The Buddha spent the second Varṣaka or rainy season retreat at Rājagṛha.[1] The rainy season retreat soon became an annual custom; a time of reflection and meditation, the

---

1. The first, according to the Mūlasarvāstivādin Vinaya.

Varṣaka observance became a strong unifying force for the Sangha. According to the Vinaya, the first sixty disciples returned from their travels to join this convocation.

Within a few years, the Sangha had established a number of other vihāras in the vicinity of Rājagṛha, including one located on the summit of Gṛdhrakūṭa, the Vulture Peak. Named both for its unusual shape and for the vultures that inhabited the region, the Vulture Peak is renowned as the site where the Buddha taught the Prajñāpāramitā Sūtras during the second period of propounding the Dharma, and where he taught most of the Ratnakūṭa Sūtras during the third period. King Bimbisāra, who came often to seek the Buddha's counsel and teachings, built a wide road to the summit, which modern pilgrims still use. The opening of the Ratnakūṭa-sūtra describes the Vulture Peak as it appeared when the Buddha gave this extensive teaching:

"Once the Buddha was residing on the Vulture Peak at Rājagṛha. Through the virtue of the Tathāgata, this monarch of mountains was bounteous and majestic and radiated splendor and beauty. Its slopes were adorned with a vast array of flowers and fruit trees; by the power of the Buddha, yakṣas and tribes of savages peacefully lived there, as did birds and wild animals of every kind.

"On the mountain, streams, lakes, and ponds were covered with lotuses, their banks fragrant with a vast variety of herbs. The rain clouds which crowned Vulture Peak were swept away by the mighty voices of the gods to reveal sparkling skies. High grasses the color of a peacock's throat covered the slopes, and the ground gave spring to the step. Lotuses the color of gold, crystal, and fire gave off incomparable fragrance in all ten directions.

"Gods, men, and nāgas gave myriad offerings of precious gems, incense, balsam, silks, and victory banners which formed clouds of brilliant color that decorated the mountain. The essence of sandalwood floated in the breeze as gods, nāgas, and gandharvas offered gifts beyond imagining to pay honor to the Tathāgata, who came forth from illusion, born from stainless action, free from defilements, manifesting the Dharma in all directions like a dream."

Rājagṛha, nestled in a small bowl-like valley encircled by five large hills, was surrounded by many pleasant groves and caves that provided the Sangha with ample sites for meditation and assembly. Among the best known of these locations, long favorite homes of ascetics and sages, were the Vaibhāra Grove, the Saptaparṇī and Indraśaila caves, and the caves on the side of the Sarpaśuṇḍikaprāgbhāra.

Śāriputra and Maudgalyāyana

During the Sangha's first year at Rājagṛha, the Buddha established the Ārya Sangha, the community of Arhats that exemplifies the benefits of following the Buddha's teachings. Among those who joined the Sangha at this time were Śāriputra and Maudgalyāyana, two of the Buddha's foremost disciples. Śāriputra, the son of a wealthy Brahmin philosopher, was born in Nālandā, a village about six miles north of Rājagṛha, and Maudgalyāyana, a Brahmin and son of a king's minister, was born in a neighboring village. Both were still youths when Śāriputra was acknowledged as surpassing even his father in understanding the Vedic scriptures, and Maudgalyāyana was given responsibility for the education of five hundred young Brahmins.

Although their parents were not on good terms, Śāriputra and Maudgalyāyana became fast friends. One day, while viewing a large festival, they began to think deeply about the transience of life and the inevitable end of all efforts at happiness. When Maudgalyāyana, against his family's wishes, decided to leave the world for a renunciate's life, Śāriputra went with him; both became disciples of Sañjaya, a prominent teacher of the Ājīvika (agnostic or skeptic) tradition.

Before Sañjaya passed away, he advised Śāriputra and Maudgalyāyana to become disciples of the Śākya teacher residing in Rājagṛha; they were not to mention their caste or family name, but to abandon pride and practice the Dharma diligently in the Buddha's Sangha. Sañjaya gave them a final teaching on the instability of human happiness and entrusted them with the guidance of his 250 followers. The two friends mourned their teacher, who seemed to have touched the threshold of wisdom, and vowed to each other that whichever one of them found the direct path to truth would first teach it to the other.

Śāriputra soon encountered the bhikṣu Aśvajit, one of the Buddha's original five disciples. Impressed by Aśvajit's appearance, Śāriputra followed the bhikṣu as he walked about Rājagṛha on his alms-round; then, when Aśvajit had finished and was leaving the village, Śāriputra asked the bhikṣu about the Buddha's teaching. Aśvajit replied with a single statement: "all things come into being and pass away through causation; the Tathāgata has explained the causes and the way to end them." These words were sufficient to convey the essence of the Buddha's teaching to Śāriputra. He brought this teaching to his friend Maudgalyāyana, who had immediate insight into its meaning.

Accompanied by Sañjaya's 250 disciples, Śāriputra and Maudgalyāyana went at once to the Bamboo Grove where the Buddha was teaching and became part of the Ārya Sangha. A few weeks later, while the Buddha was residing in the Sukarakhata Cave on the Vulture Peak, Śāriputra's uncle Dīrghanākha, "the long-nailed one," an ascetic of the skeptic school, came to judge for himself the wisdom of the Buddha. When Dīrghanākha proclaimed that he was a skeptic, and so could not accept any doctrine as conclusive, Śākyamuni showed him the inconsistency of this statement.

This teaching, known as The Questions of Dīrghanākha (NE 342), won the heart of the aged ascetic and completely freed Śāriputra from all residual attachments to worldly life. Śāriputra and Maudgalyāyana became Arhats and from that time exemplified two complementary paths to liberation:

Śāriputra became known as the disciple unsurpassed in wisdom and Maudgalyāyana as the disciple unsurpassed in psychic attainments.

The Sangha then numbered 1,250 bhikṣus: the thousand disciples of the Kāśyapa brothers and the 250 disciples of Śāriputra and Maudgalyāyana. When the Sūtras name those assembled to hear the teaching, the mention of 1,250 bhikṣus refers to this core group of the Ārya Sangha.

Mahākāśyapa

Mahākāśyapa, the Buddha's disciple foremost in ascetic practice, was born in the Brahmin village of Mahātiṣṭha, near Rājagṛha, and educated in the traditional manner. His given name was Pippalāyana, recalling his birth under a pippala tree. From an early age he was strongly attracted to the ascetic life but married at the insistence of his parents. Since his wife, Bhadrā Kapilānī, was similarly inclined to asceticism, they decided to live as brother and sister; eventually they agreed to renounce worldly life completely and began the search for a teacher.

Mahākāśyapa left home the day of the Buddha's enlightenment. When he heard that the Buddha was residing at the Bamboo Grove, he immediately set out for Rājagṛha; simultaneously the Buddha left the Bamboo Grove and went toward the village of Nālandā. When Mahākāśyapa met the Enlightened One halfway between Rājagṛha and Nālandā, he recognized him instantly and fell to the ground at his feet, declaring himself the Buddha's disciple. After ordaining Mahākāśyapa, the Buddha exchanged robes with him and gave him specific instructions for practice; following them assiduously, Mahākāśyapa became an Arhat in eight days. A strong and capable leader, Mahākāśyapa became one of the Buddha's most trusted disciples. In time, his former wife Bhadrā Kapilānī also joined the Sangha.

Where the Buddha Taught

Although most sources agree on the major events of the Buddha's life, attempts to create a precise chronology for the years between the enlightenment and the Buddha's final journey have not been entirely successful. Buddhist chroniclers of all traditions have searched the Sūtras to shape a chronological sequence of teachings and events, but much of their chronology is based on speculation.

The commentary on the Buddhavaṁsa, a text in the Theravādin tradition, names the sites where the Buddha spent the first twenty rainy seasons of his teaching years, as shown on the chart on page 90. According to the Mahāyāna tradition, the Buddha resided mostly in Śrāvastī for the next twenty-five years, either at Jeta's Grove, or nearby in the Pūrvārāma (built by the patroness Viśākhā), said to have been second only to the Jetavana in magnificence. However, other sources, specifically in the tradition known to the seventh-century pilgrim Hsüan-tsang, state that during these years the Buddha divided his time between Śrāvastī and Sāketa, where there was also a dwelling-place named Pūrvārāma built by the same Viśākhā, who was married to a rich merchant of Sāketa.

According to the Saṁskṛtāsaṁskṛta-viniścaya, as cited in the *Blue Annals*, the Buddha Śākyamuni lived for eighty years. He spent twenty-nine years in the palace and practiced austerities for six years. Having attained enlightenment, he spent the first summer retreat at Sārnāth, site of his first teaching, and the second and fourth summer retreats at Veṇuvana, the Bamboo Grove. The chart on page 91 illustrates this description of the rainy season locations.

The Mahāvibhāṣa gives the following summary (as quoted by Bu-ston):

"In the place where he swung the Wheel of the Doctrine
in Vaiśālī, in Pandubhūmi, in the realm of the gods,
in Balaghna and in Kauśāmbī,

in the wilderness, in Uśīrayicī,
in the Bamboo Grove [Rājagṛha],
and in the city of Kapilavastu–
in each of these places the Lord,
the highest of living beings, abided for a year.

Twenty-three years he resided in Śrāvastī,
four years in the place abounding with remedies
[Bhaiṣajyavana],
two years he spent in the Indraśaila Cave,
five years in the villages of Rājagṛha,
six years he underwent the practice of asceticism and
twenty-nine years he abided in his father's palace.
Thus the Lord, the holiest and highest of sages,
attained the age of eighty and departed into nirvāṇa."

As for the time of the Buddha's return to his homeland
in Kapilavastu, there are two major views: according to the
Theravādin tradition (related in the Jātaka-nidāna and other
sources), the Buddha went to Kapilavastu from Rājagṛha in
the first year after his enlightenment, after he had been away
from his homeland for six years. These sources state that the
Buddha later returned to Kapilavastu several times and observed the fifteenth rainy season retreat in Kapilavastu. In
the tradition preserved in the Mūlasarvāstivādin Vinaya, the
Buddha first returned to Kapilavastu some six years after the
Buddha's enlightenment, after teaching in Śrāvastī and con-
verting Prasenajit, King of Kosala, to the Dharma.

The sequence of sites of the Buddha's teachings presented
in the following pages generally follows the order given in
the Mūlasarvāstivādin Vinaya as preserved in Tibetan translation. The chronology given in the Buddhavaṁsa commentary has been incorporated insofar as possible, together with
teachings preserved in the Chinese and Theravādin Buddhist
traditions. For a helpful overview of the Buddha's teachings,
read the settings of the Sūtras preserved in the Tibetan bKa'-
'gyur given in Part V of this book.

Varṣaka Sites (Theravādin Tradition)

Rainy season	Location	Age of the Buddha
1	Sārnāth	35
2	Rājagṛha	36
3	Rājagṛha	37
4	Rājagṛha	38
5	Vaiśālī	39
6	Maṅkula Hill (Rājagṛha?)	40
7	Trāyastriṁśa Heaven	41
8	Bhagga (Suṁsumagiri)	42
9	Kauśāmbī	43
10	Pārileyakka Forest	44
11	Nāla (Nālanda?)	45
12	Verañja (Vairantī)	46
13	Cāliya Hill	47
14	Jeta's Grove, Śrāvastī	48
15	Kapilavastu	49
16	Ālavi	51
17	Rājagṛha	52
18	Cāliya Hill	53
19	Rājagṛha	54
20	Śrāvastī	55

Varṣaka Sites (Mahāyāna Tradition)

Rainy season	Location	Age of the Buddha
1	Sārnāth	35
2	Veṇuvana (Rājagṛha)	36
3	?	37
4	Veṇuvana (Rājagṛha)	38
5	Vaiśālī	39
6	Mt. Golāṅgula (Rājagṛha)	40
7	Trāyastriṁśa Heaven	41
8	Śiśumāragiri	42
9	Kauśāmbī	43
10	Pārileyakka Forest	44
11	Rājagṛha	45
12	Verañja (Vairantī)	46
13	Caityagiri	47
14	Jeta's Grove, Śrāvastī	48
15	Nyagrodhārāma (Kapilavastu)	49
16	Āṭavaka	51
17	Rājagṛha	52
18	Jvālinī Cave (near Gayā)	53
19	Jvālinī Cave	54
20	Rājagṛha	55
21–24	Mṛgaramātṛārāma (convent of Mother Mṛgarā, near Śrāvastī)	56–59
25–45	Śrāvastī	60–80

The Gift of the Jetavana

A few years after enlightenment, while the Buddha was staying at the cremation grounds of Śītavana in Rājagṛha, he was invited to the home of the guildmaster of Rājagṛha to partake of the midday meal. While at the guildmaster's house, the Buddha met his host's brother-in-law Sudatta, a rich merchant from the city of Śrāvastī in Kosala. Famed for his generosity, Sudatta is better known in the Sūtras as Anāthapiṇḍada, Giver of Food to the Poor. Anāthapiṇḍada listened intently to the Buddha's teaching on ethics and charity; he became a lay disciple at that first meeting and requested the Buddha's permission to provide a place for the Sangha in Śrāvastī.

Receiving permission, Anāthapiṇḍada returned home to Śrāvastī and searched for a suitable site. He selected a park owned by Prince Jeta, King Prasenajit's son, who had no desire to relinquish it. However, when Anāthapiṇḍada offered to pay as much gold as would cover the whole park, Jeta finally agreed to sell. As he promised, Anāthapiṇḍada arrived at the park with an ox-cart full of gold pieces, which covered all but a corner of Jeta's land. Seeing that Anāthapiṇḍada was willing to give such a fortune to provide a place for the Buddha, Jeta decided to retain that part of the garden so that he himself could build a shrine there and present it to the Buddha as an offering.

Jeta's park was located a short distance south of the walled city of Śrāvastī, the prosperous capital of the kingdom of Kosala. Situated at the juncture of three major trade routes, Śrāvastī was an ideal center for the Sangha. Fifty-seven thousand families were said to live within its walls, surrounded by rich wheat fields nourished by the waters of the Achiravatī (modern Raptī) River. From Śrāvastī, bhikṣus could travel the trade routes throughout northern India. To the north, a road linked Śrāvastī with Mathura, gateway to the route west across the plains to the cities of Takṣaśilā and Gandhāra. To the southwest, a trade route connected Śrāvastī with Sāketa, Kauśāmbī, Vidiśā, Ujjayinī, and Paithana on the Godāvarī River. The route to the southeast connected the countries of Kosala, Śākya, Vṛji, and Magadha; the main road southeast from Śrāvastī passed through Kapilavastu and Kuśinagara to Pāvā, continued through Vaiśālī, and ended at Rājagṛha. It was this road the Buddha had followed upon leaving his father's palace.

Soon after the purchase of Jeta's park, Śāriputra accompanied Anāthapiṇḍada to Śrāvastī to supervise the building of a vihāra. When the members of other spiritual orders (tīrthikas) saw Jeta and Anāthapiṇḍada providing so generously for the Sangha, they feared the growing popularity of the Buddha's teachings and planned ways to stop the Sangha from making a home in Śrāvastī. Śāriputra, to counter their activities, invited them to engage in a contest of spiritual powers, from which Śāriputra emerged victorious. Impressed with Śāriputra's bearing and abilities, Raktakṣa, the chief of the tīrthikas, joined the Sangha; he was followed by a great number of adepts in other traditions as well as by many townspeople of Śrāvastī.

According to the Vinaya, plans for the vihāra in Śrāvastī, sent to earth by devas of the Tuṣita Heaven, specified sixty large and sixty small halls. When Anāthapiṇḍada asked how the vihāra should be ornamented, the Buddha replied:

"On the outside door you must represent a yakṣa holding a club in his hand; in the vestibule you must depict a great miracle, representing the five divisions of beings of the circle of transmigration (wheel of becoming, bhavacakra); in the courtyard, portray scenes from the birth stories (Jātakas); on the door of the Buddha's hall, (Gandhakūṭi, Hall of Perfumes), depict a yakṣa holding a wreath; in the house of the attendants, bhikṣus and sthaviras discussing the Dharma. . . ." The Buddha continued, describing exactly what should be depicted for each area (*Life of the Buddha*, p. 49n).

When the vihāra was completed, the Buddha was welcomed to Śrāvastī with great fanfare. The Acintyaprabhāsanirdeśa-sūtra (NE 103) records that as the Enlightened One entered the city gates, wondrous signs manifested: The blind saw, the deaf heard, and the naked were clothed. All beings in the city, filled with faith in the Dharma, paid homage to the Buddha. When Anāthapiṇḍada presented the vihāra and park to the Sangha, the Buddha named the vihāra the Anā-thapiṇḍadārāma and the park Jetavana, or Jeta's Grove. For his generosity to the Sangha, Anāthapiṇḍada became known as chief among the almsgivers. Prince Jeta, delighted at the naming of the park, ornamented the shrine he had donated with all manner of precious substances.

Soon after, King Prasenajit visited Jeta's Grove. During his visit, the king asked the Tathāgata how he could claim to be a Buddha when the most respected holy men of the country did not consider themselves completely enlightened, and he, the Buddha, had only recently renounced worldly life. Śākyamuni replied to Prasenajit with the teaching known as the Kumāradṛṣṭānta-sūtra (NE 296; Pāli, Dahara-sutta). In this teaching the Buddha explained that there are four things in this world that must not be taken lightly simply because they are young: a royal prince, a serpent, fire, and a disciple of the Buddha. This teaching converted King Prasenajit to the Dharma.

Prasenajit, renowned for his respect for holy men of all traditions, became a devoted sponsor of the Sangha, as did Queen Mallikā, his wife, who never wavered in her confidence in the Buddha's wisdom. Her faith and her love for her husband were instrumental in Prasenajit's taking refuge in the Buddha, Dharma, and Sangha and becoming a true member of the lay Sangha. As accounts in the Vinaya and Sūtras alike record, Prasenajit visited the Buddha often to ask questions that clarified his understanding of the teachings. The Rājāvavādaka-sūtra (NE 221), a teaching on morality and wise government, was given especially for King Prasenajit's benefit. On the occasion of its presentation, the king had arrived at the grove with a great entourage of attendants and townspeople, accompanied by the clashing of cymbals and the sound of drums. The Prasenajit-gāthā (NE 322) relates the Buddha's responses to the king's question concerning the merit of giving offerings to the Tathāgatas.

News of the Buddha's teaching reached a Brahmin master of Śrāvastī named Puṣkarasarin, who sent his disciple Appriya to see if it were true that the Śākya master had all the characteristics of a great sage. Appriya questioned the Buddha on the pursuits of those devoted to religious practice and examined the Buddha's knowledge of the Vedas. Although Appriya had come to examine the Buddha, he returned home humbled and greatly impressed.

Appriya's praise of the Buddha greatly irritated Puṣkarasarin, who struck Appriya with his shoe in frustration and went himself to question the Buddha. Seeing that Puṣkarasarin's greatest obstacle was pride, the Buddha dispelled it; instructing Puṣkarasarin in the truths of suffering, its origin, its cause, and the eightfold path to complete liberation, the Buddha awakened Puṣkarasarin so thoroughly that the Brahmin, full of joy, took refuge in the Three Jewels and became a member of the Sangha.

The Ambaṭṭha-sutta (DN 3) preserves a similar but more detailed account of the Buddha's conversion of the young Vedic scholar Ambaṭṭha and his master Pokkharasādi. Ambaṭṭha, a Brahmin, filled with pride of his caste and family, behaved disdainfully toward the Buddha and insulted the Śākyas as being of inferior birth. Unperturbed, the Buddha engaged Ambaṭṭha in a dialogue that revealed that the Brahmin's pride was groundless; not caste or family, but knowledge elevates an individual to prominence among gods and humans. Without aspiring to perfection in knowledge and conduct, one who adheres to the brahmanic rituals and practices becomes only the servant of the one who seeks such perfection.

Questioning Ambaṭṭha, the Buddha showed the young scholar that he had not been wisely instructed, nor had he been taught how to follow the brahmanic practices. Then

Ambaṭṭha realized how great was the difference between the great Brahmin sages of old and the present conduct and practice of Brahmin teachers, and returned to his teacher Pokkharasādi full of praise for the Buddha.

Beside himself with frustration, yet deeply humbled, Pokkharasādi invited the Buddha to his dwelling, offered well-prepared food, and listened intently as the Buddha spoke of morality, the futility of desire for worldly things, and the way to lasting happiness. As the Buddha spoke, wisdom arose in Pokkharasādi's mind; when he perceived that all that arises must also pass away, confusion and doubt vanished and he saw clearly the significance of the four noble truths. Recognizing that the Buddha's teaching brought forth truly liberating knowledge, Pokkharasādi, filled with joy, took refuge in the Buddha, Dharma, and Sangha together with his disciples, friends, and family.

On many other occasions and in many ways the Buddha engaged Brahmin teachers and practitioners, opening their eyes to deeper dimensions of their actions and encouraging them to break the five fetters that chained them to the wheel of becoming: belief in personality, the skeptical mind that rejects without investigation, belief in the efficacy of rules and ritual, sensual cravings, and all residues of ill-will.

The Mahāli-sutta (DN 6) describes the Buddha's dialogue with the ascetic Nigrodha, in which he demonstrates that ascetic practices of themselves can exacerbate bondage to the five fetters and points out the view in which Nigrodha's efforts would more surely lead to liberation. Respecting that Nigrodha had his own teacher and his own path, the Buddha conveyed to Nigrodha how to avoid the pitfalls and how best to realize the goals of that particular teaching and path. In this teaching the Buddha clearly illustrated that ethics and morality, strengthened through mindful restraint and detachment from desire, counteract error arising from spiritual pride and egoistic views and provide the most favorable environment for any religious practice.

The city of Śrāvastī, where the Buddha lived the longest, nurtured the formative years of the Sangha. The Buddha spent most of the rainy season retreats with the Sangha in Jeta's Grove, where he gave nearly three quarters of the Sūtras (Pāli: Suttas) preserved in the Pāli Canon and at least 102 of the Sūtras preserved in Tibetan translation.

While Jeta's Grove served as the first substantial home for the Sangha, several other large vihāras for the Sangha were also established at Śrāvastī. After the Jetavana's central vihāra, the largest was the Pūrvārāma, or Eastern Monastery, a magnificent two-storied building with one thousand rooms built at great cost by Viśākhā, a beloved benefactress of the Sangha. Viśākhā became known as "Mother Mṛgāra" after she converted Mṛgāra, her father-in-law, and in that sense became his spiritual mother. Close by the Pūrvārāma was the Ekesalakatinduka Grove donated by Mallikā, wife of King Prasenajit, where wandering ascetics were always welcome. King Prasenajit, in turn, built the Rājakārāma, the Royal Monastery, for the Sangha.

Return to Kapilavastu

Shortly after his conversion, Prasenajit sent word to Śuddhodana, the Buddha's father, telling him to rejoice, that his son had attained his purpose and was even then quenching the thirst of humanity with the nectar of enlightened knowledge. Śuddhodana immediately sent a series of messengers to find his son and implore him to return to his homeland, but each messenger joined the Sangha and became an Arhat. Having lost all interest in worldly matters, none of them ever communicated Śuddhodana's message to the Buddha.

Finally the Śākya Udāyin promised Śuddhodana that he would return with news, even if he did join the Sangha. Although he became a bhikṣu after meeting the Buddha in Rājagṛha, he returned to Kapilavastu as he had agreed. He told Śuddhodana that the Buddha would soon return to his homeland and asked that the king prepare a vihāra on the model of Jeta's Grove outside the city. Śuddhodana prepared a vihāra in a grove of banyan trees near the Rohinī River, later known as the Nyagrodha, or Banyan Grove.

In turning homeward, the Buddha followed a tradition established long before his time. After enlightenment, all Buddhas return to the land of their birth. Hsüan-tsang, a seventh-century Chinese pilgrim to the Buddhist holy places, describes specific locations where Buddhas of the past were welcomed by their fathers; having succeeded in opening the path to the end of suffering, they offered the people of their homeland the benefits of their realization.

As the Buddha and twenty thousand disciples drew near the city, King Śuddhodana, followed by a great crowd, came out to greet him. Overcome by the splendor of Śākyamuni's appearance, the king bowed at his son's feet, much to the amazement of his people. The Pitāputra-samagamana-sūtra (NE 60), the Reunion of Father and Son, relates that on this occasion the Buddha gave an extensive teaching on the effects of previous actions. Still, Śuddhodana yearned for his son to revert to his former life and spoke of the joys of the palace. Unsuccessful in persuading his son to return, Śuddhodana sorrowfully returned to the palace.

The Śākyas were proud warriors; while they were joyful at the prince's return, they could not comprehend why he would choose to live in the wilderness and beg for alms in the streets of their city. In order to dispel their ignorance, the Buddha performed a series of magical transformations. Rising high in the air, he caused flames of fire to flare forth from the upper part of his body and streams of water to flow from the lower part. Then, reversing this flow, he caused water to come out of the upper part and fire from the lower. In such a way he convinced the Śākyas that he was a perfectly enlightened Buddha and no longer the prince they had once known. The Buddha is said to have performed this miracle two more times in the early years of his teaching: in the city of Rājagṛha and at Śrāvastī, before ascending to the Trāyastriṁśa Heaven.

The Buddha then dwelled in the Banyan Grove, where he ordained his uncle Śuklodana and seventy thousand Śākyas. Shortly afterwards he accepted into the Sangha his father's other two brothers, Droṇodaya and Amṛtodana, together with another 141,000 Śākyas. Even the great ṛṣi Kapila came to hear the Buddha, who gave the Sthānasthāpaka-sūtra (NE 333) for the sage's benefit.

Although the Buddha sent Maudgalyāyana to convert his father to the Dharma, the power of even this great Arhat could not sway Śuddhodana's mind, which was fixed on regaining his son. Then one day the devas Brahmā and Śakra, accompanied by a great number of gods and the four World-Guardians, came to the Banyan Grove to hear the Buddha's teaching. When King Śuddhodana saw the Buddha teaching this shining assembly, memories of the past fell from his mind. Now able to perceive the nature of his son's transformation, Śuddhodana also became a member of the Sangha.

The Buddha's cousins Aniruddha, Bhadrika, and Raivata, desiring to join the Sangha but fearful that Devadatta would then become king, persuaded Devadatta to enter the Sangha with them. After they issued a proclamation stating that they were relinquishing their succession to the throne, Devadatta realized too late that he had been tricked into giving up his opportunity to rule. From that moment he redirected his ambitions and sought power within the Sangha, eventually attempting to supplant the Buddha.

King Śuddhodana sent the royal barber Upāli to shave the heads and beards of the young Śākyas for their ordination. As a servant of low caste, Upāli felt it would not be appropriate to mention that he also deeply yearned to enter the Sangha. But Śāriputra, knowing that Upāli would become an enlightened Arhat, led him to the Buddha, who called out to him, "Come here, bhikṣu, and lead a life of purity." Immediately Upāli's hair spontaneously fell from his head, and he stood arrayed in the robes of a bhikṣu. The young Śākyas arrived soon afterwards and were ordained after Upāli.

The Buddha's wife, overwhelmed with desire to win him back, had a potion made that would bind whoever drank it to the person who gave it to him. She gave the potion to Rāhula, her son, who was then six years old, and asked that he give the drink to his father. Rāhula did so, but the Buddha returned it to him, and the child drank it down. After that Rāhula could not be prevented from following the Buddha, who asked Śāriputra to ordain his son.

The Vinaya mentions that at the time of the Buddha's first visit to Kapilavastu, Ānanda, son of the Buddha's uncle Amṛtodana, was six years old, the same age as Rāhula. Ānanda's father knew of a prediction that his son would become the Buddha's attendant, and at first sought to prevent their meeting. Realizing that Ānanda would become an Arhat if he joined the order, the Buddha went to Amṛtodana's house where he taught both father and son. Amṛtodana then granted permission for Ānanda to join the order. The Buddha also converted his cousin Nanda, who was very attached to his wife. The Nandagarbhāvakrānti-nirdeśa-sūtra (NE 57) relates how the Buddha showed his cousin Nanda the delights of the heavens to free him from worldly attachments, and the Nandapravrajya-sūtra (NE 328) records the Buddha's instruction to Nanda on the benefits of following a religious life.

Vaiśālī

While Śākyamuni Buddha was residing in Rājagṛha, the Licchavis of Vaiśālī, capital of the Vṛjian confederacy, were suffering greatly from an epidemic. They invited in turn each of the six great philosopher-magicians known throughout the broad plains of the Ganges basin, but none could stop the course of the plague. Hearing of the Buddha, the governor of Vaiśālī dispatched the respected courtier Tomara to Bimbisāra, king of Magadha, requesting that the Tathāgata come to heal the people of Vaiśālī. Bimbisāra agreed, on the condition that the Buddha would be treated with the same respect accorded him in Magadha.

It is said that the Buddha first sent his disciple Ānanda to Vaiśālī to dispel the epidemic and purify the city through mantras. Through the power of the Buddha, the epidemic was halted. The Vaiśālī-praveśa-sūtra (NE 312) mentions that upon arriving in the area, the Buddha and his attendants were invited to stay in the Mango Grove, which the royal courtesan Āmrapālī donated to the Sangha. The grateful Licchavis remained devoted to the Buddha throughout his lifetime. They provided a large park for the Sangha, the Mahāvana, where a group of monkeys offered a gift of honey to the Buddha and made a bathing pond for his use.

In the course of his travels, the Buddha often visited Vaiśālī. The Bodhisattvacarya-nirdeśa-sūtra (NE 184) relates the marvels that attended one of the Buddha's entries into this garden city, which resembled an earthly paradise, so great was its prosperity and the elegance of the people. The Buddha remarked that the like of this city had never been seen, even in the Trāyastriṁśa Heaven.

Vaiśālī became the site of important Mahāyāna teachings, among them the Bhadrakalpika-sūtra (NE 94), in which beings assembled from celestial as well as earthly realms to hear the extensive teaching on the thousand Buddhas of our aeon. Also in Vaiśālī, the Buddha asked the Bodhisattva Mañjuśrī to visit the ailing layman Vimalakīrti, who gave a moving teaching on the nature and path of the Bodhisattva known as the Vimalakīrti-nirdeśa-sūtra (NE 107). In the garden of Kūṭāgara, the Buddha predicted that Vimalakīrti's daughter Candrottarā would eventually become a Buddha, as mentioned in the Candrottarādārikā-vyākaraṇa-sūtra (NE 191).

Ratnajāli, son of a leader of the Licchavis, had a dream that the devas of the Tuṣita Heaven descended to praise the virtues of the Buddha. In the morning he went to the Mahāvana Park, where, on the banks of the Monkey Pond, he received the teaching known as the Ratnajāli-paripṛcchā-sūtra (NE 163) in answer to his questions. A woman 120 years old became filled with faith and asked for teachings on birth, old age, and death, which the Enlightened One gave in the Mahālalikā-paripṛcchā-sūtra (NE 171). To merchants about to depart for Takṣaśilā, the Buddha gave the Dhvajāgra-sūtra (NE 293), a teaching on the benefits of honoring the Three Jewels. Laymen and women, bhikṣus, bhikṣuṇīs, devas, and great Bodhisattvas—all received teachings here according to their ability to understand.

Sojourn at Kapilavastu

The Buddha returned to Kapilavastu upon hearing that his father King Śuddhodana was near death. This may have happened in the fifteenth year after the enlightenment, when the Buddha spent the rainy season retreat in his homeland. At his father's request on a previous visit, the Buddha had given the Āyuṣpattiyathākāra-paripṛcchā-sūtra (NE 308), describing what occurs after death. He had also told of the means of dispelling darkness in the ten directions of the world in the Daśadigadhākara-vidhvaṁsana-sūtra (NE 269). Comforting his father, he now clarified that lay disciples as well as bhikṣus may attain nirvāṇa.

The Dānapāramitā-sūtra (NE 182) tells how the Buddha, in order to benefit all the people of Kapilavastu, resided for some months in the great grove outside the city. Here, in this place filled with all varieties of fruit trees and flowers and many kinds of animals and birds, the Buddha gave a teaching on the six perfections, in which he explained the value of practicing dāna (giving), elevating generosity to the highest spiritual perfection. Here also the Buddha gave the Dharmaskandha-sūtra (NE 245), a sermon on the 84,000 components of the Dharma, and the Kṣemaṅkara-paripṛcchā-sūtra (NE 165), an explanation of the duties of a Bodhisattva. All the Śākyas soon became lay supporters of the Buddha, Dharma, and Sangha. So great was their devotion that they agreed that in every household with two or more sons, one son would enter the order of bhikṣus.

The Buddha returned to Kapilavastu at least two more times, once to settle a dispute between the Śākyas and their neighbors, and again, to ensure their liberation shortly before the destruction of Kapilavastu.

Acceptance of Women into the Order

When the Buddha first returned to Kapilavastu, Śuddhodana would not permit the Śākya women to visit the Nyagrodha Grove and listen to the Dharma. But Queen Mahāprajāpatī greatly wished to hear the teachings and invited one of the Buddha's new disciples, her kinsman Mahānāman, to teach her and her attendants about the Dharma. After hearing the teachings, the Queen did not rest until she received permission to attend the Buddha in person. At once she and five hundred Śākya women went to hear the Buddha. It was then that Mahāprajāpatī, inspired by the wish to become a bhikṣunī, implored the Buddha three times to accept women into the order. The Buddha advised her to seek perfection as a laywoman: "Be pure, chaste, and live virtuously, and you will find a lasting reward, blessings, and happiness."

While the king lived, Mahāprajāpatī patiently observed this advice. But after her husband's death, she again sought to enter the order as a fully ordained bhikṣunī. When the Buddha left Kapilavastu, she and the Buddha's wife Gopā, together with five hundred other women, shaved their heads, dressed themselves as mendicant monks, and traveled after the Tathāgata and his disciples.

Exhausted and covered with dust, they met the Buddha again in Natika, in the land of the Vṛjis on the road to Rājagṛha. After hearing the Buddha teach the Dharma, Mahāprajāpatī again asked to enter the order and went away weeping when her request was refused. Seeing the women's fervor, Ānanda sought to persuade the Buddha to change his mind. Three times he made this request, each time with greater urgency.

At length the Buddha agreed to admit women into the order, if they would agree to eight special conditions which would protect them from harm and gossip in a society where women were considered little more than chattel. These conditions required bhikṣuṇīs to adhere to conduct that the society of the day would recognize as virtuous. In outward appearance they would defer to the privileged position of men, while working toward liberation on an equal basis: The Vinaya and other sources relate many instances of women gaining the highest enlightenment. What appears to have been unique for the times was the formal establishment of full ordination for women and provisions for a female religious order within the community of wandering monks.

Dialogue with the Philosophers

While the Buddha was dwelling at Rājagṛha, he heard that the six philosopher-magicians who had failed to dispel the plague at Vaiśālī were spreading rumors that the Buddha was a charlatan. These six each represented a tradition of philosophy current in the Buddha's time: Gośālīputra was a leader of the Ājīvikas, and Nirgrantha Jñātiputra was a Jain. Pūrṇa-Kāśyapa, Sañjaya, Ajita-Keśakambala, and Kakuda-Kātyāyana were of the skeptic, materialist, and determinist traditions. Fearing that the Buddha's success in Vaiśālī had diminished their status with the people, they were asking for a public contest to establish the superiority of their powers.

The Buddha, realizing that the time had come when he could not avert a confrontation with the followers of other teachings, proclaimed that he would, in four months, meet the six at Śrāvastī, where he would demonstrate the power of the Dharma under a great mango tree. Hearing this, the six teachers had all the mango trees in Śrāvastī cut down. King Prasenajit then prepared a place for the contest between Śrāvastī and Jeta's Grove. Upon arriving, the Buddha cast a mango-seed upon the ground, and it immediately grew into a magnificent tree with great spreading branches. Standing under the tree, the Buddha demonstrated the logical flaws in the six teachers' doctrines.

Then, to fully impress those assembled with the illusory nature of reality, the Buddha performed the "miracle of the pairs" as he had done in Kapilavastu. The miracle continued through twenty-two variations of paired actions. Then the Buddha created a series of manifestations; he appeared as if walking along a jeweled walkway in the sky and replicated a great array of thousands of Buddhas filling the great arc of the heavens. While all present stood enraptured by this display, the six teachers, fearing to reveal their inferior abilities, quietly departed.

Teaching in the Trāyastrimśa Heaven

After this contest, without telling any of his followers, the Buddha ascended to the Trāyastrimśa Heaven, where he instructed his mother and a host of devas. In teaching his mother he fulfilled another traditional action of all Buddhas. Among the teachings given in the Trāyastrimśa realm were the Jñānakasūtra-nāma-buddhāvadāna-sūtra (NE 344), an instruction requested by Jñānaka, a god terrified of birth in the animal realm; the Pratītyasamutpāda-sūtra (NE 212), an Abhidharma instruction; the Trāyastrimśa-parivarta-sūtra (NE 223), a teaching on the theory and practice of Bodhisattvas; and the Caturdharma-nirdeśa-sūtra (NE 249), a teaching on the four things with which Bodhisattvas suppress and destroy the accumulation of all bad actions.

Descent from the Heaven Realms

According to the Buddhavaṁsa commentary, the Buddha dwelled in the Trāyastriṁśa Heaven during the seventh rainy season, when he was forty-one years of age. Maudgalyāyana, using his superior powers, was able to see the Buddha teaching in the Trāyastriṁśa Heaven; he told the bhikṣus and bhikṣuṇīs where the Buddha had gone and said that he would soon descend to the world at Sāṁkāśya.

Among the large crowd assembled to greet the Buddha upon his return was the bhikṣuṇī Utpalavarṇā, who was saddened, seeing that there was no way that she, a woman, could approach the Buddha in such an eager throng. Knowing the purity of her heart, the Buddha transformed Utpalavarṇā's form into that of a Cakravartin King; the crowd gave way before this splendid figure, and Utpalavarṇā became the first to welcome the Buddha upon his arrival. The Buddha returned to earth as Maudgalyāyana had predicted; he descended on a ladder made of lapis lazuli, accompanied by Brahmā on a golden ladder to his right and by Indra on a crystal ladder to his left.

Travels Outside the Madhyadeśa

The places named most frequently in the Sūtras indicate that the Buddha usually traveled along an elliptical route through the cities and countryside of Magadha, Vṛji, and Kosala, a region corresponding to modern Bihār and Uttar Pradesh. If a journey began at Rājagṛha, the route would often lead north through Nālandā, cross the Ganges River near the village of Pāṭaligrāma (later Pāṭaliputra, modern Patna), and continue north to Vaiśālī. From Vaiśālī the road wound north through the land of the Vṛjis, Mallas, and Śākyas to Śrāvastī, the capital of the great kingdom of Kosala. From Śrāvastī the route would lead south to Sāketa and Vārāṇasī, past Mt. Gayā, and back to Rājagṛha. At stopping places along these routes, or even while walking, the

Buddha gave teachings as situations arose. Thus a number of Sūtras give indefinite locations such as "the banks of the Ganges," or refer to mountain sites and villages long vanished from memory.

While traveling on the road from Rājagṛha to Nālandā, the Buddha and his disciples overheard a vigorous dialogue between the mendicant Suppiya and his student Brahmadatta, who were walking the road close behind them. While Suppiya deprecated the Buddha, his teaching, and his Sangha, Brahmadatta defended them. The Buddha and his disciples heard every word of the argument between Suppiya and his disciple, which continued through the evening, when all the travelers stayed the night together at the royal rest house in the Mango Grove near Nālandā. In the morning, all the bhikṣus gathered around the Buddha, who taught them how best to respond to praise and blame. The Buddha then discussed opinions and views rooted in eternalism and nihilism using the image of a net of sixty-two grounds; those who propound and argue such views are caught in a net of their own making; unable to get out, they can come to no resolution, no realization, and no point of truth. Like Suppiya, they can only go on struggling. The Buddha named this teaching the Brahmājāla-sūtra (NE 352, DN 1), the Net of Brahmā.

The Sūtras relate that on occasion the Buddha traveled beyond his accustomed route. During the eighth year of his teaching, the commentary on the Buddhavaṃsa records that the Buddha traveled among the Bhaggas, where he spent the rainy season in the Deer Park in the Bhesakaḷā Grove on Mt. Suṁsumāra. At that time Prince Bodhi, son of King Udayana of Vatsa, requested the Buddha to consecrate his new palace, Kokananda. After the ceremony, the Buddha answered Prince Bodhi's questions, explaining the difficulties in finding happiness through either immersion in ascetic practices or in pleasure. The Buddha compared success in religious practice to the balance needed in riding an elephant. For religious practice, it was necessary to balance faith, wholesome conduct, honesty, perseverance, and wisdom. (*Bodhirājakumāra-sutta*, MN 85)

Years earlier, Ghosita, Kukkuṭa, and Pāvāri, three merchants from Kauśāmbī, capital of Vatsa, had joined the lay Sangha in Śrāvastī and invited the Buddha to their city. Each of them built an arāma, a place for the Sangha to stay: the Ghositārāma, Kukkuṭārāma, and Pāvārikāmbavana. A fourth place, the Badarikārāma, was also built about that time. All these places, particularly the Ghositārāma, developed into major Dharma centers.

Accompanied by many disciples, the Buddha began the journey west to Vatsa, King Udayana's kingdom. Although Udayana's son, Prince Bodhi, had welcomed the Buddha warmly, King Udayana appears to have been a hot-tempered man jealous of teachers who might influence his court and his family. Udayana had a long-standing rivalry with Pradyota, the powerful king of Avanti, who had once kidnapped and imprisoned him. As the Buddha neared Kauśāmbī, Udayana was preparing for war; viewing the Buddha's approach as a bad omen, he shot an arrow toward the Tathāgata. But as the arrow flew through the air, the king heard this teaching:

"From malice is misery brought forth—
he who here gives in to strife and quarrels
hereafter will experience the misery of hell.
So put away malice and quarreling."

Immediately repenting his action, King Udayana sat down before the Tathāgata, who counseled him to concentrate on conquering the ego, the most powerful opponent of all. Drawing on the king's training as a warrior, the Buddha advised the king to view discernment as the sword, faith, charity, and morality as the fort, virtue as the army, and patience as the armor. "Taking up diligence as a spear, use meditation as the bow, and penetrate the enemy with the arrow of detachment." (*Mulasarvāstivādin Vinaya*)

According to most traditions, the Buddha spent the ninth and tenth rainy seasons in the vicinity of Kauśāmbī. The Theravādin tradition relates that finding life close to the capital crowded and harried and wearied of contentiousness among the Kauśāmbī bhikṣus, the Buddha withdrew to the Pārileyyaka Forest, where he spent the eleventh rainy season, protected and attended by a friendly elephant.

The enthusiasm for the Dharma shown by the wives of King Udayana created great tension between the king and the Sangha. Udayana was suspicious of Ānanda, who had been sent to his court, and he had tried to have Piṇḍola Bhāradvāja, the first emissary, devoured by red ants. According to the Udayanavatsarāja-paripṛcchā-sūtra (NE 73), while the Buddha was residing at Kauśāmbī, in the Grove of Melodies, the princess Syāmā, devoted to the Buddha, was wrongfully accused of harboring lascivious desires for him. Quick to anger, King Udayana believed the lies and ordered Syāmā executed. But at the time of execution, she concentrated so deeply on love and kindness that the axe did not fall, and a great light appeared to the king. Seeking the cause of this happening, King Udayana questioned the Buddha; he became converted to the Dharma as a result of the teaching he received.

Samāvatī, one of King Udayana's principal wives, developed a great interest in the Dharma, although she had no opportunity to meet with the Buddha directly. When she heard that the Buddha was in Kauśāmbī, she sent her attendant Uttarā to hear the teachings and had her report every word that was spoken. Uttarā was said to have heard more of the Buddha's teachings than any other laywoman; her devotion to serving her mistress enabled Queen Samāvatī to attain enlightenment.

Travels to the North

The Buddhavaṁsa commentary relates that the Buddha spent the eleventh rainy season at Nāla and the twelfth rainy season in Verantī, north of Kauśāmbī, at the invitation of the Brahmin Agnidatta. Although there are accounts of the Buddha using his special powers to visit more distant lands, Vairantī, on the road leading from Mathura to Takṣaśilā, appears to have been the northwest extent of the Buddha's travels on foot. It may have been on this journey that the Buddha visited Mathurā, which became a major Dharma center in the centuries following the Parinirvāṇa.

The Buddha sent his disciples to introduce the Dharma in the lands beyond Kauśāmbī, along the trade route southwest to the sea. About this time, the Brahmin Kātyāyana, a native of Avanti, became the Buddha's disciple upon hearing the teaching of the middle way, the four noble truths, and the twelve-linked chain of dependent origination. After his ordination, the Buddha sent Kātyāyana and five hundred other disciples to carry the Dharma to Pradyota, king of the western region of Mālwā, whose capital city was Ujjayinī. Also carrying the teachings west was the merchant Pūrṇa from Sopāraka, who, after being ordained in Śrāvastī, returned to the western seacoast, where he founded a Dharma community and monastery.

The Bhikṣu

As the Sangha expanded, the Buddha instructed his disciples on how to receive novices into the order and how to ordain those who were prepared to become full bhikṣus. Although the Buddha was the guide for the Sangha, the Sangha had no equivalent of a "head monk." The Buddha therefore established procedures for electing two senior bhikṣus and five kinds of teachers to carry out the preparations and ritual of ordination.

Members of the Sangha of bhikṣus shaved their heads, a traditional mark of renunciation, and retained nothing in their appearance that tended to establish caste or encourage pride. For this reason bhikṣus did not wear the sacred cord that denoted social standing in brahmanic society. The senior disciples became the model for the Sangha, and the Buddha's teaching established a clear foundation for how to live the religious life and attain the fruit of the Arhat's path. Recognizing that not everyone drawn to the Dharma would have the circumstances, motivation, and stamina to live the mendicant's life, the Buddha gave guidelines for evaluating an applicant's readiness to enter the order and explained what procedures to follow for ordination. These guidelines became more detailed over time to address specific situations that arose.

The first rules for conduct of bhikṣus were likewise general in nature; disciples such as the Kāśyapa brothers, accustomed to ascetic discipline, needed few directives. But as more disciples were attracted directly from the laity, more explicit instructions were necessary. Here too the Buddha taught the middle way between asceticism and laxity, as exemplified in the story of Śroṇa.

Śrona, the son of a rich merchant, was so pampered by his doting father that he never walked anywhere, and long tufts of golden hair grew on the soles of his feet. When he became a bhikṣu, he took up extreme ascetic practices, but did not obtain results. The Buddha questioned why he was so severe in his practice, reminding him of his experience in playing the lute. The best sounds came not from strings stretched too tightly or too loose, but from strings delicately balanced and in tune. "Excessive severity brings distraction, and too much relaxation brings indolence. Be moderate, unselfish, and devoted, and you will attain excellence." Thereafter, Śrona practiced according to the Buddha's advice and soon became an Arhat.

The Beauty of Śīla

Guidelines for ordination and the code of conduct that governed the Sangha's way of life form the substance of the Buddha's Vinaya teachings, given to develop śīla, or moral discipline. Śīla is the special quality of the bhikṣu. Cultivated through mindfulness, it manifests as sublime beauty accompanied by perfectly appropriate action free of harmful intent or results. In the Bhikṣu-priyā-sūtra (NE 302), the Buddha describes the nature and conduct of a true renunciate and the central importance of śīla:

"Those who seek virtue, who gain food by begging, who are dispassionate, who walk in the way, whose lives are correct, who have cast off passions: They who possesses these qualities are bhikṣus.

"They who are merciful, who have cast far away gold and all the other ornaments of the world, are adorned with the most precious of ornaments. The best of raiments is not the garments of the world; the best of raiments is the saffron-colored robe, the garment of the doctrine. The best of unguents is not camphor and such like; the best of unguents is morality. The most beautiful color is not white, red, or the like; the most beautiful color is faith. It is not worldliness, but application, that is the best and swiftest conveyance. Contemplation and the practice of Dharma are the best foods and have a sweeter aroma than boiled rice. . . .

"Śīla (moral perfection) is the greatest happiness, the road to freedom, the field of perfection. Śīla is the foundation of enlightenment, the chief among all good things. Watch over śīla as your most precious possession, for life itself is at stake: Foolish are they who renounce it. All things that are born have but a limited existence, but this is not true of śīla. Therefore, Upāli, and all disciples here assembled, observe the Vinaya rules with the greatest care."

Three Phases of Revelation

The Wheel of the Dharma subdues the demons
and conquers false views; it transcends
the realm of rebirth and enters the Buddha-realm.
It is perfectly known by the venerable Arhats,
understood by the Pratyekabuddhas,
comprehended by the Bodhisattvas,
praised by all the Buddhas,
and indivisible from all the Tathāgatas.

—Voice of the Buddha

For the first seven years of his teaching, the Buddha taught the foundation of the Dharma, called the First Turning Teachings. Having perceived the causes of human suffering, the Buddha concentrated on teaching the implications of impermanence and the factors that create the potential for endless rounds of frustration. During this time the Buddha emphasized the path of the Arhats, the saints whose realization stops the production of karma and frees them from bondage to patterns that perpetuate suffering.

The basis for this path is the Vinaya, the "peaceful way" that calms body and mind and removes obstacles to realization. The Vinaya established a code of moral conduct and the physical and mental discipline necessary to gain understanding of the nature of existence. With few exceptions, the Vinaya teachings were given in the vihāras near Rājagṛha and Śrāvastī.

In addition to guiding the daily life of the Sangha, the Vinaya teachings point the way to "conquer the enemy," the tendencies of mind and habits of body that keep beings ensnared in Māra's net of illusion. On progressively deeper levels, the Vinaya encourages mindfulness of every thought, word, and action: Where did each arise, how does it evolve, and to where does it lead?

In supporting mindfulness, the Vinaya provides a firm foundation for meditation and realization of the central teachings conveyed in the First Turning Sūtras, including the marks of existence, the four truths, the connection between cause and effect, and the power of karma. The Sūtras inspire meditation, which develops clarity and concentration, essential for comprehending the Abhidharma, the more technical aspects of the Buddha's teachings. Study of the Abhidharma encourages a correct understanding of mind and mental events; with this knowledge it is possible to develop the concentration that completely dries up the passions and removes all taint of greed, hatred, and delusion.

Each type of teaching supports a specific training: Vinaya promotes śīla, or moral perfection; Sūtra promotes samādhi, or concentration; and the Abhidharma develops prajñā, or discriminating wisdom. These three trainings prepare one to "enter the stream" that leads to enlightenment and support progress at every stage of the path.

The path comprises thirty-seven elements, expressed in the Abhidharmakośa as bodhipākṣa, or wings of enlightenment: the four applications of mindfulness, the four right efforts, the four foundations of miraculous power, the five strengths, the five powers, the seven branches of enlightenment, and the eightfold path. Within the First Turning teachings, the wings of enlightenment apply to the bhikṣu, and within the Second and Third Turning teachings, they form the foundation of the Bodhisattva's practice. See pp. 118–19.

Teachings of the Second Turning

After seven years, the Buddha began a new phase of his teachings called the Second Turning, in which he revealed the more profound implications of the Dharma. The first of these teachings was given to the "four assemblies": the Arhats, including Śāriputra and Maudgalyāyana; five hundred nuns with the Buddha's stepmother Mahāprajāpatī at their head; and a great host of laymen and laywomen, including the merchant Anāthapiṇḍada and the lady Viśākhā. The expanded, or great assembly included (in addition to the four assemblies) gatherings of gods, nāgas, and gandharvas, and multitudes of such highly accomplished Bodhisattvas as Bhadrapāla, Ratnasambhava, and Jāladatta. The location for these teachings was Gṛdhrakūṭa, the Vulture Peak, a high rocky hill overlooking the countryside around Rājagṛha.

In this phase of his teaching the Buddha emphasized the importance of developing understanding of śūnyatā, the essential emptiness of all elements of existence. Now it was time for those who had generated confidence in the Dharma to penetrate to the realization of ultimate truth and fully understand what it means to live in a world of constant flux, where there is no solid ground, no resting place, no substantiality, and hence no limitation and no bar to perfect freedom. To the Arhats, the pure beings, the great saints, the Buddha presented an ideal of spiritual attainment grounded in supreme compassion: The path of the Bodhisattva, once considered only possible for a very few who would become Buddhas, was shown to be open to everyone willing to set aside all vestiges of self-interest and make efforts throughout time for the benefit of others.

The teachings of the Second Turning were given in their most fully developed form in the Sūtras on the Perfection of Wisdom. The most extensive of these profound Sūtras is the Śatasāhasrikā-prajñāpāramitā-sūtra, the Teaching of Perfect Wisdom in 100,000 verses. This teaching finds expression in shorter forms as well, in the Prajñāpāramitā Sūtras in versions of 25,000, 18,000, 10,000, and 8,000 lines. There is also a verse summary of the 8,000-line Prajñāpāramitā, known as the Ratnaguṇa-sañcaya-gāthā (NE 13), which some Western scholars regard as a chapter of the 18,000-line teaching. The large Sūtras on Perfect Wisdom elaborate on how the thirty-seven wings of enlightenment speed the Bodhisattva along the path to realization. Following the path illuminated by Prajñāpāramitā, the Bodhisattva attains maturity and becomes capable of performing the Twelve Great Actions of the Bodhisattva.

Two of the Buddha's teachings on the Perfection of Wisdom, the Prajñāpāramitā-hṛdaya-sūtra (NE 21), known as the Heart Sūtra, and the Vajracchedika-prajñāpāramitā (NE 16), or Diamond Sūtra, are still memorized and recited daily by hundreds of thousands of Buddhist practitioners in order to evoke understanding of śūnyatā.

According to a number of accounts cited by Bu-ston, the Buddha taught the doctrine of śūnyatā for twelve, twenty-seven, thirty, or thirty-one years. Teachings belonging to this Second Turning of the Dharma Wheel include the basic texts that set forth the view and path of the Mahāyāna. They comprise the teachings that clarify the great vows of the Bodhisattva and the Sūtras that enumerate the stages, paths and samādhis to be understood and realized by the Bodhisattva.

The Prajñāpāramitā-sūtras, the Saddharmapuṇḍarīka (NE 113), the Śūraṅgamasamādhi (NE 132), the Lalitavistara (NE 95), and the Bhadrakalpika Sūtras all are generally considered Second Turning teachings. Many of these teachings remained concealed for centuries, awaiting the time when the minds of human beings were prepared to appreciate the cosmic play of emptiness and form.

Teachings of the Third Turning

After fully expressing the profound doctrine of śūnyatā, the Buddha revealed the full breadth of the Dharma in a Third Turning of the wheel of the Dharma. In these teachings, given at indeterminate times in such places as Mt. Malaya, Mt. Meru, and Vaiśālī, the Buddha analyzed all aspects of existence in accord with the three natures: the imaginary (parikalpita, kun-btags), the dependent (paratantra, gzhan-dbang), and the absolute (parinispanna, yongs-grub) and imparted the doctrine of Tathāgatagarbha, the Buddha nature inherent in all beings. According to the Vijñānavāda view cited by Bu-ston, the teachings of the Third Turning were given to remove tendencies toward eternalism and nihilism and to penetrate ultimate reality directly. In the Mādhyamika view also given by Bu-ston, the First and Third Turning teachings both express conventional truth and only the Second Turning teachings directly convey the ultimate meaning.

Among the teachings imparted during this period (Bu-ston cites various traditions that this period lasted seven, nine, ten, twelve, twenty-six, or twenty-seven years) are the Avataṁsaka (NE 44), Laṅkāvatāra (NE 107), and Ratnakūṭa (NE 45), as well as the ten Tathāgatagarbha Sūtras, including the Saṁdhinirmocana (NE 106). These teachings were given at various places, primarily to the host of great Bodhisattvas who required them for their complete maturation, with members of all four Sanghas—monks and nuns, laymen and laywomen—also in attendance.

An example of one such teaching is the Sūtra known as the Lion's Roar of Queen Śrīmālā (Śrīmālādevī-siṁhanāda-sūtra, NE 92). Invited by the prayers of Śrīmālā (Queen of Ayodhyā and daughter of King Prasenajit and Queen Mallikā), the Buddha traveled to Ayodhyā, an ancient city

Thirty-Seven Wings of Enlightenment

Four Applications of Mindfulness

1. Mindfulness of body

2. Mindfulness of feelings

3. Mindfulness of mind

4. Mindfulness of all dharmas (factors).

Refraining from forming discursive thoughts about the body, the Bodhisattva sets aside selfishness, envy, and sadness, and is clearly mindful and conscious of all that concerns the inner and outer body, feelings, thoughts, and all environing factors. Mindfulness of the inner body includes awareness of exactly what the body is, what the whole body is doing, whether the breath is moving out or in, and the precise position of each part of the body. Mindfulness of the outer body arises through contemplation of the body bereft of life: Once breath leaves the body, what stages of decay does it pass through, and what is its inevitable end?

Four Right Efforts

Bodhisattvas who course in perfect wisdom arouse their will, make an effort, put forth vigor, focus their thoughts, and correctly exert themselves to accomplish the four right efforts, also known as the four great restraints:

1. Whatever non-virtuous actions do not yet exist, the Bodhisattva vigorously refrains from thoughts and actions that would bring them into being.

2. Whatever non-virtuous actions already exist, the Bodhisattva strives to give them up.

3. Whatever virtuous actions have not been generated, the Bodhisattva makes an effort to bring them into being.

4. Whatever virtuous actions have been generated, the Bodhisattva makes an effort to maintain, increase, stabilize, and perfect them.

Four Bases of Miraculous Power
1. One-pointed cultivation of will
2. One-pointed cultivation of mind
3. One-pointed cultivation of effort
4. One-pointed cultivation of analysis

Five Strengths
1. Strength of faith
2. Strength of effort
3. Strength of mindfulness
4. Strength of one-pointed contemplation
5. Strength of wisdom

Five Powers
1. Power of faith
2. Power of effort
3. Power of mindfulness
4. Power of one-pointed contemplation
5. Power of wisdom

Seven Branches of Enlightenment
1. Enlightened mindfulness
2. Enlightened investigation of truth
3. Enlightened effort
4. Enlightened joy
5. Enlightened flexibility
6. Enlightened one-pointed contemplation
7. Enlightened equanimity

Eightfold Path
1. Right view
2. Right conception
3. Right speech
4. Right conduct
5. Right livelihood
6. Right effort
7. Right mindfulness
8. Right meditative concentration

Derived from *The Large Sūtra on Perfect Wisdom*, pp. 153ff.

Twelve Great Actions of the Bodhisattvas

1. Bodhisattvas possess the quality of infinite resolve: as a result of having fulfilled the six perfections, whatever they resolve to do, they accomplish.

2. Through the analytical knowledge of languages, Bodhisattvas comprehend the speech of all beings.

3. Through the analytical knowledge of speech, Bodhisattvas are able to expound the Dharma effectively at all times.

4. Bodhisattvas are always born apparitionally.

5. Bodhisattvas are always reborn in good families.

6. Bodhisattvas are always reborn in noble or Brahmin families.

7. Bodhisattvas are reborn in that clan from which the former Bodhisattvas have come.

8. Bodhisattvas are endowed with a retinue of Bodhisattvas after they have established beings in enlightenment.

9. When born, Bodhisattvas irradiate all world systems with splendor and shake them all in six ways.

10. Bodhisattvas leave home together with hundreds of thousands of niyutas of koṭis of beings.

11. Bodhisattvas obtain the miraculous harmony of the Bodhi Tree: the roots of their Bodhi Trees are made of gold, the trunks of Vaiḍūrya (lapis), the branches of all kinds of jewels, the leaves of all kinds of precious things, and the trees' fine fragrance and radiance illuminate infinite world systems.

12. A Bodhisattva's accomplishment of the fulfillment of all virtuous qualities is the perfect purity of his Buddha-field, through the maturity of the beings in it.

—Pañcaviṁśatisāhasrikā-prajñāpāramitā

west of Śrāvastī. There he received the Queen's homage, praised her meritorious actions in previous lifetimes, and predicted her attainment of Buddhahood. Then, in the presence of the Buddha, Queen Śrīmālā made ten vows of perfect conduct and three great vows expressing the Bodhisattva's commitment to the liberation of all beings. Inspired by the Blessed One, she taught the assembly of disciples and great Bodhisattvas concerning the power of comprehending the essence of the Mahāyāna. The Buddha affirmed her realization: "Just as Mount Sumeru soars above all other mountains, to hold to the true Dharma, casting aside body, life, and worldly wealth for the great teaching, is superior to any other sacrifice."

Both the Second and Third Turnings clarify the Bodhisattva nature and path. As described by the Buddha, Bodhisattvas operate from a more expansive view of śīla, samādhi, and prajñā (moral perfection, meditation, and wisdom) than the Arhat. Governed by the most altruistic compassion that has no place for self-centered views, Bodhisattvas set aside thought of a personal nirvāṇa and vow to work for the enlightenment of all beings. Aware of their close kinship with all life, Bodhisattvas willingly engage birth after birth for the purpose of benefiting others. "Without being asked, the Bodhisattva becomes a friend who teaches, comforts, and loves all living beings." (Śrīmālādevī-siṁhanāda-sūtra, NE 92)

Motivated by the sufferings of others and convinced of the possibility of enlightenment, Bodhisattvas generate the aspiration for Buddhahood and awaken bodhicitta, the mind focused on enlightenment. To develop bodhicitta, a Bodhisattva strives to understand the theoretical basis of śūnyatā and develop insight into its profound significance. The Bodhisattva takes up the sixfold practice of giving, morality, patience, vigor, concentration, and wisdom; in elevating these qualities "to perfection," carrying them far beyond ordinary virtues and attainments, Bodhisattvas simultaneously purify themselves of the most subtle obscurations and greatly extend their capacities to benefit others.

Practicing the perfections, the Bodhisattva develops complete understanding of śūnyatā, necessary to cut through dualistic modes of thought and remove all residues of egocentric views. Only when this understanding, internalized and integrated, becomes the foundation of all thought and action can the Bodhisattva embody the six perfections and be of real assistance to others. Thus the Bodhisattva acts "without basing himself on anything," fully aware that ultimately, there are no beings to be benefited and no Bodhisattva to benefit them. The realization that neither object nor subject ultimately exists does not diminish the value of the action, which determines directionality, and ultimately the nature of change.

In the Daśabhūmika-sūtra (NE 44), the Buddha described the ten bhūmis, or stages, of the Bodhisattva path. Whereas the pāramitās are like the boat that carries the traveler to enlightenment, the ten stages provide a guide through unfamiliar regions. Each stage has an appropriate practice and realization and leads naturally to the next, culminating in the union of wisdom and skillful means that enables the Bodhisattva to dedicate lifetimes of service to all beings. In the Gaṇḍavyūha-sūtra (NE 44), the Buddha expressed the Bodhisattva path in a poetical allegory of the pilgrimage of the youth Sudāna to a series of great Bodhisattvas, who each impart a teaching that deepens his understanding. The setting for the Gaṇḍavyūha-sūtra is Jeta's Grove, which the Buddha by his power transforms into a world without limit, filled with innumerable treasures.

Among the teachings of the Three Turnings, there is no concept of higher or lower: The Dharma is fully present in all of the Buddha's words. The Nyingma scholar Dudjom Rinpoche explains that each "Turning" can be viewed as emphasizing one of the three piṭakas, or collections of teachings. For the Bodhisattva, the Vinaya, Sutra, and Abhidharma teachings of the First Turning emphasize the Vinayapiṭaka, the foundation for study and practice; the teachings of the Second Turning emphasize the Sūtrapiṭaka,

Sūtras Preserved in Other Realms

Sūtra	Realm
Mahāvyavadāna-bhūmi	deva-realms
Prajñāpāramitā	
1 billion verses	king of gandharvas
Prajñāpāramitā	
ten million verses	king of the devas
Prajñāpāramitā	
100,000 verses (complete)	nāga-realms

Bu-ston, II:170.

supporting the most profound development of samādhi; and the teachings of the Third Turning emphasize the Abhidharmapiṭaka, for they provide the most complete analysis of the meaning of the teachings.

Thus, through the Three Turnings, the Buddha planted the seeds of enlightenment in three different forms, so that all beings could obtain the maximum benefit of the teachings. All who heard the Buddha's teaching understood according to their abilities and achieved results in accord with their realization and efforts. All were free to draw from this great body of Dharma, and all who turned their thoughts to the Dharma were uplifted and benefited in some way.

Although in the last two thousand years a great portion of the Buddha's teachings have been lost, thousands of teachings are still being transmitted in an unbroken lineage from the time of the Buddha. The fabric of the Dharma woven by the enlightened Buddha Śākyamuni has endured through the centuries.

Lost Parts of the Buddhadharma

Completely lost:

Duḥkha-skandha-sūtra	0
Udayana-paripṛcchā	0
Guru-sūtra	0
Sūtra of Kāśyapa	0
Sūtra of Ānanda	0

Partially lost:	**original**	**remaining**
Ratnakūṭa	100,000 chapters	49
Mahāsamaya	100,000 chapters	60
Avataṁsaka	100,000 chapters	40
Laṅkāvatāra	36,000 verses	3,600
Ghanavyūha	12,000 verses	1,300
Mahāmegha	100,000 verses	few chapters
Samādhirāja	?	15 divisions
Ekottarikāgama	1–100 topics?	1–10
Nirvāṇa	?	incomplete*
Smṛtyupasthāna	?	incomplete*
Śūraṅgama	10,000 verses	1 chapter*
Mahādhigama	incomplete*	
Candragarbha-paripṛcchā		incomplete*

*translation into Tibetan not finished; remainder lost

Bu-ston, II: 169–170.

Many of the Second and Third Turning teachings were given in realms outside Jambudvīpa. Although humans and devas alike could not normally access realms on a higher plane than their own, it was possible to transcend these barriers through the perfection of profound samādhi. Thus teachings in these realms are associated with highly developed levels of consciousness.

At least two Sūtras were given in the Akaniṣṭha Heaven, the highest heaven in the Rūpadhātu, the realm of form: the Ghanavyūha (NE 110) and the Atyayajñāna (NE 122), a teaching on how to direct the mind at the time of death. The extensive Avataṁsaka-sūtra, a teaching of the Third Turning, was given on Mt. Meru, the abode of the devas of the Trāyastriṁśa Heaven.

The Buddha also went to the palace of Sāgara, king of the nāgas, where he gave teachings for the benefit of these powerful beings. The bKa'-'gyur preserves five such Sūtras: two Sāgaranāgarāja-paripṛcchā-sūtras (NE 154–155), teachings on the nature of existence and the four dharmas; the Anavataptanāgarāja-paripṛcchā (NE 156), a teaching in answer to Anavatapta's question on the means of obtaining Buddhahood, and two Mahāmegha-sūtras (NE 234, 235), prayers for obtaining rain. The great nāgas also protected certain of the teachings given in other locations, some of which, like portions of the Prajñāpāramitā, have since been brought to the human realm. Additional teachings remain under the nāga's protection.

"The Teaching is like a precious jewel.
Sublime and indestructible,
it shows the Path of Purity.
Contemplated with reverence by the hooded nāgas,
the Teaching is like the diamonds in the nāgas' diadems,
dispersing the darkness for those
who dwell in the depths of the earth."

—*Śiṣyalekha* (Candragomin)

Blessing Future Lands of the Dharma

The Buddha traveled miraculously to distant lands to bless specific locations and predict their role in the history of the Dharma. The Vinaya records one such journey north to Lake Manasarowar (Anavatapta), which was undertaken by the Buddha and five hundred attendants. Four great rivers are said to have risen from that lake: the Ganges, the Sindhu (Indus), the Pakṣu, and the Sītā.

On the banks of the lake, the Buddha and thirty-six of his disciples related episodes from their previous lives, and the Buddha detailed the consequences of good and bad actions. Two Sūtras record a journey of the Buddha to Khotan and prophecies concerning that land: the Gośṛṅga-vyākaraṇa (NE 357), or the Prophecy of the Ox-horn Mountain, and the Vimalaprabha-paripṛcchā (NE 168), in which the Buddha entrusts Khotan to the World-Guardian Vaiśravaṇa, master of yakṣas. The Mahāvaṁsa and Dīpavaṁsa of the Sinhalese tradition relate that Śākyamuni Buddha visited Śrī Laṅkā on three occasions after the enlightenment. The Buddha is also said to have traveled to Kashmir.

Duration of the Dharma of Śākyamuni

Throughout his lifetime, the Buddha emphasized the teaching of impermanence. All that comes into being through causes and conditions will pass away; nothing—not even the Buddha's teaching—endures forever. There are various statements as to exactly how long the Dharma will continue. The Vinaya, Mahāmegha-sūtra (NE 232), Bhadra-kalpika-sūtra (NE 94), and other sources preserve one form of the Buddha Śākyamuni's prophecy concerning his Dharma: for five hundred years his teaching will endure strongly, and then continue in diminished form for an additional five hundred years. In the Karuṇapuṇḍarīka (NE 112), the Buddha predicts that his teaching will endure strongly for a thousand years and persist in diminished form for five hundred years. The Dharmatāsvabhava-śūnyatācalapratisarva-loka-sūtra (NE 128) proclaims that the Dharma will last for 2500 years, while the Maitreyavyākaraṇa-sūtra predicts five thousand years.

According to the Candragarbhaparipṛcchā-sūtra (NE 356), human awareness will darken under the influence of emotionality and self-oriented views; as conditions become less favorable to realization, persons who listen to the teachings will lack the energy to practice and apply them in their lives; those who have taken vows will be unable to maintain the Vinaya precepts.

Then false views will lead beings into confusion; the power of Māra, Lord of Illusion, will increase. All that feeds confusion will be supported, and all that promotes enlightened understanding will be undermined. After a short period of prosperity engendered by past virtuous karma, wars will erupt more frequently. Confusion, anxiety, and suffering will predominate in human affairs, until living beings are blinded by pain and selfish concerns. Then beings will no longer be able to hear the Dharma; although the outer form—texts, temples, and rituals—will remain, their meaning will be forgotten. Eventually the forms will also disappear, and not even the memory of the Dharma will remain to protect living beings. But the darkness will not last forever. At some time in the future, the Great Bodhisattva Maitreya will appear, demonstrate the path to enlightenment, and again set the Wheel of the Dharma in motion.

Some Mahāyāna texts note that while the Dharma will become inaccessible to human beings, the teaching of the thousand Buddhas, preserved in the realm of the nāga-king Sāgara, and in the Tuṣita and Trāyastriṁśa heavens, will remain until the end of our aeon.

The Suvarṇaprabhāsottama-sūtra (NE 556) relates that the Buddha will never enter final nirvāṇa and the doctrine will not decline. (Dudjom Rinpoche, *The Nyingma School of Tibetan Buddhism,* p. 943)

Extending the Dharma

Learn the principles of causality,
trust in the path of truth,
and know that although the body dies,
the Enlightened Ones who live in the Dharma
never perish. —*Mahāparinirvāṇa-sūtra*

While traditional accounts differ in detail, all agree that the Buddha traveled most widely during the first twenty years of his teaching. Around the end of this period, while staying in Śrāvastī near the Jālinī Forest, the Buddha heard that the murderer Aṅgulimālīya, He Who Wears a Garland of Fingers, was close by. Aṅgulimālīya had made a vow to kill one thousand people and wore a finger of each his victims around his neck to keep count.

The Buddha knew that Aṅgulimālīya had already killed 999 people; to open Aṅgulimālīya's eyes to the enormity of his actions, the Buddha manifested in front of him as his mother. Aṅgulimālīya tried to catch and kill her, but each time she eluded his grasp. When Aṅgulimālīya finally gave up in exhaustion, the Buddha appeared to him in his true form. Aṅgulimālīya deeply repented the suffering he had caused; although the results of that karma continued to afflict him, he became a monk and did no further harm. Accounts of the Buddha's conversion of Aṅgulimālīya are preserved in all Buddhist traditions (NE 213, T 410, MN 86). There are other stories of the Buddha's conversion of bandits and demons, including the conversion of a cannibalistic yakṣa who lived in the Ālavī Forest.

Returning to Rājagṛha, the Blessed One spent the twentieth rainy season retreat with the Sangha in the Bamboo Grove. At this time, the Buddha's cousin Ānanda became his personal attendant. Before then, the Buddha's disciples had taken turns carrying the Buddha's extra robe and alms-bowl; but now that the Buddha was nearly fifty-five years old, he wished a permanent attendant to assist him and asked that his disciples appoint someone.

Kauṇḍinya, Aśvajit, and other elder disciples at once asked for the privilege of serving the Buddha, but they were too old for this service. Maudgalyāyana then thought of the Buddha's young cousin Ānanda, who was thoroughly devoted to the Enlightened One. He and Śāriputra went to Ānanda and asked if he would accept this honored position. At first Ānanda refused, feeling incapable of carrying out such a responsibility. After a time he consented, providing that the Buddha would see fit to grant three conditions: that he should never have to partake of the Buddha's food or use his clothing; that he should not be required to accompany the Buddha when he went to a layman's house, but whatever teachings the Buddha might give in his absence, the Buddha would repeat to him; and that he might at any time see and revere the Blessed One. When the Buddha granted the conditions, Ānanda became his attendant and constant companion.

Around this time the Buddha proceeded again to Vaiśālī, then followed the Ganges River east to the city of Campā, located in the land of Aṅga, which was then ruled by King

Bimbisāra. Staying outside the city, the Buddha dwelled on the shore of Gaggarā Lake with five hundred bhikṣus. There he gave the Soṇadaṇḍa-sutta (DN 4), emphasizing the trainings of conduct (śīla) and wisdom (paññā; Sanskrit, prajña) and, on the occasion of a lunar eclipse, he taught the Candra, or Moon Sūtra (NE 331). One day, Pessa, son of an elephant tamer, accompanied by Kandaraka, an ascetic, came upon the Buddha as he was teaching. Amazed at the disciples' composed and alert appearance, Kandaraka remarked on how well the Buddha had trained them and asked if this would also be true of the disciples of future Buddhas. The Buddha explained that there were many disciples present who were completely free from defilements and had attained the state of an Arhat.

The Buddha continued, describing the four stages of mindfulness necessary to transcend the greed and despair common to worldly life. Pessa remarked that, compared with the minds of animals, the consciousness of human beings is like a thicket, very difficult to untangle. At this the Buddha explained the four types of people: those who cause suffering to themselves, to others, to both themselves and others, and those who free themselves from desires and cause no suffering to self or to others. Following the way of Dharma, "Even though they see, hear, smell, taste, feel, and touch, their minds do not cling, and they perceive joy in controlling the five senses . . . they experience tranquility, peace, and joy and live the excellent life." (*Kandaraka-sutta*, MN 51)

While in Aṅga the Buddha also visited the residence of Sumāgadhā, daughter of the patron Anāthapiṇḍada. Married to a rich merchant in an area where there was no Sangha, the lady Sumāgadhā was repulsed by the manners and teachings of the naked ascetics whom her father-in-law wished her to honor and prayed to the Buddha to introduce her husband and family to the Dharma. Her story is related in the Sumāgadhāvadāna-sūtra (NE 346).

After the Buddha was fifty-five years of age, he usually spent the rainy season in Śrāvastī, his principal residence for most of the last twenty-five years of his life. The Buddhist traditions relate that Śākyamuni continued to travel and that he miraculously visited the lands of Kashmir, Khotan, Srī Laṅkā, Northwestern India, and Lake Anavatapta.

Seeds of Dissension: Devadatta

Although the Buddha's cousin Devadatta had joined the Sangha, he continued to cause dissension. He had noticed that Maudgalyāyana and other bhikṣus had developed supernormal powers and asked the Buddha to teach these to him as well. Knowing that Devadatta's mind was not free of ignorance, hatred, and greed, the Buddha advised him to seek power over himself through the cultivation of virtue. Unsatisfied, Devadatta went to several other bhikṣus, who advised him to seek power through knowledge and meditation.

Finally Devadatta approached the great Kāśyapa, who showed him how to develop the lesser siddhis. Devadatta immediately became inflated with pride and sought to use the powers he obtained for his own benefit. He won the admiration of Ajātaśatru, King Bimbisāra's son, who bestowed many gifts upon him. Then Devadatta conceived the thought of taking the Buddha's place as the guide for the Sangha; although his powers began to decrease as he applied them for self-centered gains, so great was his pride that he did not notice.

The Buddha rebuked Devadatta for his great arrogance; from that point forward, Devadatta did his utmost to sow seeds of dissatisfaction within the Sangha. In time he persuaded five hundred bhikṣus in Vṛji to leave the Sangha under his leadership. Although Śāriputra and Maudgalyāyana eventually brought these bhikṣus back into the Sangha, Devadatta's actions became more demonic: He hired assassins to kill the Buddha, but they were won over by the Buddha's compassion; he rolled a great boulder down a mountain near Rājagṛha toward the Enlightened One, but the Buddha was only slightly wounded; he tormented and set loose the maddened elephant Nālagiri, which fell at the Buddha's feet in devotion. According to traditional accounts, when he attempted to kill the Buddha himself, the earth opened under him and he fell directly to the lowest depths of the Avīci Hell. Even after his death, however, his influence appears to have persisted. Hsüan-tsang mentions the existence of a community that followed Devadatta's teachings in Kāmarūpa as late as the seventh century.

Ajātaśatru's Remorse

At Devadatta's urging, Ajātaśatru's ambition to rule Magdha grew steadily. Seeing this, Bimbisāra sent Ajātaśatru to gain experience by governing the rich trading city of Campā, but under Devadatta's influence, Ajātaśatru taxed the people so heavily that they complained to the King. Bimbisāra gave his son all of Magadha, but even that did not satisfy him. Finally the king turned over all his holdings to Ajātaśatru, imploring his son to end his connection with Devadatta. Instead, Ajātaśatru imprisoned his father and left him to die of hunger. Ajātaśatru's mother, Queen Vaidehī, devised a means to nourish the king, but this was discovered and stopped. Ajātaśatru eventually realized his father's kindness but repented too late. The old king died in prison before Ajātaśatru came to release him.

Filled with remorse, Ajātaśatru sought solace from several sages, who advised him to commit suicide to atone for his crime. Desperate, the king took counsel with his half-brother, the physician Jīvaka, who advised him to seek forgiveness from the Buddha. Ajātaśatru's meeting with the Buddha and the Buddha's compassionate response is preserved in the Sūtra known as the Ajātaśatru-kaukṛttiya-vinodana, Dispelling the Evil-Doing of Ajātaśatru (NE 216).

The Mūlasarvāstivādin Vinaya gives another account of Ajātaśatru's meeting with the Buddha, in which the Buddha converts the king to the Dharma through the teaching known as the Śrāmaṇaphala-sūtra (T 22; Pāli: Sāmaññaphala-sutta, DN 2), the Fruit of the Mendicant's Way of Life. At the Buddha's request, Ajātaśatru describes the teachings of his realm's prominent sages, after which the Buddha relates how the bhikṣu overcomes the five fetters, attains samādhi, frees himself from defilements, realizes the meaning of the four noble truths, and attains liberation from endless rounds of birth and death. Thereafter Ajātaśatru was completely devoted to the Buddha, Dharma, and Sangha and provided for the Sangha throughout his realm. Most historians place the time of Ajātaśatru's accession to the throne at six or seven years before the Buddha entered Parinirvāṇa.

Nirvāṇa of Śāriputra and Maudgalyāyana

To assuage the pain of Devadatta, who was then dwelling in the hell realms, the Buddha in his compassion sent Śāriputra and Maudgalyāyana to visit him. There they informed Devadatta that, although he was suffering from his misdeeds, he would eventually become a Pratyekabuddha, one who realizes a limited form of enlightenment by his own efforts. While the two Arhats were in the hells, a tīrthika (non-Buddhist) master called out to them, entreating them to carry a message to his disciples: Their master was suffering in the hells for propounding views and concepts that did not lead to liberation.

Śāriputra was the first to convey this message to the tīrthika's disciples, but they ignored him. Shortly afterwards, Maudgalyāyana met the tīrthikas in Rājagṛha and told them their teacher was suffering in the Avīci Hell for teaching false doctrines. This time the disciples became enraged; they fell upon Maudgalyāyana and beat him severely. Due to the ripening of past karma, he was unable to use his extensive magical powers to escape harm. Śāriputra rescued his friend and carried him to safety. Knowing that Maudgalyāyana would soon pass away, Śāriputra returned to his birthplace in Nālandā. There, on a full-moon night, he said farewell to his mother and his disciples and quietly passed into nirvāṇa. His friend Maudgalyāyana died soon afterwards in Rājagṛha. The Vinaya account relates that 150,000 Arhats also entered nirvāṇa at this time, "like fires that have run out of fuel." Scholars estimate the time of the great disciples' deaths as the year before the Buddha's Parinirvāṇa.

Śāriputra's disciples cremated his body and carried his ashes, alms-bowl, and cloak to the Buddha, who was then residing in Rājagṛha. The Buddha then went to Śrāvastī, where Anāthapiṇḍada asked permission to build a stūpa for Śāriputra's relics. Giving his consent, the Buddha advised Anāthapiṇḍada on the proper construction of a stūpa. While the stūpa was being constructed, Anāthapiṇḍada enshrined Śāriputra's ashes in his own house, where King Prasenajit and all of Kosala paid them homage.

Death of Prasenajit

Once King Prasenajit's son, Virūḍhaka, on a hunting trip, entered a park just outside of Kapilavastu, accompanied by many attendants on elephants and horses. This intrusion enraged some Śākya youths, who, against the advice of their elders, treated the prince roughly and humiliated him before his attendants. From that day, Virūḍhaka, heir to the throne of Kosala, swore to avenge himself on the Śākyas the moment he assumed power. He began conspiring with the royal counselors and eventually gained their support.

While the Buddha was stopping in Metsurudi, a small Śākyan town, King Prasenajit, who was traveling nearby, heard of the Buddha's presence and went to pay his respects. Dismounting from his chariot, he handed his implements of royalty to his minister-of-state and entered the house where the Buddha was staying. Seeing his opportunity, the minister returned to Śrāvastī and made Virūḍhaka king. At once Prasenajit's wives, Mallikā and Varṣikā, set out on foot from Śrāvastī to find their husband; meeting him on the road, they told him of Virūḍhaka's treachery. Prasenajit asked Mallikā, the mother of Virūḍhaka, to return to the palace in Śrāvastī, where she would be well-treated. Then King Prasenajit and Varṣikā went on foot to Rājagṛha.

Arriving at one of the royal parks outside Rājagṛha, Prasenajit sent Varṣikā to ask King Ajātaśatru for assistance. Ajātaśatru immediately ordered preparations made to properly receive the king of Kosala and set out with a large retinue to provide him a royal welcome. In the meanwhile, Prasenajit, exhausted and hungry, had eaten raw turnips from a nearby field, suffered cramps, and died in the dust of the road. Ajātaśatru was deeply grieved by the inglorious death of this king, his uncle and ruler of India's most prosperous realm. He ordered that Prasenajit be buried with full honors, having consulting with the Buddha how best to care for his uncle's remains.

Destruction of Kapilavastu

As soon as Virūḍhaka became king of Kosala, his minister urged him to quickly take vengeance upon the Śākyas. Knowing of Virūḍhaka's intention, the Buddha seated himself under a leafless tree on the road leading from Śrāvastī to Kapilavastu. When Virūḍhaka saw the Buddha, his resolve to destroy the Śākyas weakened, and he turned back to his palace in Śrāvastī. But aware that Virūḍhaka would return, the Buddha proceeded on to Kapilavastu, where he gave the Śākyas a final teaching on the four truths, karma, and the path to enlightenment. Listening to these teachings, many attained liberation.

Not long after, Virūḍhaka attacked Kapilavastu with his great army. Maudgalyāyana sought the Buddha's permission to use his power to protect the Śākyas, but the Buddha told him that nothing would change the basic situation: The Śākyas would have to bear the consequences of their offenses. Having accepted the Buddha's teachings, the Śākyas had no wish to take the lives of their attackers and resolved to expel any who did from their midst. Hsüan-tsang relates that four Śākyas, not knowing of this law, wreaked great destruction on Virūḍhaka's army and were immediately exiled for their efforts. One went to the far north, where he is said to have founded the kingdom of Oḍḍiyāna. The Vinaya mentions only one Śākya named Shampaka who did battle with Virūḍhaka's army. After his exile he went to the land of Vaku, married there, and established a government based on the Buddha's teaching.

Although Virūḍhaka's army devastated Kapilavastu and most of its inhabitants, some of the Śākyas escaped to Nepal, Rājagṛha, and other places. Virūḍhaka took five hundred Śākya maidens and five hundred youths back to Śrāvastī, but his minister had the youths slain, and the maidens also perished soon afterwards. Hearing of the fate of the Śākyas, the Buddha told his disciples that the house of Kosala would be destroyed in seven days. Virūḍhaka and his minister would perish by fire; they would be reborn in the Avīci Hells and remain there until the karma resulting from their actions was exhausted.

After Virūḍhaka returned to Śrāvastī, he told Prince Jeta of his victory over his enemies. When the prince asked who were his enemies, and Virūḍhaka answered, "the Śākyas," Jeta replied, "If the Śākyas are your enemies, who then are your friends?" Virūḍhaka, enraged, had Jeta join the Śākyas in death, and the prince was reborn in the Heaven of the Trāyastriṁśa gods. As the Buddha had foreseen, Virūḍhaka could not escape retribution. Although the king spent the seventh day after the Buddha's prophecy in a house in the middle of a lake, the sun's rays passing through a looking-glass ignited the building; as everyone else escaped, the earth opened, and Virūḍhaka and his minister both fell into the bottomless reaches of the hells.

The Last Great Instruction

Bhikṣus, never forget:
Decay is inherent to all component things.
—Śākyamuni Buddha

In entering Parinirvāṇa, the final great action, the Buddha gave the most moving of all demonstrations of impermanence; having completely fulfilled his purpose, he departed the world in peace. Every Buddhist tradition preserves an account of the Buddha's last journey and Parinirvāṇa, which, with birth, enlightenment, and setting the Dharma in motion, are the four most significant events of the Buddha's life.

The Buddha's Final Months

While dwelling on the Vulture Peak, near Rājagṛha, the Buddha asked Ānanda to assemble the Sangha, after which he spoke to them of the qualities that would ensure the survival and well-being of the Sangha. The Buddha then began his last journey. From Rājagṛha, the Blessed One traveled north toward Pāṭaligrāma, a small village on the south bank of the Ganges. He came first to the Ambalaṭṭhikā Garden, where he instructed his disciples in the four truths. After stopping at Pāvārika's Mango Grove in Nālandā, he went to Pāṭaligrāma, where he spoke to the townspeople of the fivefold loss of those who do evil and the fivefold gain of those who do good. Seeing that Pāṭaligrāma was being enlarged and fortified, the Buddha prophesied that it would become the greatest of cities but would have to endure the ravages of fire, water, and internal dissension.

After crossing the Ganges into the land of the Vṛjis, the Buddha stopped at a grove north of Koṭigrāma, where he taught his disciples the meaning of moral perfection (śīla), meditation (samādhi), and discriminating wisdom (prajñā). From there he went to Nadika, where he learned of the death of nine lay disciples who used to live in that area. There he taught the members of the Sangha how to view impermanence and how to best act in accord with that knowledge. The Buddha then traveled on to Vaiśālī where he stopped at Āmrapālī's Grove outside the city. When she heard of the Buddha's arrival, Āmrapālī went to greet him, followed by all the Licchavis of Vaiśālī, eager to pay him homage and listen to his teachings.

Soon after, when the Buddha stopped to rest near the Kapala shrine near Vaiśālī, he said to Ānanda, "How pleasant is Vaiśālī, how lovely is the land of Vṛji; the sixteen kingdoms and their cities are all very pleasant. The Hiranyavatī produces much gold; the land of Jambudvīpa is as beautiful as a painting. O Ānanda, those who acquire the superhuman power of freedom could remain in this world till the end of the kalpa, should they so wish." Although the Buddha repeated these words three times, Ānanda did not comprehend their significance. The Buddha then went to one side, and sat in the shade of a great tree.[1]

---

1. From the Mahāparinirvāṇa-sūtra. This passage, including Ānanda's dream, does not appear in the Mūlasarvāstivādin Vinaya.

At that time, Māra approached the Buddha, proclaiming that this was the time for the Blessed One to enter nirvāṇa. But the Buddha reminded him that a Buddha knows perfectly well the appropriate time for taking his leave. The Buddha stated that three months from then, in a grove of sāla trees near Kuśinagara, he would enter Parinirvāṇa. With these words the earth shook, waking Ānanda. Frightened, Ānanda told the Buddha his dream that a great tree had been destroyed in a storm, with no vestige remaining. The Buddha confirmed Ānanda's fears: Three months from that day he would completely pass away. Ānanda at once recalled the Buddha's words that he could, if he wished, remain in the world till the end of the kalpa; distraught, he beseeched the Buddha to remain. But the words of a Buddha, once spoken, cannot be changed.

After Vaiśālī, the Buddha went to Beluva in the Vṛji country and stayed in a grove north of the village. But food was in short supply due to famine, so the Buddha sent all his disciples except Ānanda to spend the rainy season at Vaiśālī. The Blessed One became seriously ill at Beluva but determined to live on until after the rainy season, when he could be with his disciples. Ānanda took hope that the Buddha would regain his strength, but the Buddha assured him that he had taught the disciples unsparingly and had withheld nothing of his doctrine: "Therefore sorrow not, Ānanda, neither give yourself up to grief. . . . Ānanda, let the truth be your island; let the truth be your refuge. There is no other island, no other refuge." (*Mūlasarvāstivādin Vinaya*)

After the rainy season, the Buddha went to Vaiśālī with Ānanda and stayed in the vihāra near the Monkey Pond. His disciples having assembled at the vihāra, the Buddha began the last journey to Kuśinagara. As he left Vaiśālī, he turned for one last look at the splendid city and told Ānanda that he was about to pass away in the Sāla Grove.

The journey to Kuśinagara led through the lands of the Vṛjis and the Mallas. The Buddha and his disciples passed through the Vṛjian villages of Āmragrāma, Jambudgrāma, Bhandagrāma, and Hasthigrāma. At Bhoga-nagara, where the Buddha rested in a grove, the earth shook three times. From there the Buddha went into the country of the Mallas and stopped at the Mahāvana, the Great Grove of Jaluka, where many villagers came to hear his teaching. Cunda the metalworker invited the Buddha to his home near the village of Pāvā the next day; there, after the Buddha took his last meal, he spoke to Cunda of the four kinds of people who follow the path of Dharma: those who are victors of the path, those who are teachers of the path, those who live by the path, and those who pollute the path.

Leaving Cunda's house, the Buddha and his disciples passed through the town of Pāvā, crossed the Hiranyavatī River, and traveled north along the river to Kuśinagara. But the Buddha became ill before they reached the city and stopped several times along the way. During this time the Buddha instructed Ānanda and the disciples to be steadfast in their practice of the Dharma.

The Twelfth Great Action: Parinirvāṇa

When the Buddha and his attendants reached the Sāla Grove, Ānanda prepared a place for the Buddha between two trees; as the Buddha lay down on his right side with his head to the north, he told Ānanda, "In the middle watch of this night I will utterly pass away." Here the Blessed One gave the teaching recorded as the Mahākaruṇā-puṇḍarīka, the Lotus of Great Compassion (NE 111). This teaching records the wonders that attended the Buddha's lying down upon his final resting place: All trees, shrubs, and grasses bowed toward the Buddha, all rivers and streams stood still. All beasts and birds left off their search for food and came to the edge of the Sāla Grove. The sun, moon, and stars lost their luster; all suffering in the hell-realms was assuaged. All in misery were relieved, and gods felt displeasure with the pleasures of their heavens. From the Akaniṣṭha Heaven, Brahmā descended to pay homage; a great multitude of gods and great Bodhisattvas assembled to honor the Buddha and receive the last teaching of his Parinirvāṇa.

At the opening of the Mahākaruṇā-puṇḍarīka-sūtra, the Buddha explained to Ānanda:

"Ānanda, I taught the supreme Dharma to bhikṣus and Brahmins, to demons and gods, to Brahmā and to others. To anyone who asked three times, I taught the Dharma. So that the stream of the Buddha's teachings should flow undisturbed in the future, I have given the teachings to the Bodhisattvas, the Great Beings."

The Buddha instructed Ānanda that after the breath had left his body the monks need not trouble themselves about a funeral; there were responsible people among the Mallas of Kuśinagara who would see that the funeral was conducted properly. The monks were to be earnest and resolute, ever zealous in their practice. The Buddha then gave instructions as to how his body should be wrapped and prepared for cremation and how the relics were to be gathered and placed in a golden vase.

Unable to bear the grief of the Buddha's impending departure, Ānanda withdrew from his presence but returned when the Buddha sent for him: "Enough, Ānanda! Do not grieve or weep. Have I not told you that in all things, there is the element of transience, of separation? How then could it be possible that what is born would not pass away, that what is compounded would not dissolve? Truly, no such condition could exist!" The Buddha then continued to console Ānanda, praising the merit of his faithful attendant, who always knew the correct timing of all that concerned the Tathāgata. "You have done well, Ānanda! Apply yourself with effort, and you too shall attain nirvāṇa."

For his son Rāhula, the Buddha had also a special teaching: "Do not grieve, Rāhula. You have done whatever had to be done for your father, and I have done whatever had to be

Twelve Forms of the Buddha's Teachings (Aṅgas)

1. *Sūtra* The short sayings of the Buddha; all the words of the Tathāgata bearing the name of Sūtra.

2. *Geya* All Sūtras in verse form.

3. *Vyākaraṇa* Predictions or prophecies concerning specific events or the future lives of persons.

4. *Gāthā* Teachings entirely in verse, or which summarize a teaching in prose, such as the Ratnaguṇa-sañcāya-gāthā.

5. *Udāna* Sūtras coupled with verses expressive of religious feeling. Words spoken not to specific individuals, but for the purpose of expressing the Doctrine.

6. *Nidāna* The teaching which follows from previous circumstances, such as a guideline for conduct given after an explanation of the cause of erroneous actions.

7. *Avadāna* Accounts of events in the lives of the Buddha, his disciples, or specific individuals.

8. *Itivṛttaka* Literally, "thus it is said;" historical accounts given by the Buddha.

9. *Jātaka* Accounts of the previous lives of Śākyamuni Buddha.

10. *Vaipulya* Literally, "greatly extended, fully expanded," referring to the Sūtras which draw out the meaning, or are "of great extent."

11. *Adbhutadharma* Accounts of wondrous accomplishments of the Buddha and his disciples.

12. *Upadeśa* Teachings on topics of specific knowledge, such as topics concerning the more psychological aspects of behavior and attitudes.

According to the Abhidharmasamuccaya, the Sūtra, Geya, Vyākaraṇa, Gāthā, Udāna, Vaipulya, and Adbhutadharma are related to the Sūtrapiṭaka; the Nidāna, Avadāna, Itivṛttaka, and Jātaka are related to the Vinayapiṭaka, and the Upadeśa is related to the Abhidharma.

done for you. O Rāhula, do not trouble your mind . . . Completely renounce all that is impermanent, and earnestly seek liberation."

Although Subhadra the ascetic traveled from Kuśinagara to question the Tathāgata, Ānanda refused five times to allow him near the Buddha. But the Buddha, knowing that Subhadra would be the last monk he would ordain, asked to see him. When the Buddha spoke of the superior result attainable through the eightfold path, the dust fell away from Subhadra's eyes; with the words "come hither, bhikṣu," the Buddha accepted him into the Sangha, and with those words Subhadra became an Arhat. Then, not wishing to see the Buddha's departure from life, he asked permission to enter nirvana; upon receiving the Buddha's permission, Subhadra passed away.

Then the Buddha named the twelve parts of his teaching: Sūtrānta, Geya, Vyākaraṇa, Gāthā, Udāna, Nidāna, Avadāna, Itivṛttaka, Jātaka, Vaipulya, Adbhutadharma, and Upadeśa, and advised the disciples to study them. He asked that they assemble twice a month and recite the Prātimokṣa, the rules of conduct he had given them, and that they select from the minor matters what they viewed as important. Then he advised them on the demeanor of novices and how the elder monks should care for them. The Buddha spoke to the disciples of the four places that stūpas would be built to commemorate the major events of his life: his birthplace at Lumbinī; the place of his enlightenment at Bodh Gayā; the place of the first teaching, at the Deer Park of Sārnāth; and the place of his death, in the Sala Grove south of Kuśinagara. Three times he asked if there were questions in the mind of any disciple present. All remained silent.

With his last words, the Buddha Śākyamuni gave his final teaching: "Bhikṣus, never forget: Decay is inherent to all component things."

Then the breath completely left his body, and the Buddha passed into Parinirvāṇa.

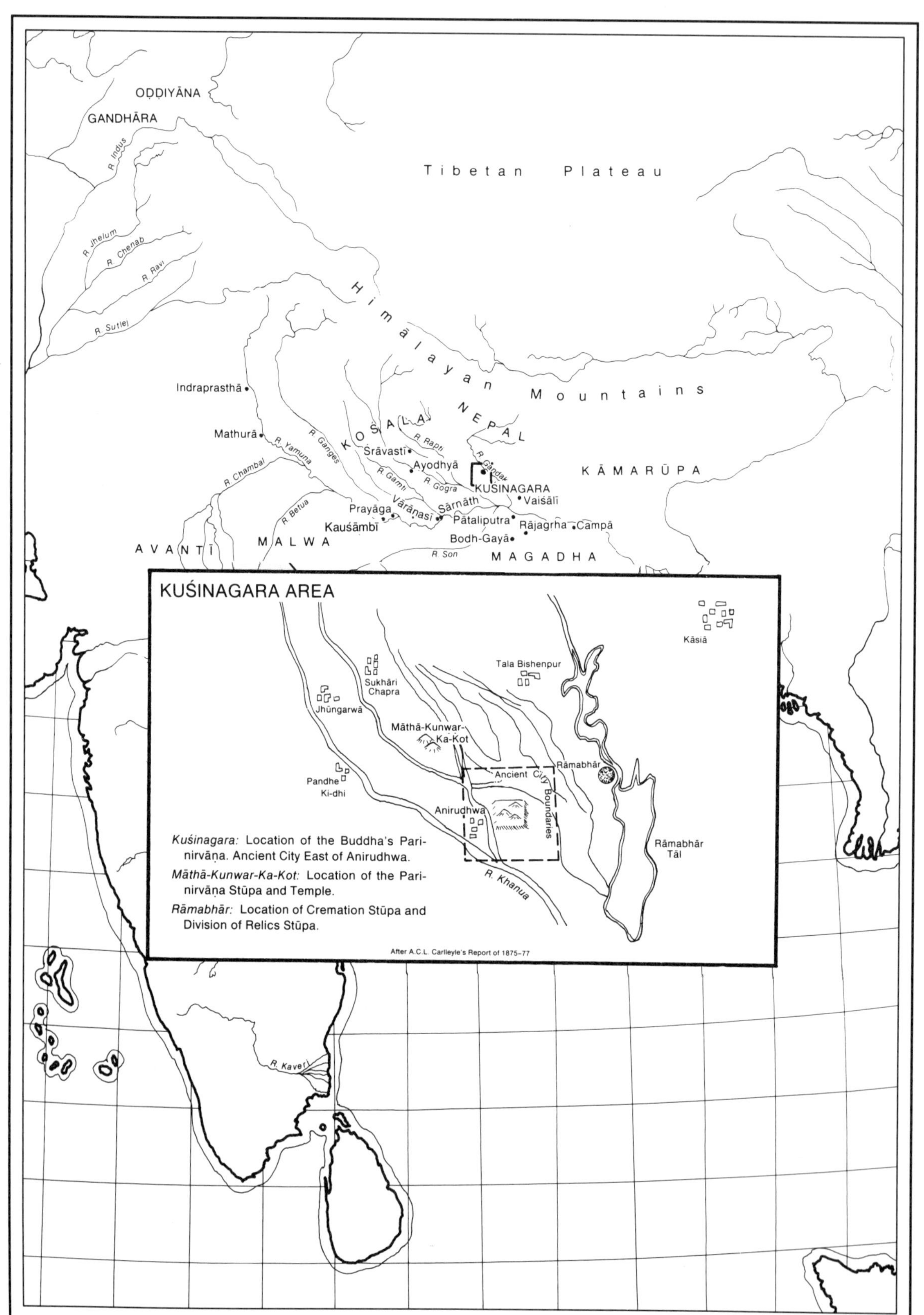

Kuśinagara: Location of the Buddha's Parinirvāṇa. Ancient City East of Anirudhwa.

Māthā-Kunwar-Ka-Kot: Location of the Parinirvāṇa Stūpa and Temple.

Rāmabhār: Location of Cremation Stūpa and Division of Relics Stūpa.

After A.C.L. Carlleyle's Report of 1875–77

Sites related to the Parinirvāṇa

"As soon as the Blessed One ceased to breathe,
the great earth shook, lightning fell,
and the gods of the heavens cried out
with the thunderous sound of a drum.
Residing in the Kalantakanivāsa Bamboo Grove
at Rājagṛha, the great Arhat Mahākāśyapa
directed his mind to the cause of this turmoil
and saw that the Blessed One had completely passed away.
Knowing the nature of things, he said,
"This is the case with every compounded thing."

—Mūlasarvāstivādin Vinaya

Distribution of the Relics

Aware that King Ajātaśatru would die from shock should he hear the news of the Buddha's Parinirvāṇa directly, Mahākāśyapa devised a means of informing him more gradually. He instructed Varṣakāra, the king's minister-of-state, to have images made of the Buddha's significant actions: the Bodhisattva's reflections in the Tuṣita Heaven, entering his mother's womb in the form of a white elephant, how he became enlightened; how, as a Buddha, he taught his doctrine in twelve ways, how he displayed great miracles at Śrāvastī, how he descended from the Trāyastriṁśa Heaven after teaching his mother, and how, after accomplishing his purpose, the Buddha entered nirvāṇa at Kuśinagara.

Then Mahākāśyapa explained to Varṣakāra how to guide the king gently, explaining each action carefully, until he reached the scene of the Buddha's nirvāṇa, at which point the king would faint from shock. After instructing Varṣakāra as to how to revive the king and save his life, Mahākāśyapa departed for Kuśinagara.

At Kuśinagara, the day after the Buddha's nirvāṇa, Aniruddha sent Ānanda into the city to inform the Mallas that the Blessed One had passed away, so that the Mallas would have the opportunity to properly honor the Buddha's remains. The Mallas requested seven days to prepare for the funeral. On the seventh day the Mallas arrived at the Sāla Grove and honored the body; they carried the bier through the city of Kuśinagara and out through the eastern gate, to the Makuṭa-bandhana shrine. While this procession was in progress, flowers fell from the sky for miles around, covering the ground up to the knees. A merchant traveling to Pāvā picked up some of these flowers; when Mahākāśyapa passed this merchant on the road and saw the flowers, he realized that the Buddha had passed away seven days before.

Mahākāśyapa arrived at the shrine while the Mallas were still attempting to light the funeral pyre, which would not catch fire. Mahākāśyapa uncovered the Buddha's body and paid homage to it, then exchanged the Buddha's shroud for a new one and covered the coffin once again. The fire burst forth immediately and consumed the remains. When the bier was completely consumed, the Mallas put out the fire with milk, placed the relics in a golden vase, and brought the relics to Kuśinagara.

The people of the lands blessed by the Buddha's teachings all sought a portion of the Buddha's relics for their country, so they could build stūpas over them and honor the Buddha in their own land. Even the Mallas of Pāvā came to claim a portion of the relics from the Mallas of Kuśinagara, since the residents of Pāvā had honored the Buddha for many years and did not think it fair for their kinsmen in Kuśinagara to retain all the relics for themselves. Then came the Bulis of Allakappa, the Koliyas of Rāmagrāma, the Brahmin of Vethadvīpa, the Śākyas, and the Licchavis of Vaiśālī, all requesting a portion of the relics. Ajātaśatru, overcome with grief, sent his minister Varṣakāra in his stead to obtain a share of the relics.

Seeing that a dispute might arise over the distribution of the relics, the Brahmin Droṇa went to each of the parties assembled, offering to divide the relics into eight parts so each might share equally. In exchange, Droṇa asked that he receive the vase that held the relics after the relics were divided, so that he might build a stūpa over the vase. The Brahmin Nyagrodha, probably of the Moriya clan, requested the embers from the cremation fire, so he could build a stūpa for them in the Pippala Grove. In all, ten stūpas were erected to commemorate the Buddha's Parinirvāṇa: eight over the relics, one over the vase, and another over the embers from the cremation fire.

The Vinaya records that of the eight measures of relics of the Buddha, seven remained in Jambudvīpa; the eighth was taken to Roruka, a city of the nāgas. The four eye-teeth relics were also dispersed. According to the Vinaya, one is in the Trāyastriṁśa Heaven, another in the town of Anumana (Gandhāra?), the third in the country of the king of Kaliṅga, and the fourth in Roruka.

Further Readings on the Life of the Buddha

Lalitavistara-sūtra. *The Voice of the Buddha: The Beauty of Compassion,* 2 volumes.

Buddha-Dharma, published by the Numata Center for Translation and Research.

Buston. *History of Buddhism,* part II, pp. 7–72.

Rockhill, W. Woodville. *The Life of the Buddha and the Early History of His Order,* pp. 14–147.

The Mahāvastu, translated by J. J. Jones. Vol. III, pp. 45–55, 93–121, 242–273, 290–343, 439–449.

Mizuno Kōgen. *The Beginnings of Buddhism.*

Thomas, E. J. *The Life of Buddha as Legend and History,* pp. 27–159.

Nakamura Hajime, *Gotama Buddha.*

Ñānamoli, Bhikkhu. *The Life of the Buddha as it Appears in the Pāli Canon.*

Part Three

Growth of the Sangha

The Sixteen Great Arhats

*At the time of the Parinirvāṇa,
sixteen Great Arhats vowed to remain in the world
to maintain the Dharma until the appearance
of the future Buddha, Maitreya.*

After Śāriputra and Maudgalyāyana passed into nirvāṇa, 150,000 Arhats, having the ability to abandon existence at will, followed them into nirvāṇa. Although there were more than eighteen thousand Arhats still living, the Buddha knew that most of these Arhats would wish to follow him into nirvāṇa. Concerned for the Sangha's welfare, the Buddha requested that sixteen Great Arhats remain in the world and watch over the Dharma as long as beings were capable of benefiting from the teachings. Since then the Sixteen Great Arhats have appeared to encourage the devoted and support confidence in the Dharma. According to the Aśokāvadāna, Piṇḍola Bhāradvāja appeared regularly to the Sangha at Pāṭaliputra in the time of King Aśoka, as witnessed by Aśoka himself. In the seventh century, Hsüan-tsang recorded an account of the great Arhat Rāhula accepting the hospitality of a devout layman at Kuśinagara.

The Arhats' most widely celebrated appearance was to the Chinese emperor T'ai-tsung (seventh century C.E.), who sent his emissary Hwa-shang to India to invite the Arhats to the Chinese court. Assuming apparitional bodies of light, the Arhats flew through the air to China with their attendant Dharmatāla and the emissary Hwa-shang. The emperor gave them silk robes and built a residence for each in honor of their presence. Sixteen statues were made in their likenesses as a reminder that the Arhats will at all times support those who wish to follow the Dharma. Paintings of these images were made and brought to Tibet by the master Klu-mes 'Brom-chung, who placed them in the Brag-yer-pa Monastery.

Accounts of the Sixteen Great Arhats and their iconographical depictions are known in all Buddhist traditions. Meditation on the Great Arhats and the Dharma symbols they carry stimulates insight into various aspects of the Buddha's teachings. Thus their representations have traditionally served as the focus of meditation and devotional practices. All are known by the Arhat's traditional title of Āyuṣman, meaning Possessing Long Life.

Āyuṣman Aṅgaja dwells on Mt. Kailāsa, with a retinue of thirteen hundred Arhats. On this most sacred of mountains the Buddha explained the law of karma, setting beings of all realms on the path to liberation. In his hands, Aṅgaja holds a bowl and whisk that have the power to liberate beings from all manner of emotional pain.

Āyuṣman Ajita lives on Mt. Drang-srong, the mountain of hermits and sages, with one hundred Arhats; some refer to his dwelling as the Crystal Wood of the Sages. He is depicted with his hands in the meditation mudrā. Seeing the Arhat in this gesture endows one with the ability to enter into profound meditation. Propitiating Ajita grants protection and steadfast devotion to practice.

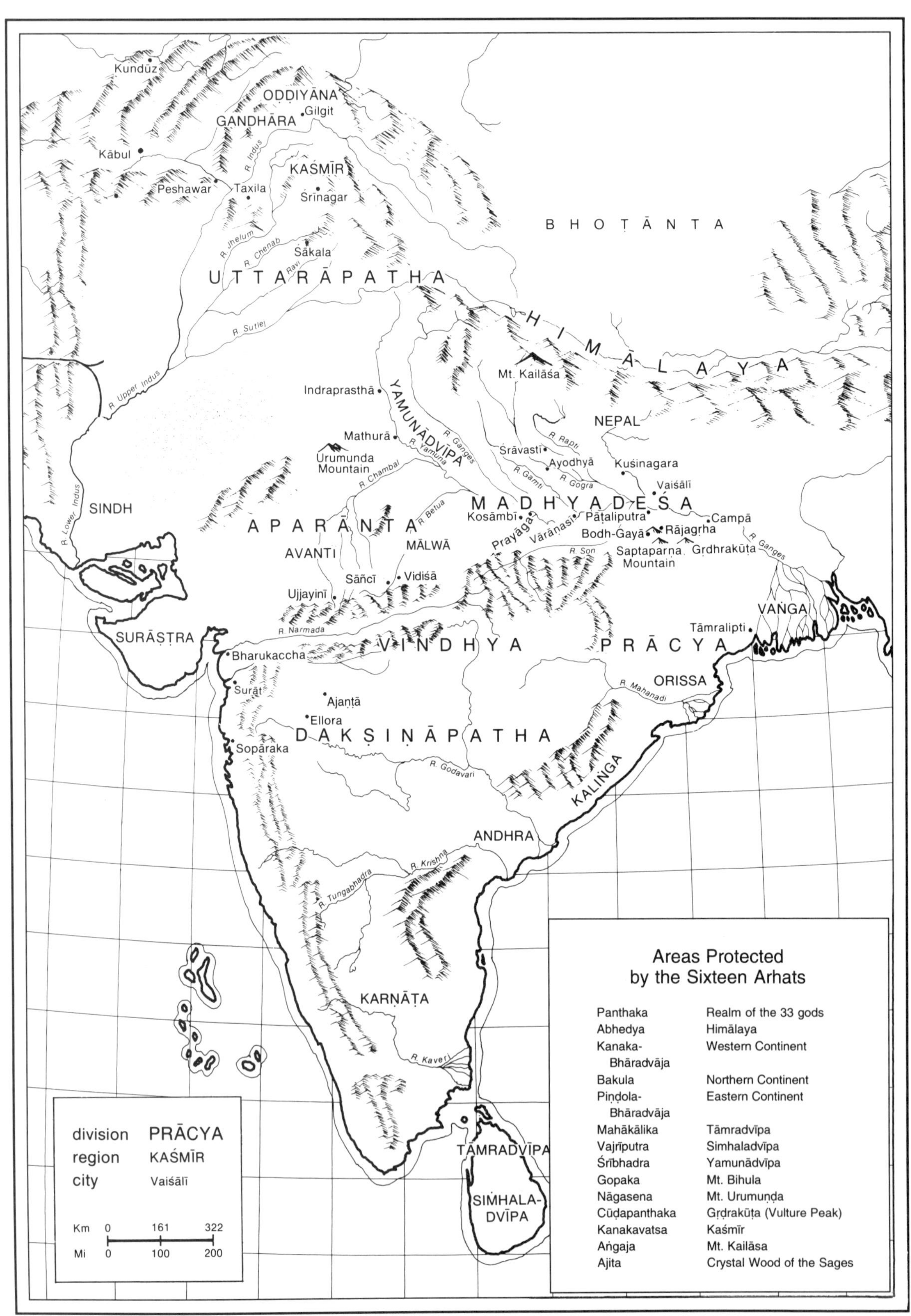

Sixteen Great Arhats vowed to remain in the world to sustain the vitality of the Dharma.

Āyuṣman Vanavāsin resides in a cave in the Saptaparṇa Mountain in Rājagṛha, near the site of the Sangha's First Council, accompanied by fourteen hundred Arhats. He holds a fly whisk in his hand; whoever feels its breeze gains the coolness of moral restraint. Those who invoke his aid obtain fulfillment of their wishes for spiritual riches.

Āyuṣman Mahākālika lives in Tamradvīpa attended by eleven hundred Arhats. He holds two golden earrings in his hands. By visualizing these ornaments, practitioners become able to penetrate illusion.

Āyuṣman Vajrīputra dwells with twelve hundred Arhats in a remote place in Śrī Laṅkā with a thousand Arhats. He holds a scented fly whisk in his left hand; his right hand displays the gesture dispelling fear. Meditation on Vajrīputra strengthens concentration and wisdom in those who work for the benefit of others.

Āyuṣman Śrībhadra, kinsman of the Buddha, dwells on Yamunādvīpa, Island of the Yamunā River, with a retinue of twelve hundred Arhats. He holds his right hand in the gesture of teaching the Dharma and his left in the meditation mudrā. Meditation on Śrībhadra develops the faculty of correct discernment, essential for understanding śūnyatā and perfecting compassion.

Āyuṣman Kanakavatsa dwells in the caves of Kashmir's Saffron Hills with five hundred Arhats. He holds a chain of precious stones given him by the nāgas. Mindfulness of Kanakavatsa develops fine spiritual qualities and strengthens the bond with one's teacher.

Āyuṣman Kanakabharadvāja lives on a mountain on the Western Continent (Godānīya), together with seven hundred Arhats. His hands are held in the meditation mudrā. Invoking Kanakabharadvāja opens opportunities for practicing the six pāramitās and developing along the Mahāyāna path.

Āyuṣman Bakula resides in a mountain cave on the Northern Continent (Uttarakuru) with nine hundred Arhats.

He holds a mongoose that conveys the power to grant understanding of all the Buddha's teachings. Those who visualize the Great Arhat Bakula acquire the boundless treasures of realization.

Āyuṣman Rāhula, the Buddha's son, lives in Prīyaṅgudvīpa, in the northern region of India, with eleven hundred Arhats. He holds a diadem in his hands that he received as an offering from the gods of the Heaven of the Thirty-three (Trāyastriṁśa). Those who invoke Rāhula's aid cool the heat of passion and enter the path to enlightenment.

Āyuṣman Cūḍapanthaka dwells with sixteen hundred Arhats on Gṛdhrakūṭa, the Vulture Peak, where the Buddha proclaimed the profound Perfection of Wisdom teachings. He holds his hands in the meditation mudrā. Those who invoke Cūḍapanthaka gain the ability to free themselves from desire, hatred, and ignorance, the three poisons that predispose beings to suffering.

Āyuṣman Piṇḍola Bharadvāja lives with a thousand Arhats in a mountain cave on the Eastern Continent (Pūrvadvīpa). He carries a book in his right hand and a begging bowl in his left. Through the aid of this venerable Arhat beings are freed from misfortune.

Āyuṣman Panthaka dwells in the Trāyastriṁśa Heaven with nine hundred Arhats. With his right hand he displays the teaching mudrā; his left hand holds a book. This Great Arhat aids those who earnestly wish to study, practice, and realize the Buddha's teachings.

Āyuṣman Nāgasena resides on Mt. Urumuṇḍa (Śīra Hills) near the city of Mathurā with twelve hundred Arhats. He holds a monk's staff in his left hand and a vase in his right. All who visualize his great staff and listen for the sound of its bells free their minds from confusion and awaken confidence in the three jewels.

Āyuṣman Gopaka lives with fourteen hundred Arhats in a cave in Bihula Mountain. He holds a book in both hands.

His blessing endows meditators with great wisdom, enabling them to teach the Dharma.

Āyuṣman Abheda dwells in the Himalaya, or some say in Śambhala, on Mt. Gangs-can, with a retinue of a thousand Arhats. He holds the enlightenment stūpa in his hands. Those who meditate on the stūpa he holds gain fortune and merit and open the way to realization.

It is said that when beings are no longer capable of understanding the Buddhadharma, and the Dharma of the Buddha Śākyamuni has disappeared from this world, the Sixteen Arhats will gather all that remains of the sacred texts and place them in a stūpa made of seven precious jewels. When this is done, they will pay homage to the stūpa, then pass from this world leaving no trace. The stūpa will sink into the earth, and no vestige of the Dharma will remain. Until the Bodhisattva Maitreya becomes enlightened and speaks with the lion's roar of the Great Buddhas, the Dharma will be heard no more in this world.

Further Readings

Dagyab, Loden Sherap. "The Sixteen gNas-brtan," in *Tibetan Religious Art*, pp. 60—118.

Crystal Mirror VI, pp. 193–195, 216–258.

The First Council of the Sangha

The limitless word of the Buddha,
He who was endowed with the ten powers,
Is now compiled in this Collection of the Dharma
for the sake of mankind.
Possessed of light, it removes
the gloom of ignorance
and the false views that obscure
and oppress all living beings.　—*Kṣudraka-vastu*

Although the Buddha charged the Sixteen Arhats with protecting the vitality of the Dharma for future generations, he appointed Mahākāśyapa to care for the Sangha after he was gone. Soon after the Buddha's Parinirvāṇa, Mahākāśyapa perceived the need to convene an assembly of Arhats to recite the Buddha's teachings. By reviewing, confirming, and fixing in mind the words of the Buddha, the teachings would be transmitted exactly as the Buddha had given them. The following account of the assembly is based on the 'Dul-ba (Mūlasarvāstivādin Vinaya).

Mahākāśyapa requested an immediate convocation of all the Arhats; he asked Pūrṇa to sound the bell for the assembly, and the Arhats immediately responded. Noting that the Arhat Gavāṁpati was not present, Mahākāśyapa sent Pūrṇa to call him from his retreat at Śirīṣaka. Told of the Buddha's Parinirvāṇa, Gavāṁpati closely questioned Pūrṇa about how the Dharma and Sangha was faring without their great leader. Pūrṇa replied:

"O Sage, in order to secure
a long existence for the Doctrine,
a congregation of the Śrāvakas has come together.
They request that you join them in their work.
The great ship, the Lord Buddha, has disappeared,
and the Mountain of Wisdom has been ravaged.
But there still survive numerous ascetics of four kinds
who have the highest teaching, and who are not idle.
I am their messenger. You must come with me
in order that the Teaching might be firmly established."
—*Kṣudrakavastu*, Bu-ston II:75

But Gavāṁpati declined to join the convocation, saying that what wise person, having attained the ability to enter nirvāṇa at will, would wish to live in the world once the Buddha was gone? Giving Pūrṇa his almsbowl and garments to offer to the Sangha, and asking forgiveness for leaving them, he vanished in a fire that burned from within. Four streams of water came out of the fire, and from these waters Pūrṇa heard Gavāṁpati's voice:

"The times have become evil
and individuals are following their own ways.
the Light of the World has passed away;
therefore all must now choose their paths themselves.

"The elements of existence, being accumulated,
disappear at once, in an instant.
Subjected to the suffering of birth, and all the rest,
and impelled by desire,

ordinary beings indulge in the conception of the self.
You must know that there is no such thing!

"He who is wise must become attentive
through constant thought,
and make effort to all that is virtuous.
For living beings in their multitudes,
all pass away and perish,
and the joys of life are liable to change.

Having had the wisdom to worship the Lord,
and brought to completion all his aims,
full of reverence and highest devotion,
Gavāṁpati has thus departed, following his Teacher."
—*Kṣudraka-vastu*, Bu-ston II:76

Pūrṇa returned to the congregation of Arhats and told them what had transpired. Mahākāśyapa praised Gavāṁpati's wisdom, but asked all the remaining Arhats to refrain from following his example. Now was the time to stay in the world and exert themselves for the sake of future generations. All the Arhats still living would be needed to continue the Buddha's teachings.

The Arhats then discussed where they would gather to recite the Dharma; Mahākāśyapa suggested Magadha, another suggested that they assemble at the Bodhi Tree, the site of the Buddha's enlightenment. But Mahākāśyapa chose Rājagṛha, for he knew that King Ajātaśatru would willingly support the Arhats throughout their convocation. The time for their gathering was to be during the rainy season. The Theravādin tradition tells that only the assembly of five hundred Arhats spent that rainy season at Rājagṛha; all others in the Sangha held the traditional rainy season retreat in a separate location. As Mahākāśyapa had foreseen, Ajātaśatru gladly agreed to supply the needs of the assembly and offered them their choice of locations. The Arhats chose the Saptaparṇī Cave in the mountains near Rājagṛha, and the king had it furnished for their use.

The question arose whether or not Ānanda would be allowed to attend the convocation of Arhats. Although Ānanda had heard all the Buddha's teachings and was blessed with total recall of all he had heard, he had applied himself so thoroughly to serving the Buddha that he had not taken time to meditate upon the teachings sufficiently to attain the state of an Arhat. However, respecting Ānanda's perfect recall and his special status as the Buddha's personal attendant, the entire assembly asked that he be permitted to join the convocation. Mahākāśyapa expressed doubt on this issue, but acceded to the wishes of the assembly.

The Mūlasarvāstivādin account relates that before the assembly opened, Mahākāśyapa asked Aniruddha if any of the five hundred bhikṣus were still subject to the passions, anger, ignorance, desire, or attachment. Aniruddha found only one: Ānanda was not yet completely free. Because of this, Mahākāśyapa insisted upon excluding Ānanda from the assembly. Ānanda pleaded to be included, saying he had never acted inappropriately nor had he done anything detrimental to the Sangha. Then Mahākāśyapa challenged Ānanda's statement, in what came to be known as the "Reprimand of Ānanda." (The seventh-century Chinese pilgrim Hsüan-tsang mentions that a stūpa was built to commemorate this event.) Specifically, Mahākāśyapa listed seven offenses:

1. Ānanda had requested that women be admitted into the order.

2. Ānanda had not asked the Buddha to remain in the world.

3. Ānanda had rested his feet on the Buddha's robe.

4. Ānanda had once given impure water to the Buddha.

5. Ānanda had not clarified with the Buddha which Vinaya rules were to be always kept and which could be sometimes set aside.

6. Ānanda had shown the Buddha's unclothed corpse to the Sangha.

7. Ānanda had shown the corpse of the Buddha to women, who profaned it with their tears.

Overcome with grief, Ānanda recalled the Buddha's instruction to him shortly before the Parinirvāṇa, not to give in to sorrow, but to trust Mahākāśyapa, to be patient, and to do as Mahākāśyapa advised: "Do not weep, Ānanda. You will increase the virtuous Dharma; you will not diminish it." As Ānanda remembered these words, Aniruddha approached him. "Go, Ānanda, and destroy every particle of the passions, become an Arhat, and then you may enter the assembly."

Ānanda's attendant, a bhikṣu of the Vṛji clan, counseled Ānanda to seat himself under a tree, focus his mind on nirvāṇa, surrender himself to meditation, and accomplish liberation from the passions. Ānanda did as his attendant advised; by daybreak he had succeeded and with great joy joined the assembly at Rājagṛha.

At the opening of the council, the five hundred Arhats requested Mahākāśyapa to preside over the assembly. Taking his place on the lion throne, Mahākāśyapa asked Ānanda to recite the Sūtras and Upāli to recite the Vinaya. He himself recited the Mātṛka, the seeds of the Buddha's Abhidharma teaching.

The Mūlasarvāstivādin account records that, upon taking the seat prepared for him, Ānanda reflected: "In considering the whole of the Sūtrānta as spoken by the Blessed One, there are the Sūtras the Blessed One spoke in the presence of the Sangha, those he spoke in the abode of the nāgas, and those he spoke in the abode of the gods. I will recite each one of the Sūtras as they took place, exactly as I heard and understood them."

Ānanda then proceeded to recount to the assembly of Arhats the place where each Sūtra was given and the person or group to whom the teaching was addressed. He then recited the entire body of Sūtras, beginning with the Dharmacakrapravartana (NE 31), the Buddha's first teaching to the five disciples at the Deer Park in Sārnāth. As Ānanda finished the first Sūtra, the Arhat Kauṇḍinya, one of the five disciples present at this teaching, arose and confirmed that Ānanda had indeed recited the Sūtra exactly as the Buddha had spoken it.

After hearing this teaching, Kauṇḍinya had become free of illusion and comprehended the implications of impermanence. Remembering that all was subject to decay, even the Buddha and his teaching, the assembly took the purpose of their council even more deeply to heart.

Then Ānanda recited each teaching, naming the villages, towns, countries, and kingdoms where they were spoken. After the recitation of each Sūtra was finished, Mahākāśyapa and the assembly confirmed that it was truly the word of the Buddha as they themselves had heard it. Then Ānanda compiled the Sūtras according to their subject and sorted them by length.

When Ānanda had finished, Mahākāśyapa asked Upāli, wise and renowned for his knowledge of the Vinaya, to recite every word of the Buddha's teaching on the rules that guided the Sangha. The recital took the form of questions and answers: Mahākāśyapa asked where the Buddha pronounced each rule, whom the rule concerned, and to what subject the rule applied. Upāli answered concerning the place, the subject, the occasion, the individual concerned, the proclamation of the Buddha, its repetition, and the fault incurred. Listening attentively, the Arhats confirmed each rule and classified them into categories from the most major to the most minor rules. This recital stated the substance of the Vinaya, later written down into seven texts: the Vinayavastu, the Prātimokṣa and its vibhaṅga, the Bhikṣuṇī-prātimokṣa and its vibhaṅga, the Kṣudraka-vastu, and the Vinaya-uttaragrantha (NE 1–7A).[1]

---

1. In the southern (Theravādin) tradition, the Vinaya texts are the Pātimokkha, the Mahāvagga and Cullavagga, the Suttavibhaṅga, and the Parivārapāṭha.

Some accounts of the Parinirvāṇa relate that at this point, rather than earlier, Ānanda reminded the Sangha that before the Parinirvāṇa, the Buddha had said that the Sangha could, if it wished, set aside the lesser precepts. However, under Mahākāśyapa's questioning, it became clear that Ānanda had failed to ascertain exactly which were to be considered the lesser precepts. Lacking certainty on this point and wishing to prevent any appearance of laxity, the entire assembly of Arhats concurred with Mahākāśyapa: "Let us change nothing of what the Buddha has said."

Then Mahākāśyapa mounted the central seat and recited the Mātṛka, the teachings intended to be developed through the bhikṣus' study and practice. As he explained, the Mātṛka clarifies what ought to be known: It comprises the four things to be continually born in mind, the four great restraints, the four bases of miraculous abilities, the five faculties, the five forces, the seven branches of enlightenment, the eightfold path, the four kinds of analytical knowledge, the four rewards of the virtuous, the four fundamental principles of the Dharma, and so forth.

According to the Saddhamma-saṁgaha, a text in the Pāli tradition, the council lasted seven months; the earth shook, and many wonders attended the completion of this great convocation. "The religion of Him who was endowed with the ten powers, has thus, by the Thera Mahākassapa, been rendered capable of lasting five thousand years."

The Mūlasarvāstivādin Vinaya relates that, at the conclusion of the council, Mahākāśyapa considered that the five hundred Arhats had accomplished their purpose. Then the yakṣas proclaimed: "The Venerable Mahākāśyapa and the rest of the five hundred Arhats have compiled the Tripiṭaka, the Three Collections of the Tathāgata; the devas will increase in number, and the asuras will diminish!"

The Buddha's teachings as compiled during this council are also known the Collection of the Five Hundred and as the Collection of the Elders. In all, the teachings covered

84,000 topics, as recorded in the southern (Theravādin) and northern (Sarvāstivādin) traditions alike.

Questions Concerning the Abhidharma

Nearly all the communities that branched out from the Buddha's original Sangha developed the Mātṛka into collections of teachings known as Abhidharma. Some traditions, however, regarded the Vinaya and Sūtra as the full expression of the Buddha's teaching and did not accept the more expanded Abhidharma as Buddhavacana, the Word of the Buddha. These views arose from various accounts of the First Council that presented the Mātṛka as a "means of preserving the sense of the Sūtrānta and Vinaya as it was spoken" and which did not clearly state that the Mātṛka was a separate collection.

Some accounts of the First Council do not mention the recital of the Mātṛka at all: The Mahīśāsaka and Mahāsāṃghika Vinayas, as well as the Cūḷavagga of the Theravādin tradition, mention neither Mātṛka nor Abhidharma. The Cūḷavagga is mostly concerned with the Vinaya recitation and minimizes even Ānanda's participation in the council. Of the Vinayas that have survived to the present day, the account of Mahākāśyapa's recital of the Mātṛka appears only in the Sarvāstivādin and Dharmaguptaka traditions. However, although the Cūḷavagga does not mention the rehearsal of the Abhidharma, the Abhidharma later found its place in the Theravādin Tipiṭaka along with the Vinaya and Sūtra collections.

Of the seven basic Abhidharma texts, only the Prajñaptiprakaraṇa (NE 4086–4088) is found in the Tibetan Canon. This omission does not appear to have been deliberate, but historical: At the time the Tibetan Canon was compiled, these texts had been lost and could be found neither in their original Sanskrit nor Prākrit, nor in Tibetan translation. However, the Mātṛkas, as described above, are all contained within the Vinaya and Sūtras preserved in Tibetan.

Council of the Great Vehicle

The Mahāyāna tradition relates that at the same time as the five hundred Arhats were rehearsing the teachings, one million Great Bodhisattvas assembled nearby on the summit of Mt. Vimalasvabhāva to recite the complete teachings of the Buddha. Maitreya recited the Vinayapiṭaka, Mañjuśrī the Sūtrapiṭaka, and Vajrapāṇi the Abhidharmapiṭaka. Dudjom Rinpoche (I:430–31) cites several traditional references to the compilers of the Mahāyāna Sūtras. One, that the original compilers were Samantabhadra, Mañjuśrī, Guhyapati, Maitreya, and others. Two, that the compiler of the teachings of the Thousand Buddhas was Vajrapāṇi. Three, the account cited above; and four, that the sections on the profound view (Prajñāpāramitā) were compiled by Mañjuśrī, and the works pertaining to the broad extent (Third Turning) were compiled by Maitreya.

Council of the Great Assembly

The Mahāsāṃghika (Great Sangha) tradition traces its origins to another council convened near Rājagṛha at the time for the First Council. Called the Council of the Greater Sangha because it was composed of several hundred thousand bhikṣus excluded from the assembly of Arhats, it included bhikṣus in training as well as those who were fully ordained. In order to express their gratitude for the Buddha and the Dharma, these bhikṣus decided to compile a Dharmapiṭaka, which they divided into five sections: Sūtra, Vinaya, Abhidharma, Kṣudraka, and Dhāraṇī.

According to Paramārtha and Chi-tsang's account, written in the sixth century C.E., the leader of the Mahāsāṃghikas was Baspa, and ten thousand participated in this assembly. A pillar commemorating the Council of the Great Assembly was erected in the time of Aśoka. Hsüan-tsang, a seventh-century Chinese pilgrim, noted the existence of this pillar in his records.

The Oral Tradition

Today we may wonder how the great body of the Buddha's teachings have been accurately preserved, when these teachings were probably not written down for several centuries. In ancient times, the spoken word was considered "close to the heart," far more sacred than we can readily appreciate today, and the mind of an aware human being was considered far more reliable than words written on perishable bark, paper, or palm leaf. The Vedic tradition had thoroughly implanted the value of memory and developed techniques to insure precise recall of elaborate ritual formulas and lengthy hymns. All religious traditions of the Buddha's time depended upon an oral tradition to preserve the most valued teachings.

For members of the Sangha, mental clarity and perfect retention of all teachings and events was a mark of spiritual attainment, a quality to be cherished and developed through mindfulness exercises and meditation. Thus Ānanda, Upāli, and Mahākāśyapa (and those who followed them) were fully capable of reciting the teachings of the Buddha, and the approval by the full assembly of Arhats insured protection against the slightest error.

Further Readings

Crystal Mirror VI, pp. 193–247.

Rockhill, W. Woodville. *The Life of the Buddha and the Early History of His Order*, pp. 148–161.

Vinaya Texts, translated by T. W. Rhys-Davids and Hermann Oldenberg. Part III (Cullavagga), chapter 11, pp. 370–386.

Poussin, Louis de la Vallée. *The Buddhist Councils*, pp. 2–29.

Patriarchs of The Dharma

After the Buddha's Parinirvāṇa, a succession of elders watched over the Dharma, establishing a lineage of Patriarchs that maintained and propagated the Buddha's teachings far beyond the Madhyadeśa.

The first Patriarch of the Dharma was Mahākāśyapa, to whom the Buddha had entrusted the Dharma shortly before his Parinirvāṇa. When the First Council drew to a close, Mahākāśyapa determined that he had done what was necessary to insure the preservation of the Buddha's teachings, and that the time had come for him to enter nirvāṇa. Entrusting Ānanda with watching over the Dharma, Mahākāśyapa told him that the next Patriarch would be Śāṇavāsika, a merchant's son, who had not yet entered the order.

Mahākāśyapa then made a pilgrimage to the four great stūpas that marked the place of the Buddha's birth, enlightenment, first teaching, and Parinirvāṇa and the eight stūpas that were built over the Buddha's relics. The great Arhat even traveled to the land of the nāgas and to Mt. Meru, abode of the Thirty-three gods, to pay homage to the eye-tooth relic preserved in each place. When Mahākāśyapa went to Rāja-gṛha to take leave of King Ajātaśatru, the king was asleep, and his servant feared to awake him. Leaving a message for the king that he was about to pass away, Mahākāśyapa climbed the southern peak of Mt. Kukkuṭapāda, where, according to the Kṣudrakavastu, he put on the Buddha's robe, vowed that his corpse would not decay until the Dharma was sounded once more by the future Buddha Maitreya, and entered nirvāṇa. The gods paid him homage and covered over the area between Kukkuṭapāda's three peaks, sealing Mahā-kāśyapa's body in the mountain.

King Ajātaśatru, who had also missed seeing the Buddha before his death, was distraught at hearing of Mahākāśyapa's departure. Accompanied by Ānanda, the king climbed the mountain to see the place where the Patriarch had passed away. The yakṣas removed the concealing cover, allowing the king to view Mahākāśyapa seated within the mountain, and the king paid homage to the great Arhat. To comfort the grieving monarch, Ānanda promised the king that he himself would not pass away without speaking with him. Ānanda then described how during the time of Maitreya, Mahā-kāśyapa's body would be brought forth and shown as the foremost among those who attain the twelve virtues of an ascetic. Ānanda advised the king to build a stūpa on this sacred site, and it was done.

When Ānanda became Patriarch, the Sangha was re-gaining strength and beginning to expand. According to the sixteenth-century Tibetan historian Tāranātha, although thousands of Arhats had entered nirvāṇa when the Buddha passed away, the disciples who had not become Arhats dur-ing the Buddha's lifetime regretted their lack of attainment and resolved to apply themselves more diligently. Those who had entered the Sangha after the Parinirvāṇa realized that it was even more important to practice diligently now that they no longer had the Buddha's direct guidance. As a result, many attained the four stages of perfection for the Arhat:

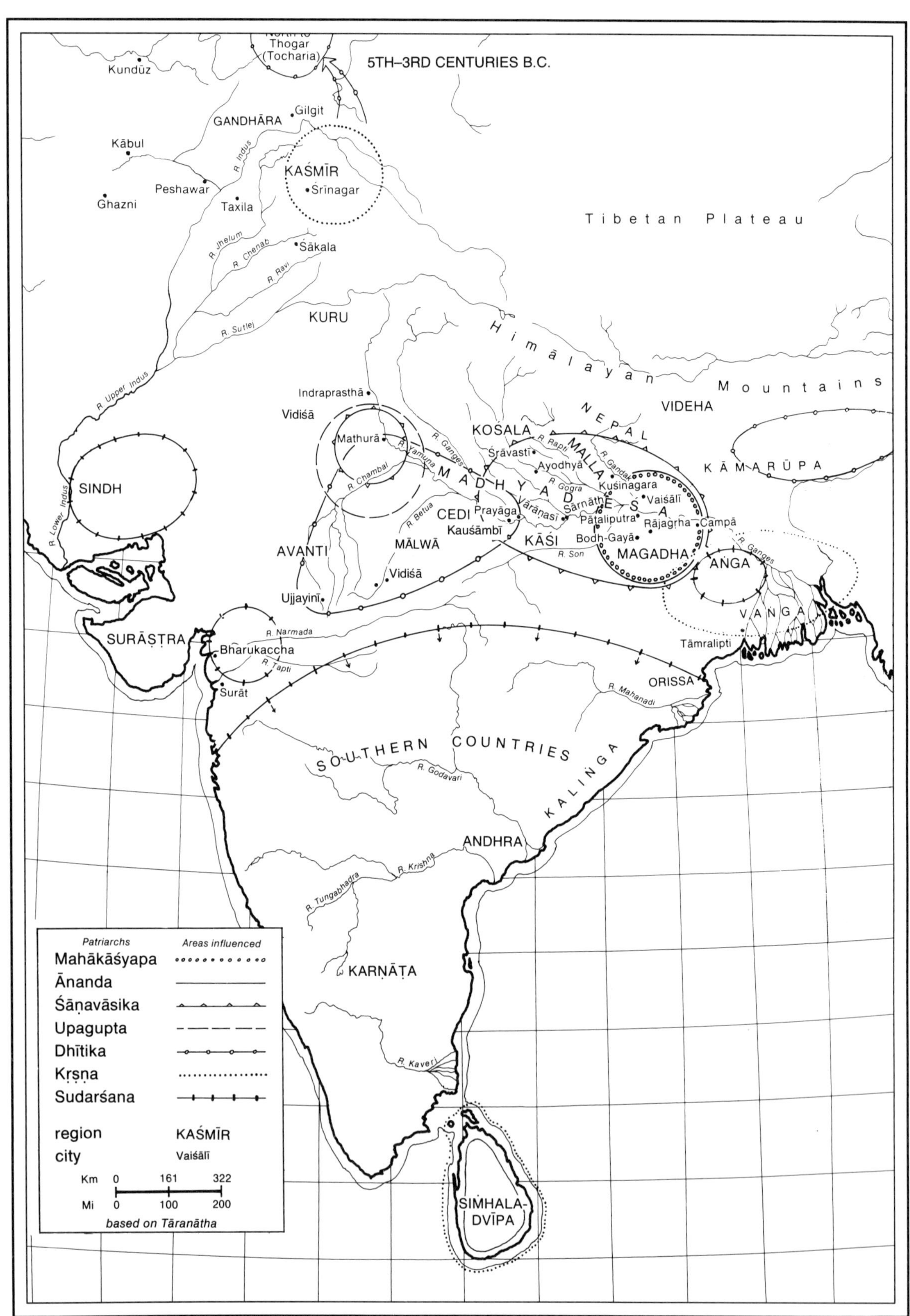

After the Buddha's Parinirvāṇa, seven great Patriarchs propagated the Dharma.

stream-enterers (those on the path to nirvāna); once-returners (those destined for but one more rebirth); non-returners (those who would attain freedom from birth and death in their present lifetime); and the state of an Arhat, the accomplished saints completely tranquil and free from defilement.

Tāranātha records that after the Buddha's Parinirvāna, the lands harboring the Sangha enjoyed peace and harmony for forty years. There do, however, appear to have been challenges to the Buddha's disciples during this period of time. Tāranātha mentions that a Brahmin from the south came to Magadha and engaged the bhikṣus in a contest of magic power that lasted for seven days. Ānanda won the contest in front of a huge gathering and through his teaching converted the entire assembly to the Buddha's way.

Eventually, as Mahākāśyapa had foreseen, Śānavāsika, a merchant's son, returned from the sea with such riches that he was able to support the Sangha for a full five years. He at once went to the Bamboo Grove asking to meet with the Buddha and was deeply grieved when Ānanda told him that the Enlightened One, as well as Śāriputra, Maudgalyāyana, and Mahākāśyapa, had entered nirvāna. Ānanda invited Śānavāsika to enter the order; Śānavāsika accepted, and Ānanda transmitted to him all he knew. Blessed with complete recall, Śānavāsika learned all the teachings of Vinaya, Sūtra, and Abhidharma, and in time became an Arhat.

According to the Āgamas, Ānanda taught the Dharma in Western India as well as in the Madhyadeśa, and on many occasions stayed in Kauśambī at the Ghositārāma, the monastery founded by Ghosita. A hundred years after the Buddha's Parinirvāna, when Yaśas sought Arhats to attend a convocation at Vaiśālī, he found many Arhats from the region of Kauśambī who had been Ānanda's disciples.[1]

Tāranātha records that Ānanda served the Sangha for forty years. According to the Kṣudraka-vastu, when Ānanda

---

1. Hirakawa Akira. *A History of Indian Buddhism*, p. 85.

grew old and saw that the time had come for him to enter nirvāṇa, he entrusted the Dharma to Śāṇavāsika. Ānanda told Śāṇavāsika that a merchant's sons, Nata and Bhaṇṭa, would build a monastery on Mt. Muruṇḍa (Urumuṇḍa) near Mathurā, where Upagupta, also a merchant's son, would enter the order of bhikṣus. According to the Aśokāvadāna, the Buddha had predicted Upagupta's ordination by Śāṇavāsika years before and mentioned that Upagupta's monastery would be known as the Naṭabhāṇṭika; it would become the finest of all the forest hermitages.

When Śāṇavāsika agreed to care for the Dharma in Ānanda's place, Ānanda sent a message to King Ajātaśatru, informing him of his intention to enter nirvāṇa and the place where he could be found. Wishing to avoid all disputation over the distribution of his relics, Ānanda decided to pass away on an island in the Ganges River, midway between Magadha, Ajātaśatru's realm, and the land of the Vṛjis. Ajātaśatru came to the southern bank of the Ganges with his whole army in attendance, and the Licchavis assembled on the northern bank. Each wished Ānanda to enter nirvāṇa on their land, but Ānanda remained steadfast in his purpose, convincing both sides that the Dharma would be best honored if each side received half of his relics.

The earth shook as Ānanda lay dying. But before Ānanda passed away, a ṛṣi with five hundred disciples came to him requesting ordination. Ānanda accepted them, and the ṛṣi and all his disciples entered the Sangha as non-returners. When Ānanda explained the Dharma further, all of them were freed from obscurations and became Arhats. Since the ṛṣi had entered the order at midday, in the middle of the Ganges, he was given the name Madhyāntika, Deriving From the Middle. The ṛṣi asked for permission to enter nirvāṇa before Ānanda, as the Buddha, upon his Parinirvāṇa, had granted this permission to his last convert Subhadra. But Ānanda refused, explaining that the Buddha had predicted that in Kashmir, a place well-suited for meditation, a monk known as Madhyāntika would establish the Dharma a hundred years after the Buddha's Parinirvāṇa. Assenting to this prophecy, Madhyāntika and his five hundred disciples departed for Kashmir.

Then, blessing the peoples of Magadha and Vṛji equally, Ānanda divided his body in two and passed away. Ajātaśatru had one half of Ānanda's relics placed in a stūpa in Pāṭaliputra, and the Licchavis, upon receiving the other half of the relics, built a stūpa for them in Vaiśālī.

Ajātaśatru died the year after Ānanda entered nirvāṇa; Tāranātha relates that he was reborn in the hell realms due to his treatment of his father but eventually passed from there and was reborn in Tuṣita Heaven, where he entered the path to liberation after hearing Śāṇavāsika teach the Dharma. Subāhu, Ajātaśatru's son, ruled in Magadha after his father; it is said that he was also devoted to the Dharma.

Traditional accounts of Madhyāntika differ slightly. The Kṣudraka-vastu relates that Madhyāntika, following the Buddha's prophecy, went to Kashmir directly after Ānanda entered nirvāṇa. Tāranātha, however, cites the Kashmiri tradition that extends Madhyāntika's stay in the Madhyadeśa for most of King Subāhu's reign (said to be seventeen years), during which time he served the Sangha as Patriarch. The Kashmiri tradition holds that Madhyāntika lived in the Madhyadeśa for fifteen years and was Patriarch before the Arhat Śāṇavāsika.

The Kashmiri tradition, which appears to have developed in relative isolation from middle India, relates that after Ānanda's nirvāṇa, the Arhat Śāṇavāsika quietly taught the Dharma in Śrāvastī, while Madhyāntika led the Sangha from a center in Vārāṇasī. Madhyāntika attracted so many disciples that Vārāṇasī's householders began to complain that they could not support so many monks. So Madhyāntika, together with ten thousand Arhats, went north to the Śīra Hill (Uśīragiri) and joined a congregation of Sanghas which the householder Aja sponsored for one year. Madhyāntika remained three years in the vicinity of Śīra Hill before departing for Kashmir. The Kashmiri tradition further states that only after King Subāhu died and his son Sudhanu became king of Magadha did Śāṇavāsika actually serve as Patriarch. Thus Madhyāntika appears after Ānanda in the Kashmiri list of eight Patriarchs of the Dharma but does not appear in the Tibetan list of Patriarchs, which follows the Kṣudraka-vastu.

While Mahākāśyapa and Ānanda concentrated their activities in Magadha and the lands of the Vṛjis, Śāṇavāsika's sphere of activity ranged further to the west. At first residing in Śrāvastī, he later received a request from King Sudhanu to travel to Magadha and relieve the people of that land from a devastating epidemic. Complying with the king's request, Śāṇavāsika went to Magadha, after which he propagated the Dharma widely to the bhikṣus and bhikṣuṇīs, laymen and women of India's six great cities: Śrāvastī, Sāketa, Campā, Vārāṇasī, Vaiśālī, and Rājagṛha.

Śāṇavāsika taught the Dharma throughout the reign of King Sudhanu, which Tāranātha gives as twenty-three years. Upon Sudhanu's death, Śāṇavāsika ordained two thousand of the king's officers and attendants. During the next rainy season they lived at the cemetery of Śītavana, where they became Arhats under Śāṇavāsika's guidance. Shortly thereafter, as foreseen by Ānanda, Upagupta, son of Gupta the incense-merchant, was ordained by Śāṇavāsika and attained the state of an Arhat within seven days.

It is said that, during his lifetime, Śāṇavāsika brought fully ten thousand disciples to a high level of understanding, and ten thousand of his disciples became Arhats. When the time arrived for his nirvāṇa, Śāṇavāsika entrusted the Dharma to Upagupta and passed away in the city of Campā.

Upagupta extended the Dharma northeast, to Videha, then to Mathurā, on the northwest boundary of the Madhya-deśa. Tāranātha states that in Videha, Upagupta resided in a monastery built by the householder Vasudhara, who had for many years supported all the Sanghas in the area. Continuing west, Upagupta taught the Dharma on the mountain variously named Gandha, Gandhamādana, or Gandhāra. Then he traveled to Mathurā, where he dwelled many years. As Ānanda had foretold, the merchants Naṭa and Bhaṇṭa built a monastery near Mathurā on Śira Hill (also known as Mt. Muruṇḍa or Urumuṇḍa) which they offered to Upagupta as his residence. This monastery became a thriving center for the Sangha, where many people came to hear Upagupta teach the Dharma.

Upagupta's teaching drew the attention of Māra, Lord of Illusion. At one time, when all the people of Mathurā were assembled on Śira Hill to hear the Dharma from Upagupta, Māra showered rice upon the city to induce the townspeople to return home. The next day Māra showered clothes on the city, which lured even more people away. The third day Māra created a shower of silver, on the fourth day, gold, and on the fifth day, precious jewels, until only a few people remained with Upagupta. Even these few were drawn away when Māra transformed his family into celestial dancers and musicians, who led the people back to the city.

Upagupta followed Māra's troupe to the city, where he congratulated them upon their performance and flung garlands about their necks. Immediately Māra and his demon family transformed into putrifying beings with decomposed corpses of humans and dogs hanging around their necks. Covering their noses in disgust, the townspeople turned and fled. Māra pleaded with Upagupta to release them, which Upagupta did after securing Māra's promise that he would attempt no further harm.

As Māra protested Upagupta's aggressiveness, Upagupta preached the Dharma to him, then asked Māra to perform an act of illusion: "I have seen the Teacher only in visions, not in his physical form. You, evil being, actually saw the Blessed One; therefore, please show me how the Teacher appeared in this life." Then Māra the shape-changer assumed the Buddha's form. Upagupta was filled with ecstatic joy; his hair stood on end and his eyes filled with tears. Then, forgetting who actually stood before him, Upagupta fell at the feet of the Buddha's image. Unable to bear such devotion, Māra fell down unconscious and vanished. Upagupta returned to Śīra Hill and taught the Dharma for six days without stopping; on the seventh day, one hundred eighty-thousand people attained realization. (Tāranātha, pp. 36–37)

Upagupta spent the rest of his life at the vihāra on Śīra Hill. In all, he served the Dharma for thirty-one years, for the nine years of King Mahendra's rule, and for the twenty-two years' reign of Mahendra's son, Camaśa. Tāranātha relates that only the Tathāgata surpassed Upagupta in compassion for living beings. He became, as the Buddha Śākyamuni had predicted, "a Buddha without the thirty-two marks." Upagupta entered nirvāṇa after entrusting his disciple Dhītika with the Dharma; his body was cremated and his relics taken away by the gods.

Dhītika, son of a rich Brahmin, remained a layman and mastered the eighteen branches of learning while his father remained alive but had no desire to continue a worldly life. After his father died, he became a wandering mendicant along with five hundred followers; although he traveled widely in India, he could find no one who could satisfy his questions on moral conduct. Finally, in Mathurā, Dhītika met the Patriarch Upagupta and awakened faith in the Buddha's teachings. Upagupta ordained Dhītika and his followers, and they became Arhats after seven days.

After Dhītika became a Patriarch, he traveled widely to propagate the Dharma, and, perhaps because of his family background, he was particularly successful among the Brahmins. Tāranātha describes how Dhītika went to the land of the Thogars, north of Kashmir. Seeing Dhītika flying through the air with five hundred of his disciples, the Thogars mistook him for the sky-god and greeted him with great reverence. Through Dhītika's teaching, a thousand Thogars, including their king, were converted to the Dharma, and many others attained the first stages of the path. After the rainy season was over and the routes to Kashmir passable once again, bhikṣus from Kashmir traveled north and continued to transmit the Dharma among the Thogars.[2]

Tāranātha also traces Dhītika's activities in the region of Kāmarūpa (modern Assam), where a wealthy Brahmin named Siddha, taking him for the sun-god, paid him homage and listened to his teaching. When the Brahmin was filled with faith in the teachings, Dhītika presented himself as a follower of the Buddha, and Siddha became a benefactor of the Sangha. According to this account, Siddha built a monastery called Mahācaitya, and Buddhism became widely accepted in the area. By Hsüan-tsang's time, however, no trace of such a monastery remained.

Another story connects the Patriarch Dhītika with the land of Mālwā, just west of the Madhyadeśa, where the ruler Adarpa ordered thousands of animals sacrificed daily. By miraculous actions Dhītika prevented a great sacrifice from taking place and taught all assembled there the uselessness and waste of such practices. Dhītika converted King Adarpa to the Dharma and lived in Kauśāmbī, the capital of Mālwā, for the latter part of his life. After benefiting beings for many years, Dhītika entrusted the Arhat Kṛṣṇa with the Dharma and entered nirvāṇa in the city of Ujjayinī, west of the land of Mālwā.

Tāranātha describes Kṛṣṇa as the son of a rich householder. Enamored of the sea when young, he made six voyages to Ratnadvīpa, the Isle of Treasure, in company with five hundred merchants. After his parents died, Kṛṣṇa met the Patriarch Dhītika, and became devoted to his teachings. Pressured by some merchants to make just one more voyage, Kṛṣṇa finally gave in. But this time, as the ship was returning home, a demon captured all the crew. When Kṛṣṇa prayed to Dhītika, he appeared and rescued them from the demons.

---

2. Some scholars identify Thogar with Tukharistan; the name of Mi-nar, king of the Thogars, is similar to the Greek Menandros, and the name of Mi-nar's son I-mas-sya might be a version of the Greek Hermaios.

Following Kṛṣṇa's example, the grateful merchants gave all their wealth to the Sangha and joined the order.

According to Tāaranātha, about the time that Kṛṣṇa became Patriarch, a Kashmiri bhikṣu named Vatsa was attempting to spread the doctrine of a permanent soul, which contradicted the Buddha's essential teaching of anātman. The Sangha assembled at the Puṣkariṇī Monastery in Maru, and Kṛṣṇa expounded the anātman teaching for three months, clearing up misconceptions and finally convincing even Vatsa of his error. Kṛṣṇa is also said to have flown to Śrī Laṅkā at the invitation of the Sinhalese king, who wished to hear the Patriarch teach the Dharma. Kṛṣṇa entered nirvāṇa after passing responsibility for the Dharma to Sudarśana, who was to become the last of the Great Patriarchs.

Sudarśana, born into a rich Kṣatriya family, grew up in the midst of great luxury. However, seeing an Arhat named Sukāyana, he abandoned attachment to wealth and sought to enter the order. Sukāyana refused to ordain him, however, without his father's permission. Angered by Sudarśana's request, his father began to beat him, but Sudarśana displayed such wondrous accomplishments that his father, convinced of the Dharma's power, let his son be ordained. Sudarśana was a disciple of the Patriarch Kṛṣṇa and became Patriarch upon Kṛṣṇa's death.

Sudarśana is associated with Sindh, the land around the lower Indus basin. In Sindh, he converted the yakṣiṇī Hiṅgalācī, who, upset by the death of her son, was spreading disease and exacting sacrifices from the people. Meditating on compassion and countering the yakṣiṇī's attacks through magic power, Sudarśana eased her wrath and converted her to the Dharma. Knowing that he would be the last to have such power, Sudarśana subdued some five hundred nāgas and yakṣas and taught them respect for the Dharma. Then he worked to establish the Dharma in the south and in many "small islands." He is said to have propagated the Dharma in China as well.

As for the date of the last Patriarchs, Tāranātha mentions that the latter part of Dhītika's life corresponds with King Aśoka's childhood, that the career of the Patriarch Kṛṣṇa corresponds with the time before Aśoka's conversion, and that Sudarśana was Patriarch at the time Aśoka became a Dharma king. He also refers to an ancient account by the Paṇḍita Indradatta, who records that Upagupta became Patriarch fifty years after the Buddha's Parinirvāṇa, and that the succession of the seven Great Patriarchs, known as the Mighty Elephants of the Dharma, ended after one hundred and ten years.

Bu-ston mentions another lineage of Patriarchs from a commentary on the Laṅkāvatāra-sūtra. This source follows the Vinaya account up to the time of Dhītika; after Dhītika, it names Bibhaka, Buddhananda, Buddhamitra, and Pārśva, then Pārśva's disciple, followed by Sunaśata, Aśvaghoṣa, Amṛta, Nāgārjuna, Āryadeva, Bākula, Saṃghananda, and others, up to the bhikṣu Siṃha.

The Mahākaruṇā-puṇḍarīka has yet another list, which starts with Mahākāśyapa and Ānanda, followed by Śāṇavāsika and Nandin in Mathurā. The text predicts that on Mt. Śīra, 44,000 bhikṣus would continue the Dharma; later, in Pāṭaliputra, there would be the Patriarchs Aśvagupta and Uttara. Thirteen thousand bhikṣus would arise in the province of Aṅga. Vijña and Saṃjaya would guard the Dharma in the city of Survarṇadroṇa; Mahāvīrya would protect the Dharma in the city of Sāketana, and Kāśyapa would protect it in the northern land of Gandhāra.

In this Sūtra the Buddha speaks of devoted laymen who would work for the Dharma in the future: Jāṭanika in Takṣaśilā, and Dharmavardhana, along with many other Brahmins in the north, including the Mahāyāna bhikṣu Jīvaka. At this time, when many bhikṣus would have fallen into false views, Jīvaka would restore damaged statues of the Buddha. King Agnidatta would support the Dharma in the "border-wood-land," and three thousand Arhats would live there. The

Buddha's relics would be honored in the northern borderlands, and many bhikṣus endowed with the highest morality would appear to propagate the Dharma.

Further Readings

Rockhill, W. Woodville. *The Life of the Buddha and the Early History of His Order,* pp. 161–170.

Tāranātha. *History of Buddhism in India,* pp. 20–78.

Bu-ston. *History of Buddhism,* pp. 86–95.

Hirakawa Akira. *A History of Indian Buddhism from Śākyamuni to Early Mahāyana,* pp. 76–94.

The Sangha After the Parinirvāṇa

*Then the Buddha enumerated the types of Dharma
teachings; he advised the bhikṣus to study them and
recommended that they hold half-monthly meetings
to recite the Prātimokṣa.*

—Mahāparinirvāṇa-sūtra

The early history of the Sangha testifies to the Buddha's
far-sighted wisdom and compassion. Setting forth clear
guidelines for conduct and emphasizing harmony, enlightened knowledge, and democratic process, the Buddha established a strong foundation for the Sangha's future growth.
This effort enabled the Sangha to preserve its essential unity
through millennia of expansion and diversification.

However, in every religious tradition, decisions made in
the critical years after the death of the founder profoundly
influence the course of the teaching. After the Parinirvāṇa,
preservation of the Three Jewels—the Buddha, Dharma and
Sangha—was the highest priority for the Buddha's disciples.
Fortunately for later generations, records of these critical

years were considered important enough to include in the
Vinaya section of the Tripiṭaka. Thus the Vinaya-vastu and
the Kṣudraka-vastu (and the Cullavagga of the Theravādin
Vinaya) extend our knowledge of the history of the Sangha
to the Second Council, held at Vaiśālī 100 to 110 years after
the Parinirvāṇa.

The Eightfold Sangha

The Buddha established a Sangha with two major components and eight levels of participation. The first component was the monastic Sangha, which included those who
received some degree of ordination. The second component
was the lay Sangha. The monastic Sangha consisted of the
fully ordained bhikṣus and bhikṣunīs, men and women who,
abandoning the ways of the world, were fully committed to
the religious life. It included the śramaṇas and śramaṇīs,
men and women who took the vows of the novice as well as
the śikṣamāṇas, students too young for full ordination.

The lay Sangha consisted of upāsakas and upāsikās, men
and women who remained householders but who served the
Dharma by living an ethical, morally upright lifestyle. Traditionally, the laity supplied the four basic requisites to the
renunciates—clothing, food, dwelling places, and medicines.
The Sangha of householders was also expected to serve the
monastic Sangha without favoring individual bhikṣus and
bhikṣunīs. Members of the laity could, if they wished, become upavasthas, sharing the bhikṣu's way of life by taking
temporary vows.

Essentially the monastic Sangha was expected to observe
ten fundamental precepts, rules of conduct consistent with
a path of virtue: to refrain from killing, stealing, lying, or
taking intoxicating drink; to observe chastity; to take no food
after noon, watch no entertainments, and use no personal
adornments; to sleep only on a low bed; and not to handle
money. But then, as today, the bhikṣus and bhikṣunīs agreed
to abide as well by the complete Prātimokṣa rules estab-

lished by the Buddha, which number more than two hundred for bhikṣus and more than three hundred for bhikṣunīs. In accord with the Prātimokṣa, bhikṣus and bhikṣunīs wore the robes specified for the order and gave up all but the most essential possessions.

The lay Sangha observed five precepts: to refrain from killing, stealing, lying, taking intoxicants, or engaging in sexual misconduct. Members of the lay Sangha were taught to cultivate the virtues of giving and moral conduct, patience and personal responsibility, contemplation and learning. They were encouraged to respect all forms of life. Taking the bhikṣus and bhikṣunīs as their ideal, upāsakas could strengthen their moral conduct and accumulate merit, preparing for a time when they could renounce worldly life and follow the teachings more intensively. All who took refuge in the Three Jewels—Buddha, Dharma, and Sangha—became part of this eightfold Sangha.

The Sangha of bhikṣus and bhikṣunīs was also known as the Sangha of the Four Directions, for they had no fixed home or household and thus were at home everywhere. Bhikṣus and bhikṣunīs were mendicants, or śramaṇas, expected to beg for their food, and homeless wanderers, or parivrājakas. In the earliest years of the Sangha, bhikṣus and bhikṣunīs continually traveled between Śrāvastī, Rājagṛha, Vārāṇasī, and other locations, either in company with the Buddha or individually.

While kings and lay supporters donated gardens and groves for the use of the Sangha, these places were at first temporary stopping places. The Sangha within a certain "parish" (sīmā) would assemble at one of these locations twice every lunar month, on the days of the full and new moon, to celebrate together the poṣadha, or uposatha, which was a day of fasting and especially strict observance of the Vinaya rules. Once a month the poṣadha observance ended with a recitation of the Prātimokṣa, the rules for conduct, and a public acknowledgement of transgressions by each

Prayer Upon Reciting the Prātimokṣa

With folded palms, we pay pure homage
to the Lion of the Śākyas (the Buddha).
I wish now to recite the Vinaya rules;
the Sangha should listen to them attentively.

Allow even the smallest offense
to produce great fear in the heart.
If you are guilty of a transgression,
confess it whole-heartedly
and never do it again.

Once you let loose the horse-like mind,
galloping on the path of wrongdoing,
it is difficult to control.
If you are earnest in the practice of śīla
as pronounced by the Blessed One,
your mind becomes like the horse who pays close attention
to the guiding pressure of the bridle.

The good will be able to believe and practice
the instructions uttered by the Blessed Tathāgata.
That is, when both rider and horse
have been well-trained, they are able to
defeat the army of evil dispositions.

If the Buddha's command is not accepted,
and love of śīla does not arise,
this means that neither the rider
nor the horse is properly trained;
they will be annihilated by the army of evil dispositions.

If you care for śīla
just as an ox is fond of its tail
and encourage a well-concentrated mind,
remaining earnest day and night
for the sake of obtaining true wisdom,
then, following the Buddha's doctrines,
you will be able to attain a pure life.

bhikṣu or bhikṣuṇī. The earliest assembly hall known from archaeological remains was the main hall of the Jīvakāmravana, the Mango Grove of Rājagṛha, given to the Sangha by the physician Jīvaka, patron of the Sangha and King Ajātaśatru's half-brother.

During the three-month rainy season, however, the wandering lifestyle was not practical, so the Buddha instituted the varṣaka, or rainy season retreat and established rules for selecting a proper location. King Bimbisāra, Anāthapiṇḍada, Viśākhā, Ghosita, and other patrons all built retreat centers so that the Sangha could spend the rainy season in reflection and meditation. The Sangha continued this practice after the Buddha's Parinirvāṇa, returning each year to a central location after nine months of wandering.

But the Sangha grew rapidly; within two hundred years the activities of the Patriarchs and Arhats had carried the Dharma well into Central and Western India, far beyond the boundaries of Magadha and Kosala. In time, as communities of bhikṣus developed in widely separate locations, it became impractical for the entire Sangha to come together in one central place. Bhikṣus began to observe the varṣaka in local centers or in centers more accessible on their travels.

Some members of the Sangha also adopted a more settled lifestyle, moving less frequently from place to place and establishing a more formal relationship with the laity in their regions. Gratitude for the teachings motivated patrons to provide more permanent shelters for the wandering bhikṣus, which in time became fully developed monasteries with relatively permanent monastic communities. This tendency can be seen during the time of the Patriarchs, when the merchants Naṭa and Bhaṇṭa built a mountain residence for the Patriarch Upagupta and an assembly hall to accommodate the townspeople of Mathurā who gathered in great numbers to hear Upagupta teach the Dharma. This shelter later developed into a complete monastery complex supporting a settled community of bhikṣus.

Yet the Buddha described the true renunciate as "one who wanders lonely as a rhinoceros." There were many who followed the example of the Buddha's first sixty disciples and adhered to the wandering life. The ideal of the anagārika, the bhikṣu unattached to any specific place, remains to this day.

The Council of Vaiśālī

Questions of relaxing or abolishing the minor Vinaya rules had been raised during the First Council, but the five hundred Arhats had determined that, lacking specific guidance from the Buddha, they would change none of the rules. Yet even during the Buddha's lifetime, exceptions were considered allowable in cases of hardship or where observing certain minor rules would clash unduly with local customs. Some bhikṣus took this lenience as a precedent for interpreting the rules of the Vinaya more liberally. According to the Kṣudrakavastu and the Cūlavagga, this tendency gave rise to a Second Council, which was held in Vaiśālī either one hundred and ten or one hundred years after the Parinirvāṇa. According to Tāranātha, this council was held at the time of King Aśoka, although other accounts place it at the time of Kālāśoka, or Aśoka the Black, who some historians equate with Nandin, the first king of the Nanda dynasty. Among all traditions the gathering at Vaiśālī is often known as the Council of the Seven Hundred.[1]

Momentum for this council began when the Arhat Yaśas visited the Sangha at Vaiśālī and discovered that the bhikṣus there saw no harm in permitting ten practices prohibited in the Vinaya rules.

---

1. Tāranātha mentions that according to the Vinaya accounts of some other schools, the council of Vaiśālī took place two hundred and ten or two hundred and twenty years after the Parinirvāṇa. But this tradition may have arisen from the habit of counting each solstice as a year. Historically, attempts to bring all accounts and dates into agreement have been only marginally successful; however, all accounts agree that such a council was held and that seven hundred Arhats participated.

1. proclaiming oaths such as "alala!" (alas!)

2. enjoying celebrations

3. digging the earth as in gardening or farming

4. storing salt

5. meeting and eating as a group away from the vihāra

6. eating with two fingers

7. drinking fermented drinks

8. eating milk and curds between meal-times

9. using a new mat without affixing a patch from the old

10. receiving gold or silver as alms.[2]

Concerned that these practices represented a falling away from the Buddha's teachings, Yaśas sought the advice of elder Arhats, most of whom had been direct disciples of Ānanda. Yaśas went to Sarvakarma, a venerable aged bhikṣu who had lived during Ānanda's time, and explained to him these ten practices (indulgences) permitted by the Vṛji bhikṣus. Sarvakarma recalled the classification of each offense and told Yaśas he would support him in adhering to the strict interpretation of the Dharma.

Yaśas traveled throughout the area where the Dharma was established, northwest to Sāṁkāśya and Śrughna, southwest to Māhiṣmatī, west to Mathurā and Kauśāmbī, to Pāṭaliputra and other places, explaining the ten indulgences to the eldest Arhats. Finding that all, like Sarvakarma, supported his conservative view, Yaśas convened the council of seven hundred Arhats, all of whom had been Ānanda's contemporaries, to decide whether to permit such relaxations of the Vinaya rules. Of all the indulgences, the tenth, relating to the receipt of gold and silver, appears to have aroused the greatest controversy. All seven hundred Arhats repudiated the ten indulgences and reproved the bhikṣus of Vaiśālī.

---

2. While all accounts agree on the subject of the council and its outcome, there are slight variations in the way these ten points are expressed.

Emergence of Conservative and Progressive Currents

The Second Council focused the entire Sangha's attention on the Vinaya observances of one particular region. As this council made clear, there were differences in view as to whether or not regional communities could adjust the manner of observing Vinaya rules to accord with local culture and customs. Where appropriate, the Buddha had granted such adjustments, but who would now be authorized to approve them? As differences of opinion persisted, distinctions arose between conservative and progressive elements in the Sangha. In time, these distinctions led to the first division of the Sangha into two major traditions: the Sthavira, or elders, who held fast to the perfections of the Arhat and favored a strict interpretation of the teachings, and the Mahāsāṃghika, who questioned the status of the Arhat and held broader views on Sangha and doctrine.

According to the Mahāvaṁsa, the Arhats recited the complete Tripiṭaka and performed acts of purification before closing the council. The Mūlasarvāstivādin Vinaya account of the Sangha's history ends with the reproval of the Vaiśālī bhikṣus, as do the records of other early schools preserved in Chinese. The account in the Cūḷavagga of the Sthavira (Theravādin) Vinaya ends with the Sangha reciting the Vinaya teachings only.

While it is clear from accounts of the Vaiśālī council that there were differences of opinion on minor points of observance, the sources that discuss the development of the early Buddhist schools do not agree on the precise time or the specific cause of the first formal division of the Sangha. The southern tradition, as recorded in the Dīpavaṁsa, a relatively late chronicle compiled in Śrī Laṅkā, traces this division directly to "a council at Vaiśālī," that occurred one hundred years after the Buddha's Parinirvāṇa. This account claims that the Vajjiputtas (the Vṛji bhikṣus) convened their own assembly immediately after this council, and independently compiled the collection of the Buddha's teachings as they understood them. The Dīpavaṁsa refers to these bhikṣus as Mahāsāṁghītikas. However, according to the Mahāsāṁghika Vinaya, an earlier text, the Mahāsāṁghikas clearly supported the decision of the Council of the Seven Hundred in censoring the Vṛji bhikṣus.

The Council of Pāṭaliputra

According to the Kathāvatthu, a Theravādin Abhidhamma text compiled to examine and resolve points of controversy, there was also a Third Council held at Pāṭaliputra during the time of Aśoka, who ruled over the Magadhan Empire in the second century B.C.E. The northern tradition does not record a third formal assembly of the Sangha at Pāṭaliputra. See pages 223–225 for a fuller discussion of events related to the assembly of Pāṭaliputra.

Further Readings

Rockhill, William Woodville. *Life of the Buddha and the Early History of His Order*, pp. 171–188.

Vinaya Texts, translated by T. W. Rhys-Davids and Hermann Oldenberg. Part III (Cullavagga), pp. 386–414.

Poussin, Louis de la Vallée. *The Buddhist Councils*, pp. 30–63.

Hirakawa Akira. *A History of Indian Buddhism from Śākyamuni to Early Mahāyāna*, pp. 62–68, 76–94.

Warder, A. K. *Indian Buddhism*, pp. 209–218.

Buddhism under the Dharma King Aśoka

*I have supported righteousness, that it may endure
as long as the moon and the sun, and that my sons
and my great grandsons may support it;
for by so doing they will gain
both this world and the next.*
—Aśoka, Toprā Pillar Edict (Delhi)

Although stories of the Great King Aśoka appear in all the Buddhist traditions throughout Asia, much of what is known of the dates and details of his reign are found on rock edicts that he had placed throughout the land. Rock edict XIII, for example, mentions that Aśoka sent missionaries to five kings in the West. By comparing the names of these kings with what is known of their reigns, Aśoka is now thought to have ruled from around 268 to 232 B.C.E..

Under Aśoka, the Mauryan empire reached its greatest expansion. In the northwest, the empire included the entire valley of the Indus River, the Punjab, and the former Greek lands of Arachosia and Bactria, even part of Gedrosia. In modern terms, this area encompasses all of Pakistan; its borders followed a line connecting Kābul, Ghaznī, and Kandahār. The southern boundary crossed the peninsula of India in a line stretching from Nellore on the eastern coast west to the Arabian Sea. Of the entire South Asian subcontinent, only the lands of the Satiyaputras, the Coḷas, the Pāṇḍeyas, and Kerala lay outside Aśokan influence. Most of this empire had been established by Aśoka's grandfather, Candragupta Maurya, and Aśoka's father, Bindusāra.

Even before the death of his father, Aśoka had been given responsibility for the government of part of the empire. At age eighteen, Aśoka was sent by his father to govern the western province of Avanti. Aśoka also served as viceroy of Ujjayinī and went to Takṣaśilā to suppress a revolt in the northwest. Upon his father's death, Aśoka inherited an empire that stretched from modern Bengal in the east to Afghanistan in the west.

Aśoka's only military campaign after he assumed the throne was against the Kaliṅgas who lived on the southeast coast between the Mahānaḍi and Godāvarī rivers. This territory was won at great price; a rock edict erected after the campaign confirms that "150,000 were captured, 100,000 were slain, and many times as many died." (*Rock Edict XIII*)

Aśoka probably was formally converted to Buddhism on or before the tenth year after his coronation. Observing the suffering of the Kaliṅga people during and after his conquest of them, he came to believe that war was wrong and that the only real conquest was one based on the peaceful truths of Buddhist teaching. After this insight, in the eighth or ninth year following his coronation, Aśoka lived close to the Sangha for over a year and performed religious austerities. From the rock edict at Maskī: "For more than two and a half years, I have been a lay disciple of the Buddha. More than a year ago, I visited the Sangha, and since then I have been energetic in my efforts." According to *Rock Edict VIII*, from the tenth year of his reign Aśoka practiced Buddhism con-

Aśoka's Inscriptions

Where other kings left monuments to personal grandeur and glory, Aśoka carved inscriptions on pillars and rock slabs to convey the benefits of the Dharma. The pillars, often thirty to forty feet high, were usually surmounted with a Dharma wheel or a powerful animal such as an elephant, lion, horse, or Garuda. Hsüan-tsang described several highly-polished pillars that shone as though they emanated light from within; some allowed designs to form that were used for predictions. Nineteenth-century European travelers are known to have thought the glossy stone pillars were iron.

Aśoka's inscriptions were written in the Brāhmī script, which passed out of usage about a century after Aśoka's time. After Buddhism declined in India, Aśoka and the purpose of his monuments faded from memory until the middle of the nineteenth century, when the inscriptions were identified as Brāhmī. The first inscriptions were deciphered in 1873; since then many more have been located, deciphered, and translated.

The edicts were discovered to contain a wealth of information about Buddhism during Aśoka's time. Some supported accounts in the Avadānas concerning events in Aśoka's life and contributions to the Sangha; others conveyed his ethical advice to society at large. To the modern historian, these inscriptions have provided valuable information on the precise extent of the Aśokan empire. For the Buddhist, the edicts placed on significant sites commemmorate events to be born in mind.

Discoveries of Aśokan edicts have continued. A pillar with an inscription in Aramaic was discovered at Lampaka in Afghanistan in 1949, and another in Greek and Aramaic was located in Kandahār in 1958. The most recent was a rock edict found in the city of Delhi in 1966.

scientiously and made great efforts to propagate the Dharma throughout his empire.

Aśoka added a moral and ethical dimension to the science of kingship as set forth by his grandfather's minister Cāṇakya in the Arthaśāstra, a classical textbook for politics and administration: Substituting conquest by Dharma for conquest by arms, Aśoka replaced the summons to war by a call to observe the principals of the Dharma. He assumed the role of educator; through his actions he gave his people a model of restraint, responsibility, and genuine concern for the welfare of all in his realm.

"All men are my children,
and just as I desire for my children
that they may obtain every kind of welfare
and happiness both in this and the next world,
so do I desire for all men."
—Aśoka, *Kaliṅga Edict I*

Aśoka's conviction that the "moral law" of the Dharma would ensure the ethical well-being of his people prompted him to use rock and pillar edicts in order to communicate the Dharma throughout the vast extent of his empire. In this way Aśoka emphasized the importance of the family, the value of establishing proper relationships within the family unit, and the virtue of obedience to one's elders. He also stressed considerate treatment of ascetics, Brahmins, and śramaṇas, and kindness to friends, acquaintances, companions, and servants, as well as the poor, the ill, and the disabled. For Aśoka, morality and right conduct were the "true ceremonies," more important for one's well-being than traditional religious rituals.

Aśoka advocated not only tolerance, but reverence for all spiritual traditions and set the example by extending support to all. That he took a special interest in the Dharma is shown by pillar edicts at Kauśāmbī and Sañcī, in which he specifically prohibited the sowing of disharmony in the Sangha. Sanghabheda, perpetrating words and actions that lead to

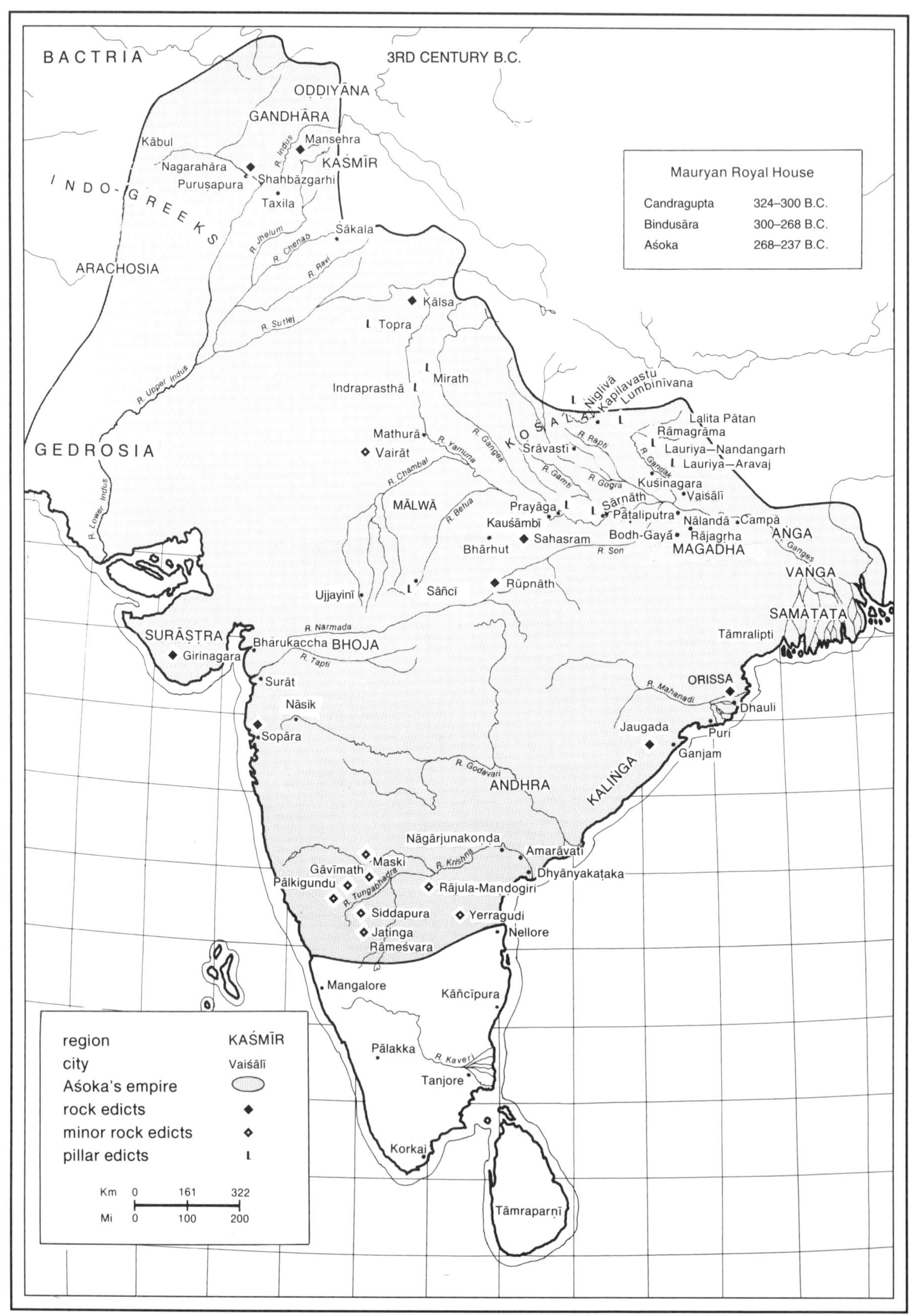

Sites of Aśokan rock and pillar inscriptions

division within the Sangha, is the first of the four unpardonable great offenses listed in the Prātimokṣa.

An advocate of total non-violence, Aśoka banned the serving of meat in his palace; he discouraged animal sacrifice, forbade hunting and other sports that harmed animals, and extended a vision of peace and harmony throughout his empire. He replaced traditional royal pleasure excursions with pilgrimages and personal inspections of remote areas of the countryside. He charged his administrators with maintaining contact with their regions and ensuring the well-being of those they governed. He left autonomous regions in his empire untouched and allowed the aboriginal hill tribes to live in freedom and peace. Throughout his empire he ruled with an even hand, treating all provinces equally.

Aśoka's benevolence and ardent support of the Dharma opened the entire empire to the Sangha. A system of roads, necessary for administering the empire and encouraging commerce, gave monks and nuns relatively safe passage. As a respected and capable ruler of an empire well-known to Greeks and Persians, Aśoka had influence far beyond the boundaries of his empire. It is likely that during his reign bhikṣus made their way along trade routes as far west as the Mediterranean Sea.

Aśoka in Buddhist Literature

Although the memory of Aśoka and his enlightened reign grew dim in India, records of Aśoka and his virtuous actions were preserved in the Buddhist traditions of China, Tibet, Śrī Laṅkā, Burma, and Thailand. Perhaps the most extensive account of Aśoka and his realm is in the Aśokāvadāna (Aśoka-sūtra), a text containing stories of Aśoka and his reign, which was translated from the Sanskrit into Chinese in 512 C.E. (A shorter text, the Aśokarājāvadāna, was translated into Chinese in 306 C.E.) Tāranātha's *History of Buddhism in India*, written in the sixteenth century, gives a short account of Aśoka. Information on Aśoka can also be found in the Lokapaññatti, Mahāvaṁsa, Dīpavaṁsa, and other Pāli texts. In the eleventh century, the Kashmiri poet Kṣemendra compiled stories of Aśoka into the Avadāna-kalpalatā, a collection of Avadānas (accounts of the Buddha and his disciples). Another collection, the Aśokāvadānamālā, awaits study and translation.

A major account of Aśoka's life appears in the Aśoka-vadāna, compiled as part of the Divyāvadāna, a large collection of Avadānas in Sanskrit preserved in the Sarvāstivādin tradition. Recently translated into English, this text traces Aśoka's association with Buddhism to a previous life, when, as a young child named Jaya who had no possessions, he offered the Buddha a handful of dirt. As the result of this gesture of respect, he was born the son of King Bindusāra. Although the king disliked him and his half-brother was Bindusāra's legitimate heir, Aśoka gained the throne with the help of his advisor Radhagupta. King Aśoka soon became known as "Aśoka the Fierce" because of his violent and cruel nature. He went so far as to create a lovely garden to entrap unwary travelers and commanded an executioner to torture and slay all who entered.

One day the Buddhist monk Samudra entered the garden; when the executioner approached to slay him, he begged for time to practice, since he had only recently become a bhikṣu. He was granted a stay of one week. Observing the horrors of that place, Samudra applied himself to the teachings and became an Arhat. Freed from delusion, Samudra had passed beyond harm, and the executioner's attempts to kill him had no effect. The executioner notified the king of this wonder. After observing the monk and the miracles he performed, Aśoka repented his harshness and became an ardent sup-porter of Buddhism. He immediately had the garden of death destroyed and changed his life to accord with the Buddha's teachings.

Soon afterwards, Aśoka heard of the patriarch Upagupta, who was considered to be—as Śākyamuni himself had predicted—a Buddha "without the marks" (the thirty-two major and sixty-four minor signs of a great being). Although Upagupta then lived on Mt. Urumuṇḍa near Mathurā, a long distance from Pāṭaliputra, Aśoka determined to visit him. But Upagupta, considering that his hermitage would not be able to support the retinue Aśoka would be bringing with him, decided to travel to Pāṭaliputra instead. Aśoka arranged for Upagupta's travel to Pāṭaliputra by boat. Upon meeting Upagupta, Aśoka bowed to his feet, overcome with reverence for the great being.

"The sight of you has doubled my faith
in this most excellent order.
Looking at you today I see in you
the incomparable Self-existent Pure One,
even though he is gone beyond.

"Now that the compassionate Jina has gone to rest,
you carry on the work of a Buddha in this Triple World.
Now that he has disappeared and closed his eyes
on this world of delusion,
you, like the sun, shine with the light of knowledge."
—*The Legend of King Aśoka*, p. 80

Aśoka then told Upagupta what he had done to further the Dharma in his empire; he spoke of his wish to honor the places where the Buddha lived and place memorials there for posterity. Upagupta agreed to be his guide and accompanied Aśoka on a pilgrimage to all the Buddhist holy places. Together they traveled throughout Aśoka's empire and erected stūpas and pillars upon all the sites sacred to the Buddhadharma. Aśoka also determined to open the eight stūpas in which the relics of the Buddha were enshrined and divide the relics into 84,000 portions to consecrate 84,000 new stūpas. According to both Hsüan-tsang and the account in the Aśokāvadāna, Aśoka succeeded in opening seven stūpas but was prevented from opening the eighth stūpa by a nāga who worshipped there daily.

The Aśokāvadāna includes details of how Aśoka converted his brother Vītaśoka to the Dharma, Aśoka's pilgrimage with the Patriarch Upagupta, his meeting with Piṇḍola Bharadvāja (one of the Sixteen Great Arhats) and the story of Aśoka's son Kuṇāla: how he was blinded through the machinations of his stepmother and how he regained his sight and his birthright.

According to Tāranātha, Kuṇāla, renowned for his piety and generosity, was sent by Aśoka to quell an uprising in Takṣaśilā. Kuṇāla was able to bring about a peaceful settlement between the governor and the people; however, his stepmother arranged that an order be sent to the governor, seemingly from Aśoka, commanding that Kuṇāla should be blinded. The governor hesitated to fulfill such an order, but when Kuṇāla insisted that it be carried out, he arranged for Kuṇāla to lose only one of his eyes. With this, Kuṇāla remembered an Arhat's teaching on impermanence and became a stream-enterer, the first stage of the Arhat's path. Leaving Takṣaśilā, Kuṇāla became a wandering musician, playing the vīnā, a kind of lute, to earn his living.

Eventually Kuṇāla was reunited with his father at Pāṭaliputra; Aśoka would have had Kuṇāla's stepmother killed for her crime, but Kuṇāla dissuaded him and through an act of truth regained his sight. Tāranātha relates that Kuṇāla was ordained into the Sangha and became an Arhat; Kuṇāla then turned over the throne to his son Vigataśoka.

The Aśokāvadāna also describes Aśoka's unfailing generosity to the Sangha, especially to the monastery of Kukkuṭārāma in his capital of Pāṭaliputra. According to tradition, Aśoka himself founded the Kukkuṭārāma, which is often referred to as the "Aśokārāma." The Arhat Yaśas was abbot of this monastery and the personal spiritual advisor to Aśoka and his court.

Aśoka continued to be exceedingly generous to the monastery even when he was old and had given over much of his power to his offspring. His grandson Sampadin, fearing the depletion of the state treasury, cut off Aśoka's ability to draw from the treasury. Still Aśoka continued to give until he had only one half of a myrobalan fruit left in his possession. Even that he offered to the Sangha. As his last gift, he used his remaining prerogatives to will the entire kingdom to the Sangha, saving only the state treasury, which he no longer controlled. After Aśoka's death, the ministers bought back the kingdom, completing Aśoka's vow to donate one hundred koṭis of gold pieces to support the Buddha's teaching.

Dharma Emissaries at the Time of Aśoka

Aśoka's fifth rock edict mentions that royal envoys were sent to introduce the Dharma among the kingdoms of the West and the Northwest, and other rock edicts record that envoys were also sent to the Tāmraparṇīyas, people who inhabited Tāmraparṇī (Śrī Laṅkā). During Aśoka's reign, trade flowed freely between India and Egypt and other lands bordering the Mediterranean; some historians even consider India the source of Egypt's embalming spices as well as of the ivory, apes, and peacocks brought to the court of Solomon. The land trade was facilitated by Syrians, Hebrews, Armenians, Caucasians, Somalis, and Parthians, and the sea routes were plied by Greeks, Romans, and Arabs.

Once the Dharma was established on India's west coast, bhikṣus had access to well-traveled routes linking Barbaricon, on the mouth of the Indus, with the Persian Gulf, and overland from there to Seleucia, Antioch, and Smyrna. The overland route lay north, from Mathurā to Kābul, north to Bactria, then west to Meshed and Rhaga, a point just south of the Caspian Sea, and from there to Seleucia and Antioch. Further archaeological research may uncover solid evidence of Buddhist communities west of modern Afghanistan, but for now we can only speculate how far bhikṣus actually ventured along these routes and study the remnants of ancient lore for clues on the westward expansion of the Dharma.

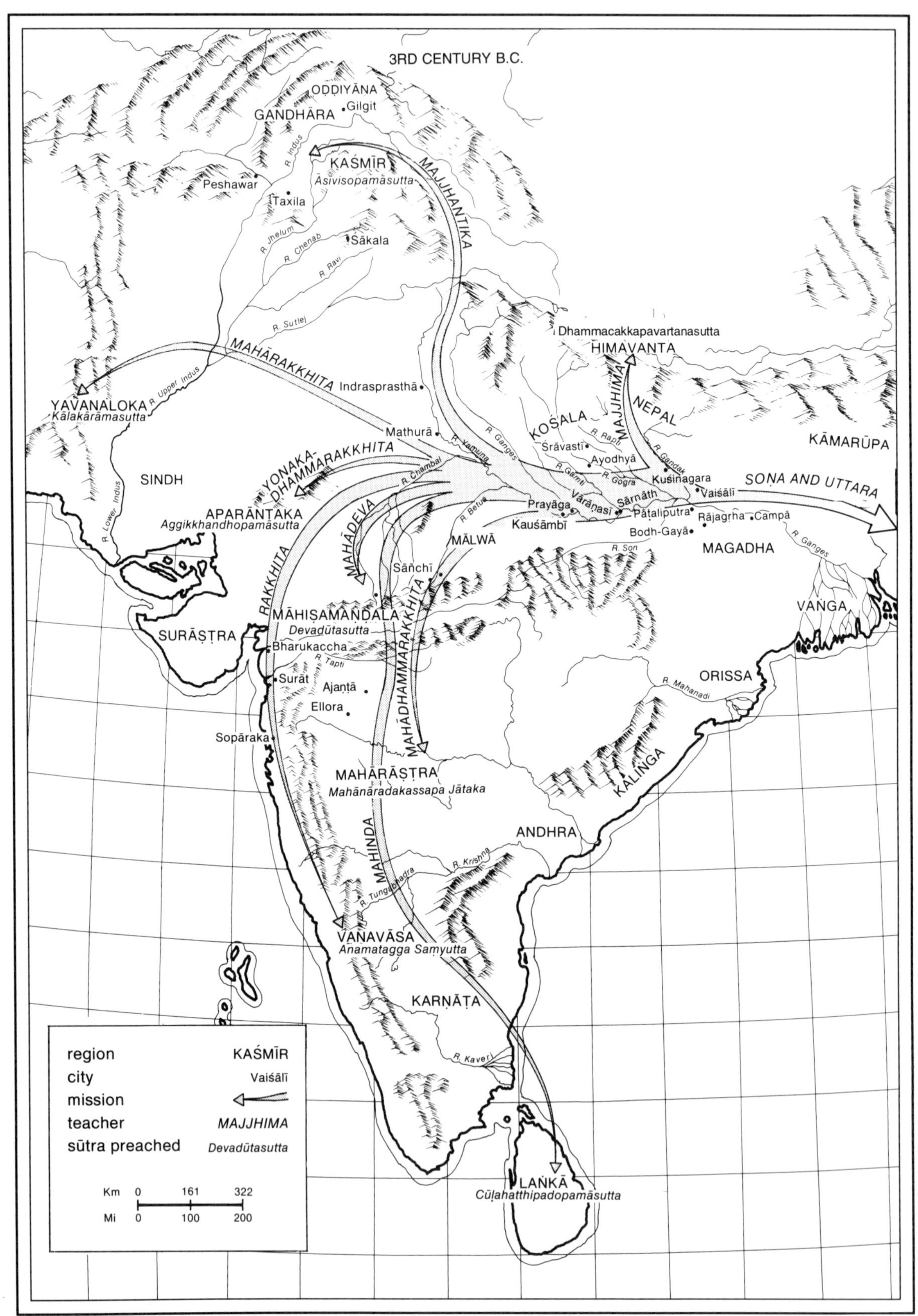

Dharma emissaries at the time of Aśoka (Sinhalese sources)

Nine Dharma Missions

The northern Buddhist traditions present the spread of the Dharma throughout the subcontinent of South Asia as a steady process begun by the Buddha and continued by the Patriarchs and their successors. The Sinhalese chronicles, however, describe the conversion of India as occurring primarily during Aśoka's reign, when the bhikṣu Mogalliputta Tissa sent emissaries from Pāṭaliputra to carry the Dharma to all parts of the empire and beyond. According to the Mahāvaṁsa, during the time of Aśoka, 236 years after the Parinirvāṇa, Mogalliputta, "looking to the future, beheld the founding of the religion in adjacent countries."

Mogalliputta sent out nine missions of Theras (elder bhikṣus) to propagate the Dharma: The Thera Majjhantika went north to Kashmir and Gandhāra, where he converted eighty thousand people; Mahādeva went to Mahisamaṇḍala (which probably lay south of Mahārāṣṭra along the Narmadā River) and brought forty thousand to the Dharma. Rakkhita went to Vanavāsī, converted sixty thousand, and founded five hundred vihāras. Yonaka (the Greek) Dhammarakkhita traveled to Aparāntaka, the lands on India's western coast; he converted thirty-seven thousand and ordained two thousand, half of them women.

Mahādhammarakkhita was sent to the region of Mahārattha (Mahārāṣṭra), located on the Upper Godāvarī River; he converted eighty-four thousand and ordained thirteen (or three thousand). Mahārakkhita traveled to the country of the Yonas (Yavanas), the lands along the Arabian Sea (Gedrosia) west of the Indus River, where he converted 170,000 (or 137,000) and accepted ten thousand (or one thousand) into the order. Majjhima was sent to the Himalayan region along with Kassapagotta, Dundubhissara, Sahadeva, and Mūlakadeva; when he recited the Sūtra describing the Buddha's first teaching (Dhammacakkapavattana), 800,000 beings entered the first stage of the path. Each of the five Theras converted an entire kingdom and ordained a hundred thousand. Sona and Uttara went to Suvaṇṇabhumi, associated with lower Burma. There they converted sixty thousand and ordained five thousand.

Aśoka's son Mahinda was sent to Śrī Laṅkā, together with four bhikṣus and his nephew Sumana. However, Mahinda decided to spend time in Western India before departing. He and his companions went West to Ujjayinī, Mahinda's birthplace, in the region of Avanti, where they dwelled six months at the Dakṣiṇāgiri Monastery. He also visited his mother Queen Devī in Vidiśā and met his cousin Bhanduka, who became a lay disciple and joined their mission. Arriving in Lanka during the reign of King Devānaṁpiyatissa, Mahinda converted 8,500 people during the first week and firmly established the Sangha in that land.

Northern accounts are silent on the missions of Mogalliputta Tissa and mention only two of the monks named in the Sinhalese accounts. Majjhantika, emissary to Kashmir, is known as Madhyāntika, although in the northern accounts he is considered to have been ordained by Ānanda, the Buddha's disciple and thus to have lived much earlier.

The other details of the conversion of Kashmir are very similar in both northern and Sinhalese accounts. Mahinda, who converted Śrī Laṅkā, is known in the northern tradition as King Aśoka's younger brother Mahendra. Mahendra is associated with Ujjayinī, his mother's home, and the nearby monastery of Dakṣiṇāgiri, where he lived before traveling to Śrī Laṅkā. Hsüan-tsang records that he saw in Malakūṭa, south of Kāñcī, an old monastery and the foundations of a stūpa said to have been built by Mahendra. This account accords with the Theravādin records of Mahinda dwelling in the west for some time before traveling to Lanka, but suggests that Mahinda made his way to Śrī Laṅkā via South India rather than by flying directly through the air.

Still, there is no doubt that in Aśoka's lifetime, traveling bhikṣus extended the Dharma further than ever before, possibly reaching even Greece or Egypt on their travels. Both Sanskrit and Pāli sources describe conditions faced by the bhikṣus in the Northwest, and travelers to other regions very likely faced similar difficulties. The Mahāvaṁsa relates that the first bhikṣus traveling to Kashmir and Gandhāra encountered 84,000 hostile nāgas, led by their king Aravāḷa or Hūṭa, as well as gandharvas, yakṣas, kumbhaṇḍakas and other non-human beings who occupied lakes and defended the mountain passes. These beings generated great storms with thunder and lightning; they blocked passage through the mountains with smoke and fire and devastated the land with floods and famine.

Throughout these attacks, the bhikṣus meditated on benevolence and compassion; the power of their meditation transformed weapons into kumuḍa flowers and won the trust of the nāga hordes. The nāga king took refuge in the Three Jewels, and the Yakṣa Paṇḍaka and his wife Hāritī, mother of five hundred demons, attained the first stage of the Arhat's realization. The Mahāvaṁsa records that the Arhat Majjhantika then blessed them saying, "Henceforth let no anger arise as of old; work no more harm to the harvest, for living beings love their happiness; cherish love for beings, and let all humanity live in happiness."

Further Readings

Aśoka. *The Edicts of Aśoka,* edited and translated by N. A. Nikam and Richard P. McKeon.

Aśokāvadāna. *The Legend of King Aśoka,* translated by John Strong.

Majumdar, R. J., ed. *History and Culture of the Indian People,* volume II, *The Age of Imperial Unity,* pp. 71–94.

Tāranātha. *History of Buddhism in India,* pp. 50–90.

Lamotte, Étienne. *History of Indian Buddhism,* pp. 223–310.

Buddhism After Aśoka

After Aśoka, the Greeks gained power in the Northwest, followed by successive waves of invasions by Central Asian tribes. Buddhism continued to expand during this time of rapid change.

The Mauryan Empire held sway in India from about 320 B.C.E., when Candragupta took power, to approximately 187 B.C.E.. These were years of rapid growth for the Sangha, which had paralleled the expansion of the Magadhan Empire from the time of Bimbisāra through the reign of Aśoka. During Aśoka's reign, it is said that the Dharma flowed like a great river throughout the whole of India, supported by the king's love for the Dharma and dedication to the well-being of his realm. King Aśoka reigned for nearly forty years and established the most peaceful and benevolent rule known to history.

However, after Aśoka's reign, which historians date from around 268–232 or 272–236 B.C.E., the empire slowly began to disintegrate. None of the later Mauryan emperors were

Aśoka's equal either in vision of empire or in application of sound government. Lacking a strong unifying ruler, local governors began to assume power in their regions, and central administrative control steadily weakened. Although the Sangha continued to flourish, it is likely that over time the fragmentation of empire affected ease of travel and communication between newly autonomous regions, isolating geographically separate Buddhist communities and fostering their growth into distinct schools.

Not much is known of the "later Mauryas," the kings who ruled during the years that elapsed between the death of Aśoka, great benefactor of the Dharma, and Puṣyamitra, who deposed the Mauryas and persecuted Buddhists. Around 187 B.C.E., Puṣyamitra Śuṅga, chief general of the Mauryan army, assassinated the last Mauryan king and established the Śuṅga Dynasty.

Buddhism Northwest of the Punjab

Tradition traces Buddhism's first appearance in Afghanistan to the time of the Buddha, long before Greeks occupied this land. The merchants Bhallika and Trapuṣa, the first to meet the Buddha after his enlightenment at Bodh Gayā, are regarded as natives of Balkh (Bāmiyān) who became the Buddha's disciples and introduced Buddhism to their homeland. Hsüan-tsang relates that they carried home with them hair and nail parings given them by the Buddha and built two stūpas over them. Balkh developed into an important Buddhist center; in Hsüan-tsang's time it was known as "Little Rājagṛha," but the reasons for this name are unclear.

Another tradition links the Śākyas to the royal lineage of Oḍḍiyāna: When Kapilavastu was destroyed near the end of the Buddha's lifetime, one of the Śākya princes made his way to Oḍḍiyāna, where he eventually became king. After the Parinirvāṇa, the Śākya king's son Uttarasena obtained relics of the Buddha and enshrined them in a stūpa in Oḍḍiyāna. The Chinese travelers Fa-hien, Sung-yun, and Hsüan-tsang all mention that a skull-relic of the Buddha was enshrined and venerated at a great temple in the vicinity of Oḍḍiyāna.

After the Second Council, the Mahāsāṁghikas established centers in the far northwest; one branch of the Mahāsāṁghikas, most likely the Lokottaravādins, settled in Oḍḍiyāna, while other Mahāsāṁghika schools established centers in Wardak and Kābul. The Sthaviras probably began to enter the lands northwest of the Punjab about the same time. The Sthavira Arhat Śāṇavāsika, who flourished a hundred years after the Parinirvāṇa, is associated with Kapiśa and Bāmiyān; Hsüan-tsang saw his hempen robe and iron pot preserved in a monastery near Bāmiyān.

In the fourth century B.C.E., when Greeks first settled in Bactria and Gandhāra, Buddhism was expanding through the Northwest, led by schools that were branching off from the Sthavira and Mahāsāṁghika traditions. The Northwest was one of the principal regions where the Dharma was actively propagated during Aśoka's reign. Aśoka's brother Majjhima sent the Arhat Majjhantika to teach the Dharma in Kashmir and Gandhāra and dispatched the Arhat Mahārakkhita to the land of the Yonas, or Greeks. Aśoka's empire included Kandahār (Arachosia), the southern region of modern Afghanistan. Stūpas and caves found in this region suggest Buddhists were active here in Aśokan times.

Buddhism and the Greeks: King Menander

The Greeks appear to have been tolerant and even supportive of the Buddhist communities developing in their lands. As they moved into the Punjab and down India's western coast, they increasingly came into contact with Buddhist teachings. The king best known to Buddhist history is King Menander (Pāli, Milinda), who came to power between 163 and 115 B.C.E. His kingdom stretched west of the Indus through the lands of Gandhāra, Oḍḍiyāna, and Sindh, and southeast through Kaccha and Surāṣṭra. Some authorities include southern Afghanistan in his kingdom, which he ruled from his capital city of Śākala (modern Siālkot), located in the Punjab.

King Menander's interest in and support of the Dharma is recorded in the Milindapañha, a contemporary text translated three times into Chinese. Carried to Śrī Laṅkā, the text was expanded and preserved also in Pāli. The Milindapañha records King Menander's dialogue with Nāgasena, a bhikṣu from the Vattaniya Monastery. Menander's previous interviews with the Dharma master Ayupāla had stimulated the king's interest, and he had sent for Nāgasena to answer specific questions.

All Dharma traditions consider Menander a Buddhist; on coin inscriptions he refers to himself as a savior, and there is general agreement that the king did indeed protect the interests of the Buddhist communities. He also sought and gained support from the middle classes, bypassing the intrigue and politics of the traditional caste system and promoting economic prosperity for his kingdom.

According to Kṣemendra's Avadānakalpalatā, Menander eventually turned over his throne to his son, joined the Buddhist order, and became an Arhat. Plutarch notes that upon his death he was cremated and that cities in the region vied for a portion of his ashes. Although the Greek (Yavana)[1] kingdoms disintegrated after Menander's death and all remnants of Greek rule ended around 30 B.C.E., the Greek legacy lived on in the northwestern territories, where Greeks served successions of new rulers as advisors and administrators.

Buddhism flourished in the northwestern countries under Greek rule. By the opening of the first century B.C.E., major Dharma centers existed far west of India's traditional cultural borders, from Takṣaśilā and Peshāwar in Gandhāra to Oḍḍiyāna on the north, and west through Kapiśa, Wardak, and Bāmiyān to Balkh, regions that fall within modern Afghanistan. The Mahāsāṃghika schools (Lokottaravādin,

---

1. Sanskrit, Yavana; Pāli, Yona (probably derived from Iona).

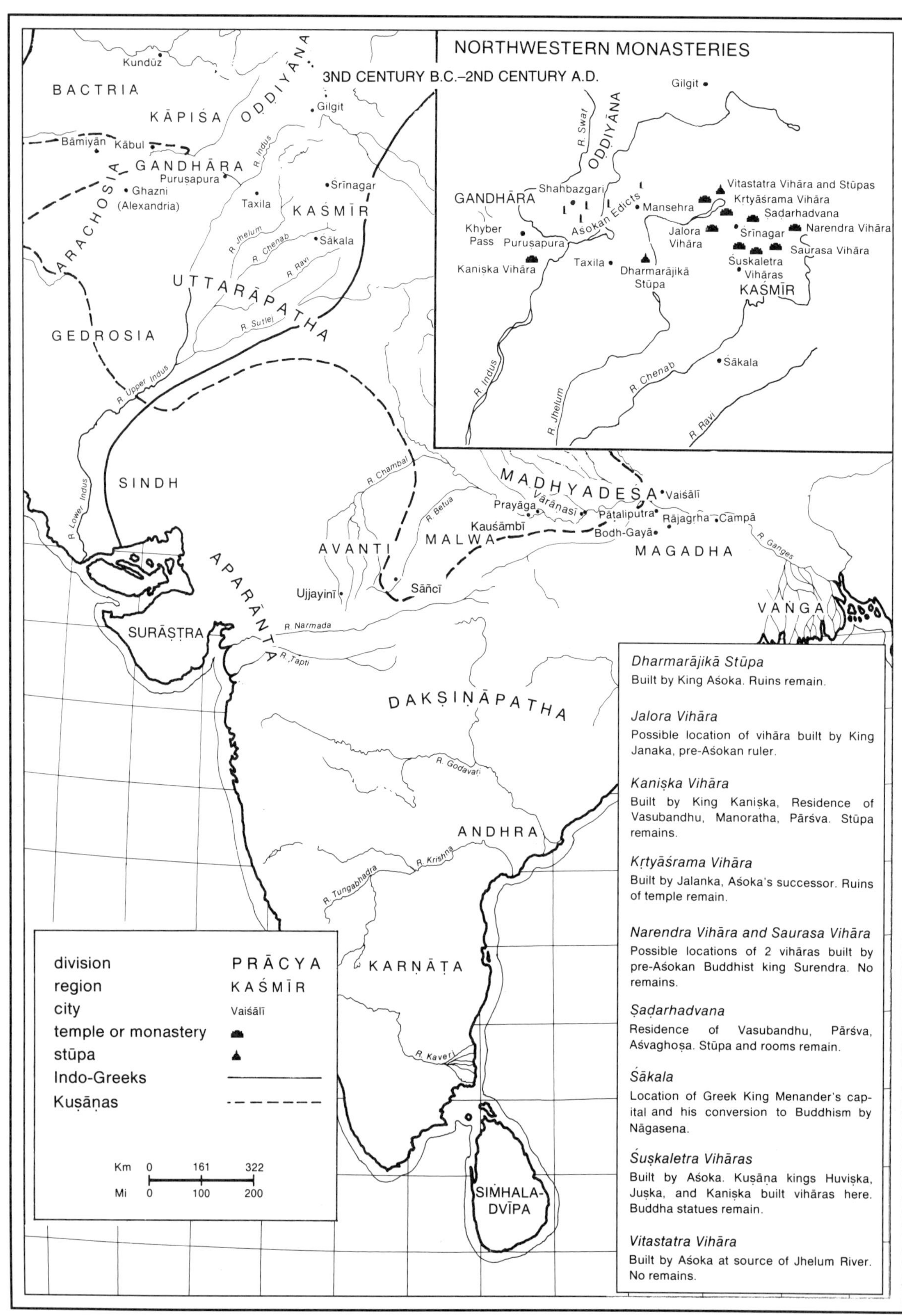

Dharmarājikā Stūpa

Built by King Aśoka. Ruins remain.

Jalora Vihāra

Possible location of vihāra built by King Janaka, pre-Aśokan ruler.

Kaniṣka Vihāra

Built by King Kaniṣka, Residence of Vasubandhu, Manoratha, Pārśva. Stūpa remains.

Kṛtyāśrama Vihāra

Built by Jalanka, Aśoka's successor. Ruins of temple remain.

Narendra Vihāra and Saurasa Vihāra

Possible locations of 2 vihāras built by pre-Aśokan Buddhist king Surendra. No remains.

Saḍarhadvana

Residence of Vasubandhu, Pārśva, Aśvaghoṣa. Stūpa and rooms remain.

Sākala

Location of Greek King Menander's capital and his conversion to Buddhism by Nāgasena.

Śuṣkaletra Vihāras

Built by Aśoka. Kuṣāṇa kings Huviṣka, Juṣka, and Kaniṣka built vihāras here. Buddha statues remain.

Vitastatra Vihāra

Built by Aśoka at source of Jhelum River. No remains.

Greek and Kuṣāṇa rulers of the northwest built monasteries and stūpas.

Ekavyavahārika, and Bahuśrutīya) were most numerous in Arachosia, Balkh (Bactria), and Bāmiyān, with the Sthavira and Sarvāstivādin centers emerging in Kashmir and Gandhāra to the east.

The Śuṅga Dynasty

Assuming power around 187 B.C.E., Puṣyamitra, the first Śuṅga king, ruled a part of India that stretched from Pāṭaliputra in the east to Jālandhara and Śākala in the Punjab, in the northwest. In contrast to Menander's benevolent rule, Puṣyamitra persecuted Buddhists and sought to strengthen the brahmanic traditions. Early in his reign, the Greek invasions had nearly cost him the entire Mauryan Empire. He suffered heavy losses in the Northwest; in the south, Kaliṅga and Andhra asserted their independence. After the Greeks withdrew from India, Puṣyamitra was able to retain the central part of his kingdom. He revitalized the brahmanic traditions to legitimatize his claim to the Mauryan Empire and reinstated the Vedic horse sacrifice to extend his influence beyond Central India.

In this elaborate ritual, a horse is selected, consecrated, and released to wander freely for a year. The horse becomes the king's divine guide, pointing out the land the gods wish the king to rule. The king's army rides close behind the horse, ready to claim for the king whatever land the horse traverses and to crush all opposition. At the end of a year the horse is brought to the capital and sacrificed in a complex ritual, completing the king's claim to all lands the horse has entered. While Puṣyamitra's army ran into difficulties when his horse crossed the boundary of the Greek territories, he was able to retrieve the horse and hold all other lands through which the horse passed.

Buddhist accounts associate Puṣyamitra with widespread destruction of monasteries and stūpas; the Sarvāstivādin Vaibhāṣa relates that he destroyed five hundred monasteries in Kashmir alone, as well as many sacred texts. But when he sought to destroy the Bodhi Tree, he was slain by the tree's protective deity. Another Sarvāstivādin account mentions that Puṣyamitra destroyed the Kukkuṭārāma (Aśokārāma) monastery in Pāṭaliputra and massacred all its monks; he finally met his end at the hands of two yakṣas. The Śāriputra-paripṛcchā gives another account, slightly different in locations and specific details.

In the Mañjuśrīmūlakalpa the Buddha predicted Puṣyamitra's enmity toward the Dharma: "In that inferior age, there will be a king, Gomimukhya, destroyer of my religion. Having seized the east and the gates of Kashmir, that madman of evil intent will destroy vihāras and venerable relics and will cause the death of monks of good conduct. Having turned northwards, he will meet his death. Under the blows of an angry Amanuṣya (demon), he, his officers, and his animal family will be struck by the edge of a mountain, and the wicked one will go to hell. After him will come a protector of the earth known as an adherent of the Buddha: Mahāyakṣa the very generous one who will delight in the Buddha's doctrine."[2]

According to Tāranātha, who places Puṣyamitra after King Kaniṣka and as contemporaneous with Nāgārjuna, Puṣyamitra instigated war and burned Buddhist monasteries from the Madhyadeśa to Jālandhara. His forces also killed a number of learned monks, but most of the monks sought refuge in other countries. Puṣyamitra died five years later in the north, and his son Agnimitra assumed the throne.

Tāranātha describes Puṣyamitra's reign as "the first hostility to the Dharma." Puṣyamitra's successors, known as the Śuṅga kings, do not appear to have been so adverse to the Dharma, and some even supported the Saṅga's recovery. Tāranātha describes a wealthy king Gauḍavardhana in Bengal who rebuilt damaged monasteries and mentions that bhikṣus and laymen alike worked to restore the Dharma.

---

2. Cited in E. Lamotte, *History of Indian Buddhism*, p. 391.

During the later Śuṅga Dynasty, political power centered around two cities: Pāṭaliputra in the east and Vidiśā, modern Besnagar, located on the road between Kauśāmbī and Ujjayinī. A small town at the time of Aśoka, Vidiśā soon became a major Dharma center. During the reign of the Śuṅga kings, Vidiśā prospered greatly; kings and wealthy laymen generously supported the building and ornamentation of large complexes of stūpas.

In modern times more than sixty stūpas have been discovered in the Vidiśā region within an area 10 × 6 miles; this group of monuments is known as the Bhīlsa Topes. Although most are in ruins, the twenty stūpas at Sañcī have survived time and invasion.

Changing Dynasties Support the Dharma

The great stūpa at Sañcī, today a famous site for religious pilgrims and tourists, symbolizes how Buddhism persisted through the periods of political upheaval in the centuries after Aśoka's reign. Monuments built by one king were often enlarged upon by the kings who supplanted them. For centuries, while rival dynasties came and went, monuments of the Dharma continued to grow. The great stūpa of Sañcī's original structure was built during Aśoka's time, probably at Aśoka's command. Under the Mauryas, Śuṅgas, and Andhras the stūpa continually expanded. The main body of the stūpa was encased in stone, ornately carved gateways were erected, and enclosed pathways were built for the devotional practice of circumambulation.

The stūpa at Bhārhut, near Sañcī, was also built around the time of Aśoka. According to inscriptions at the site, King Dhanabhūti donated a gate and a stone building to the Bhārhut Stūpa, and his son Vādhapāla donated funds for an ornamental railing at the great stūpa of Sañcī. Inscriptions indicate that Vādhapāla also donated funds for a railing at the stūpa of Mathurā.

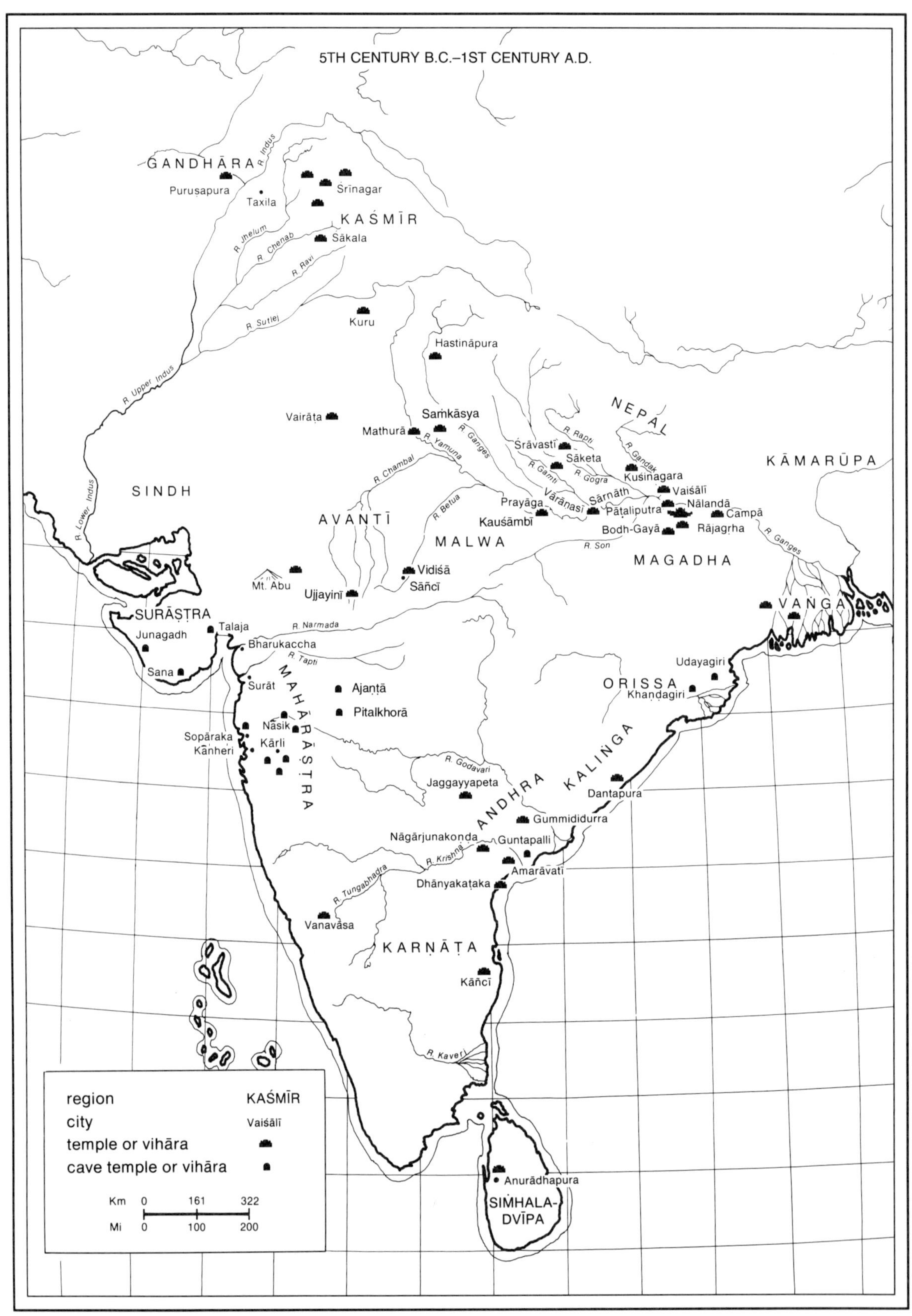

After the Buddha's Parinirvāṇa, early Sanghas established centers throughout India.

The Sinhalese chronicles name some of the monasteries in mainland India founded at the Buddha's time and still flourishing under the Śuṅgas: vihāras at the Bamboo Grove in Rājagṛha and the Ṛṣipatana in Sārnāth; the Jetavana Vihāra of Śrāvastī; the Mahāvana Vihāra in the Great Grove of Vaiśālī, also known as the Kūṭāgaraśala; and the Ghositārāma in Kauśāmbī, which had been founded by the merchant Ghosita.

The chronicles also name newer centers established by traveling bhikṣus during Aśoka's time that rose to prominence under the Śuṅgas: Dakkhiṇagiri in Ujjayinī and the Kelasa Vihāra in the Himalayan region. Also thriving were centers in Kashmir, where Majjhāntika had worked for the Dharma, and centers in Andhra, which may have been the Mahisamaṇḍala region converted by Mahādeva. The chronicles mention Dharma centers in Vanavāsa, the chief town of northern Kanara where the bhikṣu Rakkhita traveled, and Dharma centers in Alasanda Yonagara, where Mahārakkhita went to establish the Dharma.

According to a nineteenth-century reconstruction by A. Cunningham, an enclosed shrine compound at Bodh Gayā, site of the Buddha's enlightenment, was in existence during Śuṅga times. The Vattaniya Senāsana, a hermitage in the Vijhatavi Forest in the mountainous Vindhya region south of the Ganges basin was also established at the time of the Śuṅga Dynasty.

The Śuṅga Dynasty fell the way it arose, through the assassination of the last Śuṅga king by his minister Vasudeva. Vasudeva's dynasty, the lineage of Kāṇva kings, only lasted about forty-five years (approximately 75–30 B.C.E). The history of Magadha from the last Kāṇva king until the rise of the Guptas in the late third century C.E. is extremely vague. During the period between 58 B.C.E. and Gupta times, successive invaders from the northwest—the Śakas, the Parthians and the Kuṣāṇas—carved out major empires in India and opened wide the gates to Central Asia and China.

After the Śuṅga era, the Andhra tribes of the south grew in power and pushed north. During the Kāṇva Dynasty, the Andhras continued to extend their influence far into Kāṇvan lands. Although there is no clear evidence that Andhran rule ever reached as far north as the Ganges, it extended at least from the Narmadā River on the north to the Kṛṣṇa River on the south. The Andhran Empire thus linked such important Buddhist centers as Bhārhut, Sāñcī, and Bodh Gayā with Jaggayyapeṭa, Amarāvatī, and other emerging Buddhist centers in South India.

During the first through the third centuries C.E., major Mahāsāṃghika centers developed in the region between the deltas of the Kṛṣṇā and Godāvarī Rivers, known from ancient times as Veṅgī. On the Kṛṣṇā River, close to the eastern seacoast, were the monasteries of Dhānyakaṭaka and Amarāvatī, with Buddhist centers at Nāgārjunakoṇḍa lying a little to the northwest.

The artistic heritage of Bhārhut, Sāñcī, and Bodh Gayā can be traced in Amarāvatī's exquisite marble carvings and statuary that once adorned Amarāvatī's great stūpa and its railings. Amarāvatī, blessed with sculptors especially skilled in working marble, developed a distinctive flowing and graceful artistic style. During the historically opaque period in northern India between the late Kuṣāṇa and early Gupta Empires, the art of Amarāvatī, in particular, provided an artistic continuity between the Bhārhut and Sāñcī styles and the art of the Gupta period, which reached its apogee in the fifth century C.E.

Central Asians in India

Central Asia is a broad and vast expanse, inviting a population of nomadic tribes of diverse ethnic origins. High mountain ranges have been the only natural obstacle to invasion and migration from the west, Once the passes through them have been found and traversed, there is little to hinder the migration of whole cultures into India. Historically, agitation or displacement of one Central Asian tribe has immediately exerted pressure on its neighbors, creating waves of movement that alternately swept tribes far westward into Europe or eastward to the boundaries of China.

Between 174 and 129 B.C.E., the Hsung-nu, a warlike tribe on China's northwestern frontier (eastern Mongolia), attacked their neighbors to the south, known through Chinese records only as Yüeh-chih.[3] Forced southwest toward Bactria, the Yüeh-chih settled in Ferghana, in the Jaxartes River region, displacing a group of Śakas.

The Śakas, an ancient group of Central Asian tribes known to the Persian Achaemenid rulers from the eighth century B.C.E, then migrated toward the Oxus Valley. Pushed still further south, these Śakas eventually joined related Śaka tribes living in northern Persia. When Mithradates II expelled the Śakas from the Persian provinces, the Śakas moved east into the region of Sindh about 110 B.C.E.

For centuries, groups of Śakas had inhabited Sogdiana (modern Bukhara region), the plains of the Jaxartes River in Turkestan, the region north of the Black Sea, and the region of Śakastan (modern Seistan). The Celts drove them out of Europe around 300 B.C.E.; they were later pushed out of Russia and out of territories controlled by Rome. Thus between 200 and 100 B.C.E., the Śakas were moving south and east, concentrating in Iran and then moving east into India. Their language was Indo-European; some scholars associate them with Iranians, others refer to them as Indo-Iranians. The Greeks knew them as Scythians and the Iranians called them Śakas. The Indians also called them Śakas and associated them (wrongly) with the Pahlavas (Parthians).

The Parthians, who originally lived southeast of the Caspian Sea, wrested Bactria from Greek rule around 125 B.C.E.

---

3. Many identify the Yüeh-chih with the Tokharoi of the Greeks, the Tukhara of Sanskrit texts, and the Indo-Scythians of the Romans (René Grousset, *The Empire of the Steppes, A History of Central Asia*, p. 28).

and followed the Śakas into India around the beginning of the Common Era. Although their power soon came to an end, the Parthians, who were very receptive to Buddhism, played an important role in transmitting the Dharma from northwestern India, along the Silk Route, the great trade route circling the Taklamakan basin, into the heartland of China. Their skill in language and their aptitude for learning greatly facilitated the spread of the Dharma to Central Asia and China.

As a result of the efforts of Parthian Buddhists, the Sūtras of the Śrāvakapiṭaka (Āgamas) and a large number of Abhidharma texts were preserved in Chinese translation when the Sarvāstivādin monasteries of the northwest were destroyed in the centuries that followed. The Parthian bhikṣu An Shih-kao, who traveled to China during the reign of the Emperor Huan (147–167), translated many texts of the Āgama and Abhidharma collections into Chinese. Other Parthians that went to China included An Hsüan in the second century and T'an-ti, who worked for the Dharma in China in the mid-third century C.E.

After the Parthians moved into the northwest, the region was ruled by two lineages of kings: the Śaka kings Azes I, Aziles, and Azes II; and the Parthian kings Gondopharnes and his successor Pacores. Gondopharnes ruled from 21 C.E. to at least 46 C.E., but there is little evidence for the dates of Pacores' reign. At the conclusion of Pacores' reign, the Parthians of northwestern India were conquered by Kuṣāṇa kings from Bactria.

Śaka Satrapies

Throughout these changes, as Śakas yielded to Parthians and Parthians gave way to the Kuṣāṇas, some regions remained in the hands of Śaka governors or viceroys who served the dominant powers. These governors were known as satraps, a term derived from the Indian word Kṣatriya, or Shatrapa. In practice they were chieftains of varying status who deferred to the ruling powers when necessary and became more or less independent when the ruling dynasties weakened. The lands they ruled were known as the Śaka states or the Śaka satrapies. Highly adaptable to changing conditions, they persisted through the third century C.E.

The names of several mahāsatraps, or Great Satraps, stand out as supporters of Buddhism: Rājuvula (Rājula) and his son Śoḍāsa who ruled in Mathurā, and Liaka Kusūlaka and his son Pātika, who governed the region of Takṣaśilā. Pātika built monasteries for the Sangha in Takṣaśilā; later, according to a first-century B.C.E. copper plate found at a stūpa in Takṣaśilā, the satrap Pātika built stūpas in areas where none had existed before and installed the relics of Śākyamuni Buddha in them.[4] In Mathurā, Rājuvula's wife Ayasia Kamūla, together with her relatives and attendants, sponsored the building of a stūpa and monastery and donated alms to the Sarvāstivādin centers. An inscription of about 10 B.C.E. commemorates Rājula's son Śoḍāsa's donation of land to the Sarvāstivādin bhikṣus Buddhadeva and Budhila for the maintenance of cave-temples.

The Kuṣāṇas

The Kuṣāṇas are generally considered a branch of the Yüeh-chih, the people who, dislocated from their lands by the Hsung-nu, followed the Śakas south into India.[5] Like the Śakas, they seem to have spoken an Iranian-type language; ethnically, they may have been one of the Turkish tribes that populated Central Asia. The Kuṣāṇas appear to have taken over Bactria around 129 B.C.E. and to have conquered the Parthians in the last half of the first century B.C.E.

Under the leadership of Kujula Kadphises, contemporary of the Parthian king Gondopharnes, the Kuṣāṇas began their move into India sometime during the first half of the first century C.E. Wema Kadphises succeeded his father Kujula

---

4. Hirakawa Akira, *A History of Indian Buddhism*, p. 230.

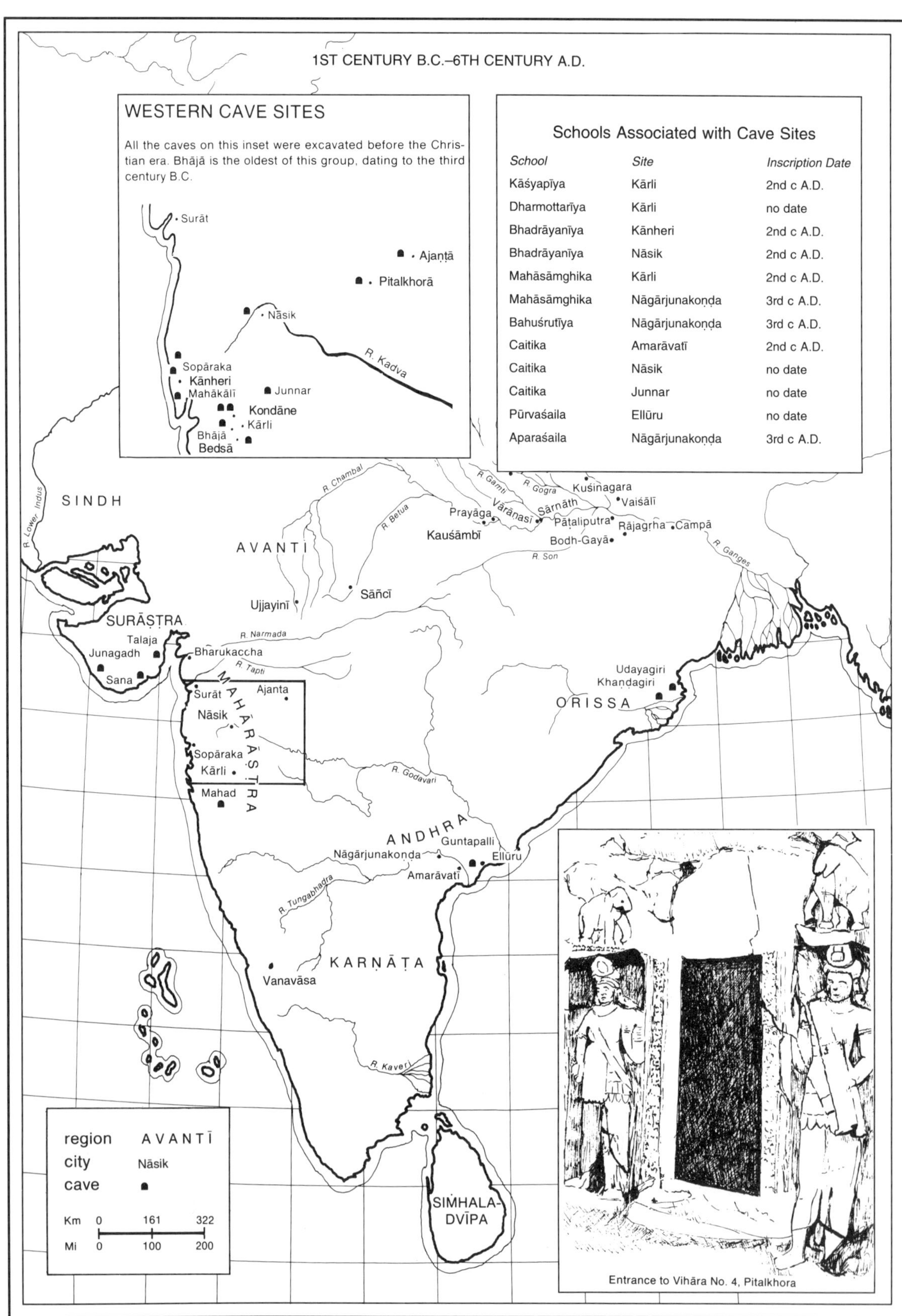

School	Site	Inscription Date
Kāśyapīya	Kārli	2nd c A.D.
Dharmottarīya	Kārli	no date
Bhadrāyanīya	Kānheri	2nd c A.D.
Bhadrāyanīya	Nāsik	2nd c A.D.
Mahāsāmghika	Kārli	2nd c A.D.
Mahāsāmghika	Nāgārjunakoṇḍa	3rd c A.D.
Bahuśrutīya	Nāgārjunakoṇḍa	3rd c A.D.
Caitika	Amarāvatī	2nd c A.D.
Caitika	Nāsik	no date
Caitika	Junnar	no date
Pūrvaśaila	Ellūru	no date
Aparaśaila	Nāgārjunakoṇḍa	3rd c A.D.

Entrance to Vihāra No. 4, Pitalkhorā

In Western India, magnificent temples carved from rock were flourishing Dharma centers.

and was known as Kadphises II. Kujula-kara appears to have been the third Kadphises, although he may have ruled only a portion of the Kuṣāṇa lands.

Kaniṣka (first or second centuries C.E.) was the next, and greatest, of all the Kuṣāṇa kings. Gaining power after the death of Wema Kadphises, Kaniṣka forged an empire that joined India on the south with Central Asia on the north, and all of Afghanistan on the west. Like the heel of a boot, Kaniṣka's Indian empire extended down the Yamunā and Upper Ganges valleys to Prayāga, Vārāṇasī, and Sārnāth; the major centers of his rule were the cities of Kapiśa, Puru-ṣapura, and Mathurā. It is likely that Kaniṣka's influence was felt as far east as Pāṭaliputra, capital of the Magadhan kings.

Although Śaka satrapies occupied the western regions of Sindh, Avanti, Kacchā, and Surāṣṭra, King Kaniṣka appears to have extended Kuṣāṇa influence over many of these regions as well. His empire, which embraced Greeks, Indians, Kuṣāṇas, Śakas, and Parthians, opened wide the routes of commerce linking India with China and the expanding Roman Empire. Following these routes, bhikṣus carried the Dharma east to Central Asia and China.

Kaniṣka was succeeded by the Kuṣāṇa kings Vāsiṣka, Huviṣka, and Vasudeva. Although the territories of the Ku-ṣāṇa Empire diminished during their reigns, the Dharma continued to flourish. During the Kuṣāṇa period, King Huviṣka built the Huviṣka Vihāra at Jamalpur, outside of Mathurā. Although it was eventually destroyed, the ruins indicate that it was a thriving and beautiful center, adorned with intricate carvings. Another monastery, the Guha Vi-hāra, was built around this time by Śoḍāsa, the Śaka gover-nor of Mathurā.

During Kuṣāṇa rule, Mathurā was home to several Buddh-ist schools, including the Sarvāstivādins, the Dharma-

---

5. The Kuṣāṇas were known to the Chinese as "Ta-yüeh-chih" or Uighurs (Hirakawa, p. 231).

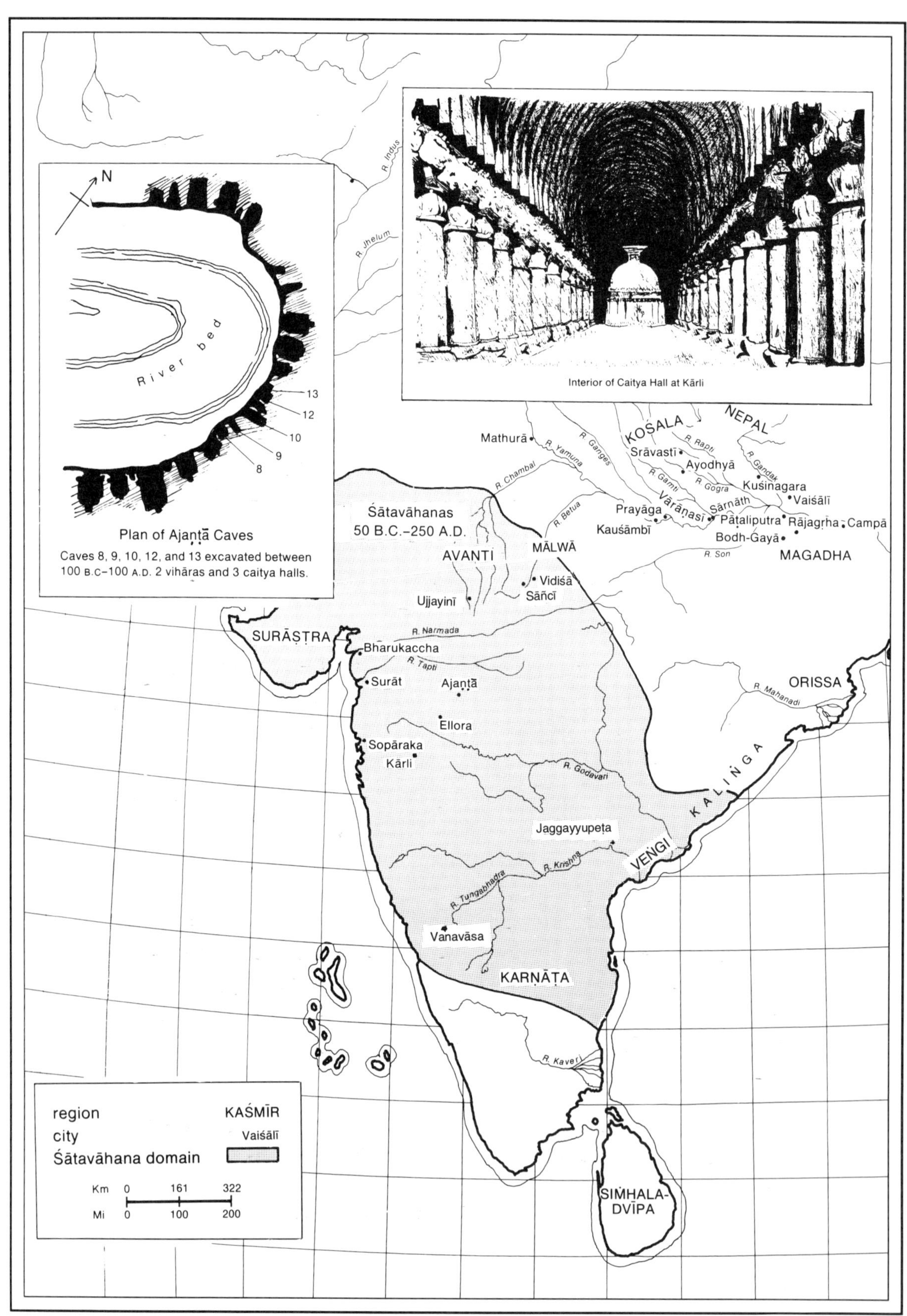

Important Buddhist sites in the Śātavāhana Empire

guptakas, the Saṁmatīyas, and the Mahāsāṁghikas. There are also many other Buddhist remains in Mathurā dating from the Kuṣāṇa period that inscriptions do not connect with any one school.

Buddhism under the Śātavāhanas

After Aśoka's death, two powers arose to claim the southern portion of the Mauryan Empire: the Śātavāhanas of the Upper Deccan (west Central India) and the Cedis of Kaliṅga. Although the Cedis did not reign for long, the power of the Śātavāhana dynasty lasted for nearly three centuries. The Śātavāhanas were Andhras, a proto-Telugu-speaking people who occupied the region south and west of the Vindhya Mountains around the third century B.C.E. and gradually extended their influence north and southeast to the modern region of Mysore.

The first Śātavāhana king, Simukha, established his empire around 30 B.C.E.. While he conquered and occupied the region around Vidiśā, his empire does not appear to have included the Ganges basin. At its greatest extent, under Gautamīputra Śātakarṇi (c. 106–130 C.E.), the Śātavāhana Empire reached to Mālwā and Surāṣṭra on the north and the Kṛṣṇā River on the south; its capital city was Dhānyakaṭaka, a major Buddhist center on the eastern seacoast near the Kṛṣṇā River. Gautamīputra Śātakarṇi and his descendant Yajñaśrī became famous for ending the power of the Śakas in Surāṣṭra and Western India between 120 and 200 C.E. The foreign influences were absorbed in these areas, which returned more fully to the cultural sphere of India.

Although the early Śātavāhana kings appear to have followed the brahmanic traditions, the Dharma flourished under their rule. In Aparāntaka, the western part of their kingdom, the Dharma first propagated by the Buddha's disciple Pūrṇa had been extended by the efforts of Yonaka (the Greek) Dhammarakkhita. When the Śātavāhana kings came to power, there were well-established Dharma centers along the western coast from Sopāraka north to Surāṣṭra.

Further south along the west coast, a Buddhist center at Konkanapura continued to thrive through the long reign of the Śātavāhana Dynasty. Konkanapura, now identified with Vanavāsa, is traditionally connected with the Arhat Rakkhita, who propagated the Dharma in Vanavāsa at the time of Aśoka. According to Hsüan-tsang, this area is also associated with the Arhat Śroṇaviṁśatikoṭi, a disciple of either Kātyāyana or Pūrṇa, who worked for the Dharma here during the Buddha's lifetime. In the seventh century C.E., Hsüan-tsang saw the stūpa built to honor Śroṇaviṁśatikoṭi, as well as a sandalwood statue of Maitreya said to have been carved by this great Arhat.

Under Śaka and Śātavāhana rule, western Buddhist communities began excavating large cave complexes, carving temples and monasteries out of the living rock in the ridge of steep cliffs known as the Western Ghats. The Mahāsāṁghikas of the eastern coast followed their example by creating cave complexes at Nāgārjunakonda, Amarāvatī, and Ellūru from the second century C.E. onward.

The earliest cave temples were relatively simple caverns cut out of the rock, with the inside pillars, beams, and arches carved to resemble the wooden structures common to aboveground temples. The excavations at Bhājā were among the earliest; estimates of the date of the first caves range from the third to the first century B.C.E.

Beginning between 100 B.C.E. and 200 C.E., and continuing for nearly seven hundred years, Buddhist monastic communities excavated complexes of caves south and east of Sopāraka, at Bedsā, Kondāne, Kārli, Kānheri, and Junnar. The cave temples of Nāsik, Pitalkhorā, Ellora, and Ajaṇṭa were excavated more inland, to the northeast of Sopāraka, and smaller cave complexes were constructed in Surāṣṭra.

The caves were often quite large, intended to accommodate temples, stūpas, and assembly halls. The vihāras, or monks' residences, usually consisted of a central courtyard surrounded by the monks' rooms, which could extend to three levels of rooms. Temples normally occupied separate caves and had a stūpa or a Buddha statue at one end. Pillars supporting a barrel vaulted roof lined the sides of the temples and curved around the stupa or statue at the back of the room (see illustration on map, p. 218). The largest cave complex is at Junnar, where 150 caves were excavated.

Inscriptions at the Nāsik caves connect the temples with the reigns of both Śātavāhana and Śaka kings, ranging from Kṛṣṇa Śātavāhana (c. 37–27 B.C.E.) to the Śaka satrap Nahapāna (119–125 C.E.). They indicate that the Nāsik caves, like other cave complexes, housed bhikṣus of different traditions. Sometimes the caves would be rennovated through cooperative efforts. The caves at Kārli were first occupied by Mahāsāṁghikas, then enlarged by Sthaviravādin bhikṣus and another group of Mahāsāṁghika monks and lay people from Dhānyakaṭaka, in southeastern India.

Further Readings

Basham, A. L. *The Wonder That Was India*, pp. 57–62.

Grousset, René. *The Empire of the Steppes; A History of Central Asia*, pp. 26–31.

Hirakawa Akira. *A History of Indian Buddhism from Śākyamuni to Early Mahāyāna*, pp. 223–246.

Lamotte, Étienne. *History of Indian Buddhism*, pp. 499–515.

Majumdar, R. C., ed. *History and Culture of the Indian People.* Volume II, *The Age of Imperial Unity*, pp. 95–153.

Puri, B.N. "Central Asia and its Peoples' Role in Ancient Indian History," in *Prolegomena to the Sources of the History of Pre-Islamic Central Asia, edited by J. Harmatta, pp. 181–186.*

Upasak, C. S. *History of Buddhism in Afghanistan*, pp. 8–18.

The Early Buddhist Communities

*Fulfilling an ancient prophecy,
several hundred years after the Parinirvāṇa,
eighteen schools arose within
the Buddhist Sangha.*

By the second century B.C.E., the Sangha had carried the Dharma throughout India and beyond, and distinct Buddhist communities had developed in culturally diverse regions from the northernmost valleys of Gandhāra and Kashmir to the island of Śrī Laṅkā. Fueled by controversies over points of doctrine, the tendencies toward separation (begun when the Mahāsāṃghikas and the Sthaviras diverged sometime after the council at Vaiśālī) persisted. According to Vinītadeva, by the time of Aśoka there were four main traditions, each with branches and subschools in widely separated regions of India. Although many of these schools arose naturally within the expanding network of Dharma centers, some divisions came about through differing emphases and approaches. However, even as the Buddhist schools were proliferating and developing their specific views and specialties, bonds of respect persisted among the different communities. United in purpose and goal, true to their vows of refuge in Buddha, Dharma, and Sangha, monks of all traditions lived peacefully side by side, often in the same monasteries.

The Five Points of Mahādeva

Since the time of King Kaniṣka (first or second centuries C.E.), masters of the different Buddhist traditions have written accounts of the formation and interrelationships of the early Buddhist schools. The first known account of the schools is by Vasumitra, a contemporary of Kaniṣka. In his Samayabhedavyūha-cakra (NE 4138), a record of the divisions of the schools, Vasumitra states that the cause of the first division of the Sangha into Sthavira and Mahāsāṁghika was five theses, or doctrinal principles, propounded by the bhikṣu Mahādeva. These five principles directly related to the status of the Arhat:

1. Arhats can be sexually tempted (because an Arhat is always subject to a certain form of physical impurity).

2. Arhats are not free from the subtler forms of ignorance.

3. Arhats are still subject to doubt.

4. Arhats can still be instructed by others.

5. Entry into the path can be accompanied by a vocal utterance.

According to Vasumitra, these principles were considered in an assembly held in Pāṭaliputra. The majority of bhikṣus present accepted them, but a group of senior bhikṣus refused to associate themselves with these points of doctrine, which they considered heretical. These elder bhikṣus distinguished themselves from the majority by forming the school known as Sthavira, or the Elders; the larger body of bhikṣus then became known as the Mahāsaṁgha, or Greater Assembly.

The Sthaviras maintained the spiritual perfection of the Arhat and strictly adhered to the fully renunciate life as the only means of attaining enlightenment. The Mahāsāṃghikas held that for even an Arhat there were different stages of spiritual development. They also accepted the possibility of enlightenment for lay members of the Sangha.

Opinions on the First Division of the Sangha

Vasumitra places the first division at the time of Aśoka, which he gives as being one hundred years after the Parinirvāṇa. He also refers to a second Mahādeva, who lived two hundred years after the Parinirvāṇa. This Mahādeva was known as a heretic who abandoned the world and joined the Mahāsāṃghika school. He lived alone on Mt. Śaila and propounded the five theses to the Mahāsāṃghikas. As a result of his teachings, the Mahāsāṃghikas subdivided further into Caityaśailas, Uttaraśailas, and Aparaśailas.

According to Paramārtha (sixth century C.E.), who explicated Vasumitra's writings on the early schools, at the time of Aśoka dissension arose in the Sangha at Pāṭaliputra concerning the five points of Mahādeva. King Aśoka called for an assembly of the Sangha to settle the disagreement by majority vote. The elders, who were Arhats, were outvoted but were not willing to relinquish their position and abide by the majority decision. When these dissenting Arhats asserted their authority through supernormal transformations, they frightened the community, and Aśoka exiled them from Pāṭaliputra. The dissenting Arhats then went to Kashmir.

After Mahādeva's death, Aśoka invited the Arhats back to Pāṭaliputra. But when the Sangha convened to recite the Buddha's teachings, the Arhats objected to some texts that they claimed Mahādeva had inserted into the Tripiṭaka. Unable to reach agreement with the majority, the Arhats formed a separate community. The seventh-century pilgrim Hsüan-tsang gives a similar account but states that Aśoka, unable to persuade the Arhats to return to the capital, gave them the land of Kashmir for their home.

Both Tāranātha and Bu-ston cite a Saṃmatīya account (recorded by the fifth-century scholar Bhavya) that describes the first division of the Sangha into Sthaviravādins and Mahāsāṃghikas as occurring 137 years after the Buddha's Parinirvāṇa, during the reign of the Magadhan kings Nanda and Mahāpadma. Bhavya agrees with Vasumitra that this division came about through disagreements in doctrine, specifically the five principles concerning the status of the Arhat. Vasumitra ascribes these five principles to a bhikṣu named Bhadra and considers Bhadra the founder of the Mahāsāṃghikas.

According to Dudjom Rinpoche's *History*, the first divisions of the Sangha were based on differences that developed among the communities in the recitation of the Prātimokṣa. These differences led to Mahādeva's formulation of five points, which were propounded after Mahādeva's death by a bhikṣu named Bhadra. Dissension concerning these points grew steadily from the time of Vīrasena, Aśoka's grandson, through the reign of King Kaniṣka, when the elder bhikṣu Nāga again stirred up the controversy. This was when the Mahāsāṃghikas, Sthaviras, and Saṃmatīyas separated from the original Mūlasarvāstivādin tradition, forming the four major early schools. Later, an influential teacher by the name of Sthiramati (not the disciple of Vasubandhu) again brought up these questions, provoking further division, until there were eighteen subdivisions of these schools: seven branches of the Mūlasarvāstivādins, five branches of the Mahāsāṃghika, and three branches each of Saṃmatīyas and Sthaviras.

After the controversy on Mahādeva's five points had died down and the eighteen schools were well established, a council was held (either in Kashmir or in Jālandhara) under King Kaniṣka's patronage. The doctrines of all schools were listed and reviewed, and the council unanimously agreed that all eighteen schools were valid Dharma traditions. During this council, some of the Arhats present described a prophetic dream told by the Buddha Śākyamuni in the Ārya-svap-nanirdeśa-sūtra (NE 48): During the time of the Buddha Kāśyapa, King Kṛkin had a disturbing dream. Eighteen men were pulling on a single cloth, and each came away with a piece of it; yet the cloth itself remained undamaged. Kāśyapa calmed the king's fears, saying the dream did not relate to the fortunes of King Kṛkin's realm but to the Dharma of the future Buddha Śākyamuni. From the teachings of Śākya-muni eighteen schools would arise and emphasize different aspects of his doctrines, but the Dharma itself would remain whole. The confusion created by the "five points" was re-solved, and the purity of all eighteen schools was established.

The Third Council

The council convened by King Kaniṣka is known to the northern traditions as the Third Council, whereas in the Theravādin tradition, "Third Council" refers to the earlier assembly at Pāṭaliputra held at the time of Aśoka, and there is no mention of King Kaniṣka or the council convened at his request. The Mahāvaṁsa, a Theravādin text, describes how Aśoka reformed the Sangha in Pāṭaliputra, dismissing from the order those who were lax in their observances or who fostered schismatic tendencies. Then, in the eighteenth year of his reign, Aśoka convened a council of one thousand monks, with Moggaliputta Tissa presiding.

When the council ended, Moggaliputta Tissa compiled the Kathāvatthu, or Points of Controversy, to clarify the doc-trines of the followers of the orthodox tradition known as the Vibhajjavādins. The Kathāvatthu mentions that heretical doctrines were taught by the Pubbaseliyas, Aparaseliyas, and others but does not mention Mahādeva as their proponent. Since this council at Pāṭaliputra is not mentioned in the northern traditions, it may have been an assembly only of the Vibhajjavādin (Sanskrit, Vibhajyavādin) community.

The issue of the councils is complex; both ancient and modern scholars of East and West alike have written extensive studies comparing different traditions. Consult the references on p. 233 for more detailed information.

The Eighteen Schools

Tradition numbers the various Sangha communities or schools as eighteen, although the number of schools that appear in the traditional lists is actually greater—largely because of the different names assigned to the same schools by different traditions. In each of the extant traditions, the eighteen schools are each identified by a characteristic feature. Some were known by the name of their founder, others after their location, still others by the specific doctrines they emphasized, or by the composition of their assembly, as shown in the chart on page 228.

Tāranātha mentions the following schools that are known by more than one name: the Kāsyapīyas, also known as Suvarsakas; the Tāmrasātīyas, also known as Samkrāntikas or Uttarīyas; and the Caityakas, also known as Pūrvasailas. The Lokottaravādins are also mentioned as Kukkūtagirikas, after Mt. Kukkūtapāda, and the name Ekavyavahārika is said to refer generally to the Mahāsāmghikas.

The differences between these schools was often quite minor. As the seventh-century Chinese traveler I-tsing observed, "There are small points of difference such as the skirt of the lower garments is cut straight in one, and irregular in another, and the folds of the upper robe are, in size, narrow in one and wide in another. . . .

"When the bhiksus lodge together, there is a question whether they are to be in separate rooms or to be separated by partitions made by ropes, though both are permitted in the Dharma. There are other cases: when receiving food, one group will take food with the hand, while another will mark the ground where the giver should place food, and both are

Schools Named after Their Doctrines

Sthaviravāda Those who follow the doctrine of the Elders

Ekavyavahārika Those who hold to only one, considering saṁsāra and nirvāṇa as fictitious denominations.

Lokottaravāda Those whose doctrines are based on supramundane views

Prajñaptivāda Those who follow the doctrine of separation between real teaching and fictitious denomination

Vibhajyavāda Those who are concerned with distinctions

Saṁkrāntivāda/Sautrāntika Those who consider that the five skandhas carry over from existence to existence; those who accept only the Sūtras as authority

Schools Named after Their Assemblies

Mahāsāṁghika The great assembly

Bahuśrutīya Those who have heard much

Dharmottarīya Those who elevate the Dharma

Bhadrāyaṇīya Those who adhere to the Vehicle of the Wise

Schools Named after Their Location

Haimavata Those who live on the snowy mountains

Ṣaṇṇagarika Those who live in the dense forest

Pūrvaśaila Those who dwell on the eastern mountains

Aparaśaila Those who dwell on the western mountains

Schools Named after Their Founder

Mahīśāsakas Founded by Mahāsasaka

Vātsīputrīyas Founded by Vātsīputra

Dharmaguptaka Founded by Dharmagupta

Tāmraśāṭīyas Founded by Tamraśata

Kāśyapīyas Founded by Kāśyapa

Tāranātha, p. 341.

in the right. Each school has traditions handed down from teacher to pupil, each perfectly defined and distinct from the other." (I-tsing, pp. 6–7)

Affiliations of the Eighteen Schools

Lists of the eighteen schools begin to diverge from an early date, and there is no evidence that they derive from a single common tradition. The schools were geographically distant from each other, and any one writer's list tends to reflect the schools with which he was most familiar.

Vasumitra's Samayabhedavyūha-cakra (NE 4138) lists schools from the perspective of the Sarvāstivādins. The Dīpavaṁsa, Mahāvaṁsa, and Buddhaghosa's commentary on the Kathāvatthu (fifth century) present the schools from the Theravādin perspective. The Śāriputra-pariprcchā gives a Mahāsāṁghika list, while the sixth-century master Bhavya presents a total of three lists (I. Sthavira, II. origin not mentioned, III. Saṁmatīya) in his Nikāyabheda-vibhaṅga-vyā-khyāna (NE 4139). There is also an early list of schools in the Mañjuśrī-pariprcchā, which exists only in Chinese translation. The Samayabhedoparacanacakre-nikāya-bhedopa-deśana-saṁgraha (NE 4140), a work by the eighth century master Vinītadeva, summarizes the Samayabhedavyūha-cakra of Vasumitra. The list of Dharma communities it includes appears to represent the Mūlasarvāstivādin tradition.

Lists which date from the seventh century forward are essentially preserved versions of earlier lists. These include Chinese versions, Tibetan summaries made by Tāranātha of Bhavya's and Vinītadeva's lists, and the Bhikṣu-varṣāgra-prcchā, a text of unknown authorship preserved in the Tibetan bsTan-'gyur (NE 4133). Charts of the relationships of the eighteen schools as described by representatives of the Mūlasarvastivādin, Mahāsāṁghika, Sarvāstivādin, Thera-vādin, Sthavira, and Saṁmatīya traditions appear on the following pages.

Vinītadeva (Mūlasarvāstivādin)

Mahāsāṃghika

Pūrvaśaila	Aparaśaila	Haimavata
Lottaravādin		Prajñaptivādin

Sarvāstivādin

Mūlasarvāstivādin	Kāśyapīya	Mahīśāsaka
Dharmaguptaka	Bahuśrutīya	Tāmraśāṭīya
Vibhajyavādin		

Sthavira

Jetavanīya	Abhayagirivāsin	Mahāvihāravāsin

Saṃmatīya

Kaurukullaka	Avantaka	Vātsīputrīya

Śāriputraparipṛcchā (Mahāsāṃghika)

Mahāsāṃghika

Vyavahāra	Lokottara	Kukkulika
Bahuśrutaka	Prajñaptivādin	Mahādeva
Caitika		Uttaraśaila

Sthavira

Sarvāstivādin	Vātsiputrīya	Kāśyapīya
Sūtravādin		Saṃkrāntika

From the Sarvāstivadins arose the Mahīśāsaka, Dharmaguptaka, and Suvarṣa schools.

From the Vātsīputrīya arose the Dharmottarika, Bhadrāyanīya, Saṃmatīya, and Ṣaṇṇagarika schools.

Vasumitra (Sarvāstivādin)

Mahāsāṃghika

Ekavyavahārika	Lokottaravādin	Kukkuṭika
Bahuśrutīya	Prajnaptivādin	Caityaśaila
Aparaśaila		Uttaraśaila

Sthaviravādin

Mūlasthavira	Sarvāstivādin

From the Sarvāstivādins arose the Vatsīputrīya, Mahī-śāsaka, Kāśyapīya, and Sautrāntika schools.

From the Vatsīputrīyas arose the Dharmottarīya, Bhadrā-yanīya, Saṃmatīya, and Saṇṇagarika schools.

From the Mahīśāsakas arose the Dharmaguptaka school.

Mahāvaṃsa (Theravādin)

Mahāsāṃghika

Gokulika	Ekavyohārika

From the Gokulika arose the Paṇṇatti and Bahulikā.

From the Bahulikā arose the Cetiya school.

Theravādin

Mahiṃsāsakā	Vajjiputtaka

From the Mahiṃsāsaka arose the Sabbattha and Dhamma-guttika schools.

From the Sabbattha arose the Kassapiyā school.

From the Kassapiya arose the Saṃkantika school.

From the Samkantika arose the Suttavāda school.

From the Vajjiputtaka arose the Dhammuttariyā, Bhadra-yānika, Candāgārika, Saṃmitī, and Vajjiputtiya schools.

According to the Sthaviras

Mahāsāṁghika

Mūla-mahāsāṁghika	Ekavyavahārika	Lokottaravādin
Bahuśrutīya	Prajñaptivādin	Caityaka
Pūrvaśaila		Aparaśaila

Sthavira

Mūla-sthavira	Sarvāstivādin	Vātsīputrīya
Dharmottarīya	Bhadrayānīya	Saṁmitīya
Mahīśāsaka	Dharmaguptika	Suvarṣaka
Uttarīya		

According to the Saṁmatīyas

Mahāsāṁghika

Mūla-mahāsāṁghika	Ekavyavahārika	Gokulika
Bahuśrutīya	Prajñaptivādin	Caityaka

Sarvāstivādin

Mūla-sarvāstivādin	Vibhajyavādin	Mahīśāsaka
Dharmaguptaka	Tāmraśāṭīya	Kaśyapīya
Saṁkrāntika		

Vātsīputrīya

Mūla-vātsīputrīya	Dharmottarīya	Bhadrāyaṇīya
Saṁmitīya		

Haimavata

Source: Tāranātha, pp. 339–340.

Further Readings

Bu-ston. *History of Buddhism*, pp. 96–101.

Dudjom Rinpoche. *The Nyingma School of Tibetan Buddhism*, volume I, pp. 440–442.

'Gos Lo-tsā-ba. *The Blue Annals*, pp. 27–32.

Masuda Jiryo. "Origin and Doctrines of Early Indian Buddhist Schools," *in Asia Major* 2 (1925):1–78.

I-tsing. *A Record of the Buddhist Religion as Practised in India and the Malay Archipelago*, pp. 6–7.

Lamotte, Étienne. *History of Indian Buddhism*, pp. 529–548.

Rockhill, W. Woodville. *The Life of the Buddha and the Early History of His Order*, pp. 181–202. (Translations of the Nikāyabheda-vibhaṅga-vyākhyāna, by Bhavya, the Samaya-bhedoparacanacakre-nikāya-bhedopadeśana-saṁgraha, by Vinītadeva, and the Bhikṣu-varṣāgraprcchā [anon.]).

Tāranātha. *History of Buddhism in India*, pp. 339–342.

Bareau, André "Trois traités sur les sectes bouddhiques," *Journal Asiatique* 242 (1954):229–266; 244 (1956):167–200.

Dispersion of the Eighteen Schools

Between the second century B.C.E. and the third century C.E., centers related to the eighteen schools developed throughout India.

Knowledge concerning the development and dispersion of the early Buddhist communities is largely based upon modern archaeological findings, remains of ancient inscriptions, entries in court chronologies describing patronage of various Sanghas, and the accounts of Chinese pilgrims such as Fa-hien (399–414), Hsüan-tsang (629–645), and I-tsing (671–695). Inscriptions on stūpas, reliquary boxes, the bases of statues, ritual objects, and dedicatory tablets of monasteries and temples often provide names of donors and schools followed by the resident Sangha. Gathering all available information, historians have matched names and dates of known kings with names of donors and have calculated probable dates of these early communities. At least sixty-three such inscriptions dating from 100 B.C.E. to 200 C.E. have been found in sites throughout mainland India; however, the communities that lived at these sites were probably well-established by the time these inscriptions were carved.[1]

According to Tāranātha, all the eighteen schools were active in India at the time of the great master Vasubandhu, generally considered to have lived toward the end of the fourth or in the early fifth century C.E. Some of the schools lost ground during the first hostility to the Dharma at the time of Puṣyamitra, the first Śuṅga king. Gradually controversies among the schools and various other misfortunes contributed to the disappearance of all but seven of the schools by the seventh century C.E. Still active were two branches of Mahāsamghikas (Prajñaptivādin and Lokottaravādin), two branches of Sammatīyas (Vātsīputrīya and Kaurukullaka), two branches of Sarvāstivādins (Mūlasarvāstivādin and Tāmraśāṭīyas), and the Sthavira school.

Of these seven schools, the lineages of two survive to the present day: the Sthavira, in the Theravāda tradition of Śrī Laṅkā and Southeast Asia, and the Mūlasarvāstivādin, in the Vinaya of the Tibetan Buddhist schools.

The Four Main Branches[2]

1. Sarvāstivādins, centered in Mathurā and Kashmir

2. Sammatīyas, centered in Central India

3. Mahāsāmghikas, centered in Andhra, in the south

4. Sthaviras, centered first in Magadha, then in Śrī Laṅkā

Sarvāstivādin

During Aśoka's reign, a group of bhikṣus in Mathurā developed certain convictions about the Buddha's teachings concerning existence that distinguished them from the rest of the Sangha. They became known as the Sarvāstivādins,

---

1. Étienne Lamotte, *History of Indian Buddhism*, pp. 523–526.
2. As enumerated by Vinītadeva, Hsüan-tsang, and I-tsing.

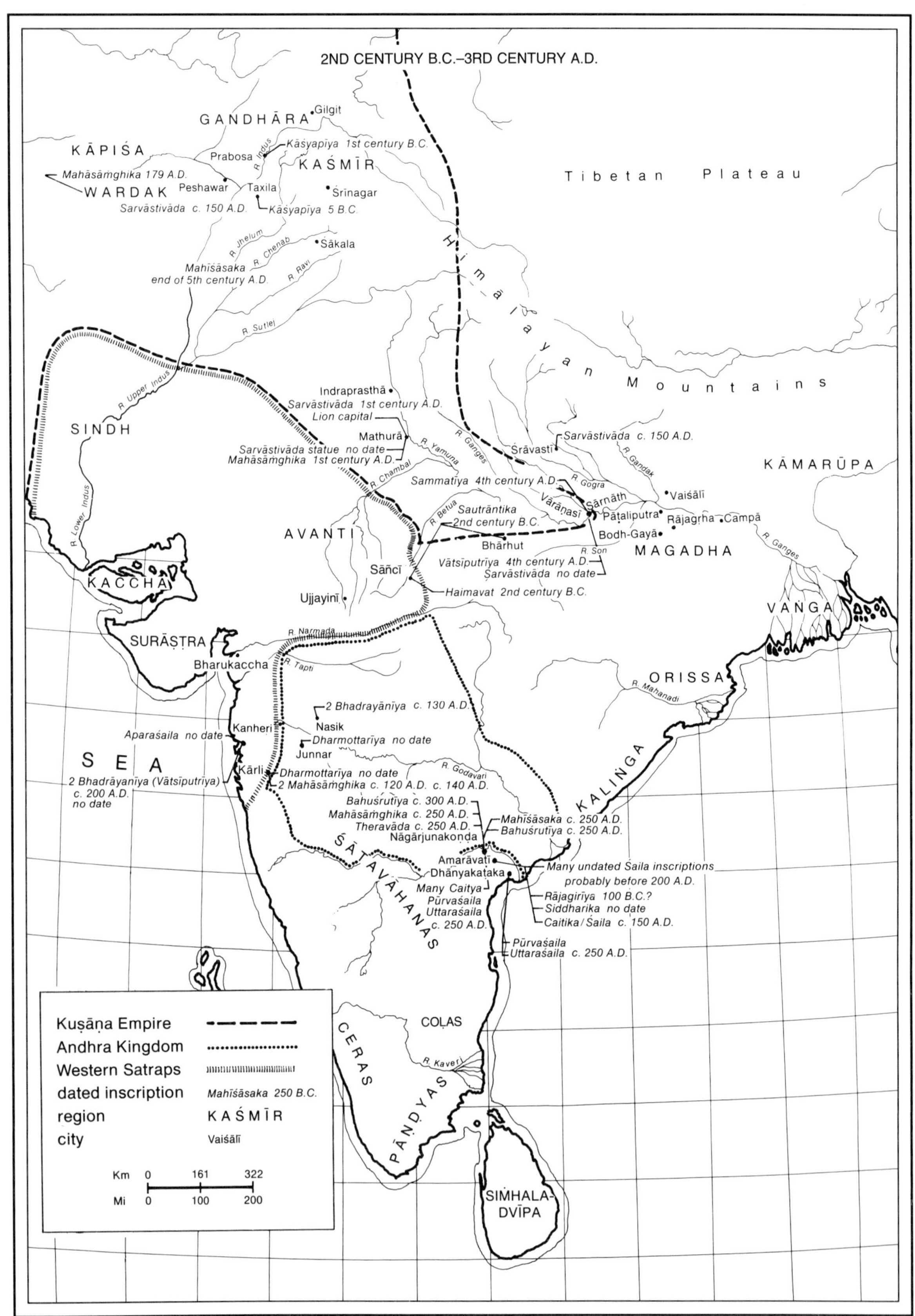

Contemporary inscriptions record locations and dates of early Sanghas.

Those Who Hold That Everything Exists. While the Sarvāstivādins later established monasteries in Śrāvastī and Vārāṇasī, Mathurā, where the Patriarch Upagupta worked for the Dharma, was their first major center. During Mauryan times, Sarvāstivādin bhikṣus traveled from Magadha to the far northwestern part of Aśoka's kingdom, to Gandhāra and Kashmir, where for centuries they refined the Abhidharma teachings in isolation from the centers in India proper. Both Hsüan-tsang and I-tsing reported that the Sarvāstivādins were also active in the Madhyadeśa during the seventh century, although not very numerous.

According to I-tsing, the name Mūlasarvāstivādin, or Root Sarvāstivādins) came into use around the seventh century as a way of distinguishing the "original" Sarvāstivādins from the schools that arose later within the Sarvāstivādin fold. Bu-ston, however, states that the name Mūlasarvāstivādin was used because the Sarvāstivādins were the "root" or basis of all the Dharma traditions.

I-tsing, himself a Sarvāstivādin master, noted that there were four subdivisions of Sarvāstivādins: Mūlasarvāstivādin, Dharmaguptaka, Mahīśāsaka, and Kāśyapīya. By the seventh century, the Dharmaguptakas, Mahīśāsakas, and Kāśyapīyas could no longer be found in India proper; these three schools, like the Sarvāstivādins of Kashmir, continued their tradition in communities they had established in the far northwestern regions of Oḍḍiyāna (Swat Valley), Kundūz, and Kusthāna. From these regions the Dharmaguptakas, Mahīśāsakas, Kāśyapīyas, and Sarvāstivādins spread eastward and established communities in parts of southern China. The Sarvāstivādins were also strong in the Southern Islands (modern Indonesia), and some communities existed in Champa (Cochin China). Of all four schools, the Dharmaguptakas were the most widely established Buddhist tradition in China, especially in the eastern and western regions.

According to I-tsing, all the Buddhist centers in India's north central region were Sarvāstivādin; there were some

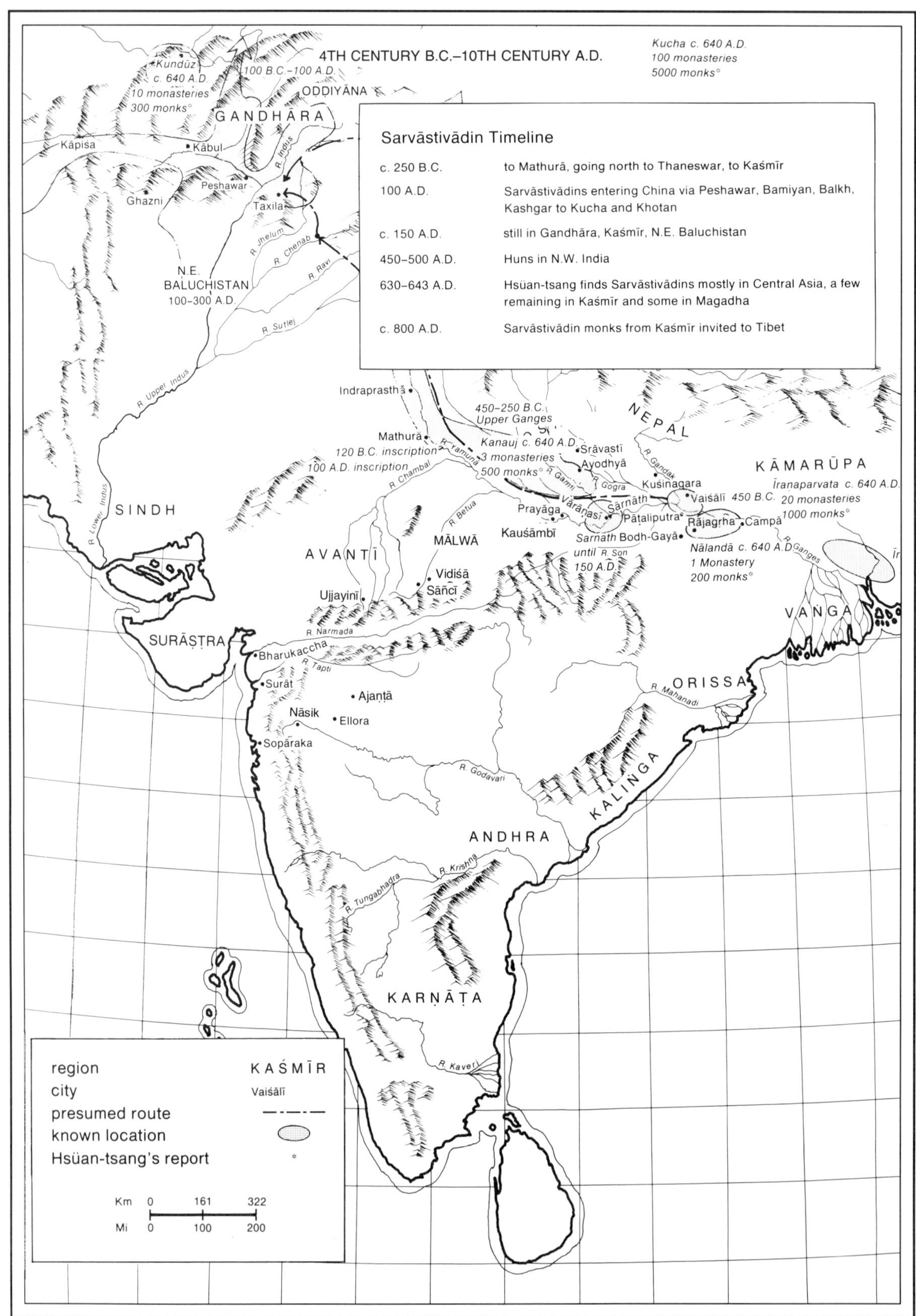

Major Sarvāstivādin centers

Sarvāstivādin monasteries in Magadha, and a few Sarvāstivādin communities in Western and South India. In Eastern India, Sarvāstivādins existed side by side with the other Buddhist traditions, especially at the great university of Nālandā. A generation earlier, Hsüan-tsang had counted at least 158 Sarvāstivādin monasteries in India and Central Asia housing 23,700 bhikṣus. Of these, thirty monasteries with three thousand bhikṣus were in Vārāṇasī, but very few were found elsewhere in the Ganges basin.

The Dharmaguptakas, at first centered in Aparānta, in the west, expanded further to the west and north; they founded communities in Bāmiyān (modern Afghanistan) and possibly even in Iran. They became well established in Oḍḍiyāna (Swat Valley) and from there entered Central Asia where they established major centers in Kuchā and Khotan. The Dharmaguptakas, one of the first traditions to enter China, began arriving in China early in the second century C.E. and were widely established there in the seventh century, especially in the eastern and western regions. Their Vinaya tradition was the one followed by most of the Chinese Buddhist traditions. As of the seventh century, Dharmaguptakas were no longer in India; they continued only in the Swat Valley (Oḍḍiyāna), Central Asia, and China.

In the Northwest, the Mahīśāsakas had communities in western Vahika in the Salt Range, while the Kāśyapīyas established communities in Gandhāra, possibly at such sites as Takht-ī-Bahī, Takṣaśilā, and Pālāṭū Dherī, where inscriptions indicating their presence have been found. From the Northwest, Mahīśāsaka and Kāśyapīya bhikṣus followed the Silk Route circling Central Asia to enter China. The Mahīśāsakas also established Dharma centers on the west coast near Bombay, as well as in Śrī Laṅkā, where they appear to have eventually merged with the Sthaviras. As of the seventh century, neither of these schools existed in India proper. Like the Dharmaguptakas, they survived only in isolated areas of Central Asia and China. Of all these traditions, only the Mūlasarvāstivādins survived to the twelfth century.

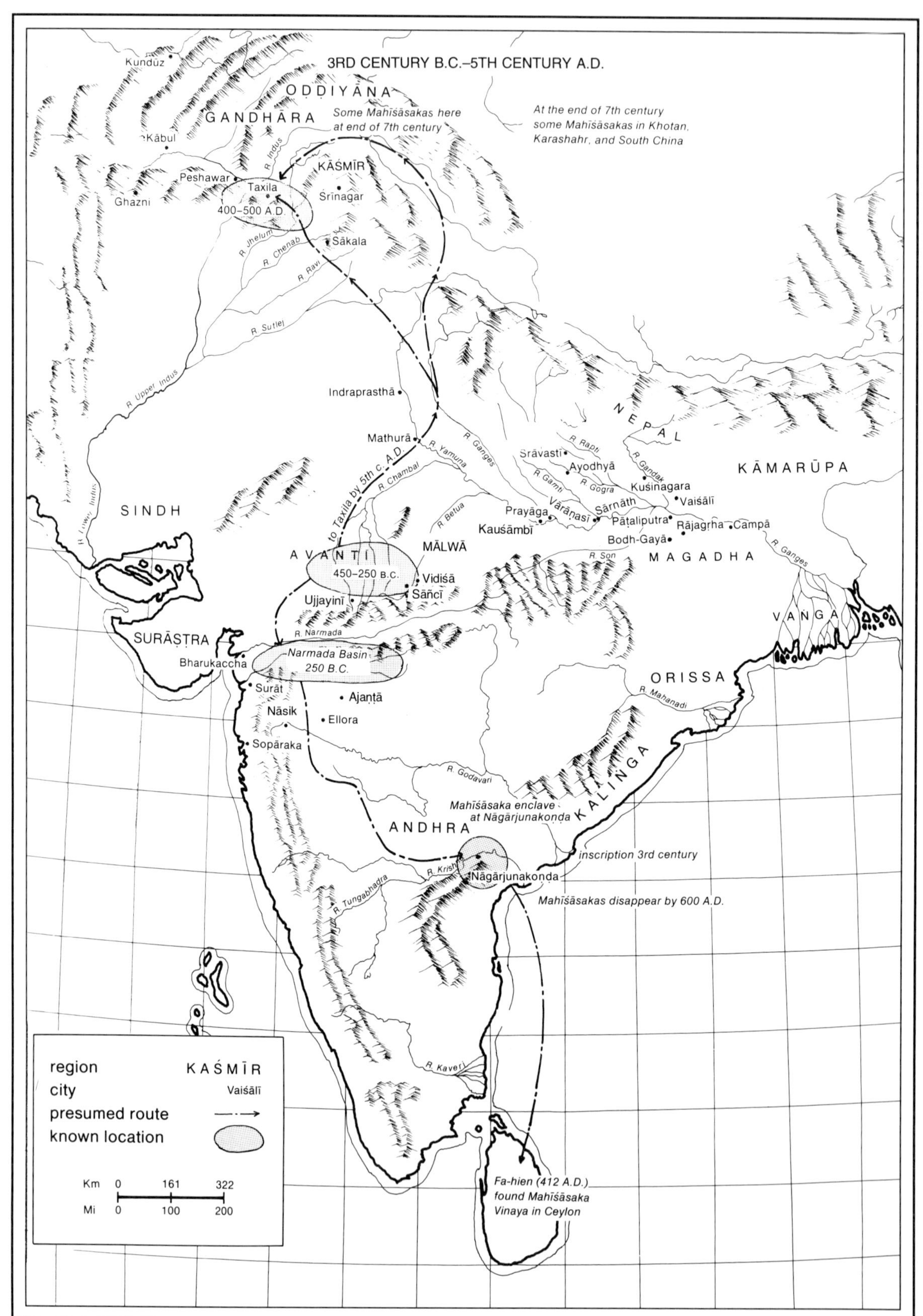

Major Mahīśāsaka centers

As previously mentioned, their Vinaya lineage continues to the present day in the Tibetan Buddhist traditions.

Sammatīya

The Sammatīyas were among the first of the schools to move as far west as Surāṣṭra (modern Gujarat), where they established centers as early as the second century B.C.E.. They were strong in both Surāṣṭra and the Madhyadeśa through the early seventh century, but appear to have declined shortly thereafter. I-tsing notes that the Sammatīyas had four subdivisions, but does not provide their names. (Vinītadeva gives these three subdivisions: Kaurukullaka, Avantaka, and Vātsīputrīya) According to I-tsing, there were a few Sammatīyas in South India, none in the North, and Sammatīyas existed side by side with the other Buddhist traditions in Eastern India.

A generation earlier, Hsüan-tsang had found Sammatīyas the most numerous of all the schools: He counted 1,351 Sammatīya monasteries in India housing 66,500 bhikṣus. According to I-tsing, there were no Sammatīyas in Śrī Laṅkā or in China proper, but Sammatīyas were in the majority in Champa (Cochin-China), and there were a few Sammatīyas in the Southern Islands (modern Indonesia).

The Vātsīputrīyas, whom Vinītadeva lists as a division of the Sammatīyas, were strong in the Madhyadeśa through the time of the Pāla Dynasty (eighth–twelfth centuries). Tradition ascribes their founding to the Brahmin Vātsīputra, although this ascription is controversial. Some traditions consider that the Vātsīputrīyas arose first within the Sarvāstivādins; in turn, a group led by the Arhat Sammata separated from the Vātsīputrīyas, forming the Sammatīyas. Subschools of the Vātsīputrīyas, the Dharmottarīyas and the Bhadrāyanīyas, developed in Western India. The Dharmottarīyas were known around the thriving port city of Sopāraka on India's western coast, and the Bhadrāyanīyas lived in eastern Mahārāṣṭra, the region around Nāsik. While

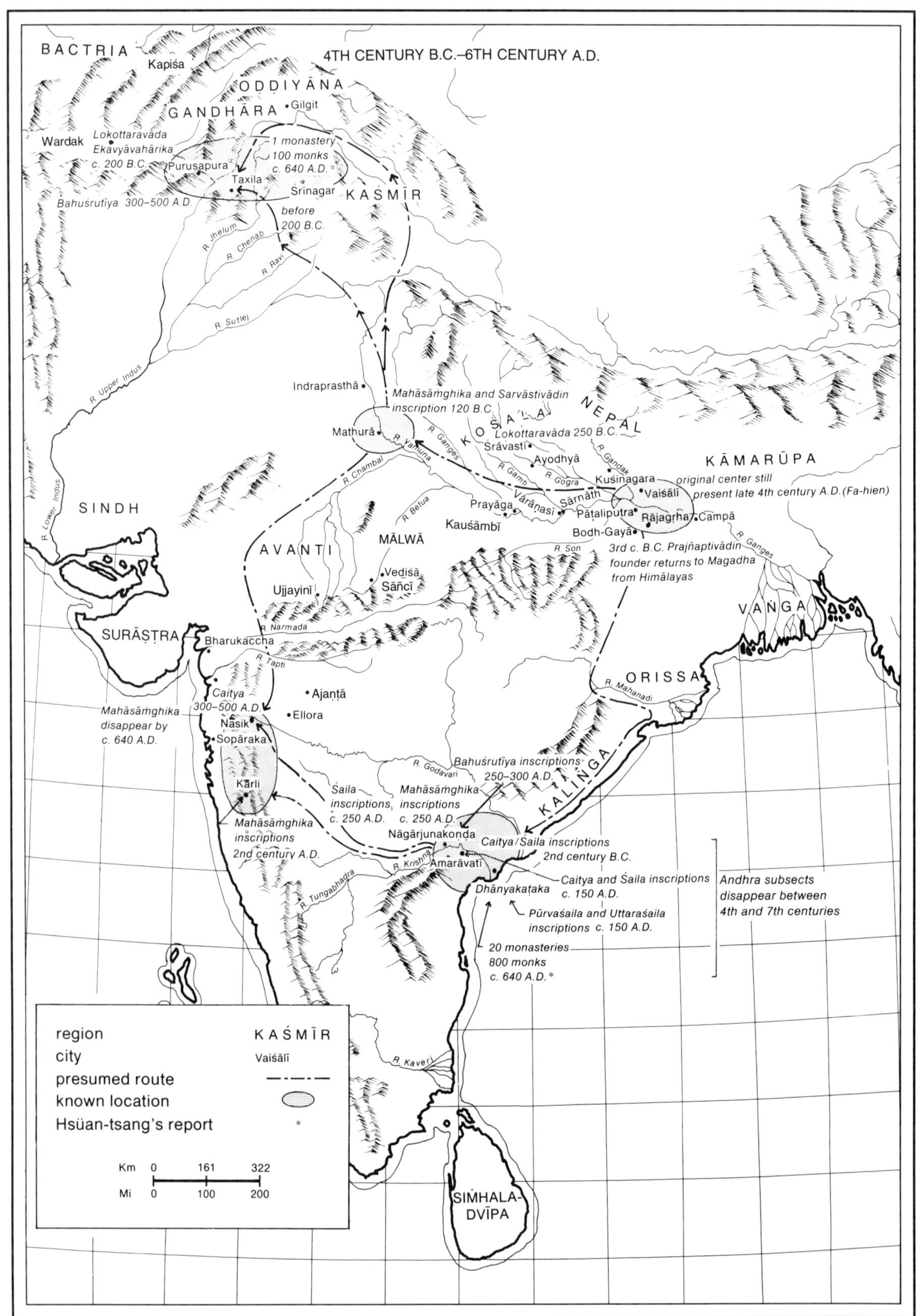

Major Mahāsāṃghika centers

both schools flourished up to the third century C.E., they seem to have disappeared from India by the seventh century.

Mahāsāṁghika

The Mahāsāṁghika, or Great Assembly, one of the earliest of the schools to develop, was represented in Mathurā by 120 B.C.E., as evidenced by an inscription on a lion-topped pillar. Inscriptions discovered during this century reveal that the Mahāsāṁghikas founded communities as far northwest as Bactria (Balkh), Wardak and Kapiśa, all in modern Afghanistan; they were also represented in the cave temples of Kānheri and Kārli in the Western Ghats, near Bombay. By the seventh century, the Mahāsāṁghikas had become the most widespread of all the communities. They had maintained a strong center in Magadha, while branching to the north, west, and south, and through Orissa to Andhra, where they prospered and branched into new communities.

In the north, two Mahāsāṁghika schools, the Ekavyavahārikas and the Lokottaravādins, established communities near Puruṣapura around 200 B.C.E. Other branches of the Mahāsāṁghikas, the Caityakas, (also known as Śailas), the Pūrvaśailas and the Aparaśailas, arose in the south as early as the second century B.C.E.. These schools are known through numerous inscriptions on pillars, sculptures, and temples at Amarāvatī and Nāgārjunakoṇḍa. The name Pūrvaśaila refers to the eastern branch of the Caityakas, and the Aparaśaila refers to the western branch.

Based on firm archaeological evidence, scholars today regard Dhānyakaṭaka as the main center of both branches of Caityakas, which seem to have been amply supported by the lay Sangha in the area. The Caityakas appear to have expanded to the northwest, along the Godavarī River at least as far as Nāsik on the Deccan Plateau. Patrons of the Caityakas from Dhānyakaṭaka contributed to enlarging the cave temples at Kārli, near Bombay; their inscriptions also appear in the cave temples of Kānheri.

Other branches of the Mahāsāṃghikas migrated to or developed in other regions: The Bahuśrutīyas were known in Kosala (Madhyadeśa) and Nāgārjunakoṇḍa (Andhra) as well as in the northwestern site now known as Pālāṭū Ḍherī (Gandhāra). The Gokulika, also known as Kaurukullakas, and the Prajñaptivādins were only known in the Madhyadeśa. (The affiliation of the Bahuśrutīyas is in question; while the earliest treatises consider the Bahuśrutīyas as Mahāsāṃghika, the eighth-century Kashmiri master Vinītadeva lists them as a Sarvāstivādin school.)

In the seventh century, Hsüan-tsang and I-tsing noted that there were seven subdivisions of the Mahāsāṃghika, although the school in general was in decline. In Magadha and Eastern India, Hsüan-tsang noted at least twenty-four Mahāsāṃghika monasteries housing about 1,100 monks. According to I-tsing, there were a few Mahāsāṃghikas in Western, Northern, and South India, but none in Śrī Laṅkā. The Mahāsāṃghikas had some followers in western China and had recently entered Sumatra, Java, and other islands of modern Indonesia.

Sthavira

The course of the Sthaviras can be traced westward from Pāṭaliputra to Vidiśā and Sañcī in Avanti, where they were known as Mūlasthaviras and as Haimavatas. In Aśokan times they spread south into Mahārāṣṭra, through Andhra and southeast along the river valleys to Kāñcī. They founded monasteries in Kāñcī and in Śrī Laṅkā, which eventually became their major center. According to inscriptions, several branches of the Sthavira community (Dharmottarīyas and Suvarṣakas) contributed to the site renovations at Kārli.

Although the Sthaviras maintained a presence in Pāṭaliputra and had monasteries in Vārāṇasī, Kauśāmbī, and the region north of Mathurā, they began to decline in the north as they grew stronger in South India and Śrī Laṅkā. From their center in Śrī Laṅkā the Sthaviras propagated the

Dharma in Samaṭata (modern Bengal) and Kaliṅga (modern Orissa). In the seventh century, Hsüan-tsang noted thirty Sthavira monasteries in Samaṭata with a total of two thousand bhikṣus. Hsüan-tsang also mentioned the presence of ten "Mahāyāna-sthavira" monasteries in Kaliṅga housing more than five hundred bhikṣus. The Mahāyāna-sthaviras mentioned by Hsüan-tsang are generally considered to refer to the Abhayagirivāsins, a school that separated from the more conservative Sthaviras in Śrī Laṅkā. Hsüan-tsang also counted sixty Mahāyāna-sthavira monasteries that housed 3,300 bhikṣus on India's west coast, but he does not mention the large Sthavira centers of Vidiśā and Sañcī, and he found no Sthavira monasteries north of Vidiśā. In all, Hsüan-tsang wrote that there were 401 Sthavira monasteries in India and Śrī Laṅkā housing a total of 36,800 bhikṣus.

I-tsing, in the late seventh century, noted that there were some Sthavira bhikṣus in Magadha and in areas further east. At that time nearly all South Indian Buddhists were Sthavira, and Sthaviras were the only school in Śrī Laṅkā. He also commented that the Sthaviras had only recently entered the islands of the southern sea and noted that there were no Sthaviras in China.

Further Readings

Fa-hien. "Fo-kwo-ki," in Hsüan-tsang. *Si-Yu-Ki: Buddhist Records of the Western World*, pp. ix–lxxxiii.

Hsüan-tsang. *Ibid.*, throughout.

I-tsing. *A Record of the Buddhist Religion as Practised in India and the Malay Archipelago*, translated by J. Takakusu, pp. xxii–xxxvii; 1–15.

Lamotte, Étienne. *History of Indian Buddhism*, pp. 523–529.

Languages of the Buddha's Time

I authorize you, monks, to learn the
Buddha's words each in his own dialect.
—Śākyamuni Buddha

According to the Kashmiri paṇḍita Vinītadeva, the four major branches of the eighteen schools were associated with specific languages: the Sarvāstivādins with Sanskrit, the Saṁmatīyas with Apabhraṁśa, the Mahāsāṁghikas with Prākrit, and the Sthaviras with Pāli. This association, whether based on geographical location, the background of the schools' major teachers, or the styles of expression these schools chose to adopt, reflects the rich cultural and linguistic diversity of India. In ancient times, as today, every tribe, every region, and often each religion had its own language or dialect. Although the vast array of differences can be confusing, within this diversity can be found patterns of development to help us understand the basic relationships of India's complex net of cultures, languages, terminologies, and scripts.

India's religious leaders and philosophers have long been aware of the relationship of sound to conceptual patterns and by extension to the expression of reality. The Brahmins, who preserved the Vedas as well as the religious and social systems based on them, accorded the study of sound, word, and language a high priority; they evolved sophisticated systems of grammar and included language and grammar among the five classical sciences.

While the speech of the local populace was vigorously evolving and diversifying, the Brahmins attempted fairly successfully to keep the language spoken by the educated classes (mostly Brahmins) close to the language of the Vedas, their sacred texts. By the time of the Buddha there were two parallel streams of language development: the slowly evolving language of the educated classes and the languages of the general populace. At some point the language of the educated classes became known as Sanskrit (from saṁskṛta, well-formed, polished, following the rules of grammar) and the language of the masses became known as Prākrit (from prakṛta, natural).

The sophistication and specificity possible through Sanskrit made Sanskrit the natural choice of philosophers; since philosophy before the Buddha's time was the province of the learned classes, Sanskrit was adopted by the Brahmins and literary masters from early on. Prince Gautama, the Bodhisattva, would have mastered this language as part of his education. It would have been the obvious language that the Brahmins Arāḍa Kālāma and Rudraka the son of Rāma, to whom the Bodhisattva went after leaving home, used to express their philosophies.

In the fourth century B.C.E., the grammarian Pāṇini wrote the Aṣṭadhyāyī, a text which defined Sanskrit so completely that the language was effectively frozen and changes thereafter were extremely rare. The Aṣṭadhyāyī formulated four thousand grammatical rules in a concise, nearly mathematical mode of expression, setting a model followed by Indian grammarians to this day. While Sanskrit underwent certain types of elaborations, especially after the twelfth century, it continued to adhere to the Pāṇinian system.[1]

In the Buddhist tradition, Indra, Pāṇini and Candra-pa are regarded as the three great Sanskrit grammarians. Tibetan scholars trace the origin of Sanskrit grammar to Indra, also known as Tuṣita Sarvajñādeva, chief of the gods of the Trāyastriṁśa Heaven. His grammar, the Indravyākaraṇa, is said to be the progenitor of all Sanskrit grammatical traditions. Pāṇini and Candra-pa, who formulated a more flexible grammatical system favored by Buddhist scholars, are named in the lineage stemming from Indra. Candra-pa's major work, the Candra-vyākaraṇa, essentially agrees with the system of Pāṇini.

The term Prākrit applies generally to the rapidly evolving languages of the people of northern India. Vararuci (c. third to fifth century C.E.), the first Prākrit grammarian, named four major Prākrits, and later grammarians identified numerous subdivisions. Modern grammatical analysis derives Prākrit from the language used by the people of the Vedas, since Prākrit has some remnants of the Vedic language that were not retained in the Sanskrit. As spoken languages tend to become simpler with time, Prākrit dropped consonants at the end of words, simplified clusters of consonants, and tended to consolidate the number of cases and verb forms.

Since this process devolved differently in different regions, with more or less admixture of local words and idioms, different forms of Prākrit developed in various regions. The Prākrits closest to Sanskrit, spoken in the brahmanic heartland of India, had the greatest prestige, while Prākrits spoken in areas such as Magadha and Aṅga, the homeland of the Dharma, had far less stature. In the sixth century

---

1. The modern sciences of phonetics and linguistics arose from the discovery of Pāṇini's grammar. The work of Pāṇini, Candra-pa, and other Indian grammarians had no equal in grammatical literature anywhere in the world up to the nineteenth century.

B.C.E., Magadha and Aṅga had only recently been brahmanized. Magadha, then rising in power, was formerly a land of shepherds, peoples not particularly diligent in observing the customs of the Vedas. While the republican tribes north of the Ganges were generally accorded the status of Kṣatriya, the ruling class, most of them may not have been ethnically related to the Vedic peoples.

India at the time of the Buddha was also the home of other languages, such as Apabhraṁśa and Paiśācī, each of which developed different dialects over time. Among the Apabhraṁśa were languages of Āryan and non-Āryan origins, such as Pañcāla, Mālava, Kaliṅgya, Karṇataka, and Drāviḍa, the languages of the janapadas of Pañcāla, Mālava, Kaliṅga, and Andhra. The indigenous languages or their survivals in the local idioms were often known as deśya or deśi-bhāṣā, "country speech." For these languages also, those nearest to the "pure" languages of the Vedic peoples had the greatest prestige, and those furthest away were relegated to the status of demonic or animal speech.

The term Pāli simply refers to a "line of letters" or "the texts," and there are wide differences of opinion concerning what language is meant by this term. Pāli has been compared to Māgadhī, the Prakrit spoken in the kingdom of Magadha, but Pāli is much closer to Sanskrit and the more ancient Vedic than the Māgadhī described by ancient grammarians. Comparisons of the language of the Pāli texts with the detailed descriptions of Prākrits given by the ancient grammarians indicate that Pāli has the closest affinity with the languages spoken in the area of Sāñcī and Ujjayinī.[2]

There are no surviving examples of any Indian writing from the fall of the Harappan culture around 1,500 B.C.E. to the time of Aśoka. The Vedas, Brāhmaṇas, and Upaniṣads do not mention writing, although the Buddhist Sūtras refer

---

2. This was the home area of Mahendra, Aśoka's son who carried the Dharma to Śrī Laṅkā. Sāñcī was a strong Sthavira center around the time of Aśoka.

to written language and the prosperous mercantile trade in the Buddha's time would very likely have required some form of written documents and records. The scripts carved on the stone Aśokan pillars are perfectly adapted to Indian sounds, reflecting a long period of development. Noting this, some scholars have suggested that a form of writing may have existed centuries earlier than Aśoka's reign. However, the issue of when writing actually came into use in India remains unresolved.

Aśokan inscriptions use two kinds of script: the Brāhmī and the Kharoṣṭhī. The origins of Brāhmī are uncertain and controversial; however, there is agreement that Kharoṣṭhī developed from the Aramaic alphabet and was read right to left in the same manner. Kharoṣṭhī was the script favored by the Kuṣāṇas; after Kuṣāṇa influence waned, the use of the script survived in Central Asia, where it was employed for copying manuscripts of Buddhist texts.

Languages of the Buddha

The Sūtras clearly state that the Buddha knew the languages of all manner of beings, from all the human languages of his day to the languages used in the non-human realms. The Sūtras also refer to the Buddha's mastery of scripts used to express these languages, asserting that he knew "The Brāhmī, Kharoṣṭhī, and Puṣkarasārī scripts. . . . the scripts of Aṅga, Vaṅga, and Magadha. . . . the Maṅgalya, Mānuṣya, and Aṅgulī scripts. . . . the scripts of Śakārī, Brahmavalī, Drāviḍā, Kinarī, Dākṣina, and Ugra. . . . the scripts known as Saṅkhyā, Anuloma, or Ardhadhanus. . . . and those known as Madhyākṣaravistara and Puṣpa." (*Voice of the Buddha* I:189)

There has been much discussion among Western scholars about the "original language of the Buddha," upon which there is no universal agreement. Recently some authorities have pointed out the pitfalls of choosing one language over another as somehow closer to the Buddha's "actual speech."

Since the teachings were transmitted orally in various languages for hundreds of years, there is no inherent superiority of one language over another by virtue of one being an "original" language, even if we could ascertain that there was one. Where proponents of one language might claim a closer historical connection, another more developed language could assert its greater precision and clarity in conveying the Dharma's subtle meanings.

"Two monks, brothers, Brahmins by birth, of fine language and eloquent speech, came to the Buddha and said, 'Lord, here monks of various names, clan-names, castes, and families are corrupting the Buddha's words by repeating them in their own dialects. Let us put them into Vedic [implying chanting them in the Vedic manner as well as the actual language].' The Lord rebuked them: 'Deluded men! How can you say this? This will not lead to the conversion of the unconverted' . . . And he delivered a sermon and commanded all the monks: 'You are not to put the Buddha's words into Vedic (khandasoāropemā). Whosoever does so shall be guilty of an offence. I authorize you, monks, to learn the Buddha's words each in his own dialect (sakkaya-niruttiyā).'" (Cullavagga 5:33)

It is clear from early accounts of the Buddha's life that he chose to express his teachings in languages that all beings could understand. In a broad perspective, this presents no difficulty: By virtue of his attainment of the ten powers of a Buddha, the Enlightened One knew the hearts and minds of all beings; he could teach beings of human and non-human realms simultaneously, each hearing according to their custom and their level of comprehension.

For practical purposes it seems best to consider that the Buddha followed his own guidelines and spoke the languages appropriate to his listeners, whether they be gods, nāgas, kinnaras, or human beings of different cultures and social levels. Thus it is reasonable to assume that in Vaiśālī the Buddha spoke in Licchāvī; in Kuśinagara, in the Śākyan dialect; in Kosala in Kosalese; and in Magadha, in Māgadhī. He also encouraged his disciples to use the languages of the people they were teaching.

The Buddha's teachings (Tripiṭaka) were transmitted orally for many centuries. So respected and accurate was this oral tradition that it persisted long after the Buddhist scriptures were written down. Exactly when the Buddhist communities began to transcribe their collection of sacred texts is uncertain. The Tipiṭaka, which was written down in Pāli in Śrī Laṅkā in the first century B.C.E., is the oldest known written collection of the Buddha's teachings. The Pāli Tipiṭaka has supported the Theravādin traditions of Śrī Laṅkā and Southeast Asia to the present day.

Accounts of the council sponsored by King Kaniṣka strongly suggest that the sacred texts of the northern traditions were codified and written down as a result of that council. (A fuller discussion of this topic begins on p. 285.) From the second to fourth centuries C.E., the languages used for transcribing texts in the north appear to have been Prākrit and a form of "mixed Sanskrit," which incorporated both Prākrit and Sanskrit elements to a greater or lesser degree. By the fourth century, Prākrit and mixed Sanskrit were replaced by "Buddhist Sanskrit," which was closer to the classical Sanskrit defined by Pāṇini. (Since Buddhist Sanskrit was never codified and frozen as strictly as classical Sanskrit, the term "Buddhist Sanskrit" encompasses a wider range of variations.)

In the northwest, where the Sarvāstivādin schools emphasized the Abhidharma teachings, the use of Sanskrit served two major purposes: its precision enabled precise expression of sophisticated concepts, and the use of Sanskrit gave Dharma masters a way to effectively address the shortcomings of Brahmin philosophers, who were quite strong in the northwest. Highly respected Brahmin philosophers, overcome in debate, added their skills to the Dharma, as did Mātṛceṭa, who composed elegant poetry in pure Sanskrit.

The great poet Aśvaghoṣa, whom some traditions equate with Mātṛceṭa, also wrote the Buddhacarita, a compelling epic of the life of the Buddha, in eloquent Sanskrit. Works such as these, together with the Sarvāstivādin Abhidharma texts and the writings of learned Mahāyāna masters, firmly established Sanskrit as a Buddhist language.

Further Readings

Basham, A. L. *The Wonder That Was India*, pp. 386–399.

Burrow, T. *The Sanskrit Language*, new revised edition, pp. 1–66. London: Faber and Faber, 1973.

Edgerton, Franklin. *Buddhist Hybrid Sanskrit Grammar and Dictionary*, volume I, pp. 1–14.

Lamotte, Étienne. *History of Indian Buddhism*, pp. 272–292; 517–593.

Buddhism in Śrī Laṅkā

*The Master of Boundless Wisdom, looking to the
salvation of Laṅkā in time to come . . . visited this
fair island three times . . . Therefore this isle, radiant
with the light of truth, came to high honor among
the faithful.*
—*Mahāvaṃsa*

According to the Mahāvaṃsa, the Great Chronicle of the
Theravādin tradition, in the time before the Parinirvāṇa
of the Buddha, Śrī Laṅkā was inhabited only by yakṣas,
nāgas, and other non-humans. The first human inhabitants
of the island are said to have been seven hundred refugees
from India who arrived in Śrī Laṅkā on the very day of the
Buddha's Parinirvāṇa. The leader of the seven hundred (all
of whom had been exiled because of their violent dispositions), was Vijaya, son of Sīhabāhu, king of the Vaṅga country (modern Bengal).

The tradition relates that the seven hundred émigrés
came under the protection of Śakra, king of the gods; with
the help of a female yakṣa, they overcame all the yakṣas in

the region they wished to settle. The refugees then built settlements on this forested isle and named them Anurādhagāma (Anurādha's village), Upatissagāma (the village of Upatissa), Ujjenī, Uruvelā, and Vijita. After a time the seven hundred men sent emissaries with rich offerings to South India in search of wives. The Paṇḍu king of the city of Madhurā agreed to send his daughter to Vijaya and arranged for many maidens to accompany her. The settlers anointed Vijaya their king; thereafter he abandoned his violent behavior and ruled Lankā in peace and righteousness.

Having no heir, Vijaya sent to India for his brother Sumitta to rule after his death. But Sumitta already ruled a kingdom in South India, so he sent his son Paṇḍuvāsudeva to Lankā in his stead. Subhaddakaccanā, daughter of a Śākya noble, became Paṇḍuvāsudeva's queen, connecting the royal family of Śrī Lankā with the Buddha's clan. It was prophesied that one of their descendants would establish the Buddha's religion in Śrī Lankā. The three kings who ruled after Paṇḍuvāsudeva—Abhaya, Paṇḍukābhaya, and Miṭasiva—established the Simhala Dynasty, named after the Simhala (Lion) clan. The island they ruled became known as Simhala; the people who inhabited the island became known as Simhāli and their language as Sinhalese.[1] Between 236 and 276 years after the Buddha's Parinirvāṇa, Devānampiyatissa came to the throne; it was he who welcomed Aśoka's son Mahinda and supported the establishment of the Dharma in Śrī Lankā.

The Buddha's Three Visits

According to the Mahāvamsa, the Buddha traveled three times to the land of Śrī Lankā. During the first year after his enlightenment, when the Buddha was residing at Uruvelā (Uruvilvā) awaiting the appropriate time to convert the Kāśyapa brothers, he visited the land of the Kurus in the

---

1. Lankā, or Śrī Lankā, has also been known in India as Tāmraparṇī, Simhaladvīpa, and Ceylon.

north and then, nine months after the enlightenment, traveled south to Śrī Laṅkā. The Tathāgata foresaw that Śrī Laṅkā would become a land hospitable to the Dharma, but first he had to expel the yakṣas, fierce beings incapable of responding to the Dharma, who were making the island impossible for human habitation.

The Mahāvaṃsa relates how the Buddha arrived at Śrī Laṅkā just as all the yakṣas were gathered in a great assembly; hovering over their heads, the Buddha caused a great storm to arise, filling the yakṣas with terror. In return for releasing them from their fear, the yakṣas gave the Tathāgata the entire island of Śrī Laṅkā, and the Buddha enabled them to move to another island.

At that time, a multitude of devas assembled on Śrī Laṅkā to praise the Buddha, and the Enlightened One spoke to them of the Dharma. After thus setting the Dharma in motion in the land of Śrī Laṅkā, the Buddha gave some of the hairs from his head to Mahāsumana, the leader of the devas, and then returned to Uruvilva. Mahāsumana had a stūpa built in the place where the Buddha first taught the Dharma and enshrined the hair-relics within it. After the Buddha's Parinirvāṇa, Sarabhu, the disciple of Śāriputra, brought a collarbone relic to Śrī Laṅkā and placed it within this same stūpa. This stūpa, enlarged through the years by the Dharma kings of Śrī Laṅkā, became known as the Mahiyaṅgana-thūpa.

Five years after the enlightenment, while he was residing at Jeta's Grove in the city of Śrāvastī, the Buddha traveled a second time to Śrī Laṅkā to prevent war between two nāga leaders. Arriving in the region of Nāgadīpa, he converted the nāgas to the Dharma and planted a rājāyatana tree to commemorate the event. Three years later, the powerful nāga-king Maṇiakkhika formally invited the Buddha and the Sangha to Śrī Laṅkā. Leaving Jeta's Grove, the Tathāgata, accompanied by five hundred bhikkhus (bhikṣus), set out for the island and arrived at Kalyāṇi. During this visit the

Buddha visited several places which later became sacred sites. Among them were Mt. Sumanakūṭa, where the Buddha left traces of his footprints, and the future sites of the Mahāmegha Monastery, the Bodhi Tree, the Great Thūpa (Stūpa) of Anurādhapura, and the Thūpārāma, the monastery connected to the Great Thūpa.

Aśoka's Emissaries

Approximately 236 years later, when Devānaṁpiyatissa became king of Śrī Laṅkā, his realm so abounded in treasures said to result from the king's great merit that it became known as the Jewel Island. The Mahāvaṁsa records that Devānaṁpiyatissa sent a large shipment of priceless gems as a gift to the Dharma King Aśoka, and Aśoka responded with gifts of friendship to the Śrī Laṅkan king.

Soon afterwards, Aśoka either sent or supported sending bhikkhus out to propagate the Dharma in lands beyond the boundaries of Magadha. Among these bhikkhus was his son, the great Thera Mahinda, who traveled to Śrī Laṅkā from Vedisa (Vidiśā), accompanied by five disciples, Mahinda's nephew Sumana, and the lay disciple Bhaṇḍuka. Archaeological research verifies the Mahāvaṁsa's account: Inscriptions found at Vidiśā in Central India confirm that Aśoka and Devānaṁpiyatissa were contemporaries and that bhikkhus traveled from Vidiśā to Śrī Laṅkā at that time.

The Mahāvaṁsa records that Mahinda and his disciples traveled to Śrī Laṅkā through the air, landing at Missaka Mountain (modern Mihintale). King Devānaṁpiyatissa, out hunting a stag, came upon the shaven-headed bhikkhus and at first mistook them for supernatural beings. Finally convinced that the bhikkhus were indeed human, the king took refuge in the Dharma along with five hundred of his attendants. With great respect, he welcomed the bhikkhus into Anurādhapura, his capital city, and invited them to teach the Dharma to him and his subjects.

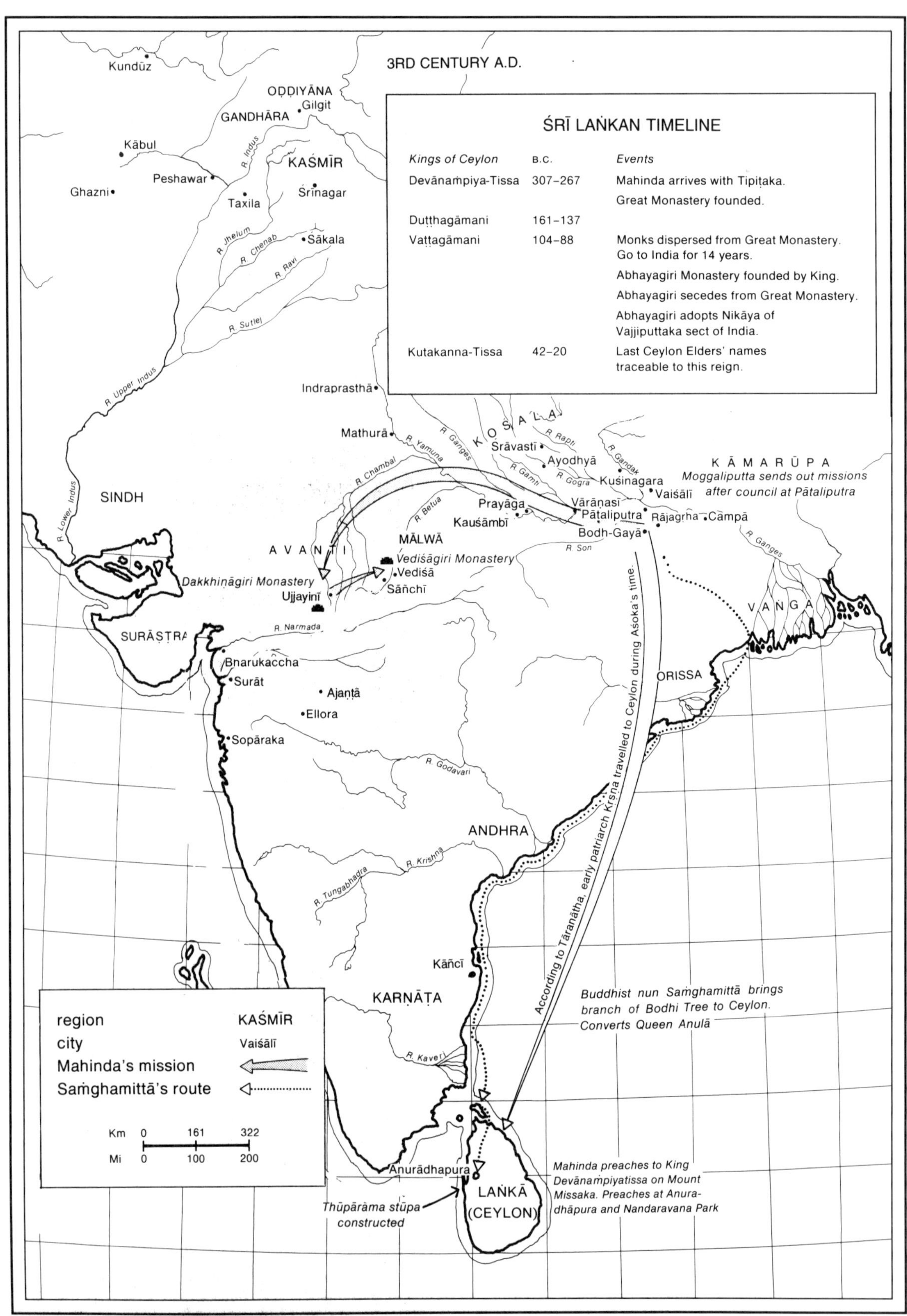

King Aśoka's son Mahinda established the Dharma in Laṅkā.

A great multitude assembled to hear the teachings, and eight thousand people attained the first stage of liberation. When the Queen Anūlā and her five hundred attendants requested ordination, Mahinda, unable to ordain women, sent to Pāṭaliputra for his sister, the bhikkhuṇī Saṁghamittā.

To the Sangha King Devānaṁpiyatissa gave his garden named Mahāmegha, the Great Cloud, and the earth shook to mark the event. Mahinda explained that in ages past, this place had been visited by four different Buddhas. Each had asked that a branch of their Bodhi Tree be brought to that place by a bhikkhuṇī and planted by the king. At Mahinda's request, Saṁghamittā brought with her to Śrī Laṅkā a branch of the Bodhi Tree, and the king planted it in the garden of Mahāmegha, where Bodhi trees of past Buddhas had stood. The Mahāvaṁsa records that the planting of the Bodhi Tree took place in the eighteenth year of King Aśoka's reign. Many auspicious signs occurred during the planting ceremony; the Bodhi Tree prospered in the land of Śrī Laṅkā, and great trees grew from its seeds, which were planted among the vihāras built for the Sangha.

The king had a great monastic complex of buildings, gardens, and ponds built in this area, which became known as the Mahāvihāra, the great dwelling place of the Sangha. The king also built a vihāra on Mt. Missaka for the Sangha's observance of the rainy season retreat. So many temples were built on Mt. Missaka that it became known as the Cetiya (Temple) Mountain, and the first vihāra constructed there was named the Cetiyapabbata Vihāra.

In the first year of the Dharma in Śrī Laṅkā, King Devānaṁpiyatissa performed twelve great actions on behalf of the Sangha: In Anurādhapura he constructed the Mahā-vihāra, Cetiyapabbata Vihāra, and the Thūpārāma; he planted the Bodhi Tree, erected a beautiful stone pillar, enshrined the collarbone relic, and built the Issarasamaṇa Vihāra, the Tissa Pool, the Paṭhama Thūpa, the Vessagiri Vihāra, and the first two bhikkhuṇī-vihāras, Upāsikā Vihāra and Hatthāḷhaka Vihāra. The king continued his good works for the rest of his life.

Aśoka's daughter Saṃghamittā ordained Queen Anūlā and her five hundred attendants, and her brother Mahinda ordained Ariṭṭa, Devānaṃpiyatissa's son, together with his five hundred followers. Both Anūlā and Ariṭṭa, as well as Ariṭṭa's fifty-five brothers, became Arhats, and the Sanghas of bhikkhus and bhikkhunīs were firmly established.

On the day when the relics of the Buddha's collarbone were enshrined in the Thūpārāma, there were thirty thousand bhikkhus in attendance. When the Bodhi Tree was planted, Queen Anūlā with five hundred maidens and five hundred harem women attained Arhatship, as did Ariṭṭha, the king's nephew, along with five hundred attendants. At the king's invitation, Mahinda led the recital of the Dhamma (Suttas) and Vinaya, and Ariṭṭha spoke on the source of the Vinaya. In the Theravādin tradition, this is known as the Fourth Council, the assembly that established the roots of the Sangha in Śrī Laṅkā.

King Devānaṃpiyatissa reigned forty years. After his death his younger brother Uttiya became king; in the eighth year of Uttiya's reign the great Arhat Mahinda, then sixty years of age, passed away at the Cetiyapabbata Vihāra during the rainy season retreat. King Uttiya had Mahinda's relics collected and built a temple to hold half of them; the other half he enshrined in stūpas he had built on the mountain and in all the monasteries. The place where Mahinda was cremated was named Isibhūmaṅgaṇa, the Courtyard of the Sage.

Mahinda's sister, Saṃghamittā, passed away a year later at the age of fifty-nine. She was cremated with full honors in sight of the Bodhi Tree as she had requested, and the king had a stūpa erected in that place.

King Uttiya reigned ten years; he was followed by his younger brothers, Mahāsiva and Sūratissa, who also reigned ten years each. This dynasty was then interrupted for twenty-two years, when Sena and Guttaka, sons of a Damiḷa (Tamil) horse-merchant, usurped the throne. At that time Asela, Devānaṁpiyatissa's youngest brother, defeated the usurpers and ruled for ten years, after which Eḷāra of the Damiḷa tribe, a noble from the South Indian kingdom of Coḷa, seized the throne and ruled forty-four years.

The Builder-Kings Duṭṭhagāmaṇi and Vaṭṭāgāmaṇi

Eḷāra and thirty-one other Damiḷa rulers were eventually overthrown by Duṭṭhagāmaṇi, who united all of Laṅkā under one rule. Duṭṭhagāmaṇi vigorously supported the Sangha's expansion. Next to the Mahāvihāra, he built the nine-storied Lohapāsāda, inlaid with coral and precious jewels; he also built the Maricavaṭṭi Vihāra and began construction on the Mahāthūpa, the Great Stūpa requested by Mahinda. It is said that the gods themselves assembled the materials for its construction. Completed by Duṭṭhagāmaṇi's son and successor Saddhātissa, this stūpa, recently restored, is known today as the Ruvanveli Dāgaba. Saddhātissa ruled from 80–62 B.C.E. and was followed by four other Sinhalese kings. In 44 B.C.E., an ambitious general overpowered the king but was displaced by the king's son, Vaṭṭagāmaṇi.

A few months later, however, the Damiḷas of South India invaded and drove Vaṭṭagāmaṇi from the throne. Śrī Laṅkā was then ruled by a succession of five Damiḷa kings; political chaos and famine ensued, devastating the populace and the Sangha alike. Many bhikkhus left Śrī Laṅkā at that time to live in Buddhist communities in India. After fourteen years, Vaṭṭagāmaṇi, supported by the royal ministers and the Sangha, overcame the last Damiḷa ruler and restored Siṁhāli rule to Śrī Laṅkā in 29 B.C.E..

The Saddhamma-saṁgaha relates that fifty-seven years after the founding of the Great Thūpa, the king of Śrī Laṅkā, Vaṭṭagāmaṇi-abhaya (Vaṭṭāgāmaṇi the Fearless) built the great vihāra of Abhayagiri and near it a magnificent stūpa;

The Pāli Canon

Vinaya Piṭaka

Suttavibhaṅga (Rules of conduct)

Khandaka (Supplementary rules and rituals)

Parivāra (Summaries and classification of rules)

Sutta Piṭaka

Digha Nikāya (Long Suttas)

Majjhima Nikāya (Middle length Suttas)

Samyutta Nikāya (Topically-grouped Suttas)

Anguttara Nikāya (Numerically-grouped Suttas)

Khuddaka Nikāya (Small books)

Abhidhamma Piṭaka

Dhammasaṅganī (Enumeration of dharmas)

Vibhaṅga (Further analysis of dharmas)

Dhātukathā (Discussion of elements)

Puggalapaññatti (Description of individuals)

Kathāvatthu (Points of controversy)

Yamaka (Treatises on psychological subjects)

Paṭṭhāna (Causation and interrelation of phenomena)

—From *An Analysis of the Pāli Canon*

later enlarged to a height of 105 meters, the Abhayagiri Stūpa is the largest in all of Śrī Laṅkā. Vaṭṭagāmaṇi then donated the Abhayagiri Monastery to the Thera (Elder) Mahātissa, who had supported him throughout fourteen years of exile. However, this gift to an individual rather than to the Sangha was unprecedented; it instigated a long-standing rivalry between the conservative bhikkhus of the Mahāvihāra and the bhikkhus of the Abhayagiri Vihāra, who were from the outset more open to new insights and developments.

From this rivalry two factions emerged within the Theravādin tradition—the Mahāvihāravāsins and the Abhayagirivāsins. Soon after, the Mahāvihāravāsins expelled the Abhayagirivāsins from their community, arousing the king's displeasure. New subschools arose within the Abhayagirivāsins; in the fourth century, one of these new schools moved into the Jetavana Monastery recently founded in Anurādhapura, from which they became known as Jetavanīyas. Eventually the Mahāvihāravāsins, who maintained close relationships with the Śrī Laṅkan rulers, prevailed, and the Abhayagirivāsins ceased to exist as a distinct school.

Transcribing the Pāli Canon

During the reign of King Vaṭṭagāmaṇi, the bhikkhus decided that the time had come to transcribe the sacred texts to ensure their preservation. Up to that time in Śrī Laṅkā the scriptures had been preserved exclusively in an oral tradition. In response to the bhikkhus' request, the king built a hall in the Mahāvihāra especially for the purpose of transcribing the sacred texts. To accomplish this work, many hundreds of thousands of bhikkhus selected one thousand elder bhikkhus, "expert in the learning of the three Piṭakas, advanced in analytic insight, able to refute the threefold knowledge (of the Vedas)."[2] Following the example of the earlier councils, the Elders rehearsed the Sūtras and Vinaya.

---

2. Saddhamma-Saṁgaha, in B.C. Law, *The Buddhist Historical Traditions*, p. 66.

Within one year all of the sacred texts were written down in Pāli, and all the explanations and commentaries were written down in Sinhalese. According to the Dīpavaṁsa, thus it was ensured that the Sangha would endure for five thousand years. The earth quaked at the completion of this work, and many wonders manifested in the world. In the Theravādin tradition, this assembly is known as the Fifth Council.

Buddhaghosa, Buddhadatta, and Dharmapāla

Throughout the third and fourth centuries C.E., Buddhism in Śrī Laṅkā was advanced and supported by monks who traveled to the island from India. In the fifth century, during the reign of King Mahānāma, three Indian scholars—Buddhaghosa, Buddhadatta, and Dharmapāla—traveled to Śrī Laṅkā in search of the ancient commentaries (Aṭṭhakathā). These commentaries, transmitted by the great Theras since the time of the Buddha Śākyamuni, were then preserved only in Śrī Laṅkā.

Buddhaghosa undertook the journey to Śrī Laṅkā at the request of his preceptor, the Thera Revata, who asked that he translate the commentaries into Pāli and bring them to India. The Saddhamma-saṁgaha relates that just as Buddhaghosa left India to sail to Śrī Laṅkā, the learned Thera Buddhadatta left Śrī Laṅkā to return to India; they are said to have met each other through miraculous means. Buddhadatta would later return to Śrī Laṅkā to continue Buddhaghosa's work.

Buddhaghosa met the Thera Saṁghapāla at the Mahāvihāra in Anurādhapura; upon hearing monks recite the Aṭṭhakathā, Buddhaghosa was convinced that these commentaries were indeed true to the Buddha's teaching, and he requested permission to translate them. In order to test Buddhaghosa's qualifications, Saṁghapāla gave him only two verses to translate and demonstrate how he would explicate these teachings. Consulting the three Piṭakas and their commentary, Buddhaghosa wrote the Visuddhimagga, a major summary of Buddhist doctrine. The Saddhamma-saṃgaha relates that the devas made the Visuddhimagga disappear two times; as a result, Buddhaghosa had to write down the entire text three times. The devas then restored the first two copies, so that the Śrī Laṅkan scholars could compare all three versions of the Visuddhimagga. It is said that so clearly had Buddhaghosa understood the meaning of the teaching that no difference whatsoever could be found between the three texts.

Greatly esteemed for this feat, Buddhaghosa received complete access to the Aṭṭhakathā; from these commentaries he prepared the Samantapāsādikā, an extensive commentary on the Vinayapiṭaka, and the Kaṅkāvitaraṇī, a commentary on the Pātimokkha, as well as commentaries on each of the five Nikāyas of the Suttapiṭaka.

Turning next to the Abhidhammapiṭaka, Buddhaghosa composed a commentary on two of the seven basic texts: the Aṭṭhasālinī, a commentary on the Dhammasaṅgaṇi, and the Saṃmoha-vinodanī, a commentary on the Vibhaṅga. He also composed the Pañcappakaraṇa-aṭṭhakathā, a commentary on the five remaining Abhidhamma texts. According to the Saddhamma-saṃgaha, all these works were completed within the span of a single year. After Buddhaghosa's commentaries were accepted, the Sinhalese Aṭṭhakathās were either lost or destroyed.

It is not known whether Buddhaghosa actually returned to India, or whether his works became known to the Sthavira/Theravādin communities on the mainland of India. His work was continued by the Great Theras Buddhadatta and Dharmapāla. Both masters were natives of South India, and both probably spent their early years in a monastery in Kāñcī, a prominent center of Buddhist culture and learning. Buddhadatta is highly regarded for his work in translating and systematizing the Abhidharma; he may also have been responsible for preparing the Uttaravinicchaya, a compendium of Vinaya.

Dharmapāla completed the great work of editing and translating the ancient commentaries into Pāli; specifically, he prepared the Paramāṭṭhadīpanī, Elucidation of the Ultimate Meaning, a commentary on the Thera- and Therīgāthās (Psalms of the Brethren and Psalms of the Sisters), as well as commentaries on other books of the Khuddaka Nikāya. He also composed at least six subcommentaries, three of which appear to be lost today.

Theravāda Buddhism Becomes the State Religion

Śrī Laṅkā attracted masters from all Buddhist traditions, and all flourished briefly on the island around the third and fourth centuries. In the third century, the Mahāyāna teachings found a receptive audience among the bhikkhus of the Abhayagiri school, and the Vajrayāna, based on the Prajñā-pāramitā and Tantra teachings, took root in the eighth and ninth centuries. But all traditions depended on royal support for survival; most Sinhalese kings favored the Theravādin tradition as upheld by the more conservative Mahāvihāra bhikkhus.

When communication with the mainland weakened, traditions unable to generate local support could not survive. The Vajrayāna tradition was strong for a time but disappeared after King Vijayabāhu revived Theravāda as the state religion in the eleventh century. The Abhayagiri school persisted the longest; it was finally absorbed into the Mahāvihāra tradition in the twelfth century. Since that time, the island of Śrī Laṅkā has been exclusively Theravādin.

The eleventh century ushered in a series of foreign invasions that seriously weakened Sinhalese rule as well as the Sangha. Hindu Tamils, Portuguese, Dutch, and English occupied the island in turn, with adverse effects on the study and practice of Buddhism. Three times the Vinaya lineage had to be revitalized by bhikkhus from other Theravādin countries. A new period of revival began under British rule during the eighteenth and nineteenth centuries, supported by Western interest in the Buddhist teachings. Today the Theravādin tradition continues strongly in Śrī Laṅkā, upholding a tradition more than two thousand years old.

Further Readings

Mahāvaṁsa, or The Great Chronicle of Ceylon, translated by Wilhelm Geiger, pp. 1–18, 51–271.

Saddhamma-saṁgaha. *A Manual of Buddhist Historical Traditions,* translated by Bimala Churn Law, pp. 46–82.

Lamotte, Étienne. *History of Indian Buddhism,* pp. 266–271, 360–371, 483–486.

Law, B.C. *The Life and Work of Buddhaghosa.*

Webb, Russell, ed. *An Analysis of the Pāli Canon,* pp. 1–42.

The Dharma In Kashmir

The Blessed One has said of Kashmir,
one hundred years after the Buddha's Parinirvāṇa,
there will be a bhikṣu known as Madhyāntika;
he will introduce the Dharma into this country.
—Mūlasarvāstivādin Vinaya

Kashmir, a high valley that lies in India just north of the Himalayas, is bounded by the Kharakhorum Mountains on the northeast, Himchal Pradesh on the south, and the Vitastā (Jhelum) River on the west. Two main rivers, the Indus and Vitastā, flow through the valley. The Candrabhāga (Chenab), the third of the five rivers that gave the Punjab its name (Pañca-ab, five waters), defines the valley's southern border; its northern boundary extends beyond the Indus River to the base of the Little Pamir range.

While in centuries past, Kashmir's boundaries fluctuated somewhat with the tides of empire, Kashmir was generally larger than it is today. Ancient Kashmir bordered the outpost satrapy states of Persia and Greece, as well as Central Asia and Tibet. However, the passes into Kashmir from the north and west were especially difficult to traverse. To the west, the Khyber Pass connected Takṣaśilā with Kābul and from Kābul west and east to the whole civilized world. Invaders as well as merchants streamed through this route very close to Kashmir's southwestern border, but narrow river valleys and mountainous terrain protected Kashmir from all but the most determined visitors or conquerors. Although Hsüan-tsang relates that the land was protected by a dragon, the inhabitants of Kashmir appear to have augmented this protection through their own efforts. The Kashmiris learned early to protect their land and were said to have guarded the passes with great vigilance.

Although Kashmir was far distant from Magadha and Kosala and isolated by great rivers and high mountains, its connection with the Madhyadeśa traces to ancient times. The Mūlasarvāstivādin Vinaya records that the Buddha regarded Kashmir as "the best place for meditation that one could wish for." He predicted that a bhikṣu named Madhyāntika would conquer the nāga Hulunta and introduce the Dharma to that land, which was then populated by nāgas, water-loving snakelike beings capable of changing their shapes and wreaking great havoc on those who disturbed them. Having received this prophecy from the Buddha's disciple Ānanda, Madhyāntika went to Kashmir in the fiftieth year after the Buddha's nirvāṇa. He sat down in meditation, knowing that this would surely attract the nāgas' attention. As his mind focused in concentration, the earth trembled, and the nāgas drew upon their powers to distract him.

They caused rain to fall in great torrents and then physically attacked him, but Madhyāntika concentrated on compassion, and the nāgas could not move even a part of his garment. Then the nāgas caused arrows to fall from the sky upon him, but the arrows turned into a shower of fragrant flowers. Thunderbolts, huge arrows, and swords and axes followed, but all these fell on Madhyāntika in the form of blue lotus blossoms. Astonished, the nāgas approached the bhikṣu and asked what he wished from them. Madhyāntika told them of the Buddha's prediction and asked that the nāgas grant him the land of Kashmir.

The nāgas agreed only to give Madhyāntika all the land he could cover when seated in vajrāsana (meditation posture). Through the power of his meditation, Madhyāntika was able to cover an area encompassing nine valleys. The nāgas agreed to surrender the land if Madhyāntika could bring five hundred Arhats there to establish a Sangha. Madhyāntika also requested permission to bring householders to settle on the land, for they would be needed to support the Sangha. The nāgas agreed, on the condition that when the Dharma had run its course in the world, they could live in the great lake that would once again cover Kashmir.

So provinces were laid out, villages built, and householders brought to settle the land. Madhyāntika built five hundred monasteries, one for each of the five hundred Arhats. To give the householders a basis for prosperity, Madhyāntika took them to the Gandhamādana Mountain and told them to gather saffron plants to cultivate in their fields. The nāgas of that region became very upset, but Madhyāntika calmed them, and they agreed that as long as the Buddhadharma endured, they would allow the inhabitants of Kashmir to take saffron plants from the mountain. The householders then planted the saffron in their fields; Madhyāntika blessed the plants, and the saffron flourished.

Madhyāntika worked for the Dharma in Kashmir until the end of his days. When he entered nirvāṇa, his body was cremated and his relics enshrined in a stūpa built to receive them. The Chinese scholar and pilgrim Hsüan-tsang adds that after the death of Madhyāntika, the Kritīyas, the people he had brought to settle the land, began to view themselves as the real rulers of Kashmir. However, around this time, King Aśoka began to build a series of Buddhist monasteries in Kashmir and gave the whole country to the monks as a gift.

Indian rulers have long recognized the strategic value of Kashmir and regarded it as an integral part of India, although Kashmir has been autonomous for much of its history prior to modern times. Candragupta Maurya, Aśoka's grandfather, brought Kashmir into his empire, and Aśoka carefully maintained it as part of his realm as well.

According to tradition, Aśoka founded the capital of Śrīnagarī south of the present Śrīnagar, at a site known as Pandretthan. Theravādin accounts relate that during Aśoka's reign a group of Sthavira Arhats left Pāṭaliputra and established their center in Kashmir. The accounts also state that Mogalliputta Tissa sent the Arhat Majjhantika to convert the lands of Kashmir and Gandhāra. Hsüan-tsang relates that Aśoka built a stūpa there; at the time of his visit, this stūpa held a tooth relic of the Buddha.

The traditional Buddhist accounts of the early history of Kashmir are echoed in the Rājataraṅgiṇī, the chronicle of early and medieval Kashmir compiled in the twelfth century by the Kashmiri historian Kalhaṇa. This source mentions the story of Madhyāntika and notes that the inhabitants of Kashmir belonged to three tribes that migrated from Dardistan to the north: Nāgas, Piśācas, and Yakṣas. Rivers, lakes, and streams provided an ample water supply; the land abounded with wildlife, especially snakes, which were simultaneously objects of fear, admiration, and worship. When the Āryan tribes later migrated into the valleys of Kashmir, they met with great resistance from the Nāga tribes. These same tribes, however, appear to have been very receptive to the Buddhist teachings.

Buddhism prospered in Kashmir under the Kuṣāṇa kings, who held suzerainty over Kashmir from the first century B.C.E. to the middle of the second century C.E. The Kuṣāṇa rulers founded the cities of Kaniṣkapura (modern Kaniṣpur) and Huviṣkapura (modern Uṣkur), which became an important Buddhist center. The Kuṣāṇa king most associated with Buddhism was King Kaniṣka, although traditional sources do not agree on the extent of Kaniṣka's Empire nor the nature of his influence in Kashmir.

Tāranātha relates that Kaniṣka, king of Jālandhara, hearing of the Arhat Simha Sudarśana, formerly a king of Kashmir, became full of respect and came to Kashmir to pay his respects. At that time the Arhat Sañjaya was also teaching the Dharma in Kashmir, where the Sangha numbered numbered twenty thousand.

Strongly attracted to the Buddhist teachings, Kaniṣka convened a council of the Sangha in either Kashmir or Jālandhara, a province south of Kashmir proper between the Beas and the Sutlej rivers. Hsüan-tsang relates that when the council was over, King Kaniṣka again officially bestowed the kingdom of Kashmir on the monks before returning to his capital at Peshāwar in Gandhāra. After Kaniṣka's death, the Kritīyas took over the government, banished the monks, and persecuted religion.

When the king of Himatala, a descendant of the Śākyas expelled from Kapilavastu, heard of the Kritīyas' actions, he disguised his warriors as merchants, led them into Kashmir and took possession of the kingdom. He brought many monks back to Kashmir and built a monastery for them, then returned to his own country. But a century later the Kritīyas returned to power. Hsüan-tsang cites this account as the reason the Kashmiri king of that time strongly supported the non-Buddhist traditions.

After the Kuṣāṇa Empire had fallen, Kashmir enjoyed relative autonomy until the invasion of the Huns in the early sixth century. Although many of the Kashmiri kings did not support the Dharma, the Rājataraṅgiṇī mentions that a King Meghavāhana abolished the killing of animals in his realm and was a patron of Buddhism. One of his wives, Queen Amṛtaprabhā, built the Amṛtabhāvana Monastery for the Sangha, and his other queens sponsored the building of many more vihāras.

Kashmir as a Center of Education

The Sarvāstivādins who lived in Kashmir developed their monasteries into distinguished centers of learning. Although historical documents for this period are scanty, Kashmiri tradition holds that the great master Nāgārjuna lived for a time at Sadarhadvana (modern Harwan), and that his knowledge greatly enhanced Kashmir's reputation as a center of learning. But when Buddhism lost royal patronage at the time of King Abhimanyu, Nāgārjuna went to live in South India, where he went into retreat and eventually passed away at Śrī Parvata.

With the route to Central Asia having been secured by Kuṣāṇa rule, Kashmiri Sarvāstivādin bhikṣus traveled north to Khotan, then along the Silk Route that encircled the Taklamakan basin, terminating at Tun-huang on the northwestern border of China. Sarvāstivādin as well as Mahāyāna bhikṣus established monasteries near major oasis cities along the way—Kashgar, Khotan, Kuchā, and Niya—often carving monasteries and temples out of caves in the mountains and cliffs. During the fourth century, when Tun-huang became a major translation center, it is likely that Kashmiri bhikṣus contributed their scholarship there as well.

Kashmiri scholars became widely respected. The valleys of Kashmir nurtured the development of the Sarvāstivādin Abhidharma, the systematic analyses of experience that provided the foundation of Buddhist philosophy. Kashmir was the home of the Sarvāstivādin masters Kātyāyanīputra and Vasumitra; the Vaibhāṣika teacher Dharmatrāta; the Sautrāntika masters Mahā-bhaṭṭāraka Sthavira and Śrīlābha (Śrīlāta); and the Vaibhāṣika Saṁghabhadra, teacher of Vasubandhu. The Kashmiri laity appears to have appreciated the growth of scholarship in their land. Tāranātha and Bu-ston both mention a wealthy Brahmin named Śūdra or Sūtra, who generously supported the bhaṭṭārakas at the time of Kaniṣka's council.

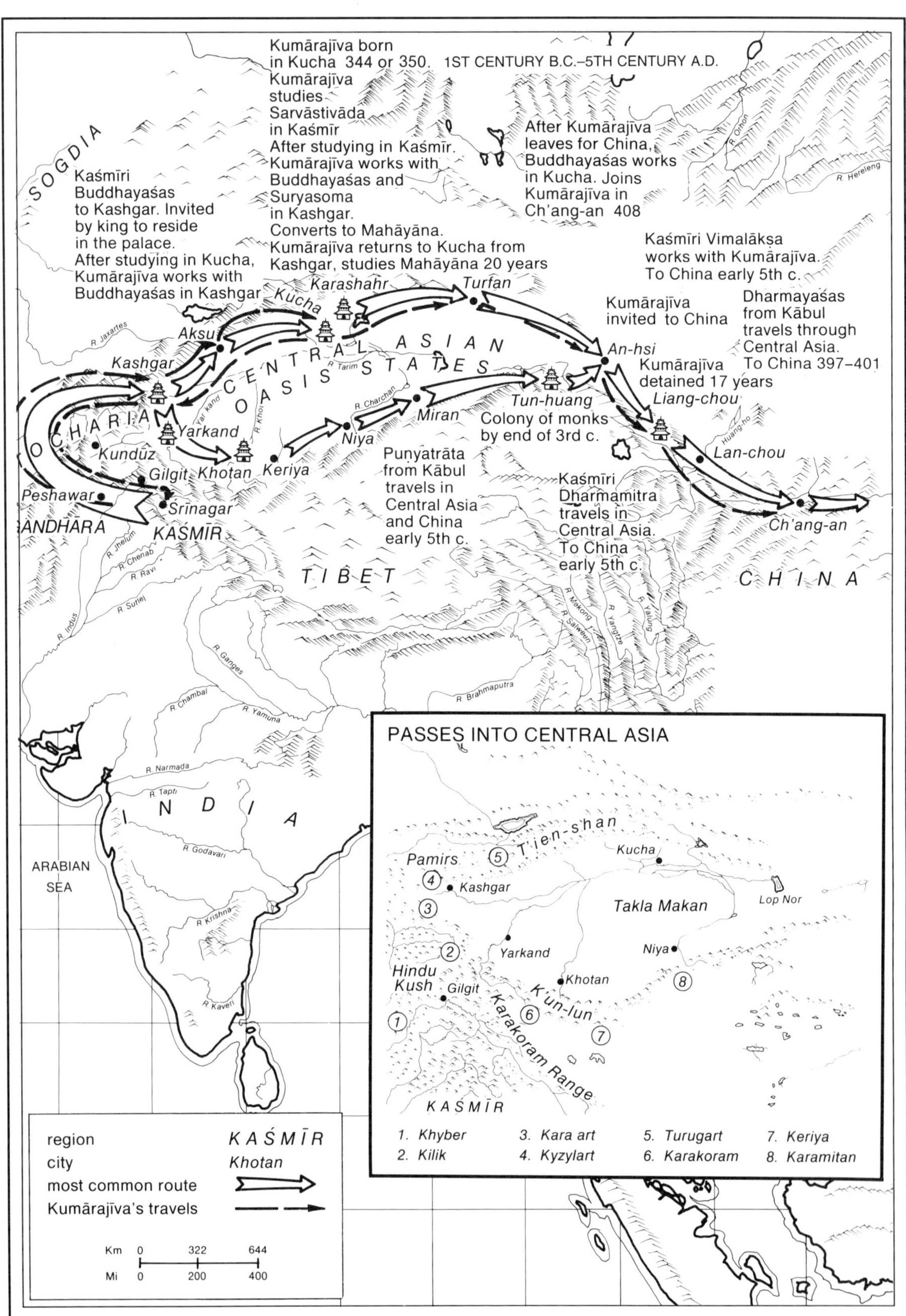

Kashmiri and Central Asian bhikṣus propagated the Dharma throughout Central Asia.

Outstanding masters educated in Kashmir were instrumental in translating the Dharma into the languages of Central Asia and China. One of the most famous Kashmiri-educated translators was Kumārajīva, son of a Brahmin and a Khotanese princess. As a youth, Kumārajīva (344–413) traveled to Kashmir with his mother where he studied the Āgamas with the master Bandhudatta. When he returned to Central Asia, he met the Kashmiri paṇḍita Vimalākṣa in Kuchā. Kumārajīva continued his studies with Vimalākṣa until the Chinese conquest around the turn of the century, when both master and disciple were taken into China at the order of the emperor. Thereafter, Kumārajīva directed the translation center the emperor established in Ch'ang-an, capital of the Chinese empire.

Kumārajīva's contemporary, Buddhabhadra, who with Fa-hien translated the Mahāparinirvāṇa-sūtra into Chinese, completed his education in Kashmir under the guidance of Buddhasena, a master known for his expertise in dhyāna, a form of yogic meditation. At the end of the fourth century, interest in dhyāna was growing in China, and teachers like Buddhasena began to attract Chinese as well as Central Asian students. Dharmabhikṣu, a fifth-century Kashmiri dhyāna master, also attracted students from China.

However, Buddhism in Kashmir suffered greatly from the invasion of the Hephthalites or White Huns in the early sixth century. According to the seventh-century pilgrim Hsüan-tsang, the Hun leader Mihirakula sought refuge in Kashmir after losing ground in the northwest, then assassinated the Kashmiri king and used Kashmir as a base to conquer Gandhāra, completely destroying all the Buddhist monasteries there. Mihirakula may be the Turuṣka leader Gomi mentioned in Tibetan accounts; he appears to have destroyed religious monuments indiscriminately, both Buddhist and Hindu. The savagery of the Huns, their hostility to the Dharma, and their persecution of monks was well-remembered through the centuries in Kashmir. As Hsüan-tsang witnessed just a little over a century later, the Huns' destruction of Buddhist monasteries and temples had been quite thorough.

After the death of Mihirakula, his son Baka (known to Tāranātha as Mahāsammata, to the Mañjuśrīmūlakalpa as Buddhapakṣa, and to Bu-ston as Bhadanta) is said to have rebuilt many vihāras and temples destroyed by his father.[1] During the reign of King Pravarasena, the king's uncle Jayendra sponsored a vihāra; the ministers of Pravarasena's son Yudhisthira II also built temples and monasteries.

By the time of the first Kārkoṭa king, Durlabhavardhana (602–638), Kashmir's influence extended north through the regions of Simhapura and Uraśa, and south to Punach and Rājapuri. Durlabhavardhana's reign heralded a renaissance of prosperity and support for the Dharma. Around the year 630 this king welcomed the Chinese pilgrim Hsüan-tsang. Although Hsüan-tsang's sorrow at seeing so many Buddhist sites in ruins pervades his account of Kashmir, he still counted one hundred active Buddhist monasteries with five thousand monks in Kashmir proper and noted the presence of three monasteries with three hundred Mahāyāna monks in Simhapura.

Hsüan-tsang personally visited the ruins of the monastery where Samghabhadra instructed Vasubandhu in the Abhidharma, as well as still active monasteries where masters such as Pūrṇa, Bodhila, and Skandhila worked for the Dharma. Most of the active Buddhist centers of that time were Sarvāstivādin; Bodhila's monastery, housing about one hundred bhikṣus, was Mahāsāmghika, and about thirty Mahāyāna monks were living near the ruins of Samghabhadra's monastery.

Hwui Li, a contemporary of Hsüan-tsang, preserved the names of some masters active in Kashmir during the seventh century: the Sarvāstivādin masters Sugatamitra and Vasumitra; the Mahāsāmghika masters Sūryadeva and Jinatrata,

---

1. B. N. Chaudhury, *Buddhist Centers in Ancient India*, p. 131.

and two Mahāyāna masters, Viśuddhasiṁha and Jina-bandhu. Hsüan-tsang himself resided in the Nāgaradhana Monastery for two years, where he studied Abhidharma with the Sarvāstivādin master Candravarma.

Further Readings

Hwui Li. *Life of Hiuen-T'siang*, translated by Samuel Beal, pp. 68–72.

Chaudhury, Binayendra Nath. *Buddhist Centres in Ancient India*, pp. 127–141.

Hsüan-tsang. *Si-Yu-Ki: Buddhist Records of the Western World*, pp. 148–164.

Naudou, Jean. *Buddhists of Kashmir*, p. 1–43.

Rockhill, W. Woodville. *Life of the Buddha and the Early History of His Order*, pp. 167–170.

Beginning of
Buddhist Philosophy

*All things have the nature of mind. Mind is
the chief and takes the lead. If the mind is clear,
whatever you do or say will bring happiness
that will follow you like your shadow.*

—*Dhammapada*

For all Buddhist schools the heart of the teaching has
always been the Buddha's word (Āgama). As the schools
proliferated and established centers throughout India in the
centuries after the Parinirvāṇa, the masters of all traditions
were universally concerned with preserving the purity of the
Buddha's teachings. At the time of the First Council, the
teachings had been classified into collections (piṭaka); while
most schools recognized three collections, the Vinaya, Sūtra,
and Mātṛka (Abhidharma), some communities held to a two-
fold division of the Buddhadharma into Vinayapiṭaka and
Sūtrapiṭaka; they preserved the Mātṛka, the more concise
and technical teachings, in the Sūtrapiṭaka without making
the Mātṛka a separate collection.

The Mātṛka consisted of the Buddha's seed statements on topics such as the nature of existence, mind, and causality, topics meant to be considered deeply and elaborated upon through meditation experience. As the bhikṣus followed the Buddha's advice to seek their salvation with diligence, they saw more clearly the need to cultivate these teachings.

Śāriputra, the Buddha's disciple renowned for his intellect, was the first to penetrate the meaning of the Mātṛkas; others arose to follow in his footsteps. Later, as Buddhist communities formed throughout India, each school tended to develop its own form of Abhidharma in the course of systematizing its specific doctrines. While not all schools recognized a separate Abhidharma piṭaka, the bhikṣus of some schools began to specialize in the study and practice of Abhidharma.

The Abhidharma appears to have been developed most strongly within the Sthavira and Sarvāstivādin traditions, both of which maintained an Abhidharmapiṭaka composed of seven texts. The Sthavira, the precursor of the modern Theravādin school, traditionally ascribed their seven Abhidharma texts to the Buddha and included them in the Pāli Tipiṭaka. In the order they were arranged by the fifth-century scholar Buddhaghosa, the Theravādin Abhidharma texts are: Dhammasaṅgaṇi (Buddhist Psychological Ethics), Vibhaṅga (The Book of Analysis), Kathāvatthu (Points of Controversy), the Puggalapaññati (Description of Human Types), Dhātukathā (Discourse on Elements), Yamaka (The Book of Pairs), and Paṭṭhāna (Conditional Relations).

The Sarvāstivādins considered the seven texts to be extended versions of the very concise Mātṛka, in full accord with the Buddha's teachings. However, unlike the Sthaviras, they attributed their seven Abhidharma texts to the specific persons who had compiled or developed them. Of these seven Abhidharma texts, the Jñānaprasthāna by Kātyāyanīputra summarized and systematized Sarvāstivādin doctrines and established the identity of the Sarvāstivādins as a distinct school. This treatise was considered the body or the main Abhidharma text, while the remaining six Abhidharma texts became known as the pada or feet. According to Yaśomitra's Sphuṭārtha-abhidharmakoṣavyākhyā (NE 4092), the six pada texts and their authors are the Prakaraṇapada, by Vasumitra; Vijñānakāya, by Devasarman; the Dharma-skandha, by Śāriputra; Prajñaptiśāstra, by Maudgalyāyana; the Dhātukāya, by Pūrṇa, and the Saṁgītiparyāya, composed by Mahākausthila.[1]

The earliest Sthavirin Abhidharma commentaries were the Aṭṭhakathās written in Sinhalese in the first and second centuries C.E.; next to appear were the works of the Indian masters Buddhaghosa, Buddhadatta, and Dharmapāla, who lived during the fifth century C.E. Buddhaghosa's Visuddhi-magga, The Path of Purification, is the most succinct statement of the Abhidharma of the Mahāvihāra school, which became dominant in Theravāda Buddhism. Since the Sthavira's development as a school mainly occurred in Śrī Laṅkā, in relative isolation from the other early schools, the Sthavira Abhidharma appears to have had little influence on the mainland traditions.

The Sarvāstivādins developed the Abhidharma early on in three major stages: They drew upon the Sūtras to clarify topics to be explicated, defined the content of Abhidharma, and forged the Abhidharma into a system and a path to realization. Generally speaking, the seven Sarvāstivādin Abhidharma texts reflect these three stages: the Saṁgīti-paryāya, Dharmaskandha, and Prajñapti, which are ascribed to the Buddha's disciples, belong to the earliest stage; the Vijñānakāya and Dhātukāya, which define the content of the

---

1. The Chinese translations of all seven Sarvāstivādin Abhidharma texts are preserved in a special supplement to the Nyingma Edition, texts 5089–5095, together with the Mahāvibhāṣā, text 5096. Only one text, the Prajñaptiśāstra, is preserved in Tibetan (NE 4086–88). According to Hirakawa (p.132), the Chinese Prajñaptiśāstra is a partial translation; the Tibetan translation includes all three sections of this text. (The Chinese tradition lists the compilers of the seven Abhidharma texts differently.)

Abhidharma, belong to the intermediate stage; and the Prakaraṇa and the Jñānaprasthāna, which systematize the Abhidharma, belong to the third stage.

Many Sarvāstivādin masters were attracted to the study of Abhidharma through their efforts to penetrate the implications of the Buddha's teachings on impermanence, the absence of self, and the nature of mind and reality. Directing their thoughts and their meditation towards analysis of these teachings, they began to chart their discernments. This emphasis on research and scholarship, pursued for roughly two hundred years, gave rise to a school of commentators that specialized in explicating Abhidharma. At some point these commentators became known as Vaibhāṣikas.

By the first century C.E., when the Sarvāstivādins had elaborated upon the Buddha's teachings concerning existence and were working out systems of classification, doctrinal differences began to emerge between the Sarvāstivādins of Kashmir and Gandhāra, with the Kashmiris maintaining the more conservative views.

At the time of King Kaniṣka, the need to consider differing views and arrive at true knowledge led to the compilation known as the Mahāvibhāṣa, The Great Explication. The Mahāvibhāṣa seems to have begun as a definitive commentary on the Jñānaprasthāna. It has been suggested, however, that the compilation of the Mahāvibhāṣa, which grew into a gigantic compendium of Abhidharma, may have continued over several centuries until it received its final form in the third century C.E.[2] Thus it is likely that work on the Mahāvibhāṣa was already in progress in the late first or early second century C.E., when King Kaniṣka convened a council of Buddhist masters.

The Mahāvibhāṣa, which survives today in Chinese translation (Taishō 1545, two hundred fascicles in length), bears witness to an immense amount of scholarship invested in

---

2. Hirakawa Akira, *A History of Indian Buddhism*, p. 135.

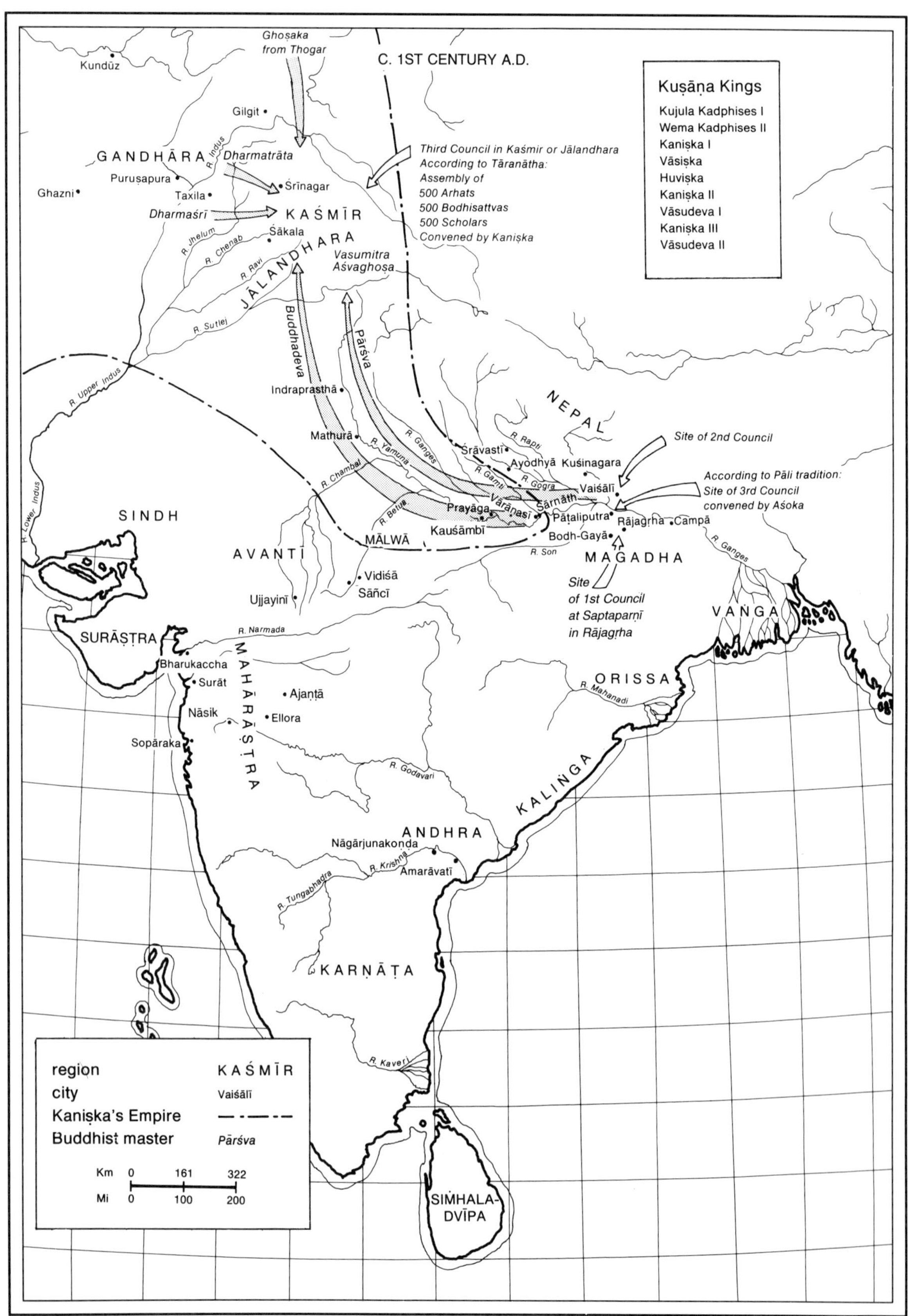

King Kaniṣka convened Arhats and Bodhisattvas to review the Buddhist doctrines.

detailing the views of all schools, including doctrines of non-Buddhist philosophers. The Chinese tradition attributes its compilation to the five hundred Great Arhats assembled at Kaniṣka's council. Although the Mahāvibhāṣa is strongly oriented toward the Sarvāstivādin view, the most developed analytical thought of that time, it is also the most complete encyclopedia of the doctrines of all the Śrāvaka schools (those who rely on the First Turning teachings).

The Council of King Kaniṣka

Hsüan-tsang relates that King Kaniṣka attained the throne of Gandhāra four hundred years after the Buddha's Parinirvāṇa; modern research tends to place Kaniṣka toward the end of the first century C.E., or even somewhat later. This powerful Kuṣāṇa ruler, whose empire stretched beyond Mathurā on the east and the valley of the Oxus River on the west, took a strong interest in the Buddha's teachings.

According to Hsüan-tsang (who follows the account of Paramārtha, a sixth-century master and translator from Ujjayinī), King Kaniṣka invited a monk to preach the Dharma at the royal palace every day. Observing differences in view amongst the Buddhist schools, he became afflicted with doubt. To resolve these doubts and ascertain the true teaching, the king convened a great assembly of Buddhist masters. Hsüan-tsang relates that the Sarvāstivādin Arhat Kātyāyanīputra figured prominently in implementing the king's directive, and that the council was held in Kashmir. After the council was over, the king went back to his capital at Peshāwar (Puruṣapura) in Gandhāra.

Hsüan-tsang describes the multitude that assembled for the council as "numerous as the stars" and relates that the king considered this assembly too unwieldy to accomplish the task he had set to them. Although the king requested that only those who were Arhats should remain, the congregation was still far too large. Three times more the king narrowed requirements for attendance, until there were 499 Arhats present. After the assembly agreed to hold the council at a place of the king's choosing, the king built a monastery specifically for this council.

Tāranātha cites two traditions as to the site of the council, one naming the Karṇikavana Monastery in Kashmir, and the other citing the Kuvana Monastery in Jālandhara, a northwestern Indian province. Dudjom Rinpoche mentions that many places are named as the council's location, including the Kusumakūṭārāma in Jālandhara, the Kuvana Monastery in Kashmir, and Śrāvastī, located in the Madhyadeśa (*The Nyingma School of Tibetan Buddhism* I:430).

Both Tāranātha and 'Gos Lo-tsā-ba (the fifteenth-century Tibetan author of the *Blue Annals*), state that the council included Bodhisattvas and scholars as well as Arhats. According to 'Gos Lo-tsā-ba, the council included five hundred Arhats with Pārśva at their head, four hundred bhaṭṭārakas (scholars) led by Vasumitra, and five hundred Bodhisattvas. Tāranātha mentions a tradition that lists five hundred each of Arhats, Bodhisattvas, and scholars for a total of fifteen hundred masters but considers that it is safer to follow the Śrāvaka tradition of five hundred Arhats and five thousand great scholars. Among the scholars assembled, Tāranātha specifically mentions Ghoṣaka from Thogar, Dharmaśrī from Gandhāra, and the Arhat Pārśva and Buddhadeva from the Madhyadeśa.

Hsüan-tsang relates that just before the assembly was to convene, the Arhats barred the venerable Vasumitra from joining the council on the grounds that Vasumitra was still subject to the kleśas (and therefore was not an Arhat). Vasumitra replied that his mind was directed toward becoming a Buddha; the condition of an Arhat was irrelevant to his purpose, but if Arhatship was necessary to enter the assembly, he would become an Arhat before the ball he was holding could fall to the ground. When Vasumitra released the ball, a deva halted the ball in mid-air and asked why Vasumitra sought this small result when he was capable of attaining Buddhahood. Seeing this, the Arhats apologized to Vasu-mitra and made him the head of the assembly. However, according to Hsüan-tsang, Pārśva presided over the meeting. (Tāranātha, p. 92, describes Pārśva as an Arhat "who had reached the limit of scriptural knowledge.")

Accomplishments of Kaniṣka's Council

As mentioned in the previous chapter, the council con-vened at King Kaniṣka's command put to rest long-standing controversies over the status of the Arhat and validated all the Buddhist schools as representing the Buddha's teaching. This council also attracted attention to the place of scholar-ship in Buddhism; it drew upon the skills of bhaṭṭārakas, learned masters who were not necessarily Arhats, and added momentum to intellectual currents already stirring within the northern Buddhist schools.

According to Hsüan-tsang, who cites the Chinese tradi-tion, the primary purpose of the assembly was to examine the entire Buddhadharma and explain all aspects of its teachings. To this purpose, a group of five hundred masters composed an Upadeśa śāstra in one hundred thousand stan-zas to explicate the Sūtrapiṭaka, a Vinaya-vibhāṣa śāstra in a hundred-thousand stanzas on the Vinaya Piṭaka, and an Abhidharma-vibhāṣa śāstra in a hundred thousand stanzas on the Abhidharma-piṭaka. ". . . from the deepest to the smallest question, they examined all, explaining all minute expressions, so that their work has become universally known and is the resource of all students who have followed them." (Hsüan-tsang I:155)

Tāranātha also emphasizes the extent of this council's efforts: "All those assembled jointly purified the Dharma; they codified the Vinaya and the parts of the Sūtrapiṭaka and Abhidharmapiṭaka which were not yet codified. The portions which were already codified were revised." (Tāranātha, p. 95)

Transcription of the Śāstras

Paramārtha relates that Aśvaghoṣa, the author of the Buddhacarita, was asked to edit the Vinaya, Sūtra, and Abhidharma śāstras and to express them in a sophisticated literary form. According to Hsüan-tsang, King Kaniṣka ordered these śāstras to be engraved on sheets of red copper and had the copper sheets placed in a stone receptacle; after he sealed the receptacle, he built a stūpa and enshrined the sheets within it. The king commanded the yakṣas to protect the area and prevent heretics from removing the śāstras but allowed those who lived in that region to study them.

Thus, traditional descriptions of this council point to the production of written commentaries and possibly to the compilation of a written Canon. Bu-ston, in speaking of this council, relates that after the teachings were recited, the word of the Buddha was then transcribed; until that time the teachings had been recited from memory, and no written texts existed.

However, Bu-ston also cites the Mañjuśrī-mūlatantra, which prophesied that the word of the Buddha would be transcribed during the reign of Upa, son of Ajātaśatru. He goes on to cite the Vimalaprabha, which mentions that the teachings of all three vehicles were written down after the Buddha's Parinirvāṇa. Dudjom Rinpoche, in *The Nyingma School of Tibetan Buddhism* (I:430), clearly states that the Vinayapiṭaka was transcribed at this council for the first time, as were the parts of the Sūtra- and Abhidharma-piṭakas not previously committed to writing. "This was the purpose of the Third (Kaniṣka's) Council."

Although the council included masters of different traditions and examined the views of all schools, the Sarvāstivādins were by far the most numerous and, by most accounts, the best represented. Most authorities agree that whatever writings were produced as a result of this council, the language used was most likely Sanskrit, the language of choice among the Sarvāstivādin schools.

The Sanskrit Tripiṭaka

It is now generally accepted on the basis of manuscript evidence that the Sarvāstivādins possessed a written Tripiṭaka in Sanskrit, ranging from a highly Prākritized mixed Sanskrit to a form closer to the classical Sanskrit used by such writers as Aśvaghoṣa, a master of literary style. Through the activities of Sarvāstivādin bhikṣus, the Tripiṭaka texts were carried throughout Central Asia and became well-known in China. As a result, although only fragments of the Sarvāstivādin Canon survive in Sanskrit, a large number of Sarvāstivādin texts are preserved in Chinese: all the Āgamas (Sūtras) and Vinaya, as well as the Vinaya-vibhāṣa, translated between the fourth and fifth centuries; one section of the Prakaraṇapada and an Abhidharma-vibhāṣa, translated in the fifth century; and the remaining Abhidharma texts (including the Mahāvibhāṣa), which Hsüan-tsang himself brought to China and translated in the seventh century.

Vaibhāṣika: Foundation of Buddhist Philosophy

After the council of Kaniṣka, the history of Buddhist doctrine in India centers on the formation of four philosophical schools: the Vaibhāṣika and Sautrāntika, which developed from the Śrāvaka traditions of Kashmir and Gandhāra, and the Yogācāra and Madhyamaka, which arose from within the Mahāyāna. The Vaibhāṣikas grew out of the Sarvāstivādin traditions of Kashmir; they took their name from the word vibhāṣa, meaning commentary or explication. Their doctrines and practice were grounded on the seven fundamental Sarvāstivādin Abhidharma texts and the Mahāvibhāṣa, the Great Explication. The first Buddhist school to systematically analyze the nature of existence, the Vaibhāṣikas provided the essential foundation for further analyses. They identified fifty-one mental events, a classification basic to Buddhist psychology, and categorized them into those that supported liberation, those that led to confusion and pain, and those that were neutral. These and other lines of inquiry provided a basis for the growth of insight into the nature of mind, reality, experience, and causality.

Once the Vaibhāṣikas began to express their analyses and theories in technical writings known as śāstras, their ideas could be further investigated, analyzed, and adjusted to guard against misinterpretation. After the Mahāvibhāṣa was completed, Vaibhāṣika scholars began to prepare shorter summaries to facilitate the study and memorization of key Abhidharma topics. The most acclaimed of such summaries, the Abhidharmakoṣa, was prepared in the late fourth century by Vasubandhu, brother of Asaṅga and a native of Gandhāra, who went to great lengths to master the Vaibhāṣika doctrines. Through Vasubandhu's efforts, the Vaibhāṣika Abhidharma became widely known throughout northern India.

The Vaibhāṣika emphasis on the Abhidharma śāstras was not universally shared by all Sarvāstivādin scholars. Some turned away from the Vaibhāṣika concentration on the Abhidharma compilations and chose to rely solely on the Buddha's direct teachings as preserved in the Sūtras. For this they became known as Sautrāntikas, Those Who Follow the Sūtras. Since few of their writings have been preserved and their doctrines are expressed mainly in the writings of other schools, very little is actually known of the Sautrāntikas as a whole. However, it is clear that some masters of this tradition were keenly interested in critiquing the Vaibhāṣika's central doctrines.

Dharmatrāta, Buddhadeva, and Ghoṣaka were probably the first scholars to question the Vaibhāṣika view of existence. Their views, rejected in the Mahāvibhāṣa, were continued by scholars of the Sautrāntika school. The Sautrāntikas continued their inquiry through the second and third centuries, when the masters Śrīlāta and Kumāralāta began to formulate the Sautrāntika insights into a system.

By the fourth century, in the person of Vasubandhu, the Sautrāntika approach engaged the Vaibhāṣika system in a productive dialogue. In presenting the Sautrāntika view of the Vaibhāṣika system, Vasubandhu's commentary (Bhāṣya) on the Abhidharmakoṣa (his own work), exemplifies how Buddhist philosophy began to grow in a vigorous progression of investigations, analyses, and critiques, penetrating ever more deeply into the profound depth of the Buddha's teachings and the nature of mind and existence.

Having pointed out the difficulties in the Vaibhāṣika's view of reality, the Sautrāntikas probed deeper into the nature of mind and consciousness. Questions concerning how we know came to the fore, clarifying the central importance of ascertaining the proofs of valid knowledge and guarding against error. In addressing these questions, the Sautrāntika inquiries gave rise to a new science of knowledge and sophisticated systems of logic. Within the Mahāyāna traditions, the Cittamātra/Vijñānavāda and Mādhyamika schools went more deeply still. The Cittamātra/Vijñānavādins recast the Abhidharma in the light of śūnyatā, the essential openness of existence, and developed a more sophisticated understanding of mind and consciousness. In concentrating on śūnyatā, negating all statements and positions, Mādhyamikans held an unwavering mirror to the central experience of enlightenment.

The development of Buddhist philosophy was a natural outcome of centuries of realization and attempts at expressing this realization. From the outset, the Buddha had instructed his disciples to hold up his teachings to the light of reason, practice them with diligence, and to discard what was proven not to accord with reality. The rise of the great philosophical traditions, each building upon the other, adhering to what proved valid and discarding what was disproved, was fully attuned to the Buddha's directive.

Takṣaśilā, Center of Learning

Takṣaśilā, located just south of Kashmir on the main route linking Central India with Bactria and Central Asia,

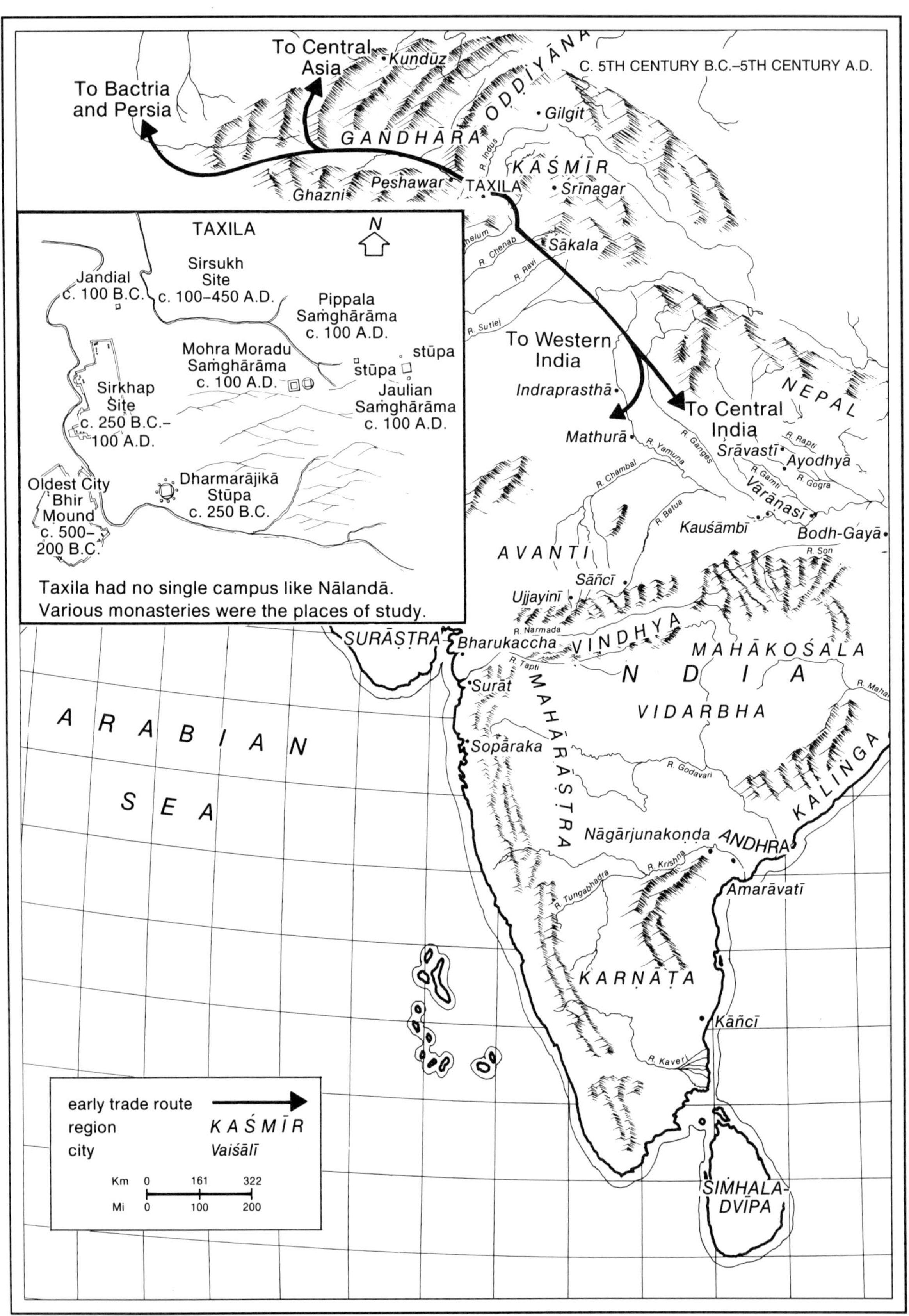

Takṣaśilā (Taxila) became an early center for the study of Buddhism.

was the traditional capital of Gandhāra and an important crossroads of the ancient world. By the time of Aśoka's grandfather, Candragupta Maurya, Takṣaśilā was already a respected center of learning, a place where the sons of ministers and kings were sent to complete their education in the Vedas, grammar, medicine, and the arts.

Candragupta Maurya brought Takṣaśilā into his empire; he linked it by roads to his capital at Pāṭaliputra and connected it to routes traversing the Indus to Kapiśa. From Kapiśa the road led west to Bactria, where it connected with ancient routes to the Mediterranean Sea. Under Aśoka's rule, Takṣaśilā became a major Buddhist center, home to the Sarvāstivādin, Kāśyapīya, Mahīśāsaka, and Bahuśrutīya traditions. Aśoka supported the growth of Buddhism in this important corner of his kingdom; he built the majestic Dharmarājika Stūpa and, next to it, a monastery with a large commemorative stone pillar.

Around 112 B.C.E., with the opening of the Silk Route, the major trade route linking China with Mesopotamia, Takṣaśilā became a prosperous center of commerce. In succeeding centuries, during the reign of the Śakas, Parthians, and Kuṣāṇas, Buddhist monasteries at Takṣaśilā attracted students from India and Central Asia. Linguistic skills were honed by exposure to the languages of the Parthians, Persians, Sogdians, Khotanese, and various Indian languages that commingled in this thriving cosmopolitan center. As the Dharma was carried through the northwest into Central Asia and established in the oasis states circling the Taklamakan basin, the monasteries of Takṣaśilā grew in importance as centers of learning.

Although Takṣaśilā is often referred to as a university, it had no central campus or unified curriculum. Knowledge was conveyed between master and student on an individual basis and not in an assembly hall setting. Students would go to different monasteries for different types of instruction. It was possible for a student to complete a full range of classi-

Takṣaśilā Timeline

500–400 B.C.E.*	Brahmins, princes, physicians from all regions of India study the Vedas and classical sciences.
275 B.C.E.	Aśoka serves as viceroy under King Bindusāra.
260 B.C.E.	King Aśoka builds the Dharmarājika Stūpa.
170–150 B.C.E.	Bactrian Greeks rebuild Takṣaśilā (Sirkap site).
100 B.C.E.–100 C.E.	Buddhist temple built near the palace in Sirkap. Additions made to Dharmarājika Stūpa.
40 C.E.	Parthian King Gondophares rules in Sirkap. St. Thomas visits his court.
100 C.E.	Kuṣāṇas in Takṣaśilā (Sirsukh). Buddhist monasteries Mohra Moradu, Pippala, and Jaulian built. Sarvāstivādins and Kāśyapīyas active in Takṣaśilā.
400 C.E.	Dharmarājika Stūpa refinished, small shrines and two colossal Buddha statues added. Large monastery built near Dharmarājika. Additions made at Pippala and Jaulian.
450 C.E.	Takṣaśilā destroyed by the Huns.

*All dates are approximate.

cal Vedic studies here, then enter one of the Buddhist orders; after a period of basic instruction, a student could go to teachers at the various Buddhist centers and attain mastery in the Śrāvakapiṭaka, the collection of teachings maintained by the eighteen schools.

When Fa-hien passed through Takṣaśilā in the early fifth century, Buddhism was flourishing throughout Gandhāra. But in the latter part of the fifth century, the whole region was ravaged by the Hephthalite Huns. The date of the Hun invasion was established by the Chinese pilgrim Sung-yun, who recorded in 520 C.E. that Gandhāra had been devastated by the Ye-tha (Hephthalites) two generations before. The destruction wrought by the Huns was thorough; although Buddhism experienced a strong revival of scholastic traditions under the Kārkoṭa kings of Kashmir, Takṣaśilā never regained prominence as a Buddhist educational center.

Further Readings

Banerjee, A. C. *Sarvāstivāda Literature*, pp. 51–75.

Bu-ston. *History of Buddhism*, pp. 96–98.

Dudjom Rinpoche. *The Nyingma School of Tibetan Buddhism*, volume I, pp. 429–430.

Guenther, Herbert V. *Buddhist Philosophy in Theory and Practice*, pp. 1–154.

Hirakawa Akira. *A History of Indian Buddhism from Śākyamuni to Early Mahāyāna*, pp. 127–138.

Hsüan-tsang. *Si-Yu-Ki: Buddhist Records of the Western World*, pp. 151–156.

Tāranātha. *History of Buddhism in India*, pp. 91–95.

Webb, Russell, ed. *An Analysis of the Pali Canon.*

Part Four

Mahāyāna

Rise of the Mahāyāna

May I work for the welfare of all beings
as long as the lands and the roads exist
in the ten directions, relieving anxiety,
dispelling pain, and assisting all beings
on the six paths of transmigratory existence.
    —*Samantabhadra-praṇidhāna*

During the Buddha's lifetime, many of his disciples, following the injunction to "strive for liberation with diligence," were able to achieve the purity of body and mind necessary to join the ranks of the Arhats. But when the Buddha introduced the profound Prajñāpāramitā, the doctrine of śūnyatā and the path of the Great Bodhisattvas, the Saddharmapuṇḍarīka-sūtra records that hundreds of Arhats fled in terror, unable to cope with the implications inherent in these teachings. Yet the teachings of śūnyatā and the path of the Bodhisattva held great significance for the future of Buddhism.

In time, many of the Śrāvakas would extend the boundaries of their realization. Having broken through to a greater vision and understanding, they would awaken the aspiration to become fully enlightened Buddhas. They would set aside all thought of self and resolve to walk the path of the Bodhisattva; they would open heart and mind to the full extent of suffering in the world and dedicate their efforts to the salvation of all sentient beings. Through their words and actions they would demonstrate the depth and breadth of the Buddha's teachings and bring the blessings of the Mahāyāna, the Great Vehicle to enlightenment, into clear view.

For followers of the Dharma, the Mahāyāna brought into focus a wider vision of path and goal. Its purview embraced the monasticism of the Śrāvakas and reached out to encompass the lay community, engendering the notion of universal responsibility: that salvation was only possible through ensuring the salvation of others. With this understanding, the compassionate way to strive for liberation with diligence was to facilitate the enlightenment of all living beings. From the perspective of the Mahāyāna, both the Śrāvakayāna (Vehicle of the Listeners) and the Pratyekabuddhayāna (Vehicle of the Self-Enlightened), became known as the Hīnayāna, the Small Vehicle.

Roots of the Mahāyāna

As there was no clear schism that created a distinct Mahāyāna school, the origins of the Mahāyāna have eluded modern scholars, who tend to look for its roots among the eighteen early schools. Yet no one school—not even the Mahāsāṁghikas, the most often suggested—appears to have transformed itself into a Mahāyāna school as such. The Mahāyāna that emerged between the first and second centuries C.E. disseminated teachings shared by many of the early schools. It may be more accurate to consider that openness to the Mahāyāna view developed within the Buddhist traditions as a natural unfolding of spiritual capacities, and only

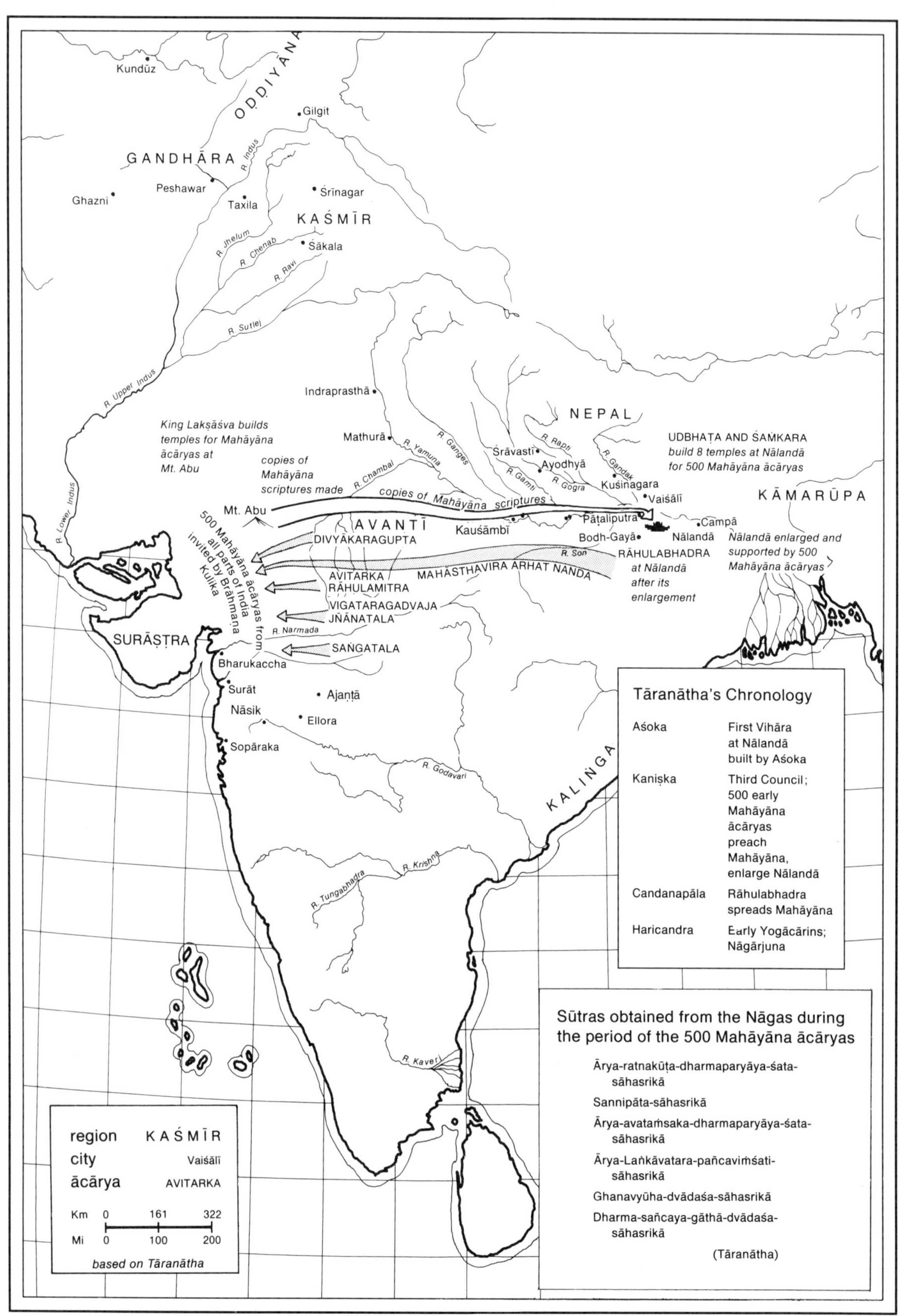

Following King Kaniṣka's council, Bodhisattvas propagated the Mahāyāna.

later took on its distinctive identity. As late as the seventh century, monks of both the Mahāyāna and Śrāvakayāna traditions lived in the same monasteries and followed the same basic Vinaya rules. The traveler Hsüan-tsang distinguished the traditions on one basis only: Followers of the Hīnayāna (Śrāvakayāna) studied the Sūtras of the First Turning, and adherents of the Mahāyāna studied the scriptures of all three turnings.

According to Tāranātha, the first Mahāyāna Sūtra reappeared in the world during the reign of King Kaniṣka, when Mahāpadma was ruling in Magadha. At that time, the Bodhisattva Mañjuśrī, in the guise of a monk, visited the palace of Candrarakṣita, king of Oḍivisa (Orissa), preached the Mahāyāna doctrines, and left at the palace a copy of the Aṣṭasāhasrikā-prajñāpāramitā-sūtra (NE 12).

Tāranātha also relates that monks who had attained the stage of anutpattikadharma-kṣānti presented Mahāyāna teachings at the council convened by King Kaniṣka to review the doctrines of all the Buddhist schools. This was the council variously said to have been held in Kashmir or in Jālandhara, a province south of Kashmir proper, known in the Tibetan tradition as the Third Council and to many Western scholars as the Fourth Council. The conservative Arhats and scholars from the different schools are said to have noted these differences on points of doctrine, but, considering that only a few masters propounded these teachings, refrained from contesting them at that time.

Although King Kaniṣka passed away some time after the council, his successors continued to support the Sangha, and the Mahāyāna views gradually became more widely known and accepted. Among the prominent proponents of Mahāyāna views, Tāranātha mentions the great Sthavirin Arhat named Nanda who was a native of Aṅga, the region east of Magadha. Accounts of Nanda's teaching reached the Brahmin Kulika in Surāṣṭra, a region far to the west. Eager to learn more of the Mahāyāna, Kulika invited Nanda to his homeland to preach the Mahāyāna teachings.

Throughout India there now appeared, seemingly all at once, hundreds of masters able to comprehend the view of the Mahāyāna. The great Bodhisattvas who had preserved the teachings since the time of the Buddha—Maitreya, Avalokiteśvara, Guhyapati, Mañjuśrī, and others—now taught the most advanced of this "new" Sangha.

Thus the masters Avitarka, Vigatarāgadvaja, Divyākaragupta, Rāhulamitra, Jñānatala, Saṅgatala, and others—five hundred in all—attained the samādhi known as dharma-śrota-anugata, which opened their minds to the profound meaning of the Buddhadharma, and they began to disseminate the Mahāyāna doctrines themselves. Then Mahāyāna Sūtras, including the Ratnakūṭa (NE 45–93), the Sannipāta-sāhasrikā, the Avataṁsaka (NE 44), Laṅkāvatāra (NE 107), Ghanavyūha (NE 110), and the Dharmasaṁcaya-gāthā were released from the realms of the nāgas, gods, gandharvas, and rākṣasas and came into the possession of these Mahāyāna masters.

According to Tāranātha, the Brahmin Kulika of Surāṣṭra, the patron of the Arhat Nanda, invited the five hundred Mahāyāna masters to his home in western India. Then Lakṣāśva, king of that land, delighted that so many masters had come to his realm, built five hundred temples on top of mount Abu, one for each of the five hundred teachers. The king had five hundred of his best qualified people ordained for the purpose of studying and realizing the Mahāyāna teachings. Soon there were fifteen hundred Mahāyāna followers assembled on Mount Abu: the five hundred teachers, five hundred listeners who had come with them, and the five hundred former attendants of the king. Tāranātha relates that the king had the Mahāyāna Sūtras written down and had copies made for donating to all the monks.

Tāranātha emphasizes that all of these Mahāyāna practitioners had been originally ordained within the eighteen Śrāvaka schools, and that even though they were now practicing different forms of meditation, they continued to live among the Śrāvakas. As the views and practices of the Mahāyāna became better known, the Śrāvakas who were unable to comprehend the Mahāyāna teachings began to express concern that the Mahāyāna teachings did not accord with the Buddha's teaching. But by that time the Mahāyāna had awakened great confidence in the hearts of those who had realized its scope and depth. Although the Śrāvakas were far more numerous than the Mahāyāna practitioners, those who studied the Mahāyāna were not disturbed by the Śrāvakas' doubts.

Tāranātha writes that about this time in Magadha the Mahāyāna doctrines became popularized by two brothers, Udbhaṭasiddhisvāmin and Śaṁkarapati, who had studied the philosophy of the Buddhists and non-Buddhists alike. After extensive consideration, both realized that only the Buddha's teachings transcended the realm of saṁsāra, and they concentrated on mastering the Dharma. Udbhaṭa composed the Viśeṣa-stava (NE 1109) and Śaṁkarapati the Devātī-śaya-stotra (NE 1112) to clarify the differences between Buddhist and non-Buddhist philosophies. Since these works were written in verse, they were easily recited as songs, and they became widely known "from the marketplace up to the king's palace" (Tāranātha, p. 101).

The two brothers supported both the Śrāvakas and the Mahāyānists; they provided sustenance for five hundred Śrāvakas at Bodh Gayā and five hundred followers of the Mahāyāna at Nālandā, the birthplace of Śāriputra and the place where the great Arhat entered nirvāṇa together with eighty thousand Arhats. Although Tāranātha does not specifically say that these five hundred Mahāyāna teachers were the same as those who assembled on Mt. Abu, he does say that Avitarka, one of the original five hundred, was at Nālandā, and it is likely that many of the five hundred came from Mt. Abu to Nālandā to establish a center in the heartland of the Dharma.

Nālandā: First Home of the Mahāyāna

In the time of Śāriputra, Nālandā was a small settlement of Brahmin families located a few miles from Rājagṛha, the capital of Magadha. After the capital was moved to Pāṭaliputra sometime around the fourth century B.C.E., the political importance of Rājagṛha declined, and many of its inhabitants moved away. When the capital moved, Nālandā must have also declined, for Tāranātha mentions that the settlement there was in ruins at the time of Aśoka; only the stūpa honoring Śāriputra remained untouched. When Aśoka visited Nālandā on his pilgrimage to the holy places, he worshipped at the stūpa and built a temple nearby.

In selecting an appropriate location for their center, the first five hundred Mahāyāna masters had narrowed their choice to two sites: the birthplace of Śāriputra, the disciple foremost in intellectual accomplishment, and the birthplace of Maudgalyāyana, the disciple foremost in psychic attainments. While both sites had great appeal, through meditation the Mahāyāna masters came to know that if they chose Śāriputra's birthplace, the Mahāyāna would be broadly transmitted, and if they made Maudgalyāyana's birthplace their center, the Mahāyāna would become very powerful for a time, but its doctrine would not spread widely. In light of the Mahāyāna's great benefit to beings, the masters chose as their center Śāriputra's birthplace in Nālandā, from which the doctrine of the Great Vehicle would spread throughout the known world.

Thus, on the site where Aśoka had built Nālandā's first temple, Udbhaṭa and Śaṁkarapati, the two brothers greatly learned in philosophy, built eight new temples for the five hundred Mahāyāna masters. From the outset, Nālandā, with its central location, its temples, its collection of Mahāyāna teachings, and its nucleus of five hundred teachers, attracted India's outstanding intellects. The scholar Rāhulabhadra came to Nālandā in Avitarka's lifetime, where he was ordained by either the bhaṭṭāraka Rāhulaprabha or by the bhaṭṭāraka Kṛṣṇa (whom Tāranātha states is not the same as the Patriarch Kṛṣṇa).

Rāhulabhadra, who held the Vinaya lineage which had come down directly from the Buddha through Śāriputra and Rāhula, mastered the texts of the Śrāvakas, then heard the Mahāyāna doctrines from Avitarka and other masters. Excelling in study and exposition of the Dharma, Rāhulabhadra eventually became the abbot of Nālandā. His greatest disciple was Nāgārjuna, the foremost of those who studied the Mahāyāna Sūtras and penetrated the meaning of śūnyatā.

According to Tāranātha, this was the period when King Candanapāla, a patron of the Buddhist Sangha, began his long rule in the western province of Aparāntaka. Visukalpa was king of Oḍvisa (Orissa), and Haricandra, said to have been a siddha, an accomplished Buddhist yogin, was king of Bengal. In Kuru, in Central India, the Brahmin Dharmika sponsored the building of 108 Mahāyāna temples, and in Hastināpura, the Brahmin Vīrya established 108 centers for the Vinaya. Around this time the bhaṭṭāraka Suviṣṇu established 108 temples at Nālandā dedicated to propagating the Abhidharma.

Foundations of Mahāyāna Philosophy

Tāranātha refers to eight great masters of the Madhyama, the Middle Way, who lived during Kaniṣka's reign, among whom were Kamalagarbha and Ghanasa. Tāranātha also mentions five hundred masters of Yogācāra who lived at this time, three of whom—Nanda, Paramasena, and Samyaksatya—wrote treatises "adhering to the standpoint of Yogācāra." Tāranātha states that these three became known in the later Mahāyāna tradition as the early Yogācārins, to distinguish them from the later Yogācārins, who based their study and practice on the teachings transmitted by Maitreya and Asaṅga.

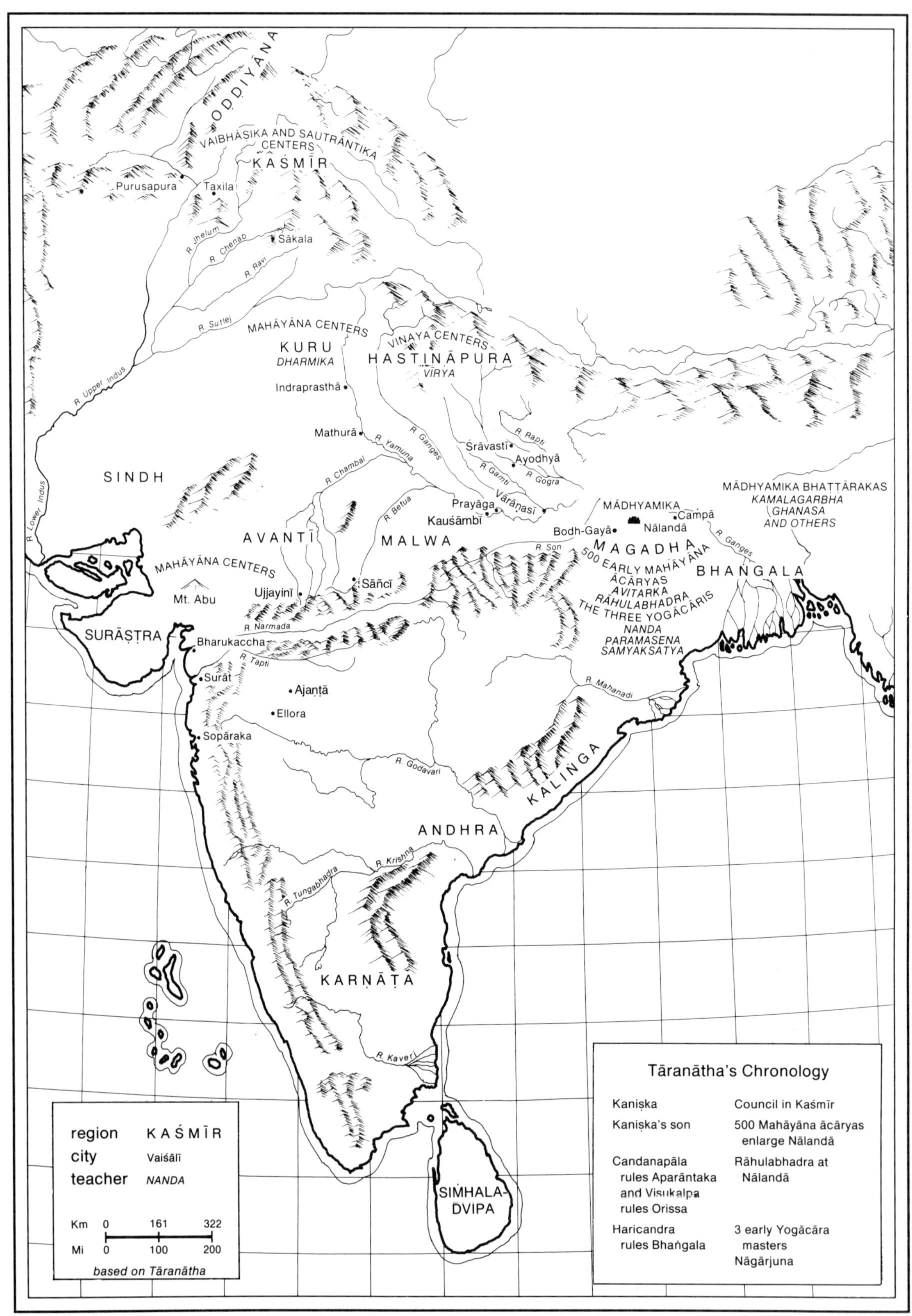

Major centers of philosophical activity in the centuries after King Kaniṣka

The Mahāyāna doctrines grew increasingly popular with the Sangha as treatises and commentaries systematized and clarified their profound and vast meaning. As understanding of the Mahāyāna increased, more Mahāyāna Sūtras were discovered and brought to Nālandā for study. Among these Sūtras was the Mahāsannipāta-dharmaparyāya, an extensive teaching in one thousand chapters. Only a portion of this Sūtra survives today in Tibetan translation (NE 230).

According to Tāranātha, it was at this time that Puṣyamitra became king of Magadha and disrupted Buddhist activities as far west as Jālandhara. Nāgārjuna left Nālandā to teach in the south of India, where he converted King Udayana. Little is known of Nālandā during Puṣyamitra's reign. However the kings who succeeded Puṣyamitra supported the Dharma, and it soon regained its momentum in Magadha.

Tāranātha mentions the Sthavira Sambhūti, who propagated the Śrāvakapiṭakas extensively and established sixty Dharma centers in Magadha at this time. In Vaṅga, in the east, the Brahmin Kāśījāta provided support for sixty-four Dharma teachers and their students to help heal the damage to the Dharma. At Nālandā, the masters who followed the Mahāyāna teachings gradually developed the monastery into the leading educational center of all of northern India.

While it is difficult to establish exact dates important to early Mahāyāna history, Mahāyāna Sūtras were being disseminated on the northwestern borders of India at least by the middle of the second century C.E.. The Kuṣāṇa monk Lokakṣema went from northwestern India to China where, between 147 and 186 C.E., he translated a number of Mahāyāna Sūtras, including the Aṣṭasāhasrikā-prajñāpāramitā (T 224), the Sukhāvatīvyūha (T 361), Drumakinnararāja-paripṛcchā (T 624), Bhadrapāla (T 418), and Kāśyapaparivarta-sūtra (T 350)—teachings that contain such central Mahāyāna teachings as the perfection of wisdom, the six perfections, the nature of the Buddha, and the qualities necessary for a mature Bodhisattva.

Wherever the Bodhisattvas traveled they carried with them the Prajñāpāramitā. As a result, the Prajñāpāramitā Sūtras were the first Mahāyāna Sūtras to become widely known beyond the borders of India. Among the first Dharma teachings to enter China, Korea, Tibet, and Japan, they became the foundation of meditation systems and sophisticated schools of philosophy in all these lands. In India the Prajñāpāramitā provided the root of the two great Mahāyāna philosophical systems: Mādhyamika, based on the śāstras of Nāgārjuna, and Cittamātra, based on the treatises of Maitreya and Asaṅga and doctrines expressed in Sūtras of the Third Turning.

Bodhisattva-Teachers of the Mahāyāna

For followers of the Mahāyāna, it became important to dedicate the merit of positive actions to others. This shift from self to others brought forward the ideal of the Bodhisattvācārya, the teacher who is also a Bodhisattva, a great being who opens the door to enlightened knowledge and action. In the Mahāyāna, perfection—even enlightenment—is merely the prerequisite for the Bodhisattva's real work.

The teachings of the Great Vehicle, "vast, profound, and difficult to fathom," brought forth teachers willing to dedicate their lives to communicating the vision of the Tathāgatas. Setting aside self-centered concerns, they focused their full capacities on unfolding ever more subtle implications of the Buddha's teachings. Where the west tends to separate intellectual from intuitive and devotional development, Mahāyāna masters often excelled in all of these spheres. Most of the great philosophers were monks whose philosophy emerged from meditative realization. Many combined an astounding range of talents including dialectical analysis, poetics, logic, and highly developed mental powers to point out the facets of the Mahāyāna view and path. Grounding their work on the Buddha's teachings, guided by the efforts of their predecessors, these Bodhisattva-teachers became links in a chain of enlightened knowledge that stretches to the modern day. Through their writings they left a living legacy of wisdom; through the lineages they founded or continued, they kept alive the vision of enlightenment and the path to its realization.

Further Readings

Bodhicaryāvatāra. *Entering the Path of Enlightenment,* translated by Marion L. Matics.

Bodhicaryāvatāra. *A Guide to the Bodhisattva's Way of Life,* translated by Stephen Batchelor and Sherpa Tulku.

The Large Sūtra on Perfect Wisdom, translated by Edward Conze, pp. 45–86.

Tāranātha. *History of Buddhism in India,* pp. 96–105.

Dudjom Rinpoche. "The Greater Vehicle" in *The Nyingma School of Tibetan Buddhism,* volume I, pp. 160–177.

Bu-ston. "The Consideration and Fulfillment of Rules Prescribed for Study and Teaching," in *History of Buddhism,* pp. 58–90.

Establishing The Mahāyāna

Rely upon the friend who is well-disciplined,
self-controlled, having perfectly calmed the passions,
endowed with surpassing merit, energetic, and rich
in the knowledge of Dharma, perceiving truth,
skillful in speech, merciful by nature,
and never weary to teach.

—*Sūtrālaṃkāra (Maitreya)*

As the Mahāyāna gathered momentum, two outstanding Bodhisattva-teachers penetrated the significance of the Second and Third Turning teachings and inspired future generations with their writings. Traditionally known as the Two Charioteers, Nāgārjuna and Asaṅga inspired the Mādhyamika and Cittamātra, the two main currents of Mahāyāna philosophy. Nāgārjuna's work was continued and explicated by his principal disciple Āryadeva, while Asaṅga's contributions were further developed by his brother, the great philosopher Vasubandhu.

The Bodhisattvācārya Nāgārjuna

"After I, the Buddha, have passed away,
Four hundred years will elapse,
And then a monk called Nāga will appear.
He will be devoted to the Doctrine,
And greatly extend its influence.
That great being will attain the Stage of Perfect Bliss,
Live for six hundred years,
And secure the mystic knowledge of the Mahāmāyūrī.
He will know the subjects of the different sciences,
And, after he has cast away this bodily frame,
He will be reborn in the realm of Sukhāvatī.
In time, he will certainly become a Buddha."

—Mañjuśrīmūlakalpa-sūtra

According to Bu-ston, Nāgārjuna was born in Vidarbha, in South India, four hundred years after the Buddha's Parinirvāṇa. Upon his birth, astrologers told Nāgārjuna's family that the child would not live longer than seven years; although his rich Brahmin father spared no expense in attempting to find ways to prolong his life, the time came when the child would die. Unable to bear the impending death of their son, Nāgārjuna's parents sent him away with a servant. Eventually Nāgārjuna came to the gates of Nālandā, where the master Saraha heard him reciting the hymns of the Samaveda. Saraha took him in, telling him that if he would become a monk, it would be possible to prolong his life.

After Nāgārjuna became ordained, he diligently prayed to Amitāyus, Buddha of Infinite Life, and overcame the early death predicted. Upon receiving instruction from Saraha (also known as Rāhulabhadra), he was ordained as the monk Śrīman. Nāgārjuna continued Rāhulabhadra's lineage and ensured its transmission through his skill in expressing the profound meaning of the Buddha's teachings. He became a renowned scholar, regarded as a great master by all the Buddhist schools.

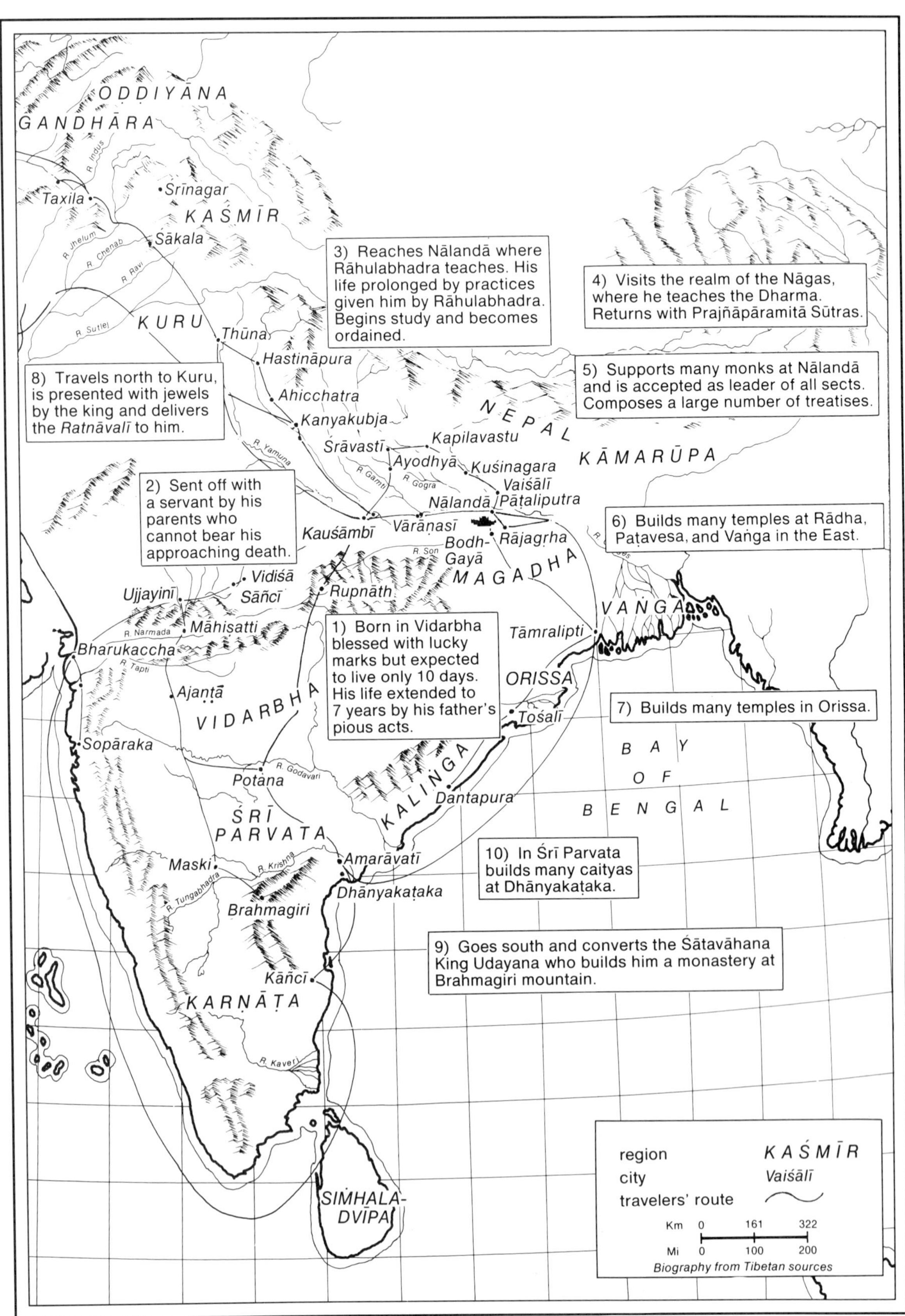

Major events in the life of the great master Nāgārjuna

Nāgārjuna was accepted as the leader of all schools of the Dharma. Dedicated to the Vinaya, he won the admiration of the Śrāvakas by expelling eight thousand bhikṣus who had great influence in the Sangha but who had lapsed in their discipline. Centuries before Nālandā attracted the generosity of royal patrons, Nāgārjuna worked tirelessly to support its teachers and establish its educational standards. He built many temples and also took steps to protect important holy places. When elephants began to damage the Bodhi Tree, he surrounded the Bodhi Tree with a stone wall and built around it one hundred and eight shrines with sacred images. When the river damaged the eastern side of Bodh Gayā, Nāgārjuna made a dam from huge blocks of stone carved with images, which became known as the Seven Sages of the Dam. In the south, Nāgārjuna built the boundary wall surrounding the great stūpa at Dhānyakaṭaka, as well as one hundred and eight temples within the wall. In the eastern regions he is said to have built temples in Oḍivisa (Orissa), Bhaṅgala (Vaṅga), and other locations.

According to Tāranātha, Nāgārjuna retrieved from the realm of the nāgas the Prajñāpāramitā in One Hundred Thousand Verses, the most complete expression of the Buddha's profound Second Turning teachings. So great was his understanding of the Prajñāpāramitā view and the Bodhisattva path that, having received Rāhulabhadra's teachings, he set forth the madhyama, the middle way between nihilism and eternalism, and established the doctrinal basis of the Mahāyāna on a sound philosophical foundation.

Nāgārjuna systematized teachings presented in the Prajñāpāramitā into śāstras, commentaries so brilliantly composed that they became the model for philosophical dialogue throughout India. In six major śāstras (Mūlamadhyamaka-kārikā, Yuktiṣāṣṭhikā, Vaidalyasūtra, Śūnyatāsaptati, Vigrahavyā-vartanī, Vaidalya-nāma-prakaraṇa, NE 3824–3028, 3030) Nāgārjuna explicated the Mahāyāna doctrines of śūnyatā and the two truths. Challenging all doctrines of realty current in his day and demonstrating their fallacies, he extended the powers of reason to their limits, pointing beyond concepts to the immediate experience of reality. The extensive Mahāprajñāpāramitā-śāstra, which summarizes the central Abhidharma teachings and goes on to explicate the Mahāyāna view and the Bodhisattva path, has traditionally been attributed to this great master. This text is preserved only in Chinese (T 1509, NE 5088).

Heir to the Vinaya lineage of the Buddha's son Rāhula, outstanding philosopher, writer, teacher, alchemist, and expert in the art of medicine, Nāgārjuna composed works that illuminated every aspect of the Buddha's teachings and alleviated the most subtle forms of suffering. For the welfare of the many who could benefit from his teaching, Nāgārjuna used his medical and alchemical knowledge to extend his lifetime to the six hundred years predicted in the Mañjuśrīmūlakalpa-sūtra. According to Tāranātha, toward the end of his long life, Nāgārjuna lived on Śrī Parvata, a mountain in the south, where he continued his work on behalf of sentient beings. He is said to have converted the Sātavāhana King Udayana, who built a monastery for him at Mt. Brahmagiri.

During this time, when Puṣyamitra, king of Magadha, destroyed monasteries from the Madhyadeśa as far west as Jālandhara and persecuted the Buddhists in North India, Nāgārjuna continued to propagate the Dharma in the south. His great knowledge of the Vedas and tīrthika philosophies earned him the respect of the Brahmins there, who became convinced of the superiority of the Dharma, converted to Buddhism, and supported teachers of the Mahāyāna. According to Tāranātha, from the time Nāgārjuna became a siddha on the fifth level of development, his complexion became jewel-like. Through his meditation on Śrī Parvata he attained the first stage of the Bodhisattva and his body manifested the thirty-two marks of a great being. About 140 of his writings are preserved in Tibetan translation.

Centuries later, Candrakīrti expressed the great value of Nāgārjuna's work in his Prasannapadā (NE 3860):

"I bow before Nāgārjuna, who has rejected
adherence to the two extreme points of view,
who took birth in the ocean of the Buddha's wisdom,
and has, out of compassion, exposed all the depths
of the treasury of the highest Doctrine
as he has realized it himself.

"The fires of whose Doctrine consume the fuel
that consists of every hostile, disagreeing view,
and dispel up to this very day
the world's mental darkness."

In Nāgārjuna's Footsteps: Āryadeva

According to Tāranātha, Āryadeva was born in Simhaladvīpa (Śrī Laṅkā); the seventh-century master Candrakīrti states that Āryadeva was the son of King Pañcaśṛṅga, and tradition holds that he refused the throne, wishing to lead a religious life. He was ordained in Śrī Laṅkā, where he completed his basic education and memorized the entire teachings of the Śrāvaka tradition. He then made a pilgrimage to the temples and shrines of India and met Nāgārjuna shortly before the great master retired to Śrī Parvata. He became Nāgārjuna's disciple and accompanied him to Śrī Parvata.

Nāgārjuna conferred upon Āryadeva responsibility for continuing his lineages. After Nāgārjuna's death, Āryadeva remained at Śrī Parvata studying and meditating upon all that Nāgārjuna had taught. He is said to have built twenty-four monasteries, each of which became a Mahāyāna center.

Word of Āryadeva's skill in dialectic reached Nālandā, where the tīrthika philosopher Durdharṣakāla was challenging the Buddhist masters to debate; so skilled was he in the use of language that no one there could defeat him. Tāranātha relates that this philosopher-poet was doing much harm to the doctrine of the Buddha, for it had become the custom that, should the person challenged not be able to

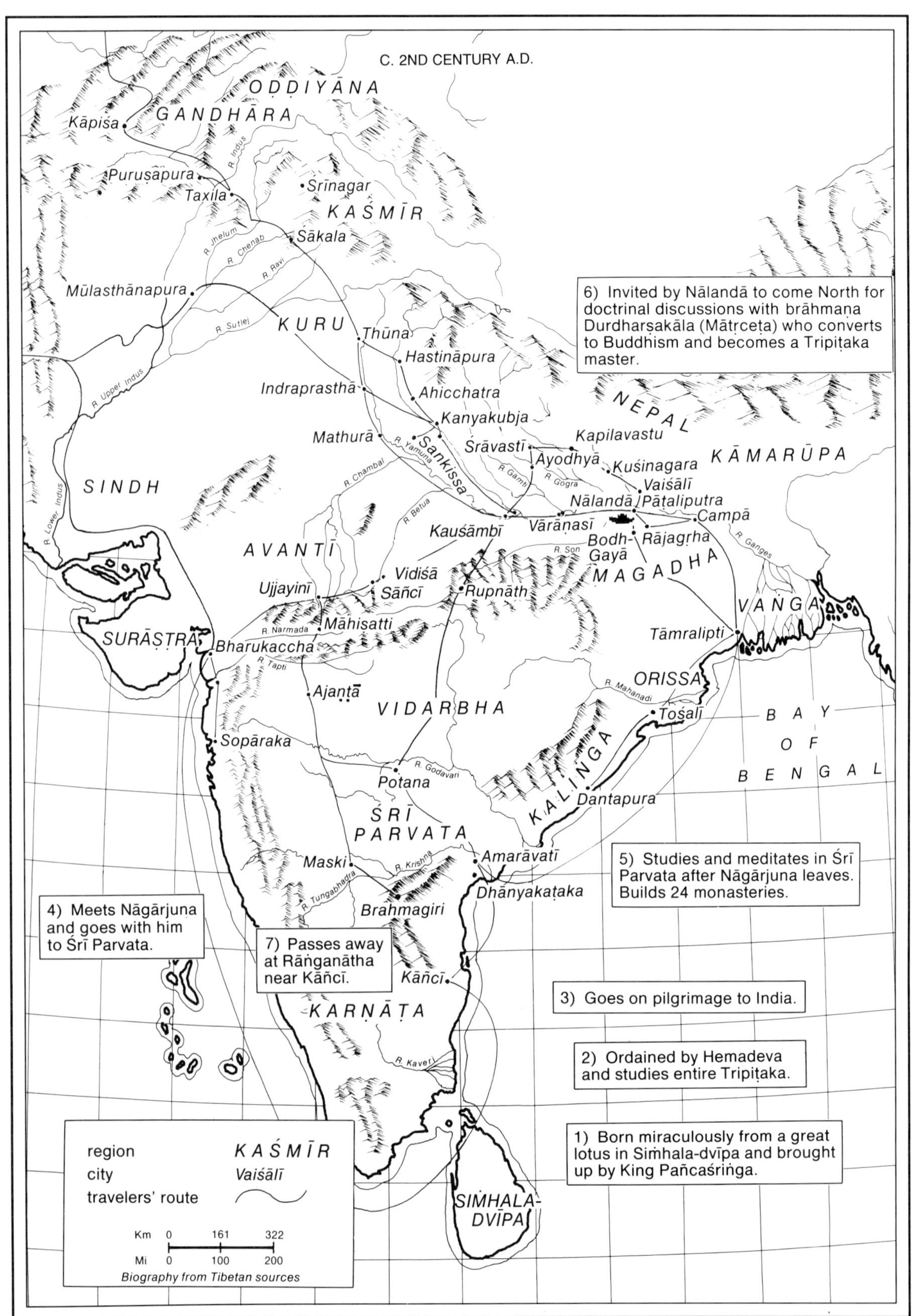

Major events in the life of Āryadeva, Nāgārjuna's foremost disciple

present his views clearly and defend them skillfully, he was obliged to become the disciple of his challenger. This kind of challenge was new to Buddhism; Nāgārjuna and Āryadeva were the first Buddhist masters known to have developed and exercised the skills needed for such debates.

Bu-ston relates that the bhikṣus of Nālandā invited Nāgārjuna there to defend the doctrine, but Āryadeva volunteered to go in his place. Arriving at Nālandā, Āryadeva effectively demonstrated the fallacies of the tīrthika's views not once, but three times. Tradition relates that Āryadeva used his powers to prevent the humiliated Durdharṣakāla from running away and gave him the opportunity to read the Mahāyāna Sūtras instead of forcing him to unwillingly convert to Buddhism. In time, Durdharṣakāla found within these texts a prophecy that he would eventually use his skills on behalf of the Dharma; his heart opened to the Buddha's teachings, and he requested ordination into the Sangha.

After mastering the entire body of Mahāyāna teachings, Durdharṣakāla worked tirelessly to communicate them to others. Many Brahmins, having seen even the great Durdharṣakāla completely won over to the Buddha's teachings, followed his lead and devoted their skills in analysis and language to disseminating the Dharma. Thus the lineage of Nāgārjuna, transmitted through such masters as Āryadeva and Durdharṣakāla, entered the mainstream of the learned classes, attracting their admiration and support.

Durdharṣakāla was known by different names to adherents of different philosophical traditions. In the Tibetan tradition he is known as Mātṛceṭa or Aśvaghoṣa. Outside of Tibet, Mātṛceṭa and Aśvaghoṣa are often considered separate masters, although very little is known of their lives or of their disciples.

If modern estimates of Kaniṣka's dates are correct, Mātṛceṭa was writing near the end of the first century C.E. The Chinese master Hsüan-tsang considers Āryadeva and Aśvaghoṣa as contemporaries; if Mātṛceṭa is indeed Aśvaghoṣa, Āryadeva and Aśvaghoṣa can be tentatively placed near the end of the first century C.E. The Buddhacarita, an elegant and poetic retelling of the life of the Buddha, is attributed to Aśvaghoṣa. Mātṛceṭa is considered the author of various stotras, songs of realization that communicate the power of devotion to awaken aspiration for Buddhalike enlightenment. He also wrote the Mahārāja-kaniṣka-lekha, A Letter to the Great King Kaniṣka (NE 4184).

I-tsing, who translated a hymn by Mātṛceṭa into Chinese, writes: "The author treats generally of the Six Pāramitās and expounds all the excellent qualities of the Buddha, the World-honored One. These charming compositions are equal in beauty to the heavenly flowers, and the high principles which they contain rival in dignity the lofty peaks of a mountain. Consequently in India all who compose hymns imitate his style, considering him the father of literature" (I-tsing, p. 157–158). According to I-tsing, everyone who became a monk at Nālandā, whether they followed the Hīnayāna or Mahāyāna tradition, learned Mātṛceṭa's hymns as soon as they were able to recite the precepts.

Āryadeva, recognized as Nāgārjuna's spiritual son, composed many works that emphasized the nature of the Bodhisattva path and explicated the view set forth by Nāgārjuna. Āryadeva's works include the Catuḥśataka-śāstra (NE 3846), the Hastavāla-prakaraṇa (NE 3845), the Skhalita-pramathana-yukti-hetusiddhi (NE 3847), and the Jñānasāra-samuccaya (NE 3851). These works further established the śāstra style of drawing out the central teachings of the Sūtras and systematizing them for maximum clarity and ease of study. Āryadeva worked for the Dharma at Nālandā for many years; toward the end of his life, he propagated the teachings in the south. Tāranātha records that he passed away at Raṅganātha, near Kāñcī.

The śāstras of Nāgārjuna and Āryadeva established the value of intellectual analysis as a means of penetrating conceptual barriers and moving closer to the view of the fully enlightened Buddhas. This approach to knowledge was continued by a lineage of masters that included Āryadeva's disciple Rāhulamitra, then Nāgamitra and Saṃgharakṣita, the teacher of Buddhapālita and Bhāvaviveka, whose writings bridged the fifth and sixth centuries. By the fifth century, the Madhyamaka approach to comprehending reality had given rise to the Mādhyamika school; the proponents of this school became known as Mādhyamikans.

After Āryadeva left Nālandā, Tāranātha relates that Nāgahvāya, another of Nāgārjuna's disciples, became Upādhyāya (principal teacher) of Nālandā. Nāgahvāya, also known as Tathāgatagarbha, is said to have visited the realm of the nāgas seven times and to have extensively expounded Mahāyāna Sūtras. Following Tāranātha's account, it was about this time that Nālandā was severely damaged in Turuṣka raids and was restored with help given by King Buddhapakṣa. Still, Nālandā's recovery from the disruption and the loss of valuable manuscripts was slowed by the general chaos the Turuṣkas inflicted on India's heartland.

The Bodhisattvācārya Asaṅga

"A monk bearing the name of Asaṅga,
well-versed in the meaning of the scientific treatises,
will, in different forms, explain
the conventional and the direct meaning of the Sūtras.
By his nature he is to be one
who teaches the Sublime Science to the living beings,
and reveals the meaning of the Sacred Texts."

—Mañjuśrīmūlakalpa

Asaṅga (fourth century C.E.) was born in Puruṣapura, the Indian name for Peshāwar, King Kaniṣka's old capital in Gandhāra. Asaṅga's mother was an educated Brahmin and his father a Kṣatriya. From his mother, Asaṅga received a highly proficient understanding of the eighteen branches of learning, including grammar, debate, medicine, and the fine

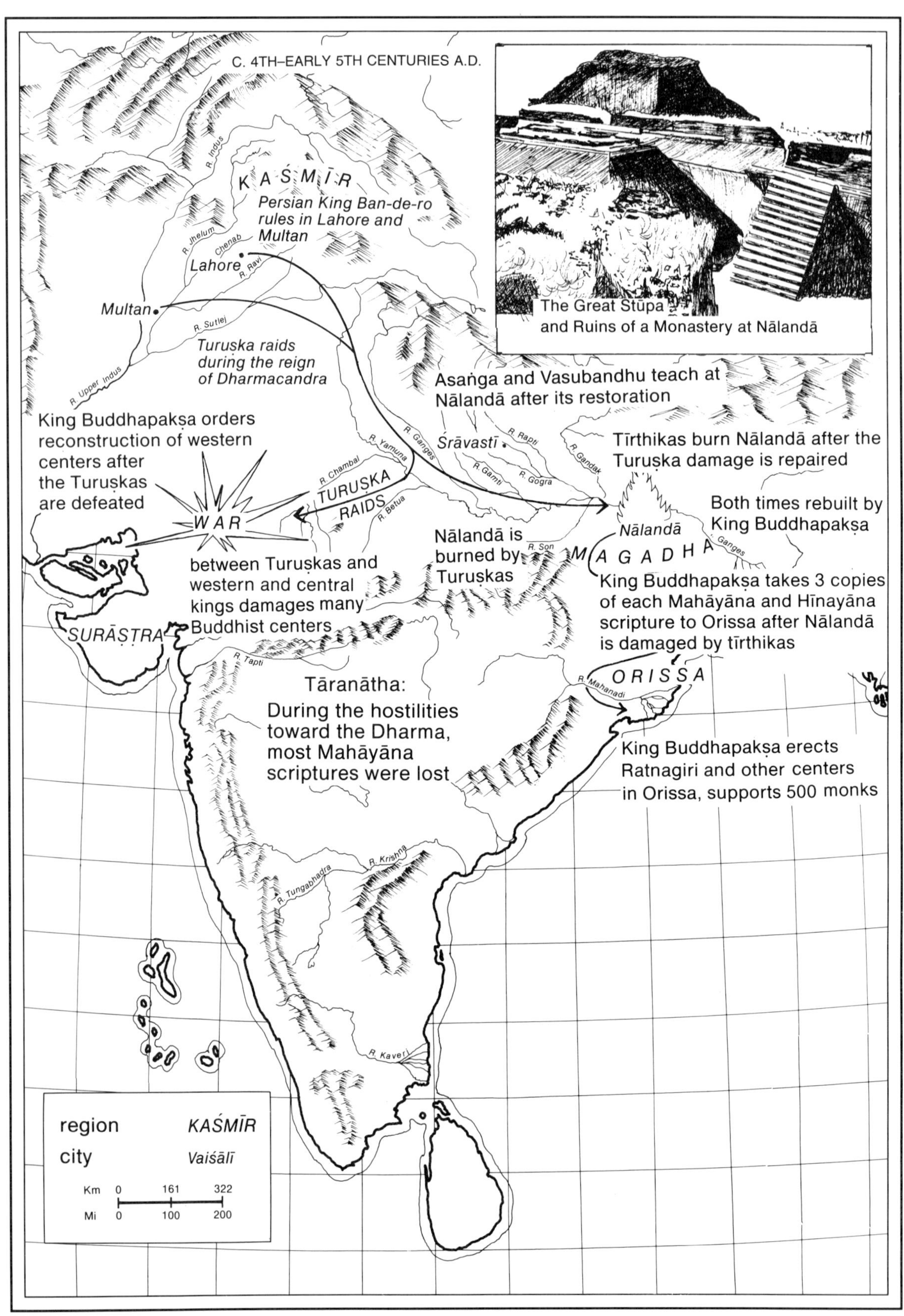

The Dharma survived destruction by Huns and tīrthikas (Tāranātha).

arts. When it came time to take up a profession, his mother instructed him to enter the Sangha and devote himself to transmitting the Dharma. Asaṅga obeyed her directives and entered the Sangha through the Mahīśāsaka school. He studied the Tripiṭaka intensively for five years, memorizing a hundred thousand ślokas every year. Learning came to him easily; only one teaching—the profound Prajñāpāramitā—presented difficulties he could not surmount. According to Tāranātha, Asaṅga then sought a meditative vision of the Great Bodhisattva Maitreya, in order to penetrate these obstacles to understanding.

Asaṅga retired to a cave on Mt. Kukkuṭapāda near Rājagṛha, where he spent twelve years in meditation. Twice he nearly gave up after he despaired of making any progress, but each time he started to leave his cave, he drew encouragement from signs that persistence eventually produces significant change. When he finally did yield to despair, he emerged from his cave to see before him a miserable dog badly infested with maggots. This sight evoked a great upwelling of compassion; as he knelt down and attempted to remove the maggots with his tongue so as not to harm them, compassion melted the last obstacle to inner vision, and he was able to see Maitreya directly.

Bu-ston records that for some years thereafter Asaṅga studied with Maitreya in the Tuṣita Heaven, where he thoroughly mastered the samādhis that enabled him to comprehend the whole of Maitreya's teachings as well as all the Buddha's Second and Third Turning Teachings. When Asaṅga returned to India, he built the Dharmāṅkura Vihāra in the Veṇuvana, the Bamboo Grove in Rājagṛha, where he set down in writing the five major treatises of Maitreya: the Abhisamayālaṁkāra (NE 3786), a text that systematizes the Prajñāpāramitā teachings under eight major topics; the Mahāyāna-sūtrālaṁkāra (NE 4020), which summarizes the practice of the Bodhisattva and explains ultimate reality as "thusness" (neither existing or non-existing); the Madhyānta-vibhaṅga (NE 4021), a work clarifying the extremes to be

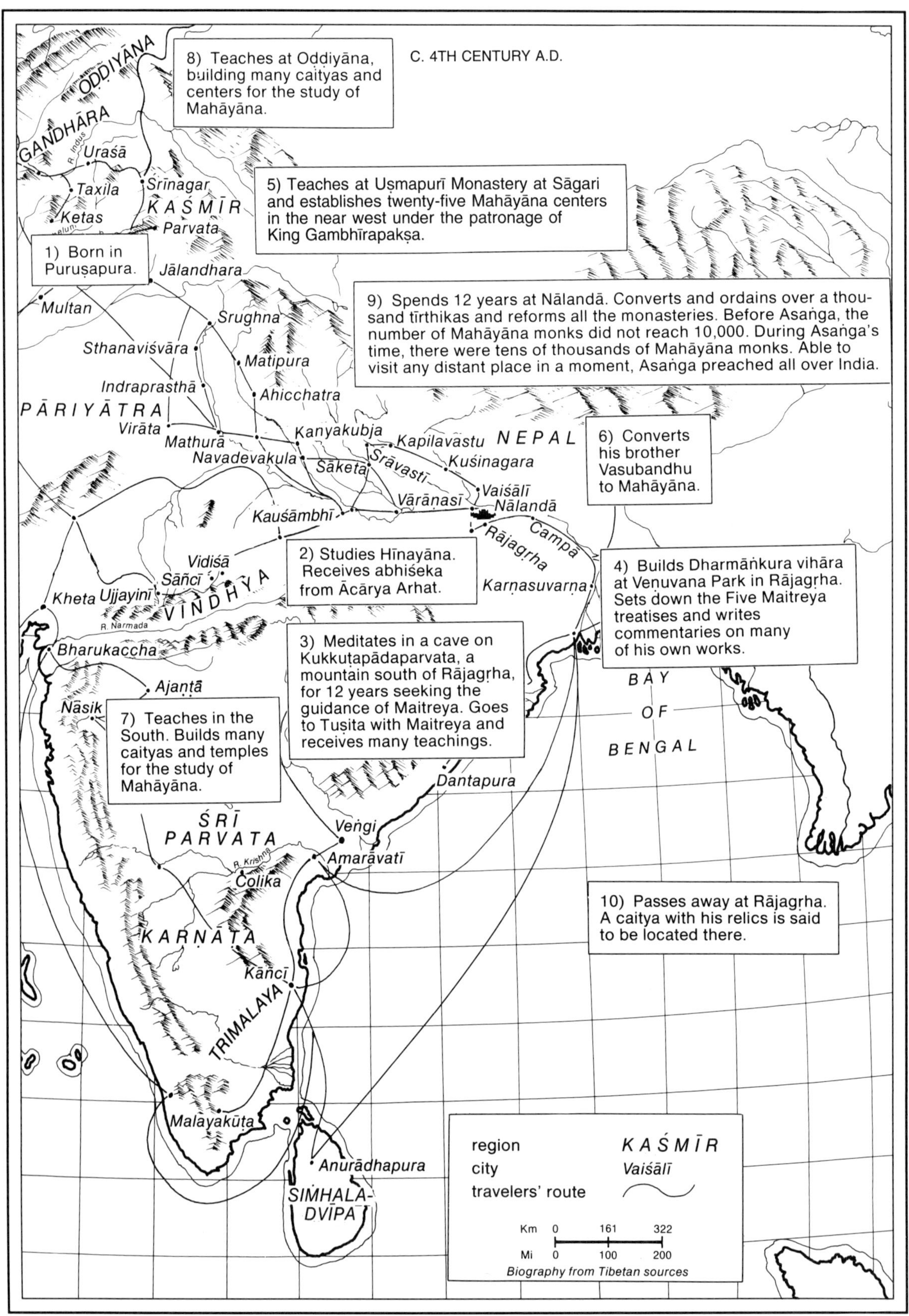

Major events in the life of the great master Asaṅga

avoided; the Dharmadharmatā-vibhaṅga (NE 4022), which ex-
plicates ultimate reality (dharmatā) and illusory principles
(dharma); and the Mahāyānottaratantra-śāstra (NE 4024),
also known as the Uttaratantra or Ratnagotra-vibhaṅga.

Asaṅga wrote commentaries on the Saṁdhinirmocana-
sūtra (NE 3981), a central teaching of the Third Turning, as
well as an explication of Maitreya's Mahāyānottaratantra
(NE 4025) and the Mahāyāna-saṁgraha (NE 4048), a treatise
that addresses the concept of ālaya-vijñāna, the matrix-con-
sciousness which stores past actions as seeds (bija) that create the potentiality for future events. In the Abhidharmasamuccaya (NE 4049), another masterful work, he revised the
Sarvāstivādin Abhidharma in light of śūnyatā, establishing
for centuries to come the standard of investigating mind and
mental events from a Mahāyāna perspective. This śāstra and
those which carried forth its teachings became known as the
Higher Abhidharma.

Asaṅga was an effective and inspiring teacher, said to
know the minds of others. At the monastery of Uṣmapurī in
the western city of Sāgari, Asaṅga taught the monks of all
traditions, instructing each at the level of his understanding.
To some he taught the Sūtras of the Śrāvakas, while to others he taught the Mahāyāna Sūtras. King Gambhīrapakṣa
supported this great assembly of at least one thousand
monks, who all eventually awakened understanding of the
Mahāyāna teachings. Through such intensive teaching efforts Asaṅga revitalized the Mahāyāna, which had declined
in the Madhyadeśa in the wake of the damage inflicted on
Nālandā during the Turuṣka raids.

According to Tāranātha, King Gambhīrapakṣa, greatly
devoted to the Prajñāpāramitā, devised six questions to test
the extent of Asaṅga's knowledge. Asaṅga responded so fully
that the king granted his request for the building of twenty-
five centers dedicated to the Mahāyāna teachings, with each
of the centers to house one hundred teachers and their students. Tāranātha mentions that Asaṅga also taught in the

Northwest (Oḍḍiyāna) and in the south; he had a great number of temples and monasteries built in both places as well as in Magadha, so that the Mahāyāna would be widely disseminated. It was said that there was practically no one interested in the Mahāyāna who did not listen to him teach at least one Sūtra.

Where Nāgārjuna pointed to the "other shore" of enlightened vision and removed the concepts binding one to incorrect views, Asaṅga's teaching established a systematic path to realization. Inspired by Maitreya's Madhyānta-vibhaṅga, Asaṅga composed the Yogācāra-bhūmi (NE 4035–4042), in which he described the stages of the path, what obstacles arise on each stage, what antidotes to apply, and what realizations indicate success. His method of study and practice became known as the Later Yogācāra; it incorporated teachings of consciousness (vijñāna) and the central importance of mind (mind-only), based on the Third Turning Teachings. Following Asaṅga's approach, many were able to "cross over" to the enlightened view communicated in the deep and profound Prajñāpāramitā.

As a result of Asaṅga's teaching, the number of Mahāyāna monks grew to at least ten thousand. Tāranātha adds that "still, the number of disciples who were constantly attached to this master did not exceed twenty-five." These twenty-five disciples formed the foundation from which the lineage of Maitreya would be transmitted throughout Asia and beyond. According to Tāranātha, Asaṅga passed away in Rājagṛha, while Paramārtha states that Puruṣapura, Asaṅga's birthplace, was also the place of his death.

The Master Philosopher Vasubandhu

Asaṅga's foremost disciple was his younger brother Vasubandhu, who was born a year after Asaṅga's ordination. Vasubandhu's father was a Brahmin vastly learned in the three Vedas; like Asaṅga, Vasubandhu was trained into scholarship from an early age and encouraged to pursue study and meditation in the Buddhist Sangha. Vasubandhu was ordained at Nālandā, where he completed his basic education and mastered the Śrāvaka Tripiṭaka. Keenly intellectual, he became interested in Abhidharma; since the Sarvāstivādin school of Kashmir had developed the Abhidharma studies most extensively, Vasubandhu went to Kashmir to study with Saṁghabhadra, the foremost Sarvāstivādin master of his time. From Saṁghabhadra Vasubandhu learned the doctrines of the eighteen schools and all branches of knowledge transmitted by the Sarvāstivādin tradition. Gifted with a photographic memory, he memorized the Mahāvibhāṣa, mastered the six classical philosophical schools of the tīrthikas, and practiced the techniques of debate.

Vasubandhu eventually returned to Magadha, where he taught the Abhidharma teachings he had mastered in Kashmir. Thus the complete Sarvāstivādin Abhidharma, developed for centuries in relative isolation from other Buddhist communities, became known outside of Kashmir for the first time.

Paramārtha relates that yakṣas guarded the sole passage into Kashmir and had permitted no one to take the Sarvāstivādin doctrines out of that country. Vasubandhu managed to do so only by convincing the Kashmiris that he was insane. After leaving Kashmir, he resided in Ayodhyā, capital of the Gupta rulers, where his students transcribed the Abhidharma teachings he had memorized.

According to Paramārtha, once, when Vasubandhu was away from Ayodhyā for a time, the tīrthika Vindhyavāsa, skilled in the Saṁkhya system, rang the bell of appeals outside the king's palace, asking to debate with the Buddhist masters. But only Buddhamitra was left to respond to the challenge; although he was a learned master, his memory was enfeebled by age. He presented the doctrine capably, but, unable to follow the tīrthika's refutation, he ended confused and humiliated.

When Vasubandhu returned, he sought out the tīrthika to redress Buddhamitra's embarrassment, but the tīrthika had died, and his body had been transformed into rock through a yakṣa's power. In this way Vindhyavāsa hoped to remain forever undefeated. But Vasubandhu, determined to refute the tīrthika's doctrines, composed seventy verses that so thoroughly discredited Vindhyavāsa's doctrine that it "fell to pieces like broken tiles, from beginning to end, leaving no sentence which could hold together" (Paramārtha). Greatly impressed, King Vikramāditya, who had generously supported the tīrthikas, gave Vasubandhu a large sum of gold. With this gift Vasubandhu built three monasteries in Ayodhyā: one for bhikṣuṇīs, one for the Sarvāstivādins, and one dedicated to the study of Mahāyāna. The king further honored Vasubandhu by making him a minister-of-state. Even the crown prince and his mother became Vasubandhu's students. When the prince became king, he generously supported Vasubandhu and the Sangha not only in Ayodhyā, but throughout his kingdom.[1]

One well-known story of Vasubandhu's scholarship revolves around his composition of the Abhidharmakoṣa-kārikā and bhāṣya (NE 4089–4090). When lecturing on the Vibhāṣa, it is said that he made a verse summary of the teaching at the end of each day; the verse summary was then engraved on a copper plate which was publicly displayed. When he had completed the summary of the Vibhāṣa in six hundred verses (Abhidharmakoṣa-kārikā), he sent the verses together with fifty pounds of gold to the Vaibhāṣika masters in Kashmir. The Vaibhāṣikas were delighted to see their doctrines systematized so succinctly. However, since the verses were very concise, they did not fully understand all of them. So they raised donations of fifty pounds of gold, added it to

---

1. If Vasubandhu lived in the mid-fourth century, as is generally accepted, the Vikramāditya of Paramārtha's account could well be the powerful King Samudragupta, son of Candragupta I (*HCIP* III:14). According to Tāranātha, Vasubandhu was a contemporary of the Tibetan king Lha-tho-tho-ri.

the fifty pounds Vasubandhu had sent them, and sent the gold and the verses back to Vasubandhu requesting that he write a prose explication.

Vasubandhu later prepared an extensive commentary (bhāṣya) on the Abhidharmakoṣa-kārikā, which reviewed the Sarvāstivādin teachings from the perspective of the Sautrāntika school. (The finished version, the Abhidharmakoṣabhāṣya, together with the original kārikās, are collectively known as the Abhidharmakoṣa-śāstra.) The Vaibhāṣika masters were upset at the refutation of their doctrines. Saṃghabhadra then wrote the Abhidharma-śāstra-kārikā-bhāṣya in response, a text that has survived to the present in Tibetan translation (NE 4091).

Paramārtha relates that a tīrthika philosopher, angered by Vasubandhu's refutation of his treatise on grammar, invited Saṃghabhadra to come personally to Ayodhyā and challenge Vasubandhu to a public debate. This placed Vasubandhu in the awkward position of potentially humiliating his own teacher. The debate, however, never took place. Vasubandhu made it clear he considered that all the relevant points had been brought out in the Abhidharmakoṣa and in Saṃghabhadra's two treatises; scholars of the future could examine them for themselves and evaluate which of the treatises was correct.

Paramārtha and Tāranātha state that Vasubandhu, secure in his knowledge of the First Turning Teachings, disparaged the Mahāyāna. Wishing to open Vasubandhu's mind to the profound Mahāyāna, Asaṅga asked his brother to visit him, either in Puruṣapura (Paramārtha) or in Magadha (Tāranātha). Although Paramārtha and Tāranātha explain Vasubandhu's conversion to Mahāyāna slightly differently, both agree that once Vasubandhu opened his mind to the meaning of the Mahāyāna, Vasubandhu's formidable intellect was drawn irresistibly to its subtlety and depth, and he quickly became convinced of the validity of the Mahāyāna view and path.

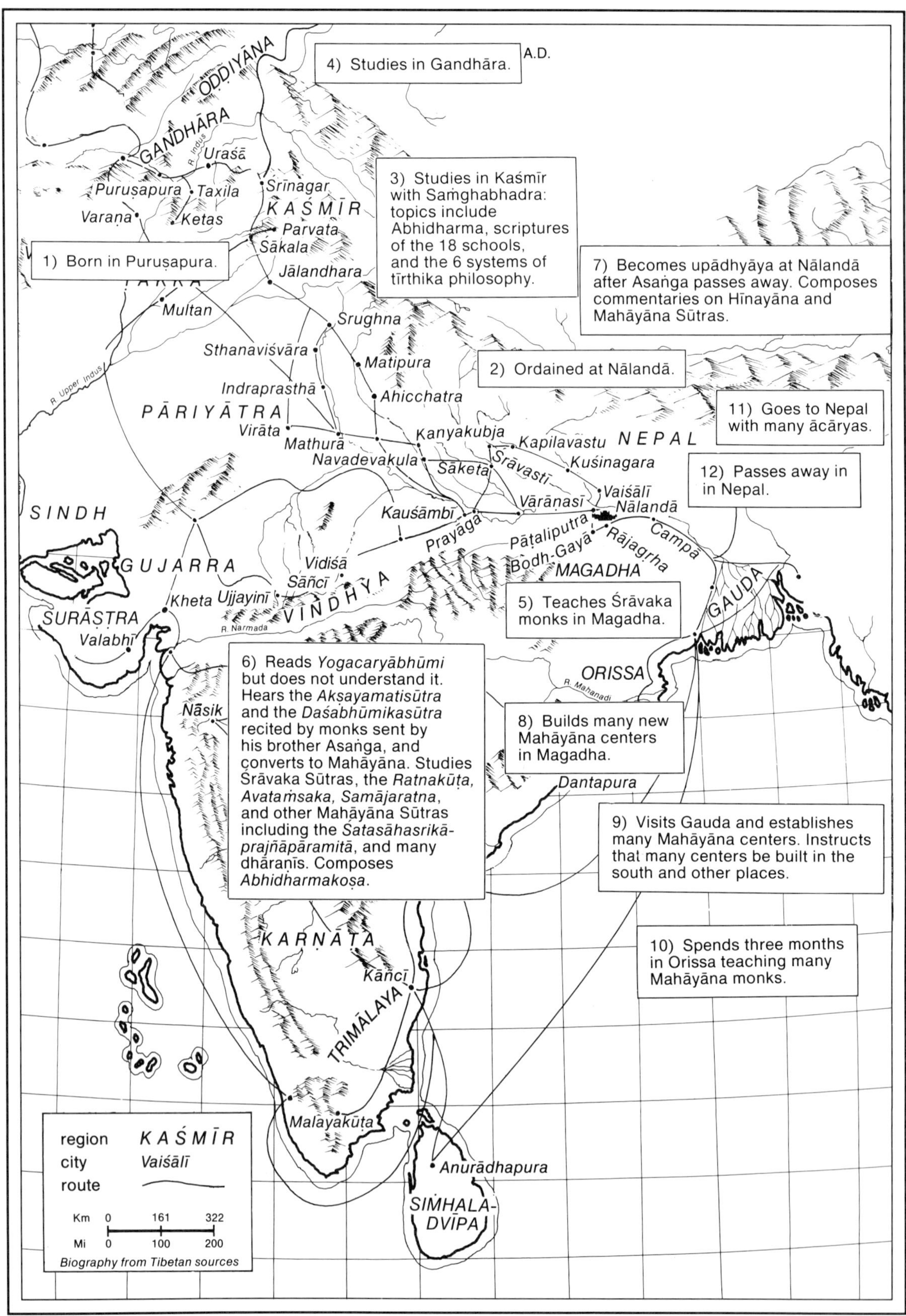

Major events in the life of the great master Vasubandhu

Humbled by this insight, Vasubandhu regretted the arrogance of mind that had hindered his understanding and asked Asaṅga how he could atone for his error. He offered to cut out his own tongue, but Asaṅga told him that his error was so great that even if he cut out his tongue a thousand times, he could not take back his disparaging words. Asaṅga asked him to use his tongue more creatively, by preaching the Mahāyāna extensively and writing skillful commentaries on the Mahāyāna Sūtras and their doctrines.

Vasubandhu's conversion to the Mahāyāna inspired five hundred scholars to follow his example. Vasubandhu then learned all the Mahāyāna Sūtras and proceeded to compose commentaries on the Daśabhūmika (NE 3993), Buddhānu-smṛti (NE 3987), the Pratītyasamutpāda (NE 3995), and other Sūtras; on the works of Maitreya and Asaṅga, such as the Sūtrālaṁkāra-vyākhyā (NE 4026), the Madhyāntavibhaṅga-ṭīkā (NE 4027), and the Dharmadharmatā-vibhaṅga (NE 4028); and basic expositions (prakaraṇas) of Vijñānavāda doctrines in the Viṁśaka- and Triṁśikā-kārikās (NE 4055–57) and the Pañcaskandha- and Karmasiddhi-prakaraṇas (NE 4059, 4062). It is said that after the nirvāṇa of the Buddha, there was none as profoundly learned in all the scriptures as the great master Vasubandhu. Tāranātha states that Vasubandhu knew by memory all the Śrāvaka Sūtras, the forty-nine Ratnakūṭa Sūtras, the Avataṁsaka, and the Mahāsamaya-sūtra, as well as the extensive Prajñāpāramitā teaching in 100,000 lines, five hundred other Mahāyāna Sūtras, and five hundred Dhāraṇīs.

After Asaṅga's death, Vasubandhu became Upādhyāya of Nālandā; his presence may have been a factor in the great surge of royal support for Nālandā's expansion into a university where all schools of the Dharma maintained centers of teaching. Tāranātha states that Vasubandhu stayed mostly in Magadha and filled the whole of that country with 108 Mahāyāna centers. The Brahmin Makṣika invited Vasubandhu to Orissa, where he established another 108 Mahāyāna centers. Tāranātha mentions that he also visited South

India and established a total of 654 monasteries in all. Vasubandhu is said to have also traveled to Nepal, accompanied by a thousand Mahāyāna teachers, and to have established Buddhist centers in that land as well. As a result of Vasubandhu's efforts, the number of Mahāyāna monks increased from ten thousand during Asaṅga's time to sixty thousand. According to Paramārtha, Vasubandhu died in Ayodhyā at the age of eighty. Tāranātha relates that Vasubandhu passed away in Nepal, where his remains were enshrined in a stūpa built by his disciples.

Bu-ston relates that Vasubandhu had four great disciples: Sthiramati, who excelled in Vijñānavāda; Dignāga, who excelled in Pramāṇa (science of knowledge); Vimuktasena, who excelled in the Prajñāpāramitā; and Guṇaprabha, who excelled in Vinaya.

Further Readings

Bu-ston. *History of Buddhism,* pp. 122–132; 136–147.

Lineage of Diamond Light, pp. 53–70.

Paramārtha. *The Life of Vasu-bandhu,* translated by J. Takakusu, in T'oung Pao, Série II, tome V (1904), pp. 269–466.

Tāranātha. *History of Buddhism in India,* pp. 106–175.

Majumdar, R. C. ed. *The History and Culture of the Indian People.* Volume III: *The Classical Age,* pp. 374–381.

Nālandā and the Mahāyāna Lineage

Under Nālandā's supportive umbrella, two general movements evolved within the Mahāyāna: the elaboration of analysis, dialectic, and doctrine during the fifth and sixth centuries and a turning toward synthesis and consolidation during the eighth century.

During the Buddha's lifetime, Nālandā was a small Brahmin settlement on the main route from Rājagṛha, King Bimbisāra's capital, to Vaiśālī, Śrāvastī, and the cities along the Ganges River. The Mahāparinibbana-sutta relates that the Buddha passed through Nālandā many times on his travels, often stopping at the Mango Grove to give teachings. After the Magadhan capital was moved to Pāṭaliputra, the village of Nālandā sank into obscurity. For several centuries thereafter, Nālandā is known for only one event: King Aśoka visited the area on his pilgrimage to holy places, paid homage at the stūpas of Śāriputra and Maudgalyāyana, and built a temple next to Śāriputra's stūpa.

As described in a previous chapter, the early Mahāyāna teachers chose Nālandā as their center, and the brothers Udbhaṭa and Śaṁkarapati provided for the support at Nālandā of five hundred monks. Here Rāhulabhadra and his disciple Nāgārjuna served as the monastery's head preceptors and established a model of educational excellence. Mātṛceṭa, whose name is synonymous with elegant prose and poetry, also expanded Nālandā's educational program. During the fourth century, the masters Asaṅga and Vasubandhu taught at Nālandā, which became a center for the transmission of the Prajñāpāramitā, Yogācāra, Vijñānavāda, and Cittamātra lineages.

The lineages transmitted by Nāgārjuna and Asaṅga gave rise to the two main Mahāyāna philosophical schools, the Mādhyamika and Cittamātra. Complemented and supported by new approaches to logic, these schools gained prominence in the fifth and sixth centuries. The growing emphasis on philosophy required a new approach to education, exemplified by the transformation of Nālandā in the fifth century from a monastic complex to a fully developed university with extensive libraries, said to have occupied three multi-storied buildings. This transformation was aided by kings of the Gupta Dynasty, who sponsored the building of monasteries and endowed Nālandā with imposing architecture and expressive sacred art.

The Gupta Kings and the Hun Invasions

Samudragupta, the king who established the Gupta Empire, accommodated and supported diverse religious traditions. Buddhism flourished during his rule, and the monastery of Nālandā began to grow into the major educational and cultural center for all of India. Since Samudragupta ruled from approximately 340–380 C.E., it is possible that he was the Gupta ruler who appointed the Buddhist master Vasubandhu as one of his religious preceptors and donated funds for the building of Buddhist monasteries. When the

Śrī Laṅkan ruler requested permission to establish a monastery at Bodh Gayā, Samudragupta readily acquiesced and facilitated the arrangements.

Samudragupta's son Candragupta II extended the empire; he drove the foreign Śaka rulers from Western India and reunited all northwestern lands south of the Candrabhāga River under one rule. His reign stands out as a time of peace and general well-being, when, as the Chinese pilgrim Fa-hien reported, bhikṣus and pilgrims could travel the realm in peace. During the reign of Candragupta II (380–415 C.E.), his son Kumāragupta (415–455 C.E.), and the four Gupta rulers who followed him, literature and art experienced a renaissance of creativity that had a tremendous influence on all aspects of religion and culture in India. Royal patronage of the arts stimulated the creation of magnificent art and sculpture with both religious and secular themes.

During the reign of Kumāragupta's son Skandagupta (455–467?), a nomadic Central Asian tribe known as Huns or Huṇas conquered Gandhāra and continued eastward; they began to ravage Buddhist monasteries through most of the Northwest and soon penetrated into India as far east as Nālandā. From their leader's family, they became known as Ye-tha, Hephthalites or Ephthalites, or simply as White Huns. (Tāranātha refers to invaders from the north as Turuṣkas and relates that they burned Nālandā and other Buddhist sites during the "second hostility to the Dharma.")[1] After Skandagupta defeated them decisively and drove them out of India, peace returned to the empire. Support for education and the arts continued, and Buddhist intellectual accomplishments greatly expanded. Yet defeat did not deter the Huns for long. Gathering strength in the Northwest

---

1. Tāranātha describes three hostilities to the Dharma: The first hostility was inflicted by Puṣyamitra, the first Śuṅga king; the second by the Turuṣkas under their leader Ban-de-ro, and the third by tīrthikas bent on avenging an insult, which occured after the previous damage had been repaired. The second and third hostilities took place during the reign of King Buddhapakṣa.

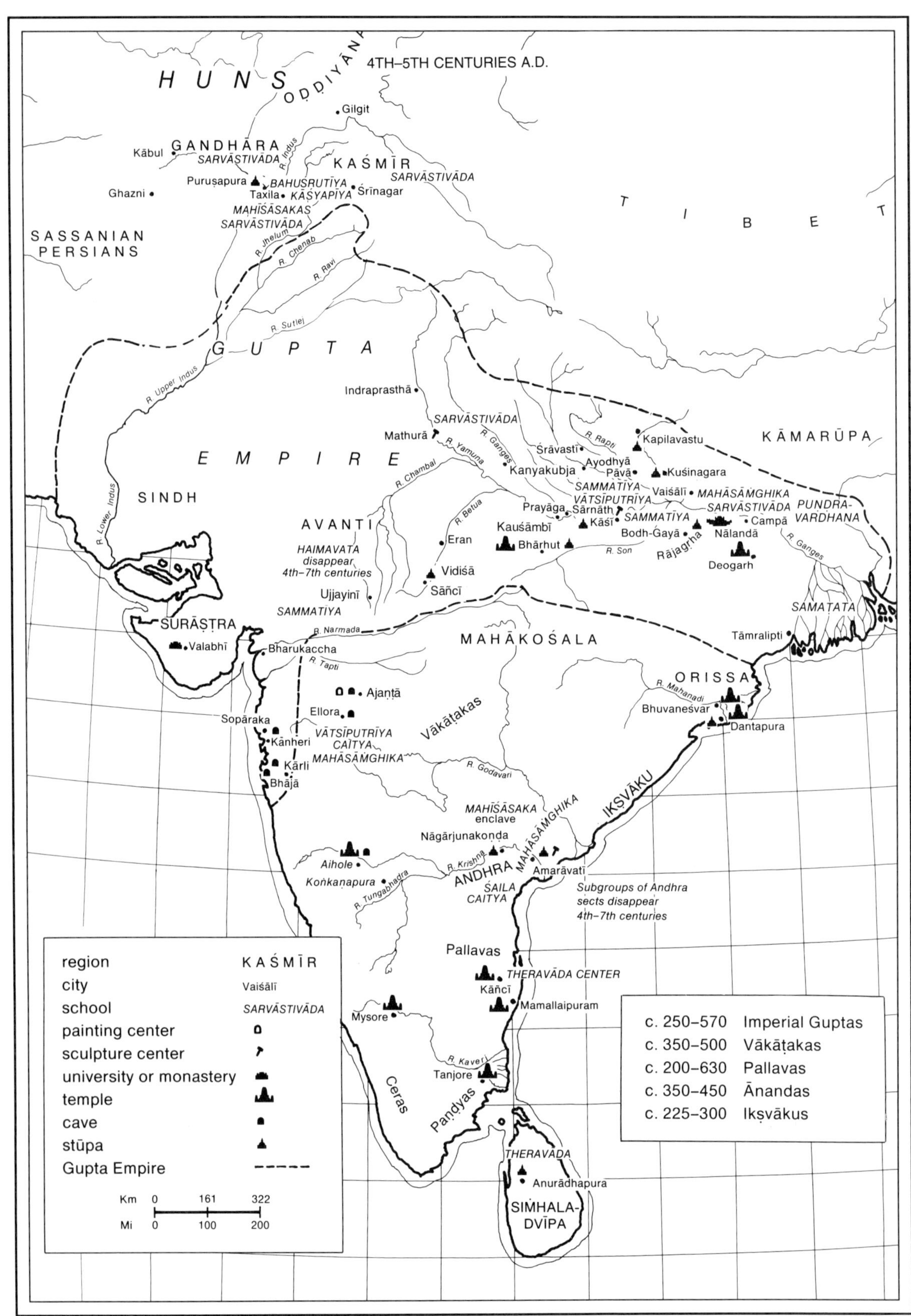

Major Buddhist centers at the time of the Gupta Empire

under the leadership of Toramāṇa, they invaded Western India as far as Eran, a city north of Sañcī. But their main destructiveness in India occurred under the leadership of Toramāṇa's son Mihirakula, who assumed power in 515 C.E. According to Sung-yun, Chinese ambassador to the Hun king of Gandhāra in 520 C.E., the ruler of that time (most likely Mihirakula) was a vicious man and very antagonistic towards Buddhism:

"The disposition of this king was cruel and vindictive, and he practiced the most barbarous atrocities. He did not believe the law of Buddha but worshipped demons. The people of the country belonged entirely to the Brahmin caste; they had great respect for the law of Buddha and loved to read the sacred books, when suddenly this king came into power, who was strongly opposed to anything of the sort." (Hsüan-tsang I:c)

From physical evidence of widespread destruction throughout Northwest India, as noted by Hsüan-tsang in the seventh century, there is little doubt that the Huns had penetrated Gandhāra, Bāmiyān, Kapiśa, Oḍḍiyāna, Takṣaśilā, Kashmir, and neighboring regions and had held on to these areas for some time. From the Northwest, Mihirakula continued to push into India; in a short time he was ravaging Magadha and compelling even Narasiṁhagupta, nephew of the great Skandagupta and ruler of the Gupta Empire, to pay him tribute.

Finally, unable to tolerate Mihirakula's cruelties and destructiveness, Narasiṁhagupta mounted an heroic effort and drove Mihirakula's Huns from his realm. In 567 C.E., the Turks and Persians cooperated to demolish the central Hun Empire on the Oxus River, completely ending the Hun threat to India. Narasiṁhagupta, also known as Bālāditya, meaning the Sun of Strength, was also very likely the ruler Bālāditya who patronized Buddhism and built a temple at Nālandā. An eighth-century inscription at Nālandā refers to "Bālāditya, the great king of irresistible valor," who, after having vanquished all his foes, erected a "great and extraordinary temple at Nālandā." (*HCIP* III:43)

Nālandā Becomes an International University

According to Hsüan-tsang, who lived at Nālandā in the seventh century and investigated its history, the physical site of Nālanda was greatly enlarged in the fifth century through the patronage of the Imperial Gupta family. The central monastery at Nālandā was built by Śakrāditya, a king of the Gupta Dynasty "who respected and esteemed the One Vehicle." An auspicious place was located for the monastery's foundation, but when the workers began excavation, they inadvertently struck and wounded a nāga. A distinguished soothsayer told the builders that this monastery would become highly renowned; it would flourish a thousand years and become a model throughout greater India. But because the nāga had been wounded, the site would suffer disasters and much blood would be spilled there.

Writing a generation later, the Chinese pilgrim I-tsing confirmed that Nālandā's central temple was built by Śakyādita and added that the building was done for a bhikṣu of North India named Rāja Bhāja. "After beginning it, he was much obstructed by other people, but his descendants finished it and made it by far the most magnificent establishment in Jambudvīpa. The building is four square, like a city. There are four large gateways of three storeys each. Each storey is some ten feet in height. The whole is covered with tiles."[2]

Purugupta, brother of Skandagupta, may also have been a patron of Nālandā. Coin evidence equates Purugupta with Śrī Vikrama; he may have been the same King Vikramāditya who sent his son to study under Vasubandhu; he may also have been the king who allowed Vasubandhu to debate with

---

2. S. Beal, *Journal of the Royal Asiatic Society* (n.s.) 13:571.

> **Kings Who Participated in Building Nālandā**
>
> | **Hsüan-tsang** | **Possible equivalents (*HCIP*)** |
> | --- | --- |
> | Śakrāditya | Kumāragupta I (415–455) |
> | Buddhagupta | Skandagupta (455–467?) |
> | Tathāgatagupta | Purugupta (467?–?) |
> | Bālāditya | Narasiṁhagupta (535–?) |
> | Vajra | Kumāragupta II (473?) or Viṣṇugupta (?–570?) |
> | King of Central India | Harṣa of Kanauj (c. 612–647) |

the tīrthikas, an event which restored the waning prestige of the Dharma in northern India.

The Gupta rulers continued to build at Nālandā throughout the fifth century. According to Hsüan-tsang, "A long succession of kings continued the work of building, using all the skill of the sculptor, till the whole is truly marvelous to behold." He adds that Buddhagupta built a monastery to the south of the great monastery constructed by Śakrāditya; Tathāgatagupta built a monastery to the east, and King Bālāditya built a monastery to the northeast. Hsüan-tsang relates that Bālāditya convened a great assembly to celebrate the completion of this monastery, inviting adherents of all religions to the ceremony. This king later abdicated his throne and became a monk. He was succeeded by his son Vajra, who built a monastery on the west side of Nālandā.

By the close of the fifth century, Nālandā had expanded into a large complex of temples, shrines, and lecture and residential halls, with a diverse population of faculty and students administered by an abbot. As its reputation grew, Nālandā attracted scholars and students from all of India and eventually from the entire Buddhist world.

Scholars Mentioned as Upādhyāyas of Nālandā
by Tāranātha or Hsüan-tsang

Rāhulabhadra	Nāgārjuna
Āryadeva	Nāgahvāya (Tathāgatagarbha)
Asaṅga	Vasubandhu
Dignāga	Saṃgharakṣita
Candrakīrti	Dharmapāla
Jayadeva	Śīlabhadra
Sangharakṣita	

During the flowering of philosophy and literature under the early Gupta kings, Nālandā provided a central location for scholarship and meditation where students could assemble in great halls to hear outstanding masters of all traditions propound their views. Here students could study the methods of the masters and practice techniques of debate, a form of inquiry into correct knowledge that grew increasingly important as schools of philosophy proliferated and scholars expressed their views through a continual flow of commentaries. South India provided Nālandā with a steady stream of outstanding philosophers and logicians who saw Nālandā as a place to deepen their understanding and transmit their knowledge. Vajrāsana, a respected center of learning located at Bodh Gayā, often shared teachers with Nālandā.

Formation of Mādhyamika and Yogācāra

According to Tāranātha, the śāstras written by Nāgārjuna and Asaṅga's followers that explicated the Second and Third Turning Teachings formed a single body of writings up to the fifth century. At that time, the masters Buddhapālita and Bhāvaviveka analyzed the śāstras and clarified distinctions between the philosophical expressions of Nāgārjuna and Asaṅga. Classifying Asaṅga's works as applying to the doctrine of vijñāna, Buddhapālita and Bhāvaviveka followed Nāgārjuna's approach and concentrated on the doctrine of śūnyatā, while their contemporary Sthiramati focused on the Vijñānavādin doctrines based on the Buddha's Third Turning Sūtras, as developed by Asaṅga and Vasubandhu.

Since Buddhapālita and Bhāvaviveka wrote treatises extending the Middle Way (Madhyamaka) set forth by Nāgārjuna and Āryadeva, they became known as Mādhyamikans, Those Who Follow the Middle Way, and the tradition that arose from their lineage became known as Mādhyamika. The masters who developed doctrines of mind (cittamātra) and consciousness (vijñāna) described by Asaṅga and Vasubandhu formed the school known as Cittamātra, which encompasses both Cittamātra and Vijñānavāda systems. The Mādhyamika and Cittamātra schools, together with the Śrāvaka Vaibhāṣika and Sautrāntika traditions, became known as the Four Philosophical Schools.

Within the Mahāyāna, these developments reshaped the early Yogācāra, a meditative tradition that had developed within the emerging Mahāyāna communities long before the works of Maitreya and Asaṅga. Asaṅga's Yogācārabhūmi provided a graduated system of realization as the foundation of the "new Yogācāra," which incorporated the doctrines of the Cittamātra and Vijñānavāda schools and provided an integrated approach to study and practice.

Mādhyamika: Buddhapālita and Bhāvaviveka

The work of the Mādhyamika masters Buddhapālita and Bhāvaviveka established two major methods of presenting the implications of Nāgārjuna's insight into the Middle Way. After the fifth century, all Mādhyamika masters tended to follow one of these two approaches in drawing out the central teachings of the Prajñāpāramitā.

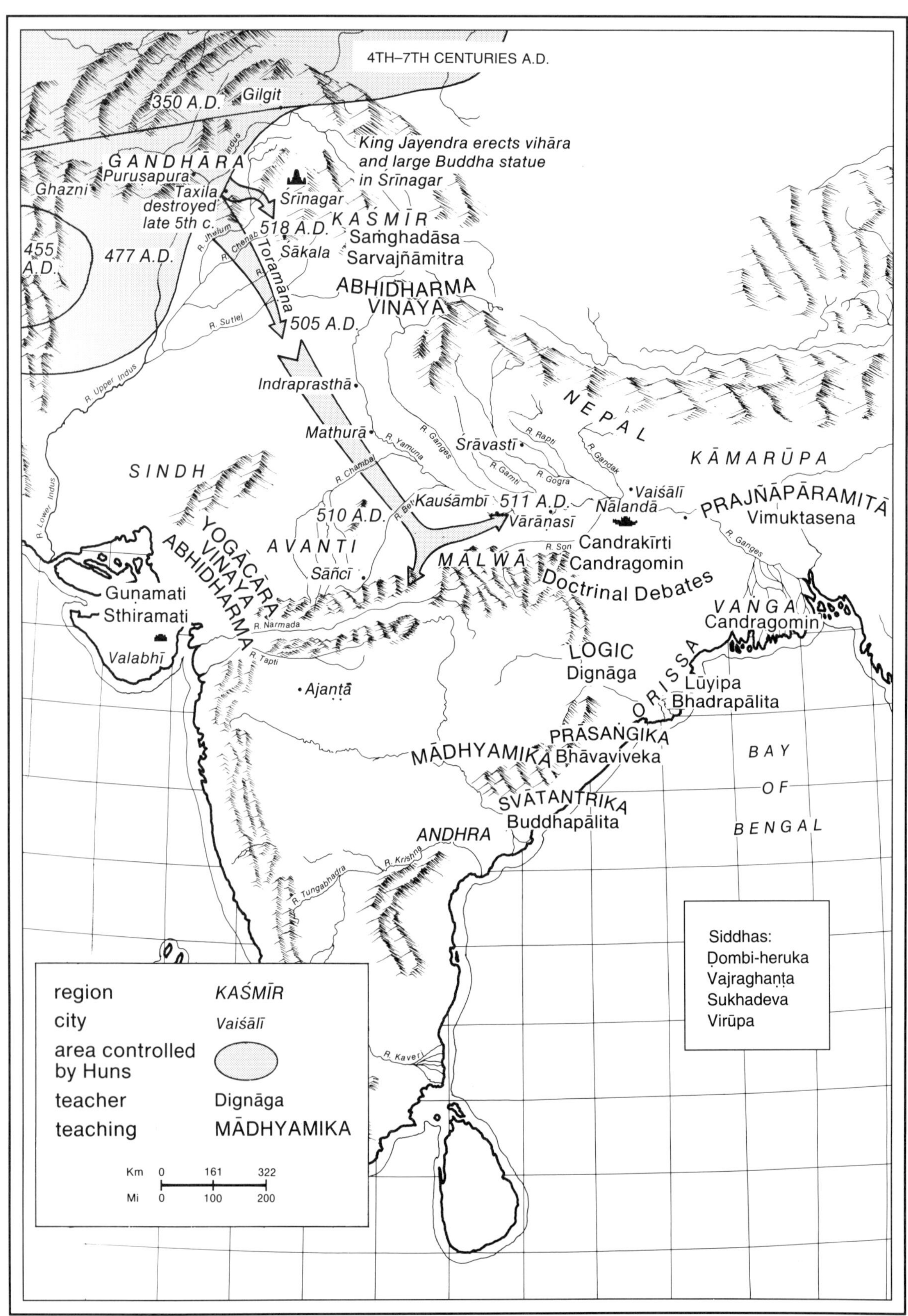

The writings of great masters established the major Mahāyāna traditions.

Both Buddhapālita and Bhāvaviveka were born in the south and went to Nālandā where they became disciples of Saṃgharakṣita, a disciple of Nāgamitra, a Nālandā scholar in Nāgārjuna's direct lineage. Buddhapālita was born in Haṃsakṛīda in the southern region of Tambala probably in the late fifth century. Ordained there at an early age, he completed the basic education of a monk and studied the teachings of the Śrāvakapiṭaka. After traveling to Nālandā, Buddhapālita mastered all of Nāgārjuna's teachings under the guidance of Saṃgharakṣita. So great was his knowledge and insight into Nāgārjuna's works that he was said to have been blessed by Mañjuśrī.

Tāranātha relates that Buddhapālita later taught the Dharma at a monastery in Dantapura, capital of Kaliṅga, and extensively propounded the works of Nāgārjuna, Āryadeva, and Āryaśūra. However, only one of Buddhapālita's works, an important commentary on Nāgārjuna's Mūlamadhyamaka-kārikā, was preserved in Tibetan (NE 3842), and only fragments of this work still exist in the original Sanskrit. In this work Buddhapālita emphasizes Nāgārjuna's use of prasaṅga, or necessary consequence, a method which carries philosophical positions to their limits, demonstrates the fallacy of a position, and points out the contradictions inherent in it.

The focus on prasaṅga as the central feature of dialectic came to distinguish the Prāsaṅgika-mādhyamika school. Taking no position whatsoever, the Prāsaṅgikas effectively concentrated on refuting all conceptual formulations. Kamalabuddhi and Śāntideva followed the Prāsaṅgika method, which reached its apogee in the late sixth or early seventh century with Candrakīrti.

Buddhapālita's younger contemporary Bhāvaviveka, also known as Bhavya, was born in Malyara, South India, where he was ordained and educated in the teachings of the Śrāvaka tradition. Upon arriving at Nālandā, he became the disciple of Saṃgharakṣita, who instructed him in the Mahāyāna

Sūtras and the works of Nāgārjuna. Returning to South India, he became head of many monasteries there and taught the Dharma extensively.

After Buddhapālita died, Bhāvaviveka studied Buddhapālita's method and took exception to Buddhapālita's complete reliance on prasaṅga. In rebuttal, Bhāvaviveka utilized logic and syllogisms to set forth proofs of the validity of the Mādhyamika view in the Madhyamaka-ratna-pradīpa (NE 3834). He went on to compose a series of commentaries supporting his approach to Nāgārjuna's works: the Madhyamakahṛdaya-kārikā and its auto-commentary Tarkajvālā (NE 3855–56), the Madhyamakārtha-saṁgraha (NE 3857), and the Prajñāpradīpa (NE 3852). His method became known as Svatantra, and those who followed this approach formed the school known as Svātantrika-mādhyamika.

After Bhāvaviveka's death, Sthiramati's writings on vijñāna became known in South India. Taking issue with Sthiramati's views, Bhāvaviveka's disciples traveled to Nālandā to debate with the disciples of Sthiramati. This debate appears to have clarified the teachings of both masters; there was no refutation, and both views were retained as valid.

Since Buddhapālita had few disciples and Bhāvaviveka had thousands of followers, the Svātantrika approach became more widely known. Elaborating on Bhāvaviveka's treatises, some Svātantrikas incorporated Sautrāntika views in analyzing reality and became known as Sautrāntika-svātantrika-mādhyamikans. Others worked to integrate the direct insight of Mādhyamika with the experiential approach of Yogācāra; this tradition eventually became known as Yogācāra-svātantrika-mādhyamika.

Candrakīrti and Candragomin

According to Tāranātha, Candrakīrti, who was to become a great Upādhyāya of Nālandā and master of Mādhyamika, was born in Samanta, South India, probably around the end of the sixth or early seventh century. As a youth he mastered the classical forms of knowledge; he was ordained into the Sangha and studied the Tripiṭaka in the South. Traveling to Nālandā, he learned the works of Nāgārjuna in the traditions of both Buddhapālita and Bhāvaviveka. From his teacher Kamalabuddhi, Candrakīrti received the lineage of Nāgārjuna as transmitted through Buddhapālita and the lineage of Bhāvaviveka through Bhāvaviveka's many disciples.

At Nālandā, Candrakīrti quickly rose to prominence due to his scholarship and skill in debate and became Nālandā's Upādhyāya, or the head preceptor. Explicating Nāgārjuna's Mūlamadhyamaka-kārikā, Candrakīrti wrote the commentary Prasannapadā, the Clear-Worded (NE 3860), which has guided students of Buddhist philosophy to understanding for more than a millennium.

In the Prasannapadā, Candrakīrti rigorously defines Nāgārjuna's view of śūnyata and relative and absolute truth. Candrakīrti further clarified the Prāsaṅgika approach in his Madhyamakāvatāra (NE 3861), an introduction to the Madhyamaka system. This great master went on to write commentaries on Nāgārjuna's Yuktiṣāṣṭhikā and Śūnyatāsaptati, as well as on Āryadeva's principal work, the Catuḥśataka (NE 3864, 3867, and 3865). In these writings, he strongly champions Buddhapālita's emphasis on prasaṅga and criticizes Bhāvaviveka's method.

Nālandā witnessed perhaps the most prolonged and famous debate of its history between Candrakīrti and the lay scholar Candragomin, a master in the lineage of Sthiramati. Candrakīrti propounded the Mādhyamika as established by Nāgārjuna and Buddhapālita, and Candragomin upheld the doctrine of Cittamātra following the view of Asaṅga. According to Tāranātha, the debate continued for seven years and attracted a large audience from the surrounding community. So equally matched were both masters, and so sound were both approaches to realization, that neither one could refute the other.

Śāntideva

Candrakīrti's refinement of the Prāsaṅgika approach has never been surpassed. Foremost among the followers in his tradition was Śāntideva, son of King Kalyāṇavarman of Surāṣṭra, in Western India. Śāntideva was probably born in the late seventh or early eighth century. According to Tāranātha, he entered Nālandā and studied under Jayadeva, who became Upādhyāya after Candrakīrti. (Hsüan-tsang states that Dharmapāla succeeded Candrakīrti and makes no mention of Jayadeva.)

Tāranātha relates that since Śāntideva worked by night and slept by day, his teachers and fellow students viewed him as indolent and unworthy. To test him, his teachers arranged for him to speak in the great assembly hall; to their astonishment, he recited from memory his eloquent treatise on the Bodhisattva path, known as the Bodhicaryāvatāra (NE 3871). In this work he masterfully applied the Prāsaṅgika view to the pragmatic methods of following the Buddhist path. Tradition relates that as he recited the last chapter, he rose in the air until he disappeared from view; only his voice was heard speaking the final verses. Later, his teachers found the Bodhicaryāvatāra and two additional treatises in his quarters: the Śīkṣā-samuccaya (NE 3939) and the Sūtra-samuccaya (NE 3934).

Vijñānavāda: Sthiramati

The late fifth century master Sthiramati was a merchant's son from Daṇḍakāraṇya. He revered Vasubandhu as a child and entered Nālandā at an early age to become his disciple. Under Vasubandhu's instruction, Sthiramati mastered the five sciences as well as the Śrāvaka and Mahāyāna systems of Abhidharma. Even with Nālandā's high standards, Sthiramati became highly respected for his scholarship and skill in debate.

Sthiramati is best known as an exponent of the Vijñā-navāda doctrine; he wrote explications of Asaṅga's and Vasu-bandhu's works, as well as commentaries on Abhidharma. It is said that he established a hundred Dharma centers and taught the Mahāyāna doctrines extensively. According to Tāranātha, Sthiramati explained Nāgārjuna's teachings in light of Vasubandhu's teaching on consciousness (vijñāna). Sthiramati is credited with developing Vasubandhu's teachings on vijñāna as presented in the Triṁśikā-kārikā into the foundation of the Vijñānavāda school, which was further developed by Paramārtha, Dharmapāla, and Asvabhāva. Sthiramati's teachings were held in especially high regard in China; Hsüan-tsang mentions that "The streams of his superior knowledge spread abroad even now."

The Science of Knowledge: Dignāga

By the fifth century, the greatest intellects of the age, both Buddhist and non-Buddhist, were focusing their attention on complex epistemological views and doctrines. Here logic came to the fore, providing the guidelines for the proofs of valid knowledge. Among the many dialecticians produced by Buddhist and non-Buddhist traditions, the master Dignāga rose to prominence as the foremost logician of his time.

Dignāga was born in Siṁhavakata, located in the Pallava country near Kāñcī. His first teacher was the Vātsīputrīya Nāgadatta, who ordained him and instructed him in the Vinayapiṭaka. But when asked to find the "indescribable self" propounded in Vātsīputrīya doctrine, Dignāga could not do so, either through reasoning or through direct examination of the physical form of a person. Nāgadatta, angered at what he considered a slight to his teaching, asked Dignāga to leave his monastery. Traveling to the north, Dignāga became a student of Vasubandhu. Under this great teacher's guidance, Dignāga became learned in both Śrāvaka and Mahāyāna doctrines, then matured his understanding through intense

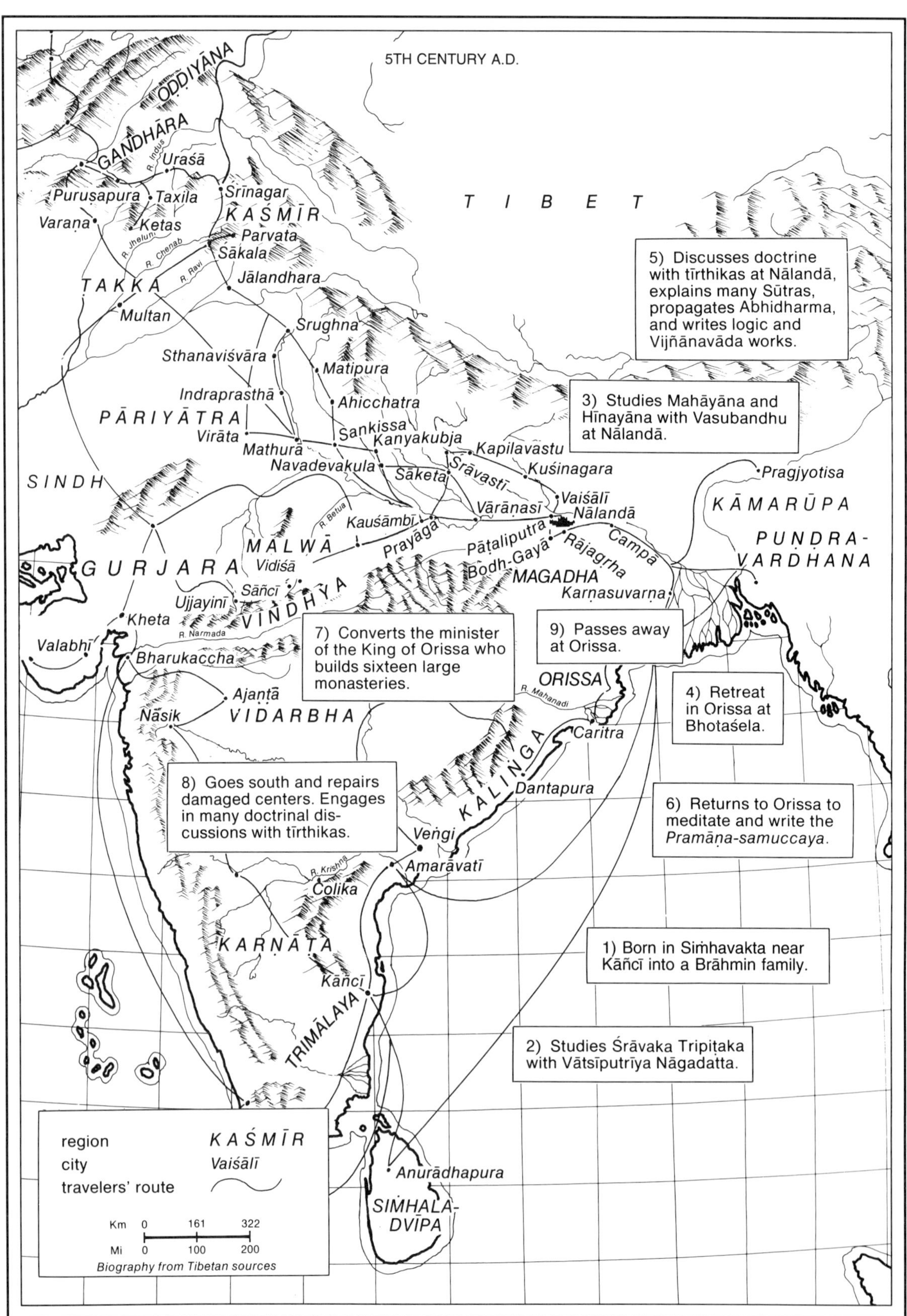

Major events in the life of the master logician Dignāga

meditation in the Bhoṭaśela Cave in the country of Kaliṅga (modern Orissa).

While Dignāga was meditating in Kaliṅga, the teachers of Nālandā were challenged by tīrthikas led by the philosopher known as Sudurjaya, Difficult to Defeat. In response to a request for his assistance, Dignāga traveled to Nālandā, thoroughly addressed the tīrthikas' doctrines and defeated them singly and collectively, not once, but three times. Many were won over to the Buddha's teachings through Dignāga's penetrating logic. He then remained for a time at Nālandā, teaching the Sūtras and Abhidharma and writing works on Vijñānavāda and logic, including the Ālambanaparīkṣā and its commentary (NE 4205–06), the Trikālaparīkṣā (NE 4207), a treatise on the three times, and the Nyāyamukha (NE 4208), an explication of inference.

Dignāga eventually resumed his meditations in Kaliṅga. Here he determined to compose a treatise setting down his whole understanding of the means of logical proofs. He began by writing a verse paying homage to Mañjuśrī and stating his purpose, but when he left his cave to gather food, the tīrthika Kṛṣṇa entered and erased his words. After this happened twice, Dignāga invited the tīrthika to debate; when Dignāga won the debate, the enraged tīrthika set fire to the contents of the cave and Dignāga barely escaped. Unable to benefit the tīrthika through the power of reason, Dignāga doubted the value of continuing this work. But, upon the urging of Mañjuśrī, embodiment of enlightened wisdom, the great master was inspired to compose the Pramāṇa-samuccaya and vṛtti (NE 4203–04), a masterful treatise with commentary that became the foundation of logical study within all Mahāyāna traditions.

Through such works Dignāga transformed the older Hetuvāda, a system of disputation, into Pramāṇa, the means of arriving at certain knowledge. In the dynamic intellectual milieu of his day, establishing a reliable theory of knowledge was a critically important contribution. Since Dignāga clarified in the Pramāṇa-samuccaya that words do not refer to real objects and expressed other Sautrāntika views as well, he is often classified as a Sautrāntika master. But like his teacher Vasubandhu, Dignāga cannot be easily held to a single classification; his work was far-reaching and monumental in its effects on all Buddhist philosophy.

Dignāga spent his later years in Kaliṅga, where he worked to repair and revitalize the Buddhist centers in that area. Although Dignāga is primarily remembered as one of the world's greatest masters of logic, and, as Tāranātha relates, "the followers of his creed filled the four directions," he is said to have had visions of the Buddhas and Bodhisattvas and appears to have spent much of his time in meditation. When the king of Kaliṅga came upon the great sage asleep in a forest, he recognized Dignāga's spiritual beauty and bowed to him in reverence.

Dignāga also inspired the king's minister and royal treasurer, the Brahmin Bhadrapālita, to follow the Dharma. According to Tāranātha, Bhadrapālita built sixteen monasteries in Kaliṅga capable of housing a large number of monks. Each monastery is said to have maintained various centers for the Dharma, which may indicate that the doctrines of several Buddhist traditions were taught at each monastery. Dignāga ended his days in Kaliṅga, passing away in his forest retreat.

During Dignāga's lifetime, a vigorous exchange of ideas came to characterize Nālandā's educational program, propelling the monastery into a full-fledged university. The proofs of knowledge that Dignāga established in the Pramāṇa-samuccaya provided a new standard for dialectic that was respected in Buddhist and non-Buddhist traditions alike. Although at his death there was no one capable of completely understanding his work, his disciple Īśvarasena preserved the lineage and transmitted it a generation later to the great logician Dharmakīrti.

Dharmakīrti

Dignāga's work came to full fruition with Dharmakīrti, who lived around 600–660 C.E. Dharmakīrti clarified and extended Dignāga's writings in his own seven treatises. The works of these two masters established a tradition of logical analysis that became an integral part of a Buddhist education and took firm root in Kashmir and Tibet.

Like Dignāga, Dharmakīrti was from the south; according to Tāranātha he was born in the kingdom of Trimalaya (Cūḍāmaṇi) and studied philosophy from non-Buddhist teachers until his conversion to Buddhism. He then traveled north to Nālandā, where he received ordination into the Sangha from Dharmapāla, a famous logician and master of debate, and completed his basic education.

Inspired by Dignāga's Pramāṇa-samuccaya, Dharmakīrti studied logic under Īśvarasena, who proclaimed him Dignāga's true disciple and asked that he compose treatises on Dignāga's śāstras. In all, Dharmakīrti produced seven treatises that clarified and elaborated Dignāga's work—the Pramāṇavārttika, Pramāṇaviniścāya, Nyāyabindu, Sambandhaparīkṣā, Saṃtānāntrarasiddhi, Vādanyāya, and Hetubindu (NE 4210–16). Together with Dignāga's Pramāṇa-samuccaya, Dharmakīrti's seven treatises became the foundation of all serious inquiries into knowledge. These works were studied by Hindu and Jain logicians as well as by Buddhist masters of all philosophical traditions.

Wishing to master all the secrets of the tīrthika (non-Buddhist) logicians, Dharmakīrti returned to South India, where he disguised himself as a servant in the home of Kumāralīla, a famous tīrthika master said to have five hundred exclusive theories. Having learning all five hundred theories, Dharmakīrti left the service of Kumāralīla after donating a large amount of money in return for the knowledge he had gained. But Kumāralīla, displeased with Dharmakīrti's deception, sought revenge. A great debate was held; when Dharmakīrti refuted all five hundred of Kumā-

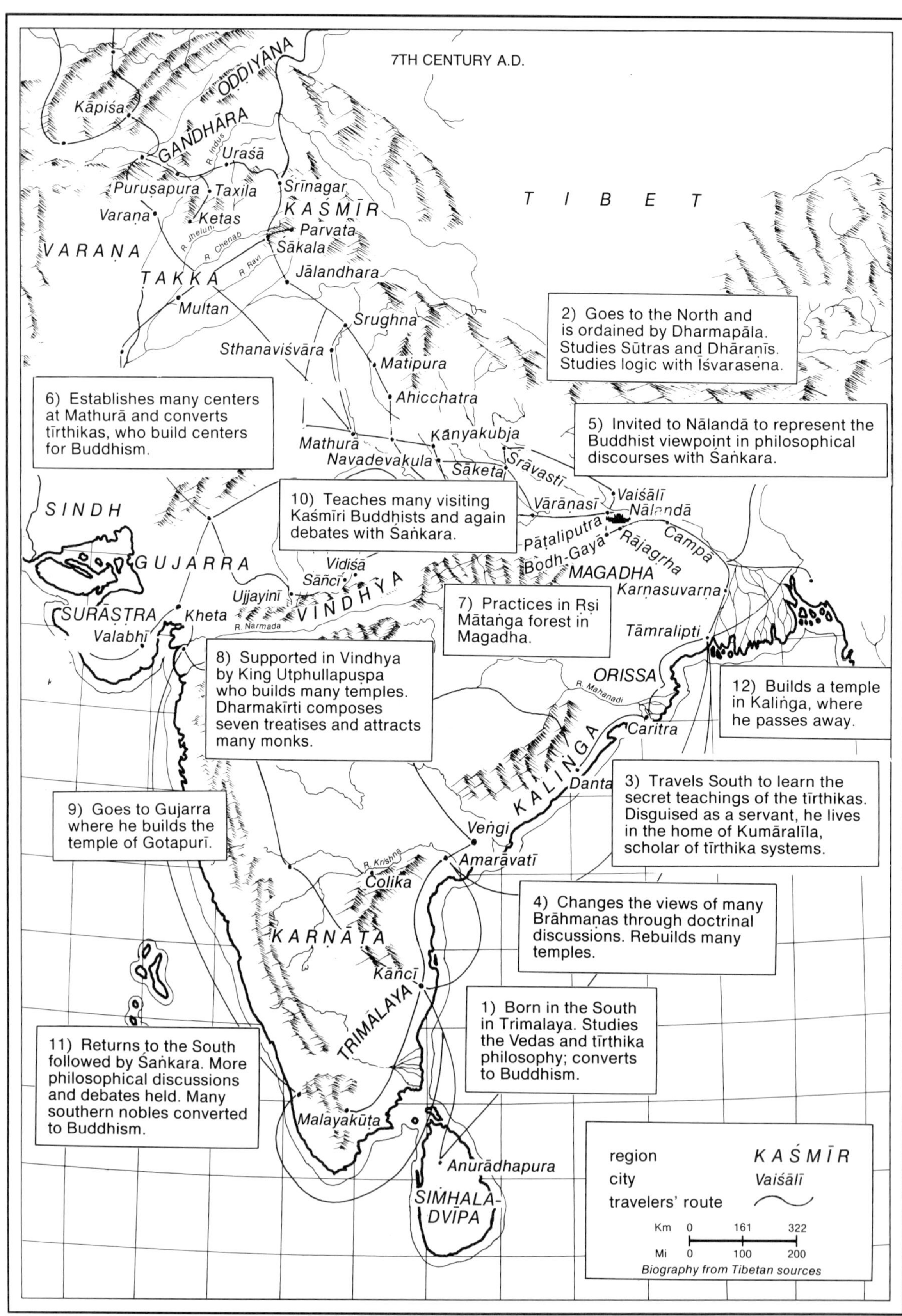

7TH CENTURY A.D.

Kāpiśa
ODDIYĀNA
GANDHĀRA
R. Indus
Uraśā
Purusapura
Taxila
Srīnagar
Varana
Ketas
KAŚMĪR
R. Jhelum
Parvata
R. Chenab
Sākala
VARANA
TAKKA
R. Ravi
Jālandhara
Multan
Srughna
Sthanaviśvāra
Matipura
Ahicchatra
TIBET

6) Establishes many centers at Mathurā and converts tīrthikas, who build centers for Buddhism.

Mathurā
Navadevakula
Kanyakubja
Śrāvastī
Sāketa

SINDH

2) Goes to the North and is ordained by Dharmapāla. Studies Sūtras and Dhāranīs. Studies logic with Īśvarasena.

5) Invited to Nālandā to represent the Buddhist viewpoint in philosophical discourses with Śankara.

10) Teaches many visiting Kaśmīri Buddhists and again debates with Śankara.

Vārānasī
Vaiśālī
Nālandā
Pātaliputra
Campā
Bodh-Gayā
Rājagrha
MAGADHA
Karnasuvarna

GUJARRA
Vidiśā
Sāncī
VINDHYA

7) Practices in Rsi Mātanga forest in Magadha.

Tāmralipti

SURĀSTRA
Ujjayinī
Kheta
R. Narmada
Valabhī

8) Supported in Vindhya by King Utphullapuspa who builds many temples. Dharmakīrti composes seven treatises and attracts many monks.

ORISSA
R. Mahanadi

12) Builds a temple in Kalinga, where he passes away.

Caritra

KALINGA
Danta

3) Travels South to learn the secret teachings of the tīrthikas. Disguised as a servant, he lives in the home of Kumāralīla, scholar of tīrthika systems.

9) Goes to Gujarra where he builds the temple of Gotapurī.

Vengi
R. Krishna
Amarāvatī
Colika

4) Changes the views of many Brāhmanas through doctrinal discussions. Rebuilds many temples.

KARNĀTA

Kāncī

1) Born in the South in Trimalaya. Studies the Vedas and tīrthika philosophy; converts to Buddhism.

TRIMALAYA

11) Returns to the South followed by Śankara. More philosophical discussions and debates held. Many southern nobles converted to Buddhism.

Malayakūta

Anurādhapura

SIMHALA-DVĪPA

region
KAŚMĪR
city
Vaiśālī
travelers' route

Km 0   161   322
Mi 0   100   200
Biography from Tibetan sources

ralīla's theories, the tīrthika master converted to Buddhism along with his five hundred followers.

Thereafter, Dharmakīrti defeated four other tīrthika philosophers—Rāhuvratī, Bhṛṅgāraguhya, Kumārānanda, and Kaṇādaroru—as well as many other masters, until there was no one left in South India who would debate with him. He rebuilt damaged Dharma centers and meditated in the solitude of the forests. Some time later, at the invitation of Nālandā's master teachers, Dharmakīrti debated with the tīrthika Śaṅkarācārya, whom no one at Nālandā had been able to defeat. In a series of debates, Dharmakīrti refuted all of Śaṅkarācārya's argumentations; shown the fallacy of their approach, many of Śaṅkara's followers accepted the Buddhist view. After a long life devoted to the Dharma, Dharmakīrti spent his last years in Kaliṅga, where he built a number of temples and inspired many to follow the Buddha's way.

Dharmakīrti's lineage was continued by his disciples Devendrabodhi and Śākyabodhi. In the eighth century, Śākyabodhi's disciple Vinītadeva, together with Dharmottara, also in the lineage of Dharmakīrti, established the study of logic in Kashmir. Tāranātha cites another account of three Kashmiri masters—Vidyāsiṁha, Devavidyākara, and Devasiṁha—who became students of Dharmakīrti; after they became proficient in the teachings, they returned to Kashmir and transmitted knowledge of the Pramāṇavārttika. Thus Dharmakīrti's works became the basis of a widely respected Kashmiri school of logic that flourished through the twelfth century. Between the eighth and tenth centuries all seven of his major treatises were taken to Tibet, translated, and incorporated into Tibet's basic program of education.

Vinaya: Guṇaprabha and Śākyaprabha

Throughout the centuries, a lineage of outstanding masters devoted themselves to upholding and expanding the knowledge of Vinaya, the foundation of the Sangha. Among the most prominent of these masters was Guṇaprabha, the disciple of Vasubandhu who excelled his master in Vinaya studies. Guṇaprabha, born into a Brahmin family in Mathurā, was distinguished for his brilliance even as a youth and became a scholar before joining the Sangha. Shortly after his ordination he became Vasubandhu's disciple and studied the Vinaya and the teachings of all the schools. His devotion to Vinaya shines through his major works, the Ekottara-karmaśataka and Vinaya Sūtra and commentary (NE 4117–4119).

Guṇaprabha's interests encompassed both Śrāvaka and Mahāyāna teachings; he was a well-known scholar of Vaibhāṣika Abhidharma and explicated the Bodhisattva path in his commentary on Asaṅga's Bodhisattva-bhūmi (NE 4044). According to Hsüan-tsang, Guṇaprabha wrote nearly a hundred treatises while residing in a monastery in Matipura, where he spent most of his life. He is said to have been a preceptor of King Harṣavardhana of Thāneśwar.

Although Śākyaprabha (eighth century) was not a direct disciple of Guṇaprabha, he provided a vital link in transmitting the Vinaya lineage to Kashmir. Born in Western India, Śākyaprabha went to Magadha where he was ordained into the Sangha by Puṇyakīrti, a renowned Vinaya scholar. Among his teachers were Haribhadra, disciple of Śāntarakṣita, and the Vinaya master Śāntiprabha. Expanding upon their knowledge, Śākyaprabha wrote an important Vinaya treatise known as the Mūlasarvāstivādin-śramaṇera-kārikā and its autocommentary Prabhāvatī (NE 4124–25).

Prajñāpāramitā: Vimuktasena

Vimuktasena, disciple of Vasubandhu and master of the Prajñāpāramitā teachings, was the first to relate the topics of the Abhisamayālaṁkara to one of the expanded Prajñāpāramitā Sūtras. In his extensive commentary on the 25,000-line Prajñāpāramitā, he established a way to investigate the Perfection of Wisdom that was emulated in the seventh century by Dharmakīrti and in the eighth century by Haribhadra and Buddhajñāna. With Haribhadra the scholastic tradition of Prajñāpāramitā reached its height. The great teacher disseminated the Prajñāpāramitā widely, systematized and elucidated its major texts, and was instrumental in establishing its study and practice in the new universities built by the early Pāla kings.

The Syncretic Movement: *Śāntarakṣita*

After Dharmakīrti, scholars in all philosophical traditions made efforts to draw upon the new logic and to use it to advance their understanding. This reliance on Dignāga and Dharmakīrti heightened tendencies of the major traditions— Sautrāntika, Svātantrika-mādhyamika, and Yogācāra—to borrow from each other; only the Prāsaṅgikas remained aloof from this movement. Engaged in continual dialogue, holding up all doctrines and concepts to the bright light of logical proofs, the traditions eventually converged in Śāntarakṣita, an outstanding master in the lineage of the Vinaya and all Mahāyāna disciplines.

Ordained at Nālandā by the Svātantrika-mādhyamika scholar and writer Jñānagarbha, Śāntarakṣita received the Vinaya lineage tracing back through Śrī Gupta to Rāhula, the Buddha's son. Śāntarakṣita went on to master the teachings of the Second and Third Turnings, as well as the works of Nāgārjuna, Maitreya, Asaṅga, Dharmakīrti, and their commentators. Holder of the lineages of all Mahāyāna philosophical traditions, he forged a synthesis known as Yogācāra-svātantrika-mādhyamika. His treatises and teachings went far toward consolidating the doctrines and views of the Buddhist philosophical traditions.

Śāntarakṣita drew strongly upon the Pramāṇa discipline established by Dharmakīrti. In his monumental work, the Tattvasaṁgraha (NE 4266), Śāntarakṣita summarized and critiqued the positions of all Indian schools, both Buddhist and non-Buddhist, establishing as valid the view of Nāgārjuna as integrated with Dharmakīrti's method of logical analysis. His disciple Kamalaśīla enlarged upon Śāntarakṣita's work in an extensive analysis and commentary (NE 4267); together, the Tattvasaṁgraha and its commentary provide a definitive overview of Indian philosophy.

The philosophical currents of eight hundred years converged in Śāntarakṣita at the same time that Tibet was reaching out to India for the Buddha's teachings. At this auspicious juncture, the whole of the Buddhist tradition entered Tibet through the master paṇḍita Śāntarakṣita and the Great Guru Padmasambhava, master of the siddha tradition.

Emergence of the Great Siddhas

In India, new currents were in motion. Scholasticism had well served its purpose of clarification and systemization; now the great siddhas arose to point the way to direct realization. This movement drew attention to the purpose underlying all Buddhist intellectual activities and served to balance and broaden access to enlightenment; it was powered by the vision of realization inspired by the Tantras, the last of the Buddha's teachings to enter the mainstream of study and practice.

The siddhas, the accomplished ones, bearers of realized knowledge, emerged from all walks of life, often within the ranks of the great philosophers. Although siddhas had been active for centuries, at least since the time of Nāgārjuna's teacher Saraha, from the eighth century onward they disseminated the teachings of their lineages more openly. Their lives and lineages are recorded in Abhayadatta's Lives of the Eighty-four Siddhas.

Further Readings

Abhayadatta. *Buddha's Lions: Lives of the Eighty-four Siddhas,* translated by James Robinson.

Bu-ston. *History of Buddhism*, pp. 147–166.

Tāranātha. *History of Buddhism in India*, pp. 176–248.

Hsüan-tsang. *Si-Yu-Ki: Buddhist Records of the Western World*, pp. 167–175.

Majumdar, R. C., ed. *The History and Culture of the Indian People (HCIP)*. Volume III, *The Classical Age*, pp. 42–45, 383–393.

Mookerji, Radha Kumud. "The University of Nālandā," in *Journal of the Bihar Research Society* 30 (1944):126–159.

Sankhalia, H. D. *The University of Nālandā*, pp. 5–126.

Nālandā and Valabhī

Expression in words causes individuals to develop the intellect according to their various circumstances and mental faculties. It leads beings from perplexity into conformity with truth, and it secures them nirvāṇa.

—I-tsing

By 635 C.E., when Hsüan-tsang arrived at Nālandā, the great university had become an international center of learning. Pilgrims were continually arriving at Nālandā not only from places throughout India—from Kashmir in the northwest to Kāñcī on the southeast—but also from China, Korea, and Tibet. Some, like Hsüan-tsang, traveled thousands of miles overland along the Silk Route: through Central Asia, the Khyber Pass, through Gandhāra and Mathurā, and to Nālandā following the Ganges basin. I-tsing and others traveled the precarious sea route: past the islands of Java, Sumatra, the Malacca Straits, up the Burmese coast, past Arakan, to Tāmralipti just south of the Ganges Delta. I-tsing arrived at Tāmralipti in 673; during his ten years' sojourn at Nālanda, he met fifty-seven pilgrims from China and Korea.

It is possible that Nālandā welcomed its first Tibetan student in the seventh century. Srong-bstan-sgam-po, king of Tibet, sent his minister Thon-mi Sambhoṭa to India to study the writing systems there and devise a script for the Tibetan language. Thon-mi Sambhoṭa is variously said to have studied with the Brahmin paṇḍita Lipidatta or with the Kashmiri Devavitsiṁha. Devavitsiṁha may have been the master Devasiṁha who studied with Dharmakīrti at Nālandā.

Hsüan-tsang mentions that Tiladaka, a large monastery located about twenty miles west of Nālandā, housed one thousand Mahāyāna monks and accommodated scholars and students from distant lands, but of Nālanda he says only that the monks numbered several thousands. Hwui-li, Hsüan-tsang's contemporary and biographer, mentions that at the time of the Chinese scholar's visit, the number of monks and students "always reached to the number of ten thousand" (Hwui Li, p. 112). I-tsing (p. 154) states that "the number of priests at Nālanda is immense, and exceeds three thousand," but he does not specify the number of students. From these sources we can conclude that in the seventh century the number of monks and students combined was somewhere between three and ten thousand, or perhaps even more.

Nālandā's Educational Program

At the height of its fame, the Nālandā university complex was comprised of six colleges with faculty and students housed in a row of eight multistoried vihāras. Opposite the vihāras were five large temples filled with images of Buddhas and Bodhisattvas. Three temples, the Ratnasagara, the Ratnodadhi, and the Ratnagañjaka housed the university's library, famed for its collection of Abhidharma and Mahāyāna texts. The Ratnodadhi is said to have housed a vast collection of Prajñāpāramitā Sūtras and Tantras.

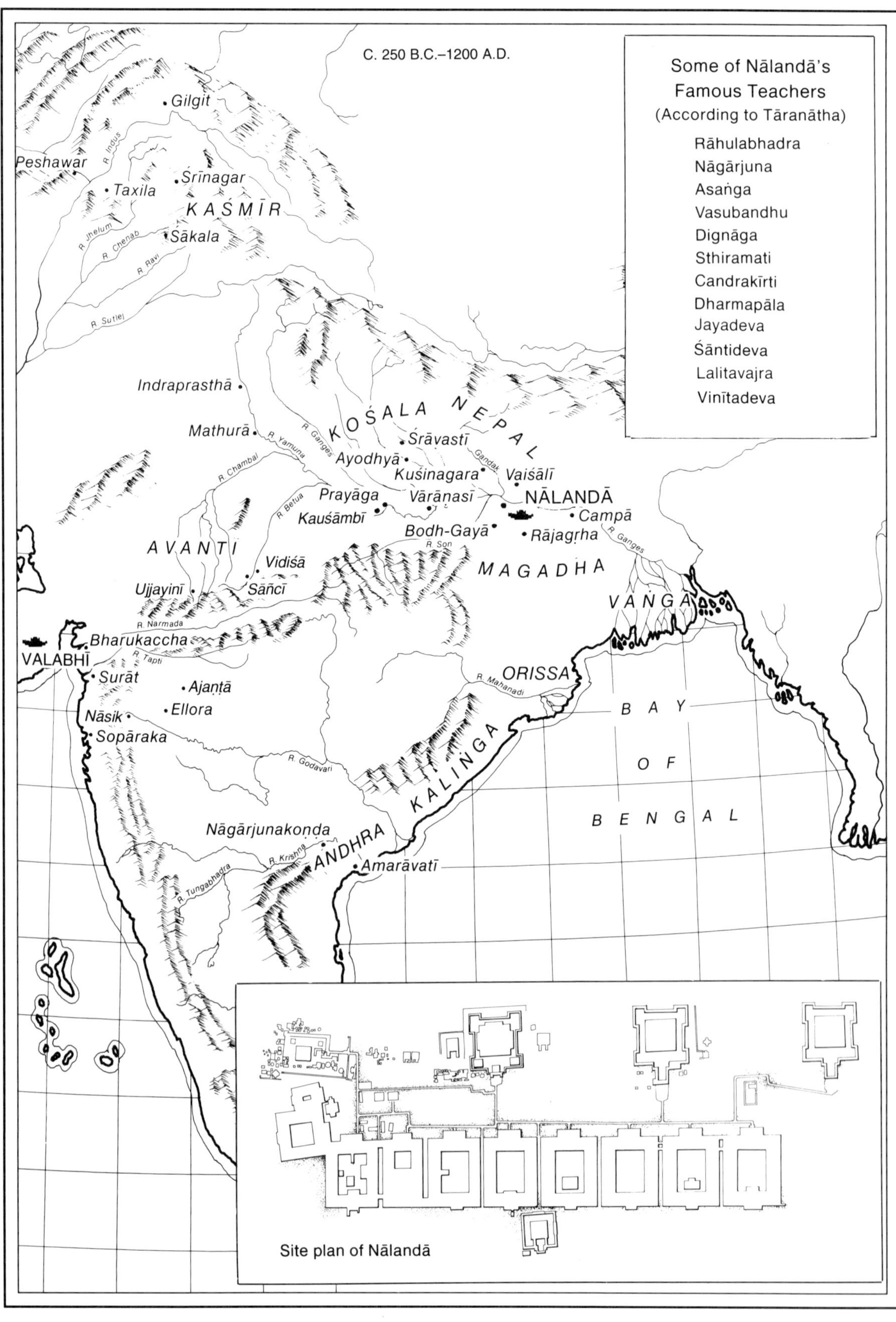

Site plan of Nālandā

I-tsing, who studied at Nālandā for ten years, described the university's curriculum. The preliminary program, which students normally entered at six years of age, was strong in grammar and logic (perceived as closely related studies in ancient India). Beginning students were expected to study Sanskrit grammar and advance toward mastery of Pāṇini's system and texts on logical analysis. Students honed linguistic and reasoning skills using techniques of debate. Encouraged by their mentors, they practiced with each other, with their teachers, and with the most highly skilled masters that their talents qualified them to engage. Preliminary education included study of the Vedas and Upaniṣads as well as the Sāṁkhya, Vaiśeṣika, and Nyāya philosophical systems.

Students read the treatises of Bhartṛhari, a contemporary of Dharmapāla, which incorporated the "principles of human life" into the basic curriculum. Bhartṛhari (early seventh century), a devout Buddhist and learned philosopher, was one of the few lay teachers at Nālandā; the rest of the teachers were ordained monks, with the possible exception of some masters who specialized in the classical sciences. Since Nālandā was also a well-known center for science, astronomy, medicine, art, and grammar, it attracted a wide range of students from all religious traditions. An education at Nālandā virtually assured the student of a respected place in society and established his reputation as a learned person.

I-tsing mentions that after mastering the basic educational program, ". . . those aspiring to become learned monks studied all the Vinaya works, the Sūtras, and the śāstras." On the advanced level, students progressed to Vijñānavāda (works in the lineage of Maitreya and Asaṅga) and Śūnyavāda (works in the lineage of Nāgārjuna), the two major systems of Mahāyāna philosophy. They also studied the Pramāṇa (science of knowledge) system of Dignāga and Dharmakīrti. At some point, at least by the eighth century but probably earlier, the study and practice of the Tantras of the Mantrayāna became available at Nālandā.

An association with Nālandā conferred great prestige and was highly prized by Buddhists and non-Buddhists alike. Students who wished to enter Nālandā, but who had not successfully completed Nālandā's basic program of studies, faced rigorous entrance examinations in the form of debate with Nālandā's gatekeepers, the masters responsible for maintaining the quality of scholarship at Nālandā. The minimum age for formal admission to Nālandā was around fifteen for young bhikṣus who had completed their preliminary studies, and the minimum age for those educated outside of Nālandā was twenty.

Instruction was largely tutorial, which encouraged a close teacher-student relationship and the perpetuation of vital lineages. I-tsing lists some of Nālandā's exemplary masters: Nāgārjuna, Āryadeva, and Aśvaghoṣa during the early period; Vasubandhu, Asaṅga, Saṁghabhadra, and Bhāvaviveka in the middle period; and Dignāga, Dharmapāla, Dharmakīrti, Śīlabhadra, Siṁhacandra, Sthiramati, Guṇamati, Prajñāgupta, Guṇaprabha, and Jinaprabha, who were closest in time to I-tsing himself.

I-tsing remarks that these great teachers were "free from covetousness; practicing self-content, they lived matchless lives." Their example was upheld by the extremely high standards of excellence maintained at Nālandā, for only masters such as these would be capable of leading others to nirvāṇa. "These men could compose a work on the spot, whatever subject was required . . . Such men could commit to memory the contents even of two volumes, having heard them only once." (I-tsing, p. 181–182). I-tsing holds up the example of the great Dharmapāla, who in a debate understood and remembered his opponent's six hundred verses from only a single recitation.

I-tsing writes that at his time (the late seventh century), the most distinguished teachers in India were Jñānacandra, of the monastery Tilaḍa (Tiladaka, modern Tilāra, west of Nālandā), in Magadha; Ratnasiṁha, at Nālandā; Divākaramitra, in eastern India, and Tathāgatagarbha, in the southernmost district. Śākyakīrti, who traveled throughout India in search of knowledge, was then teaching at Śrībhoga in Sumatra. I-tsing had personally received instruction from all these masters.

The ninth-century copperplate inscription of Devapāla records that Nālandā's qualities were manifold and that Nālandā served all levels of society. Nālandā was not only a place where venerable bhikṣus assembled from the four quarters and where Bodhisattvas well-versed in Tantras resided; it was also a storehouse of old manuscripts which learned men flocked to Nālandā to copy, as well as a hospice that supplied medicine to the sick, alms to the beggar, garments to the naked, and shelter to the homeless.

Nālandā's Style of Education: An Inner View

Hsüan-tsang's description of Nālandā provides a first-hand account of life at this great university:

"The monks, to the number of several thousands, are men of the highest ability and talent. Their distinction is very great at present, and there are many hundreds whose fame has rapidly spread through distant regions. Their conduct is pure and unblamable. They follow in sincerity the precepts of the moral law. The rules of this convent are severe, and all the monks are bound to observe them. The day is not sufficient for asking and answering profound questions.

"From morning till night they engage in discussion; the old and the young mutually help one another. Those who cannot discuss questions out of the Tripiṭaka are little esteemed and are obliged to hide themselves for shame. Learned men from different cities, on this account, who desire to acquire quickly a renown in discussion, come here in multitudes to settle their doubts, and then the streams (of their wisdom) spread far and wide. For this reason some

Education of a Monk

Vinaya

After ordination, all monks were expected to observe the ten precepts and practice in accordance with the Vinaya texts.

Āgamas

Sūtrapiṭaka (Sarvāstivādin)
(Dīrgha-, Madhyama-, Samyukta-, and Ekottara-āgamas)

Abhidharma

1. The six padas (Sarvāstivādin)
2. Mahāvibhāṣa

Logic*

1. Śāstra on the Meditation on the Three Worlds
2. Sarvalakṣaṇadhyāna-śāstra (Dignāga)
3. Ālambana-pratyadhyāna-śāstra (Dignāga)
4. Hetudvara-śāstra
5. Śāstra on the Gate of the Resembling Cause
6. Nyāyadvarataraka-śāstra (Nāgārjuna)
7. Prajñapti-hetu-saṁgraha (Dignāga)
8. Śāstra on the Grouped Information

Yogācāra/Vijñānavāda

1. Vidyāmātra-viṁśati-śāstra (Vasubandhu)
2. Vidyāmātrasiddhi-tridāsa-śāstra-kārikā (Vasubandhu)
3. Mahāyāna-samparigraha-śāstramūla (Asaṅga)
4. Abhidharma-saṁgīti-śāstra (Asaṅga)
5. Madhyāntavibhaṅga-śāstra (Vasubandhu)
6. Nidāna-śāstra (Ullaṅgha, Śuddhamati)
7. Sūtrālaṁkāra-ṭīkā (Asaṅga)
8. Karmasiddhi-śāstra (Vasubandhu)

Śūnyavādin (Mādhyamika)

Nāgārjuna's six treatises on śūnyatā and the śāstras explicating them

*Dharmakīrti's works were central to the curriculum after I-tsing's time, by the end of the seventh century.

Source: I-tsing and Tāranātha.

persons usurp the name (of Nālandā students) and in going to and from receive honor in consequence.

"If men of other quarters desire to enter and take part in the discussions, the keeper of the gate proposes some hard questions; many are unable to answer and retire. One must have studied deeply both old and new (books) before getting admission. Those students, therefore, who come here as strangers, have to show their ability by hard discussion; those who fail compared with those who succeed are as seven or eight to ten. The other two or three of moderate talent, when they come to discuss in turn in the assembly, are sure to be humbled and to forfeit their renown. But with respect to those of conspicuous talent of solid learning, great ability, illustrious virtue, distinguished men, these connect (their high names) with the succession (of celebrities belonging to the college), such as Dharmapāla and Candrapāla, who by their teaching inspired the thoughtless and worldly; Guṇamati and Sthiramati, the streams of whose superior teaching spread abroad even now; Prabhāmitra, with his clear discourses; Jinamitra, with his exalted eloquence; the pattern and fame (sayings and doings) of Jñānacandra reflect his brilliant activity; Śigrabuddha, and Śīlabhadra, and other eminent men whose names are lost.

"These illustrious personages, known to all, excelled in their attainments all their distinguished predecessors and passed the bounds of the ancients in their learning. Each composed some tens of treatises and commentaries which were widely diffused, and which for their perspicuity are passed down to the present time" (Hsüan-tsang II:170-171).

The University of Valabhī

As of the seventh century, the only place that approached Nālandā's fame as a center for culture and education was the monastic university at Valabhī, located on the peninsula of Surāṣṭra in Western India. According to a record engraved on a copper plate, the large monastery that formed the hub of this university was built by the Arhat Ācāra under the sponsorship of the princess Duḍḍā, a niece of the Maitraka ruler Dhruvasena I (reigned c. 525–545). A land grant proclaimed by Dhruvasena's nephew King Guhasena records the formal gift of this monastery to "the community of the reverend Śākya Bhikṣus belonging to the eighteen schools, who have come from various directions to the great vihāra of Duḍḍā" (*Indian Antiquary* IV:175). A later grant by Guhasena's son Dharasena II also names the Ācārya Bhadanta Sthiramati as the founder of the Śrī Bappapāda Monastery at Valabhī; Hsüan-tsang relates that Sthiramati and Guṇamati resided at the great monastery built by the Arhat Ācāra, where they composed treatises that became widely known.

Buddhism apparently was supported by the Maitraka kings of Valabhī, who welcomed the "foreign bhikṣus" from all parts of India. This hospitality was still practiced at the time of Hsüan-tsang, who noted about one hundred monasteries in the area that housed a total of six thousand monks. I-tsing wrote that Nālandā and Valabhī were the two places where youths could refine their education under the guidance of truly wise men (p. 177). Toward the end of the seventh century, Valabhī was destroyed, either by persistent Arab raids or by a combination of Arab raids and struggles for power between rival Indian rulers.

Further Readings

Hsüan-tsang. *Si-Yu-Ki: Buddhist Records of the Western World,* pp. 167–174.

I-tsing. *A Record of the Buddhist Religion, as Practised in India and the Malay Archipelago,* pp. 167–185.

Mookerji, Radha Kumud. "The University of Nālandā," in *Journal of the Bihar Research Society* 30 (1944), pp. 126–159.

Sankhalia, H. D. *The University of Nālandā,* pp. 191–206.

Buddhism and Builders of Empire

Powerful supporters of Buddhism founded new empires when Gupta power declined: Harṣavardhana of Central India and the Pāla kings of Bengal.

In the early sixth century, after the Guptas lost control of the eastern part of their empire, the kingdom of Vaṅga took shape in southern Bengal. The kingdom of Gauḍa arose in northern Bengal about forty years later; one of its kings, Śaśāṅka, a persecutor of Buddhism, figures prominently in the life of Harṣavardhana, who forged a new empire in Northern India during the seventh century. Two contemporary accounts provide valuable insights into the life and times of King Harṣa, who ruled from 606–647 C.E.: Bāṇa's Harṣacarita, which chronicles his rise to power, and the memoirs of the Chinese pilgrim Hsüan-tsang, who traveled extensively in his kingdom and visited the king toward the end of his reign.

The Reign of King Harṣavardhana

According to Bāṇa's Harṣacarita, Harṣavardhana was one of the two sons of Prabhākaravardhana, king of Sthāneśvara (modern Thāneswar), a city located along the upper Yamunā River. Prabhākara's kingdom lay directly in the path of the Huns, who still occupied the Punjab; when Gupta power waned, Prabhākara was forced to strengthen his kingdom against the danger of Hun invasions. Prabhākara's wife was a Gupta, and his daughter Rājyaśrī married Grahavarman, the Maukhari king of Kānyakubja. Prabhākara's sons Rājyavardhana and Harṣavardhana were both disinclined to rule and wished to become ascetics. But as Prabhākara lay on his deathbed, Śaśāṅka, the Gauḍa king of West Bengal, attacked Kānyakubja, imprisoning Prabhākara's daughter and killing the king, Prabhākara's son-in-law. In revenge for his sister's imprisonment, Rājyavardhana attacked Śaśāṅka but was assassinated through Śaśāṅka's treachery. Harṣavardhana then set aside his ascetic leanings, vowed to avenge Śaśāṅka's assault on his family and took up the building of empire.

Bāṇa's account ends here, without revealing the outcome of Harṣa's enmity against Śaśāṅka. By the time Hsüan-tsang met King Harṣa on his travels (630–644 C.E.), Sthāneśvara was part of a much larger empire, which Harṣa ruled from his capital at Kānyakubja. To modern historians, exactly how Harṣa came to rule in Kānyakubja remains a mystery. Some conjecture that he first ruled on behalf of his widowed sister and only later took full control of the kingdom. Yet he was in power as of 612 C.E., and, as Hsüan-tsang relates, soon enlarged his kingdom significantly.

According to Hsüan-tsang, who established a bond of friendship with the king, Harṣa had been offered the rule of Kānyakubja. Before accepting, Harṣa consulted a statue of the Bodhisattva Avalokiteśvara; as he prayed to the statue, the Bodhisattva appeared and advised him to become a just and compassionate leader. Avalokiteśvara predicted that Harṣa would become a powerful ruler if he were mindful of

the distressed and cared for them. Assisted by Avalokiteśvara, Harṣa would be invincible, but he was not to take the
title of Mahārāja, or Great King.

Harṣa then took on the duties of kingship, and called
himself Kumāra Śīlāditya, the Prince (who is the) Shining
Sun of Virtue. He assembled an army of five thousand elephants, two thousand cavalry, and fifty thousand foot-sol-
diers, and engaged in a series of conquests that brought all
of Northern India, from the eastern kingdom of Gauḍa to
the western land of Valabhī, under his influence. Hsüan-
tsang relates that during these campaigns "his elephants
were not unharnessed nor the soldiers unbelted." After thirty
years he gave up further conquest and ruled in peace.

Hsüan-tsang also relates that the king of Kāmarūpa
(modern Assam), Bhāskaravarman, was Harṣa's ally against
Śaśāṅka and a trusted friend at his court. Hsüan-tsang was
visiting the king of Kāmarūpa when Harṣa heard of Hsüan-
tsang's presence at court. Immediately Harṣa sent a message
to the king of Kāmarūpa requesting the king to come to
Kajinghara, where Harṣa was then staying, and to bring with
him the "foreign śramaṇa you are entertaining at Nālandā."
Upon meeting with Hsüan-tsang, Harṣa took a great interest
in him and asked many questions about China and its ruler.
This meeting eventually resulted in Harṣa's sending an envoy
to the Chinese emperor in the year 641.

Harṣa and the king of Kāmarūpa returned to Kānyakubja
at the head of a great procession, which followed the course
of the Ganges. At the king's invitation, Hsüan-tsang joined
the procession and recorded for posterity a detailed description of this royal display. Musicians accompanied the kings
and their retainers with drums and harps, and hundreds of
thousands of people streamed after them mounted on elephants, on horses, on foot, and riding in boats up the Ganges
River. After ninety days, the kings and their entourage arrived at Kānyakubja.

Hsüan-tsang tells how, on the west side of the Ganges, the king had constructed a monastery with a stūpa one hundred feet tall on its eastern side. In the middle of the compound was a life-size golden statue of the Buddha, with a place for washing the image nearby. King Harṣa sponsored a series of lavish ceremonies in which he made generous donations to the statues and to the assembly. However, on the last day, a great fire broke out in the monastery and stūpa. Through an act of truth, Harṣa called upon the merit of his religious activities, and the fire was extinguished soon after. Although the monastery and stūpa were seriously damaged, Harṣa's faith remained unshaken. As he surveyed the destruction, an attempt was made on his life; while his attendants watched, frozen in shock, Harṣa himself subdued the attacker. Then Harṣa learned that the fire had been deliberately set by those jealous of the king's attention to the Dharma, who had hoped to slay Harṣa in the confusion. Harṣa punished the instigators and pardoned the rest, banishing them to the frontier lands.

King Harṣa eventually ruled most of India north of the Narmadā River and the Vindhya Mountains, with the exception of Sindh and the region around Rājasthan, where the Gurjaras maintained control. At least one Gurjara ruler, King Tāta, may have been the Buddhist Gurjara king described by Hsüan-tsang. A Gurjara history mentions that this king, seeing the truth of impermanence, abdicated his throne to practice religion.

Harṣa did not rule all the lands in his empire directly; some of the old kings continued to govern their lands as King Harṣa's vassals, and at least one of these kings was related to Harṣa's court by marriage. When Hsüan-tsang visited Surāṣṭra toward the end of Harṣa's reign, he mentions that Valabhī was ruled by Dhruvapati (Dhruvasena II), King Harṣa's son-in-law. With Valabhī on the west, Kāmarūpa to the east, and all of Central India under his control, King Harṣa's empire and influence extended across the full breadth of India. To its north lay another expanding empire, the realm of Harṣa's powerful contemporary, King Srong-btsan-sgam-po of Tibet.

King Harṣa was a patron of the arts and education; he constructed a temple at Nālandā and probably enlarged the main temple there as well. Known to have favored philosophy and literature, Harṣa wrote three dramas: the Ratnavalī, the Prīyadārikā, and the Nāgānanda (The Joy of the Serpents). The Nāgānanda has a Buddhist theme; it relates the story of Prince Jimutavāhaṇa, who offers his body to end the practice of sacrificing nāgas to the garudas. This play is preserved in the Tibetan Buddhist Canon (NE 4154).

As Hsüan-tsang eloquently summarizes King Harṣa's meritorious actions: "(Harṣa) then practiced to the utmost the rules of temperance, and sought to plant the tree of religious merit to such an extent that he forgot to sleep or to eat. He forbade the slaughter of any living thing or using flesh as food throughout the five Indies on pain of death without pardon. He built on the banks of the river Ganges several thousand stūpas, each about 100 feet high; in all the highways of the towns and villages throughout India he erected hospices, provided food and drink, and stationed there physicians, with medicines for travelers and poor persons round about, to be given without any stint. On all spots where there were holy traces (of the Buddha) he raised sanghārāmas (monasteries)." (Hsüan-tsang I:213-214)

Hsüan-tsang relates that Harṣa traveled continually in administering his empire, refraining from travel only during the rainy season. He was generous to adherents of all religions and provided sustenance for all; he heard all complaints with patience, even along the roadside during his travels. As we have seen, he was fond of processions and often traveled in company with many attendants, Buddhist monks, and Brahmins.

Events recorded in Chinese chronicles indicate that Harṣa died in 647 or 648 C.E., leaving no heir to maintain his empire. Soon after his death Aruṇāśva, probably Harṣa's minister-of-state, seized the throne and attempted to consolidate power by capturing Wang Hsüan-ts'e, the Chinese ambassador to Harṣa's court. Wang escaped and fled to Tibet, where he petitioned the Tibetan king Srong-btsan-sgam-po for help. Both Srong-btsan-sgam-po and Aṁśuvarman, king of Nepal, sent armed horsemen to assist Wang Hsüan-ts'e, and Bhāskaravarman, king of Kāmarūpa, provided him with equipment and provisions. Wang Hsüan-ts'e captured Aruṇāśva and carried him off to China. Bhāskaravarman took this opportunity to extend his rule well into Magadha. For a time the powers of Northern India were in constant flux; even the Kashmiri king Lalitāditya controlled Kānyakubja, Harṣa's capital, at some point during this era.

With the passing of King Harṣa, his empire soon disintegrated, and the monasteries and temples he had supported in Central India began to decline. In 712 C.E., Arabs led by Muhammad-ibn-Qāsim moved into Sindh and used it as a base for raiding Western India. Wherever they gained a foothold, they demolished temples and forced the populace to convert to Islam. Arab incursions and rivalries among Indian rulers resulted in the destruction of the Buddhist center at Valabhī in the eighth century, and its scholars and monks moved to Nālandā and other eastern centers.

Little is known of Buddhist activity in Western or South India after Hsüan-tsang's time, but the Dharma centers there, already in decline, probably did not last long past the seventh century. Less than a hundred years after King Harṣa's death, there were only two areas of India where the Dharma still prospered: Kashmir and Oḍḍiyāna in the northwest, and the Pāla kingdom in the east.

Early Pāla Kings

During the eighth and ninth centuries, persistent Arab incursions maintained continual pressure on Western India as the network of power shifted to favor rulers who were militarily aggressive and able to maintain large armies. Arab chroniclers recorded the vigorous resistance that prevented the invaders from sweeping into Western India and which contained them in the region of Sindh for centuries. Three major powers emerged in India: the Pālas of Bihār and Bengal, the Gurjara-Pratīhāras of Kānyakubja, and the Rāṣṭrakūṭas of the Deccan, who carried on a long-standing feud with the Gurjaras.

Historians relate that the Pāla kings rose to power when the people of Bengal realized the need for a strong leader, and local chiefs subordinated their territorial claims to unite behind a popular warrior named Gopāla. Tāranātha relates that Gopāla won the respect of the people by his devotion and courage; recognizing his merit, they appointed him as their king for life. At first Gopāla ruled only Bengal; in the later part of his life he extended his power over Magadha (modern Bihār) as well.

Gopāla was a strong supporter of Buddhism, as were his successors. According to Tāranātha, he generously supported Nālandā and many new monasteries in Magadha and Bengal. Although the actual dates Gopāla ruled are uncertain, Indian scholars place his reign around 750–770 C.E.; among his contemporaries were the great Buddhist scholars Śākyaprabha, Jñānagarbha, and Śāntarakṣita.

Tāranātha gives Devapāla as the next Pāla king, but Bu-ston cites Dharmapāla as Gopāla's successor. *HCIP* agrees with Bu-ston, mentioning that Dharmapāla ruled from 770–810 C.E. Although attacked from the west by the Pratīhāras and pressured from the south by the Rāṣṭrakūṭas, Dharmapāla yielded ground only briefly. After the Rāṣṭrakūṭas drove the Pratīhāras far west into the deserts of Rājasthan, Dharmapāla moved west into lands the Pratīhāras had vacated. As a result, during the late eighth century, Dharmapāla extended his rule over Kānyakubja, the Pratīhāras' capital, as well as Bihār and Bengal.

Under Dharmapāla, Bengal emerged as the most powerful state in Northern India. Extremely popular with his people, Dharmapāla was a strong supporter of Buddhism. Tāranātha describes Dharmapāla as the patron of the great scholar Haribhadra and the founder of fifty monasteries. He is credited with sponsoring the construction of Vikramaśīla and supporting its growth into a university second only to Nālandā. He is also associated with the construction of the great monastery of Somapurī.

Devapāla, son of Dharmapāla, came to power around 810 C.E.; according to HCIP, he maintained and may have extended his father's empire as far as Kāmboja in the west and the Vindhya Mountains to the south; he is said to have also brought Prāgjyotiṣa (Assam), India's easternmost province, under Pāla rule, and to have maintained diplomatic relations with the Śailendra kings of Sumātra.

Impressed by Nālandā's reputation, the Sumatran King Bālaputradeva was inspired to build a new monastery within Nālandā's compound. According to the copper plate inscription of Devapāla, the monastery was white with a series of lofty stuccoed dwellings for the assembly of monks. At Bālaputradeva's request, King Devapāla dedicated the income of five villages to support scholars engaged in copying manuscripts at that monastery, to provide for the monks' offerings and living expenses, and to pay for the monastery's upkeep and repair. Like his father, Devapāla generously supported Buddhism, which flourished throughout his realm, and provided for the support of hundreds of monks.

Further Readings

Basham, A. L. *The Wonder That Was India*, pp. 63–78.

Majumdar, R. C., ed. *History and Culture of the Indian People (HCIP)*. Volume III, *The Classical Age*, pp. 1–121.

————. Volume IV, *The Age of Imperial Kanauj*, pp. 1–57.

Buddhism in the
Eighth Century

In the eighth century, when all the Buddhist traditions were fully developed in India and the great universities were flourishing, Tibet reached out for the Dharma, inviting outstanding masters to translate the teachings, establish the Sangha, and transmit their knowledge and lineages.

After Hsüan-tsang's and I-tsing's time, much of our knowledge of Buddhism in India relies on Tāranātha's History, supplemented by modern archaeological research. According to these sources, Nālandā reached the height of its splendor under the patronage of the Pāla kings, when it served as the model and spiritual center for the major new universities of Vikramaśīla, Odantapurī, and Somapurī. Inscriptions found at Nālandā imply that Nālandā was closely connected to these new universities and that patrons of the new centers supported Nālandā as well.

From the eighth to eleventh centuries, the Pāla kings generously supported the Buddhist holy places as well as the centers of Buddhist art and learning. Vajrāsana at Bodh Gayā, Dharmacakra at Sārnāth, Jetavana at Śrāvastī, Ratnagiri in Orissa, Trikaṭuka in Bengal, and other established centers benefited from the Pāla kings' munificence. Their patronage also enabled the building of such new monasteries as Lalitagiri, Udayagiri, and Vajragiri in Orissa and Jagaddala in Bengal.

At a time when Muslim incursions were disrupting religion and culture in Western India, the Dharma and the traditional arts flourished under the Pāla kings' protection and support. The construction of new monastic centers heightened the demand for statuary and all manner of ornamentations. Artistic expression of Buddhist themes reached new heights of elegance and spiritual grace, in a style known today as Pāla art. The Pāla Empire also facilitated close communications with neighboring countries to the north and east. For nearly four centuries Pāla art and architectural styles flowed steadily into Tibet and Southeast Asia, where they had a lasting influence on the art forms developing in those Buddhist lands.

The rise of the large universities have led many to conclude that Buddhism after the eighth century was increasingly concentrated in a few centralized locations. However, the meditative traditions, particularly those of the vidyādharas, bearers of directly realized knowledge, could be studied and practiced anywhere—in mountain and forest retreats, in the midst of daily life, in the poorest hut or the richest palace.

Since the time of Saraha and Nāgārjuna, the long-lived siddhas had traveled widely in India and beyond, quietly transmitting these special teachings to a qualified few. Gaining momentum between the fifth and eighth centuries, study of the Tantras, systematized and explicated by siddhas who were also outstanding scholars, began to enter the new monasteries and universities. By the early tenth century, Tantras had been fully integrated into the curriculum.

Odantapurī

According to Tāranātha, Odantapurī, a major center for Prajñāpāramitā and Guhyasamāja teachings, was founded during the reign of King Gopāla. Its origins trace to an interaction between a tīrthika yogi named Narada and a lay follower of the Dharma known only as Uḍya-upāsaka. The layman, having obtained his teacher's permission, assisted Narada in performing a sādhana which resulted in a magical sword and a substantial amount of gold. Narada told the layman that the gold would replenish itself continuously if the layman took care to spend it only on meritorious works. With this gold the layman built the great vihāra of Odantapurī, said to be modeled on the pattern of the cosmos, with Mt. Meru at the center and four islands reaching out like spokes toward each of the four directions. This architectural form inspired emulation in other Buddhist lands. In the eighth century, Odantapurī became the model for bSam-yas, the first Tibetan monastery built near Lhasa by King Khri-srong-lde-btsan, Śāntarakṣita, and Padmasambhava.

Replenished unceasingly by meritorious actions, the miraculous supply of gold paid for the temple and all of its statues and ornamentations and supported five hundred bhikṣus and five hundred laymen for many years. Before he died, Uḍya-upāsaka buried the gold, with the prayer that it prove useful to beings in the future. He then entrusted the care of Odantapurī to King Devapāla.

The Pāla kings were Odantapurī's most generous sponsors. Tāranātha relates that King Mahāpāla, who ruled for forty-one years, supported a Sangha of Saindhava Śrāvakas and Sinhalese bhikṣus at Odantapurī and built the Uruvasa Vihāra there for their residence. "Though allowing Vikramaśīla to retain its previous position," Mahāpāla supported Buddhist studies at Somapurī and Nālandā and made Odantapurī the primary center of veneration.

Odantapurī prospered until it fell to Ghūrid raiders at the end of the twelfth century. All its inhabitants were killed and

Pāla Kings

Tāranātha	Years of rule	Dates	HCIP
1. Gopāla	45	c. 750–770	1. Gopāla
2. Devapāla	48	c. 770–810	2. Dharmapāla
3. Rasapāla	12	c. 810–850	3. Devapāla
4. Dharmapāla	64	c. 850– ?	4. Vigrahapāla I
5. Masurakṣita	8	c. ? –908	5. Nārāyanapāla
6. Vanapāla	10	c. 908– ?	6. Rajyapāla
7. Mahīpāla	52	c. ? – ?	7. Gopāla II
8. Mahāpāla	41	c. ? –988	8. Vigrahapāla II
9. Śāmupāla	12	c. 988–1038	9. Mahīpāla I
10. Śreṣṭhapāla	3	c. 1038–1055	10. Nayapāla
11. Canaka	29	c. 1055–1070	11. Vigrahapāla III
12. Bhayapāla	32	c. 1070– ?	12. Mahīpāla II
13. Nayapāla	35	a few years	13. Śūrapāla II
14. Āmrapāla	13	c. 1077–1120	14. Rāmapāla
15. Hastipāla	15	c. 1120–1125	15. Kumārapāla
16. Kṣāntipāla	14	c. 1125–1144	16. Gopāla III
17. Rāmapāla	46	c. 1144–1161	17. Madanapāla
18. Yakṣapāla	4	c. 1161–1162?	? Govindapāla

Tāranātha refers to the following as the Seven Great Pāla Kings: Gopāla, Devapāla, Dharmapāla, Mahīpāla, Mahāpāla, Neyapāla, and Rāmapāla.

Source: Years of rule from Tāranātha; dates from *HCIP*.

its artistic treasures demolished. According to Tāranātha, the raiders used Odantapurī as a camp, from which they mounted raids on Nālandā and the surrounding area. Whatever artifacts remain of this great university lie buried under the modern village of Bihār Sharīf in the Nālandā district. Since this site is inhabited, it cannot be excavated, and Odantapurī's architectural plan cannot be confirmed. However, this same cruciform pattern described by Tāranātha was found in the Somapurī monastery excavated at Pāhārpur earlier in this century. (A diagram of the Somapurī site is printed on page 378.) A monastery excavated at Antichak, tentatively identified as Vikramaśīla, was also constructed on a cruciform pattern.

Haribhadra and the Founding of Vikramaśīla

Haribhadra, master teacher of Prajñāpāramitā, was a native of Takṣaśilā. A disciple of Śāntarakṣita and Vairocanabhadra, he became the most important commentator on the Prajñāpāramitā Sūtras and its major śāstra, the Abhisamayālaṁkara of Maitreya. His teachings and writings supported the study of Prajñāpāramitā not only in India but also in Kashmir and Tibet.

According to Tāranātha, Haribhadra became a scholar and teacher during the reign of King Devapāla and wrote his major treatises under Devapāla's successor Dharmapāla. Bu-ston relates that Haribhadra quickly became proficient in Abhidharma, Mādhyamika, and logic, but his early years of study were troubled by differing interpretations of Prajñāpāramitā. A dream led Haribhadra to travel to Khasarpaṇa, where he had a vision of Odantapurī, a major center for the study of Prajñāpāramitā and Guhyasamāja teachings. In this vision Maitreya instructed Haribhadra to study all the Prajñāpāramitā teachings and to compile his own commentary.

At this time, King Dharmapāla invited Haribhadra to Eastern India, where the great paṇḍita taught the Prajñāpāramita at the Trikaṭuka Monastery. Intensively studying the Sūtras and their commentaries, he composed the Abhi-samayālaṁkarāloka (NE 3791), a major treatise on Maitreya's systematization of Prajñāpāramitā. In another important work (NE 3790), he reorganized the Prajñāpāramitā teaching in 25,000 verses, arranging it in accordance with the system of Maitreya.

Haribhadra went on to produce a series of masterful treatises on Prajñāpāramitā, including the commentary known as Sphuṭārtha (NE 3793) and a word-by-word explication of the Ratnaguṇa-sañcaya-gāthā (NE 3792). He eventually became King Dharmapāla's preceptor and inspired Dharmapāla to build fifty Buddhist centers, twenty of which were dedicated to the study of Prajñāpāramitā. Chief among them was the great university of Vikramaśīla, where the study of Prajñāpāramitā, based on the work of Maitreya, Vimukta-sena, and Haribhadra, reached its greatest heights.

According to Tāranātha, Vikramaśīla was built on a hillock in northern Magadha on the south bank of the Ganges. There is a tradition that Dharmapāla, in a previous life as the learned Mahāmudrā master Kāmpāla, noticed the conformation of this hillock, and predicted that a great monastery would be built here under royal auspices. Reborn as the king Dharmapāla, he fulfilled this prophecy, and the monastery he built became known as Vikramaśīla. Its central temple held a life-size statue of the Buddha's enlightenment. Fifty-three smaller temples dedicated to the Guhyasamāja Tantra were built around it, together with fifty-four ordinary temples. Dharmapāla endowed the monastery with generous support for 108 paṇḍitas and four lay teachers.

Although historically there has been much speculation as to Vikramaśīla's site, modern archaeological research points to the village of Antichak in the Bhāgalpur district of Bihār as the probable site of the great Vikramaśīla monastery. Excavations at this site since 1960 have uncovered a temple and monastic complex similar in architectural details to the monastery of Somapurī. The mound comprising the ruins of the central temple stands forty-eight feet high and measures 360 feet from north to south. Four large structures which once housed large statues of the Buddha and Bodhisattvas radiate from the center in the four cardinal directions.

A square rim structure consisting of a row of about 208 rooms surrounds the monastic compound; this structure measures 1,083 feet square, and its inner wall is nearly six feet thick. According to archaeological reports, there appears to have been only one large gateway into the complex, a forty-seven-foot wide opening located on the northern perimeter wall.

Within a few decades of its founding, Vikramaśīla became, next to Nālandā, the greatest center of learning in all of India. Nālandā and Vikramaśīla appear to have maintained a close connection. Many of Vikramaśīla's paṇḍitas came from Nālandā; according to Tāranātha, the Upādhyāya (abbot or chief teacher) of Vikramaśīla was also to look after Nālandā, which indicates that both universities may have shared the same abbot. It is likely that most of the great masters of the time taught at both universities. Widely known as a center for the Mantrayāna, Vikramaśīla emphasized a balanced program of Mahāyāna philosophy, pramāṇa, and Mantrayāna teachings. Most of the scholars associated with Vikramaśīla embodied all these disciplines in their education and in their writings.

Study of the Mantrayāna flourished at Vikramaśīla under the leadership of Haribhadra's principal disciple Buddhajñāna. Buddhajñāna, the first of Vikramaśīla's twelve great Mantrayāna masters, held lineages transmitted by the Oḍḍiyāna siddha Līlavajra and the yoginī Guṇeru. He established the teaching of the Guhyasamāja Tantra at Vikramaśīla, for which this university became widely renowned. The lineages of Kriyā, Caryā, and Yoga were continued by Buddhajñāna's disciple Buddhaguhya, who transmitted all these lineages to Tibetan disciples sent to him by the Tibetan king Khri-srong-lde-btsan.

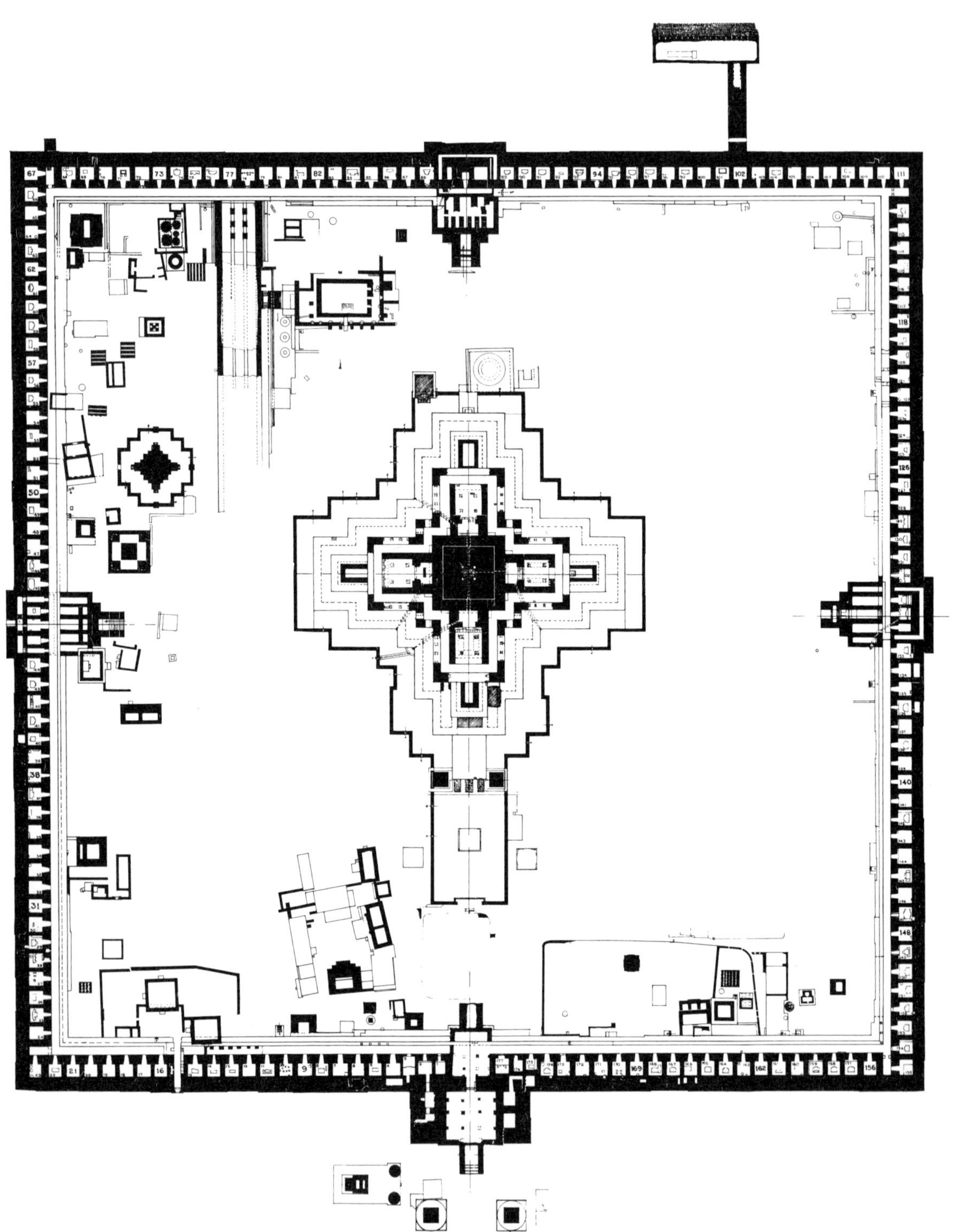

Site plan of Somapurī Monastery

The central temple of Somapurī

Somapurī

Somapurī is located in western Bangladesh, only twenty-nine miles northwest of Mahāsthan, the modern name for the ancient city of Puṇḍravardhana. Tradition relates that the Buddha once traveled from Jetavana to Puṇḍravardhana and that Aśoka built a stūpa at that site. The ruins of Somapurī lie next to a small village which is still named Dharmapurī. This village is thought to have grown up alongside the monastery and to have been named after Dharmapāla, the king who appears to have sponsored Somapurī's construction.

Somapurī, the easternmost of the great monastic universities, was situated in an area remote from the urban centers of its time. Excavations earlier this century removed layers of brush, trees, and decomposed bricks to reveal Somapurī's great temple, which even in ruins stands eighty feet high in the center of the complex. A large stūpa was on the north side and gateways opened to the other three directions. The main building rose in three terraces; a thick square outer wall twelve feet high with sides measuring 922 × 919 feet surrounded the expansive inner courtyard, and two stūpas flanked each side of the main gate to the north. Living quarters for the monks, 177 rooms in all, were built into this outer wall. With accommodations for between six and eight hundred monks, Somapurī was the largest single Buddhist monastery ever built in India.

The central temple of Somapurī was part of a much larger complex that was probably constructed in stages. The temple's foundation is laid out in the form of a viśva-vajra, a cross with arms projecting at equal distances from the center, measuring 356 feet from north to south and 314 feet from west to east. A number of the terracotta figures in the niches on the outside of the temple walls were found intact; in all, more than two thousand terracotta plaques ring the walls of Somapurī's main temple.[1] The temple's offset planes and winding pyramidical form, unique in Buddhist centers of India, most closely resembles the later temples of Burma and Java. Somapurī's architecture indicates that there was a close cultural connection between the Pālas and Southeast Asian cultures, as well as a transmission of Pāla art forms to Southeast Asia.

Although Tāranātha associates Devapāla with Somapurī's construction, terracotta seals discovered at the site indicate that Dharmapāla built the great monastery, which may have been completed or enlarged by his successor Devapāla. Tāranātha also mentions Dharmapāla as the grandson of Devapāla, whereas modern historians place Devapāla as Dharmapāla's successor. (see chart of Pāla kings on p. 374.)

Some modern Indian scholars equate Somapurī with the monastery Śrī Traikūṭaka (Tar. Trikaṭuka), long buried in

---

1. Chaudhury, *Buddhist Centres in Ancient India*, p. 215.

sand, which, according to Tāranātha, King Devapāla located and restored (*HCIP*, p. 275). In Tāranātha's description of Trikaṭuka, Mahākāla pointed out the monastery's site to Devapāla, who then discovered the monastery concealed in a sand dune. Tāranātha, however, does not directly equate Trikaṭuka with Somapurī. Haribhadra relates in the colophon of his āloka (elucidation) of Maitreya's Abhisamayā-laṁkāra that he dwelled in the excellent monastery Trai-kūṭaka, which was "adorned with learned men." Although inscriptions mention the contributions of numerous patrons over the centuries, including a temple dedicated to Tārā, historical information on Somapurī is still very sparse. In-scriptions found at Nālandā indicate that Somapurī main-tained a close relationship with Nālandā, which may have provided teachers for Somapurī as it did for Vikramaśīla.

Somapurī was the temporary home of Vikramaśīla's great paṇḍita Atīśa before he went to Tibet in the eleventh century. During his stay here he worked with Vīryasiṁha and the Tibetan lo-tsā-ba Nag-tsho to translate Bhāvaviveka's com-mentary, the Madhyamaka-ratna-pradīpa, into Tibetan. The *Blue Annals* (p. 845) mentions an Indian paṇḍita Vairo-canarakṣita, who traveled throughout Eastern India and re-ceived teachings from Śaraṇa, head of the assembly of yogins at Somapurī.

Renaissance of Buddhism in Kashmir

While Buddhism was flourishing in the early Pāla Em-pire, it was also enjoying a renaissance under the Kārkoṭa kings of Kashmir, who ruled from 602 until 1003. Durla-bhavardhana, the first Kārkoṭa king, was a contemporary of Srong-btsan-sgam-po, who ruled an expanding Tibetan Em-pire that extended over Kashmir's northern borders. Al-though Muslim forces were invading Central Asia and pushing into India as early as the eighth century, Kashmir's strong rulers and remote location protected it for centuries longer than other northwestern lands. In the early eighth century, lands to the west and northwest were being systematically conquered. By 751, the Arabs, aided by the Qarloq Turks, had defeated the Chinese in a decisive battle near the Talas River. After that conflict Buddhism gradually disappeared from the western part of Central Asia; only the Uighurs of the Tarim basin remained Buddhist.

Kashmir, however, benefited from these military conquests and actually grew in power and size during this time. The fifth Kārkota ruler, Muktāpīda-Lalitāditya (700–737), took advantage of the weakness of the Central Indian rulers to extend his sphere of influence south to Takṣaśilā and deep into India. Lalitāditya used the wealth gained through his own conquests in extensive construction projects that benefited both Kashmir and the Sangha. The king established a new capital in Parihāsapura (modern Paraspor), which the Rājataraṅgiṇī describes as "mocking the residence of Indra." In this city Lalitāditya built the Rājavihāra, a great monastery as well as a temple and a gigantic copper Buddha statue that was said to have reached the skies. Archaeological research indicates that this statue could have reached a height of ninety feet. He also had a large monastery and stūpa built at Huviṣkapura, opposite Varāhamula.

Around this time, the refugee Caṅkuna, a devout Central Asian Buddhist, became Lalitāditya's minister-of-state. The Rājataraṅgaṇī records that Caṅkuna was an alchemist who "filled the king's coffers with gold." Caṅkuna established a temple at Śrīnagar and a temple and stūpa at Parihāsapura, and his son-in-law Īśānacandra is known to have built a Buddhist temple. According to the Rājataraṅgaṇī, Kayya, the king of Lāṭa, a region adjoining Kashmir, built "the sacred Kayyavihāra, a veritable marvel," during that time. Lalitāditya's successors also supported the Dharma; his grandson Jayāpīḍa (752–783) sponsored one temple and three images of the Buddha.

During the eighth century, Kashmir was an island of calm for the Buddhists of surrounding lands, who were being continually driven from their home monasteries by the Muslim conquests. Among the refugees were artists and scholars who helped to strengthen the Dharma in Kashmir and contributed to Kashmir's art and culture. These immigrants included Mahāyāna as well as Śrāvaka bhikṣus, strengthening the growth of Mahāyāna in this largely Sarvāstivādin region. Among them were refugees from Gilgit, known through modern manuscript discoveries to have followed the Mūlasarvāstivādin Vinaya as well as the Prajñāpāramitā and other important Mahāyāna Sūtras.

The Chinese traveler Ou-k'ong (759–763) reported that Buddhism was flourishing in Kashmir in the mid-eighth century. There were three hundred active monasteries, nearly all of which were Sarvāstivādin. Ou-k'ong also mentions a few monasteries founded by the Tou-ke'ue, or Turks. These Turks, being Buddhist, were most likely refugees from lands taken over by Muslims, but their origin is unclear. It is possible that the term refers also to Tokharians, an Indo-European-speaking people of Central Asia.

By the eighth century, the writings of Dignāga and Dharmakīrti were giving new impetus to the Kashmiri interest in logic generated centuries before at the time of the Sarvāstivādin master Saṃghabhadra. According to Tāranātha, the lineage of Dignāga and Dharmakīrti was introduced into Kashmir by three Kashmiri Brahmin converts to the Dharma: Vidyākarasiṃha, Devasiṃha, and Devavidyākara, who were all directly instructed by Dharmakīrti. This lineage was further developed by Vinītadeva and Dharmottara, both educated at the university of Nālandā and singularly well-qualified to transmit the philosophical range of Buddhist logic to Kashmir.

According to the *Blue Annals*, Vinītadeva, who composed at least five treatises on Dharmakīrti's works, is sixth in the direct lineage of Dignāga, immediately after Śākyabodhi; from colophons on his writings he is known to have also been a master of Vinaya and the author of the Samayabhedoparacanacakra, a well-known history of the eighteen schools. Dharmottara, author of an extensive commentary on Dharmakīrti's Pramāṇaviniścaya (NE 4231), traveled to Kashmir in the last half of the eighth century.

Dharma Transmission to Tibet

Before the eighth century, few bhikṣus appear to have attempted the dangerous journey to the mountainous land of Tibet. However, around 430 C.E., during the reign of King Lha-tho-tho-ri, a Buddhist manuscript and several artifacts of the Dharma appeared in Tibet. Tradition relates that the king had these objects enshrined in the palace until the time came when Tibetans would be able to decipher their meaning.

The initiative for establishing Buddhism in Tibet came several centuries later from Tibet's three great Dharma kings: Srong-btsan-sgam-po, Khri-srong-lde-btsan, and Ral-pa-can, who reigned between the seventh and ninth centuries. So impressive were their lives and accomplishments that these kings were considered incarnations of three Great Bodhisattvas: Avalokiteśvara, Mañjuśrī, and Vajrapāṇi.

By the seventh century, Tibet had become a formidable power in Central Asia; its empire reached into China on the east and stretched north and west to Khotan; on the south Tibet's influence was felt throughout Nepal and well into India. Srong-btsan-sgam-po secured his strong position by allying himself through marriage with the Buddhist countries of Nepal and China. His wives from these countries were both devout Buddhists; they brought with them to Tibet two famous Buddha statues: the Jo-bo Rin-po-che, said to have been carved in Bodh Gayā during the Buddha's lifetime, and the Jo-bo-chung-ba. The king built Tibet's first temples in Lhasa for these statues and encircled his realm with 108 additional temples for blessing and protection.

At this time Srong-btsan-sgam-po sent his minister Thon-mi Sambhoṭa to either India or Kashmir to study Sanskrit and devise a script suitable for translating the scriptures into Tibetan. Upon the minister's return, Srong-btsan-sgam-po took an active role in developing a written script and used it in the Maṇi bKa'-'bum, a collection of his writings. For the welfare of his people and the stability of the empire, he prepared a constitution which included sixteen pure guidelines for conduct based on Dharma principles.

The statues of the Buddha brought by the king's wives established the Buddha's presence in Tibet; the constitution created favorable social conditions for Dharma transmission, and the written language provided the basis for education and translation. Thus the path was opened for the Dharma to enter the Land of Snow.

Five generations later, when all the Buddhist traditions were fully developed in India and the great universities were flourishing, King Khri-srong-lde-btsan initiated a comprehensive transmission of Buddhism to Tibet. To establish the Vinaya, Bodhisattva, and śāstra lineages in Tibet, the king invited Śāntarakṣita, master of all Mahāyāna philosophical traditions and holder of the Vinaya lineage that traced to the Buddha's son Rāhula. To transmit the Mantrayāna lineages, the king invited Padmasambhava, Great Guru of Oḍḍiyāna, to prepare the foundation of these teachings.

First the king and Śāntarakṣita worked to build the monastery of bSam-yas, which was modeled on the plan of Odantapurī. Padmasambhava joined them to pacify disruptive forces, and the king, Śāntarakṣita, and Padmasambhava together completed the construction of bSam-yas. Then, at the king's invitation, twelve Sarvāstivādin monks traveled from Kashmir to Tibet to assist Śāntarakṣita in ordaining the first seven Tibetan monks. The success of the seven Tibetan monks demonstrated the readiness of the Tibetans to uphold the Vinaya teachings. Soon many more Tibetans sought ordination; under the guidance of Śāntarakṣita and the Kashmiri bhikṣus, the Tibetan Sangha came into being and rapidly expanded.

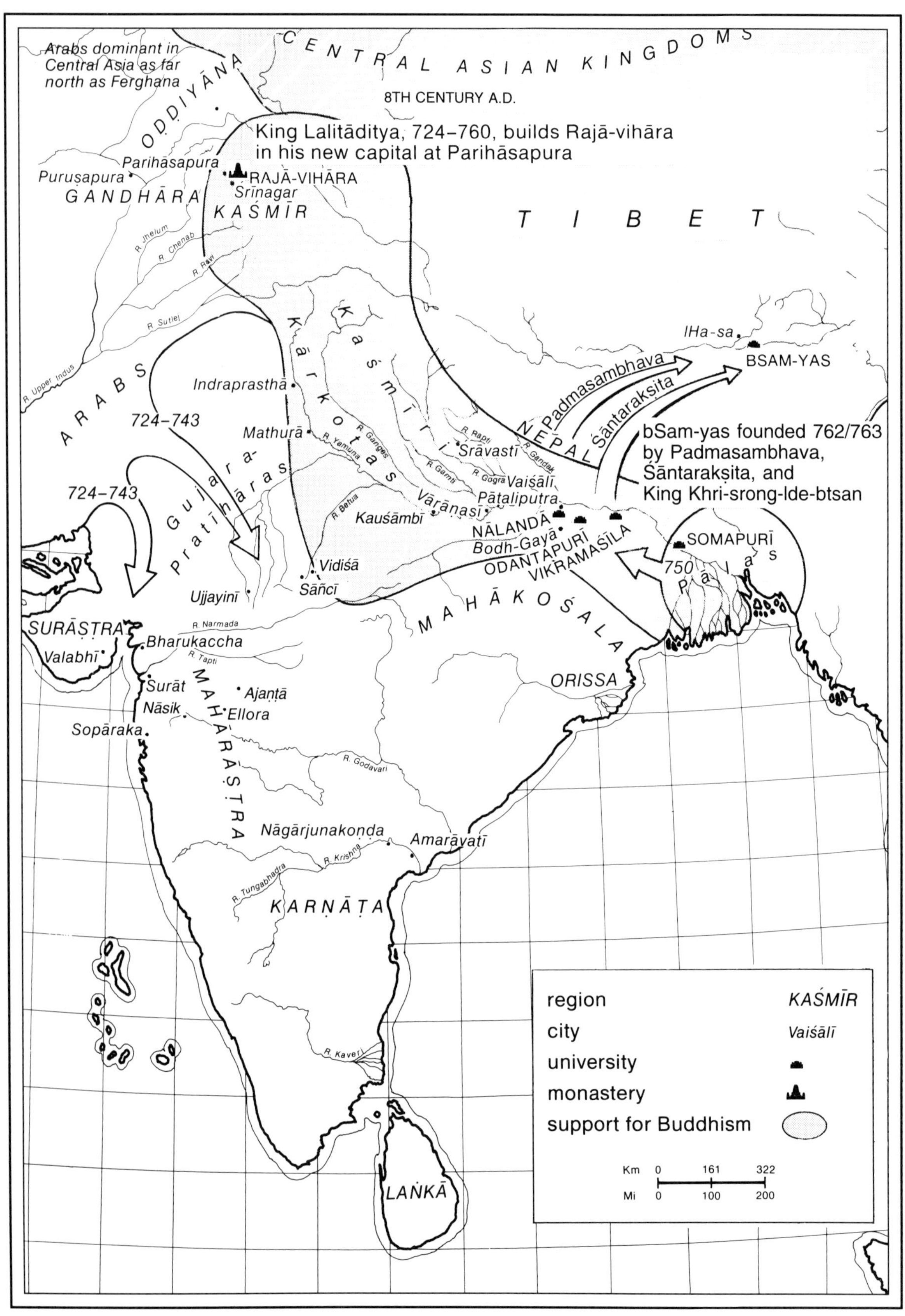

The great Buddhist universities supported Dharma transmission in Tibet.

	Tibetan Kings	**Pāla Kings**
d. 650	Srong-btsan-sgam-po	
650–676	Mang-srong-mang-btsan	
d. 667	Minister 'Gar	
676–704	'Dus-srong-mang-po-rje	
704–755	Mes-ag-tshoms	750–770 Gopāla
756–797	Khri-srong-lde-btsan	770–810 Dharmapāla
797–800	Mu-ne-btsan-po	
804–814	Sad-na-legs	
814–836	Ral-pa-can	810–850 Devapāla
836–841	Glang Dar-ma	

Tibetan kings according to *Ancient Tibet;* Pālas according to *HCIP* .

The king then invited Vimalamitra, Oḍḍiyāna's great paṇḍita and vidyādhara (bearer of directly realized knowledge). Vimalamitra and Guru Padmasambhava, together with Vairotsana-rakṣita and gNubs-chen Sangs-rgyas-ye-shes, two of Padmasambhava's Tibetan disciples, were the major vidyādharas of the Mahā, Anu, and Atiyoga teachings known in the Nyingma tradition as the Inner Tantras.

Khri-srong-lde-btsan also invited Buddhaguhya, master of the Kriyā, Caryā, and Yoga teachings known as the Outer Tantras. Buddhaguhya did not himself travel to Tibet, but Tibetans seeking his lineages studied with him at his Himalayan retreat, worked with him on translating essential texts, and returned home to establish the study and practice of the Outer Tantras in Tibet.

Soon bSam-yas became the center of intensive translation activity. Paṇḍitas from India and Kashmir collaborated with Tibetans already well-versed in Sanskrit; together they devised a process that ensured accuracy of translation. The

Kashmiri paṇḍitas Jinamitra, Sarvajñāmitra, Prajñāvarman, Śīlendrabodhi, and Dharmākara worked with the Tibetan lo-tsā-bas (translators) dPal-brtsegs, Cog-ro Klu'i rgyal-mtshan, and others to translate the Vinaya (NE 1–7) and with dPal-brtsegs and Ye-shes-sde to translate the Prajñāpāramitā (NE 8–30).

Dānaśīla, Munivarman, Devacandra, and Surendrabodhi, also from Kashmir, collaborated with Jinamitra and Ye-shes-sde to translate the Avataṁsaka (NE 44) and many other important Mahāyāna Sūtras. Jinamitra also worked with the Tibetan lo-tsā-ba Cog-ro Klu'i-rgyal-mtshan on translating important Vinaya śāstras, and with dPal-brtsegs on translating the Abhidharmakoṣa and bhāṣya (NE 4089–90). Dānaśila, Jinamitra, and Śīlendrabodhi together worked with the prolific Tibetan lo-tsā-ba Ye-shes-sde to render important Madhyamaka and Cittamātra treatises into Tibetan. This single-minded dedication produced translations of the entire Vinaya in a single generation, together with nearly 750 Sūtras, Dhāraṇīs, and śāstras, all the major Prajñāpāramitā Sūtras, and the extensive Ratnakūṭa and Avataṁsaka Sūtras.

During these years, the transmission of the Mantrayāna was set in motion by Guru Padmasambhava. The Great Guru, together with the masters Buddhaguhya, Vimalamitra, and Vairotsana-rakṣita, translated and taught to the most astute of their disciples the Outer Tantras of Kriyā, Caryā, and Yoga, and the Inner Tantras of Mahāyoga, Anuyoga, and Atiyoga.[2] Together with the Śrāvaka-, Pratyekabuddha-, and Bodhisattva-yānas, the six types of Tantras formed the Nine Vehicles of the Mantrayāna. Among the Tibetan masters who realized and continued the transmission of these teachings were rMa Rin-chen-mchog, gNyags Jñānakumāra, and gNubs-chen Sangs-rgyas-ye-shes. Passed down from master to disciple, these special Nyingma texts were compiled in the fifteenth century by Ratna-gling-pa.

---

2. The gSar-ma traditions classify the Tantras of their lineages into Kriyā, Caryā, Yoga, and Anuttarayoga.

In the ninth century, King Ral-pa-can continued and consolidated the work of his predecessors. Supporting a team of paṇḍitas and translators, he sponsored revision of the translation language and the standardization of terminology. Ral-pa-can was succeeded by his brother Glang Dar-ma, who opposed the Dharma and vigorously persecuted its adherents.

During the persecution, and the years of political chaos that followed upon Glang Dar-ma's death, practitioners of the Mantrayāna, protected by Padmasambhava's disciples, preserved the Mantrayāna lineages intact. The Vinaya lineage, essential for maintaining the continuity of the Sangha, was preserved by Rab, sMar, and gYo, three monks from dPal Chu-bo-ri Monastery, who escaped to eastern Tibet with the Vinaya texts.

Years later, with the assistance of several Chinese monks, Rab, sMar, and gYo ordained the great master Bla-chen dGongs-pa-rab-gsal. In turn, Bla-chen transmitted the lineage to Klu-mes and the monks known as the "ten men of dBus and gTsang." After peace was restored in Tibet's central provinces, Klu-mes and these ten monks returned to bSam-yas. When the lineages were reunited in the central provinces, bSam-yas was repaired, more monasteries were built, and the Sangha rapidly expanded. Once again Tibetans traveled to the heartland of the Dharma to obtain texts and teachings from India's scholars and siddhas.

Between the eleventh and thirteenth centuries, while wars and invasions were weakening Buddhism in India, the teachings flowed into Tibet in a steady stream, carried by masters such as Śrī Smṛtijñāna, Abhidharma master from Nālandā; the great scholar Atīśa from Vikramaśīla; the siddha Dam-pa Sangs-rgyas, and later, in the fourteenth century, Vikramaśīla's last abbot, Śākyaśrī.

Tibetan masters made great efforts to bring texts and lineages to Tibet, risking the difficult journey to India to study at the feet of the paṇḍitas and siddhas of Nālandā,

Vikramaśīla, and Odantapurī. Rin-chen-bzang-po traveled to Kashmir, Mar-pa lo-tsā-ba, 'Brog-mi, and Khyung-po-rnal-'byor to India, and the siddha O-rgyan-pa to Oḍḍiyāna for the teachings. Returning to Tibet after many years of study and practice, these masters transmitted all they knew to their Tibetan disciples. Their disciples founded schools based on these teachings and built monasteries for study and practice.

Three major traditions developed from these efforts; bKa'-gdams, based on the lineages brought by Atīśa and later revitalized by the master Tsong-kha-pa; bKa'-brgyud, based on the teachings transmitted through Mar-pa to Mi-la-res-pa and his disciple sGam-po-pa; and Sa-skya, founded on the lineages carried by 'Brog-mi and transmitted through 'Khon dKon-mchog-rgyal-po. The schools which based their practice on lineages brought to Tibet during the second period of transmission became known as gSar-ma, or new tradition. Those who preserved the lineages transmitted earlier then became known as rNying-ma, the ancient tradition. By the thirteenth century, when the last of the great Buddhist universities in India was destroyed by the Muslim Ghūrid tribes, the Dharma was flourishing throughout all of Tibet.

Suggested Readings

Tāranātha. *History of Buddhism in India,* pp. 257–283.

Majumdar, R. C., ed. *History and Culture of the Indian People.* Volume IV: *The Age of Imperial Kanauj,* pp. 44–55.

Bu-ston. *History of Buddhism,* pp. 156–159.

Ancient Tibet, pp. 227–303.

Dikshit, Rao Bahadur K. N. *Excavations at Paharpur, Bengal,* pp. 1–36.

Sankhalia, H. D. *The University of Nālandā,* pp. 181–190.

Prasad, Ram Chandra. *Archaeology of Champā and Vikramaśīla,* pp. 84–90.

Protecting The Light

Weakened by the destruction of the great universities, unprotected during social and political upheavals, the light of the Dharma finally faded from its homeland. Yet, transmitted to other Asian lands and nurtured through study and devotion, the Dharma continues to illuminate the hearts and minds of sentient beings.

The fortunes of the Pāla kings, who ruled in Eastern India for nearly four centuries, alternately waxed and waned. West and north of the Pāla Empire's borders, Buddhism continued to decline in all areas except Kashmir. The revival of brahmanic traditions strengthened the prestige of the warrior ethic, which may have contributed to the rising thirst for land and power that characterized the Kṣatriya clans of India between the ninth and twelfth centuries. As Muslim tribes gained strength in land west of the Indus River, India's strongest Kṣatriya families expended their resources in military campaigns against each other.

The Pāla Empire, last refuge of Buddhism in Central India, began to disintegrate in the late ninth century. According to Indian historians, Devapāla's successors Vigrahapāla and Nārāyanapāla were attracted to the religious life and disinclined to engage in power struggles with their more aggressive neighbors. Fragmentation of the Pāla Empire continued through the reigns of Nārāyanapāla and his son Rājyapala.

Buddhism at the Time of Mahīpāla

When Mahīpāla I became king around 988, he recovered nearly all of Bengal and restored the prestige of the Pāla Dynasty, earning his reputation as the second founder of the Pāla Empire, the ruler who gave the Pālas more than another century of power in Eastern India. Mahīpāla generously supported Buddhism even as he was rebuilding his empire. Important pilgrimage sites were revitalized through royal sponsorship of religious ceremonies and new construction. According to an inscription found at Sārnāth and dated 1026, Mahīpāla built and repaired temples and monasteries at this site of the Buddha's first teaching, although it is not clear if Sārnāth was actually part of his empire.

During Mahīpāla's reign, two temples were built at Bodh Gayā, and structures damaged by a great fire at Nālandā were repaired. The main temple was completely renovated; votive stūpas were built in the shrine of Tārā, and the great temple constructed by Bālāditya, nearly completely destroyed in the fire, was rebuilt by a king or chieftain from Kauśāmbī who also took the name Bālāditya.[1]

Although Tāranātha relates that King Mahīpāla favored Odantapurī and supported thousands of monks there, the king also established centers for Dharma study and sponsored religious ceremonies in the Nālandā, Somapurī, and Trikaṭuka monasteries. Under Mahīpāla's patronage, Odan-

---

1. Mullik, *Nalanda Sculptures*, p. 17.

tapurī flourished and the university of Vikramaśīla came to outshine even Nālandā.

According to Tāranātha, it was during the reign of King Mahīpāla that Piṭo Ācārya brought the Kālacakra-tantra to India, then transmitted it widely during the reign of Mahāpāla, Mahīpāla's successor, who ruled for forty-one years. Piṭo's disciple Śrī Kālacakrapāda continued the Kālacakra teachings, which entered Tibet during the second period of Dharma transmission. The Mantrayāna master and philosopher Jetāri, author of a hundred commentaries on Sūtras and Tantras, also lived at the time of Mahīpāla and became a paṇḍita of Vikramaśīla during Mahāpāla's reign.

Mahāpāla was succeeded by his son-in-law Sāmupāla and his eldest son Śreṣṭhapāla, who together ruled for fifteen years. Since Śreṣṭhapāla died early in his reign, and his brother Bheyapāla was too young to rule, his uncle Canaka ruled for a time as regent.

Paṇḍitas of Vikramaśīla

Tāranātha records that while Canaka was regent, and also during the first half of Bheyapāla's rule, outstanding paṇḍitas known as the Six Gatekeepers maintained the high standards of Vikramaśīla's educational program. As at Nālandā, the purpose of the gatekeepers was to guard the doors of admission. The gatekeepers were responsible for specific disciplines; students seeking admission were expected to demonstrate their qualifications by engaging at least one of them in debate. Among their disciples were Tibetans seeking the Mantrayāna lineages transmitted by the great siddhas. Largely as a result of Vikramaśīla's close connection with Tibet, more is known of the paṇḍitas of Vikramaśīla during these years than the masters of the other centers of learning.

The Keeper of the Eastern Gate was Ratnākaraśānti, also known as the siddha Śānti-pa. In the highest tradition of

Vikramaśīla, Ratnākaraśānti was a scholar of Prajñāpāramitā, Mādhyamika, logic, and grammar as well as a vidyādhara of the Guhyasamāja teachings. Ratnākaraśānti helped refine the study of the Mantrayāna teachings by demonstrating that Madhyamaka philosophy provided a sound basis for the practices of Mantrayāna. An outstanding teacher and scholar, Ratnākaraśānti bore the title of Rājācārya, Teacher of the King, which indicates that he may have been the royal preceptor. A colophon of the Prajñāpāramitā-piṇḍārtha-pradīpa (NE 3804) by Atīśa, the great paṇḍita who worked for the Dharma in Tibet in the early eleventh century, mentions that Ratnākaraśānti was Atīśa's teacher. Ratnākaraśānti's Tibetan disciple, 'Brog-mi Śākya-ye-shes, also carried Śānti-pa's lineages into Tibet.

Prajñākaramati, master of Madhyamaka and Prajñāpāramitā, was the Keeper of either the Western or Southern Gate. Essentially a Prāsaṅgika-mādhyamikan in Candrakīrti's lineage, Prajñākaramati prepared a definitive word-by-word commentary (NE 3872) on Śāntideva's Bodhicaryāvatāra. He also wrote commentaries on works by Haribhadra and Candragomin.

Also variously mentioned as the Keeper of the Western or Southern Gate is the paṇḍita Vāgīśvarakīrti, scholar of Mahāyāna philosophic disciplines and an accomplished Mantrayāna master. His name derives from the Vāgīśvara sādhana, through which he attained realization. Appointed as gatekeeper by the regent Canaka, Vāgīśvarakīrti is said to have built sixteen centers dedicated to specific studies: eight for the study of Prajñāpāramitā, four for the study of the Guhyasamāja, and one center each for the study of the Hevajra, Cakrasaṁvara, and Māyā Tantras. One center was dedicated to Mādhyamika and Pramāṇa, the basis for establishing correct knowledge.

Nāropa, and later, Bodhibhadra, were the Keepers of the Northern Gate. Nāropa, an accomplished scholar, is best known as the disciple of the great siddha Tilopa, who put

Upādhyāyas of Vikramaśīla (8th–12th centuries)

Early Period

1. Buddhajñānapāda
2. Dīpaṁkarabhadra
3. Laṅkājayabhadra
4. Śrīdhara
5. Bhāvabhadra
6. Bhavyakīrti
7. Līlāvajra
8. Durjayacandra
9. Kṛṣṇasamayavajra
10. Tathāgatarakṣita
11. Bodhibhadra
12. Kamalarakṣita

The Six Gatekeepers

East: Ratnākaraśānti

West: Vāgīśvarakīrti

South; Prajñākaramati

North: Nāropa, then Bodhibhadra

Central Pillars: Ratnavajra and Jñānaśrīmitra

The line of succession breaks after the Six Gatekeepers; there followed many teachers of Tantra, culminating in Atīśa Dīpaṁkaraśrījñāna. After Atīśa, there was no Upādhyāya for seven years.

Later Period

1. Mahāvajrāsana
2. Kamalakuliśa
3. Narendraśrījñāna
4. Dānarakṣita
5. Abhayākaragupta
6. Śubhākaragupta
7. Nayakapaśrī
8. Dharmākaraśānti
9. Śākyaśrī

Source: Tāranātha.

Nāropa through strenuous trials to enable him to master the Mahāmudrā system. Nāropa's teachings, transmitted to Tibet through his Tibetan disciple Mar-pa, became known as the Six Doctrines of Nāropa. Bodhibhadra, Nāropa's successor as Gatekeeper, was most concerned with sambhāra, the vows and conduct that guide the Bodhisattvas and the adepts of the Mantrayāna. While at Vikramaśīla he composed two texts on Bodhisattva-sambhāra (NE 3967 and 4083) as well as other treatises on Mādhyamika and Mantrayāna.

Ratnavajra and Jñānaśrīmitra were known as Vikramaśīla's Central Pillars. Ratnavajra, a Kashmiri scholar, traveled first to Vajrāsana at Bodh Gayā where he engaged in Mantrayāna practices. At Vikramaśīla he taught Dharmakīrti's seven works on Pramāna, Maitreya's five treatises, and the Guhyasamāja Tantra. In time he returned to Kashmir and established centers for the study of Mantrayāna. Traveling to Oḍḍiyāna, he made his way to mTho-lding Monastery in Gu-ge, where he assisted in translating Sanskrit treatises into Tibetan.

Although Jñānaśrīmitra, a Bengali scholar, is best known as a logician in the lineage of Dharmakīrti and Prajñākaragupta, he was also, like most masters at Vikramaśīla, a distinguished practitioner of Mantrayāna. Originally attracted to the Śrāvaka tradition of Buddhism, Jñānaśrīmitra's interest in philosophy led him to study the works of Nāgārjuna and Asaṅga, which converted him to the Mahāyāna. He studied with Dharmapāla and became an outstanding logician, author of twelve works preserved in Tibetan.

According to Tāranātha, after the Six Gatekeeper scholars had passed away and Neyapāla had succeeded his father Bheyapāla as king, Atīśa Dīpaṃkara became Upādhyāya of Vikramaśīla and also monitored the teaching programs of Odantapurī. Atīśa, also known as Dīpaṃkaraśrījñāna or Jo-bo-rje, was born in Bengal around 980. After completing his basic education, he studied Mantrayāna under many outstanding siddhas, including Nāropa, Avadhūti-pa, and

Ḍombi-pa, and traveled to Suvarṇadvīpa (Sumatra), where he studied Sarvāstivādin doctrine for twelve years. Upon his return, he was acknowledged as the greatest paṇḍita of his time, a master of all intellectual disciplines and an accomplished practitioner of Mantrayāna.

Once, when Atīśa was staying at the Mahābodhi Monastery at Vajrāsana, word came that Neyapāla defeated Karṇa, leader of the Kalachuris, who had invaded Magadha from the west. Although Karṇa and his army had raided Buddhist monasteries, Atīśa protected the invaders and enabled them to return safely to their homeland. After this, Atīśa worked for peace between the Pālas and the Kalachuris, traveling back and forth between the two kingdoms.

Atīśa was invited to Tibet in 1042 when he was about sixty years of age. Although he had planned on returning to Vikramaśīla after three years, he was so impressed with the Tibetans' love for the Dharma that he spent the remainder of his life teaching, translating, and writing śāstras in Tibet, where he died in 1054. In India, his work was continued by his five spiritual sons, Pi-to-pa, Madhyamakasiṁha, Kṣiti-garbha (Bhūmigarbha), Dharmākaramati, and Mitraguhya. Tāranātha relates that this was the period when thirty-seven Buddhist paṇḍitas worked for the welfare of living beings. Among them was Sthirapāla, a master of Prajñāpāramitā at Vikramaśīla, who helped his brother repair the Dharma-rājika Stūpa at Sārnāth in 1026.

Although the Dharma still flourished in the large monasteries and universities of India, paṇḍitas and siddhas alike noted that powerful destructive forces were gaining momentum. The Muslim armies were again gathering strength in the West; as early as 1034 the Persian Ghaznavids occupying the Punjab swept unopposed down the Ganges and plundered Vārāṇasī. Only dissensions among the Ghaznavids and a temporary alliance of Central Indian leaders prevented further advances. Yet leaders of Indian ruling classes tended to ignore the danger to the west and soon returned to fighting each other in age-old struggles for territory and power. Aware that the Dharma in India was endangered, far-sighted masters arose to collect, compile, and translate as many texts as possible into Tibetan, and siddhas who bore the Mantrayāna lineages made even greater efforts to transmit their knowledge to their Tibetan disciples.

Buddhism still shone brightly in Kashmir, as yet undisturbed by invasions. Although the kings of Kashmir who reigned between 700 and 1200 were Hindu, most of them were protective of Buddhism, and, with few interruptions, Buddhism continued to thrive in Kashmir. Like the Pāla Empire, Kashmir became a welcome refuge for Buddhists from surrounding areas, a valley of light in a war-torn region. During the eleventh and twelfth centuries, a steady flow of Tibetans came to study with such masters as Ratnavajra, Ganghadhara, and Śraddhavarman, and a large number of Kashmiri masters, artists, and craftsmen went to western Tibet to revitalize the Dharma there.

Kashmir became especially renowned for Mahāyāna philosophy, Prajñāpāramitā studies, several important tantric lineages, and the study of logic. In the eleventh century, the Ratnagupta and Ratnaraśmi monasteries in Anupamapura became Kashmir's most important centers of learning and culture, able to support translation of Buddhist texts in both Tibet and China.

Rāmapāla, Last of the Buddhist Pāla Kings

The reigns of Neyapāla's successors (c. 1055–1075) were troubled by invasions and weakened by internal dissensions. During this time, North Bengal passed out of Pāla control, and Somapurī was set on fire by the armies of Southeast Bengal. The Kalachuris, the Pālas' neighbors to the southwest, overran the Pālas' western borders and took over Vārāṇasī and Sārnāth. In the last part of the eleventh century, the Gāhaḍavālas, the ruling family of Kanauj, drove the

Kalachuris from Sārnāth and took over yet another piece of the Pāla Empire.

The sites sacred to Buddhism appear to have survived this succession of rulers, at least one of whom helped strengthen centers at Sārnāth and Śrāvastī in the early twelfth century. Kumāradevī, the Buddhist wife of the Gāhaḍavāla king Govindacandra, constructed a huge monastery, the Dharmacakra Jinavihāra, at Sārnāth; another patron sponsored a new casing for Sārnāth's Dharmarājika Stūpa. Still other patrons donated a large number of statues to support the revitalization of this site of the Buddha's first teaching. According to an inscription found at Saheth-Maheth, Govindacandra also dedicated the income of six villages for the support of the Sangha under Buddharakṣita, abbot of the Jetavana Monastery at Śrāvastī. Like his predecessor King Harṣa, also from Kanauj, Govindacandra appears to have been sincerely interested in the Buddha's teaching. Two of his wives were Buddhist, and his grandson, Jayacandra, converted from Vaiṣṇavism to Buddhism under the guidance of the monk Śrīmitra of Bodh Gayā.

Upon assuming power, Rāmapāla, who reigned between 1075 and 1130, formed an alliance with local chieftains to strengthen his army and brought North Bengal back under Pāla dominion. He went on to extend his rule over Assam and the areas ruled by the Varman kings of East Bengal, but attempts to expand to the northwest were frustrated by the Gāhaḍavāla king Govindacandra.

Buddhism thrived during the reign of King Rāmapāla, and the universities of the empire were well-attended. Tāranātha relates that 160 paṇḍitas and a thousand monks were permanent residents in Vikramaśīla and as many as five thousand monks attended special ceremonies there. A thousand monks, both Śrāvakayāna and Mahāyāna, were in permanent residence at Odantapurī, which held occasional gatherings attended by as many as twelve thousand monks. It was also under Rāmapāla's rule that the monk Vipula-

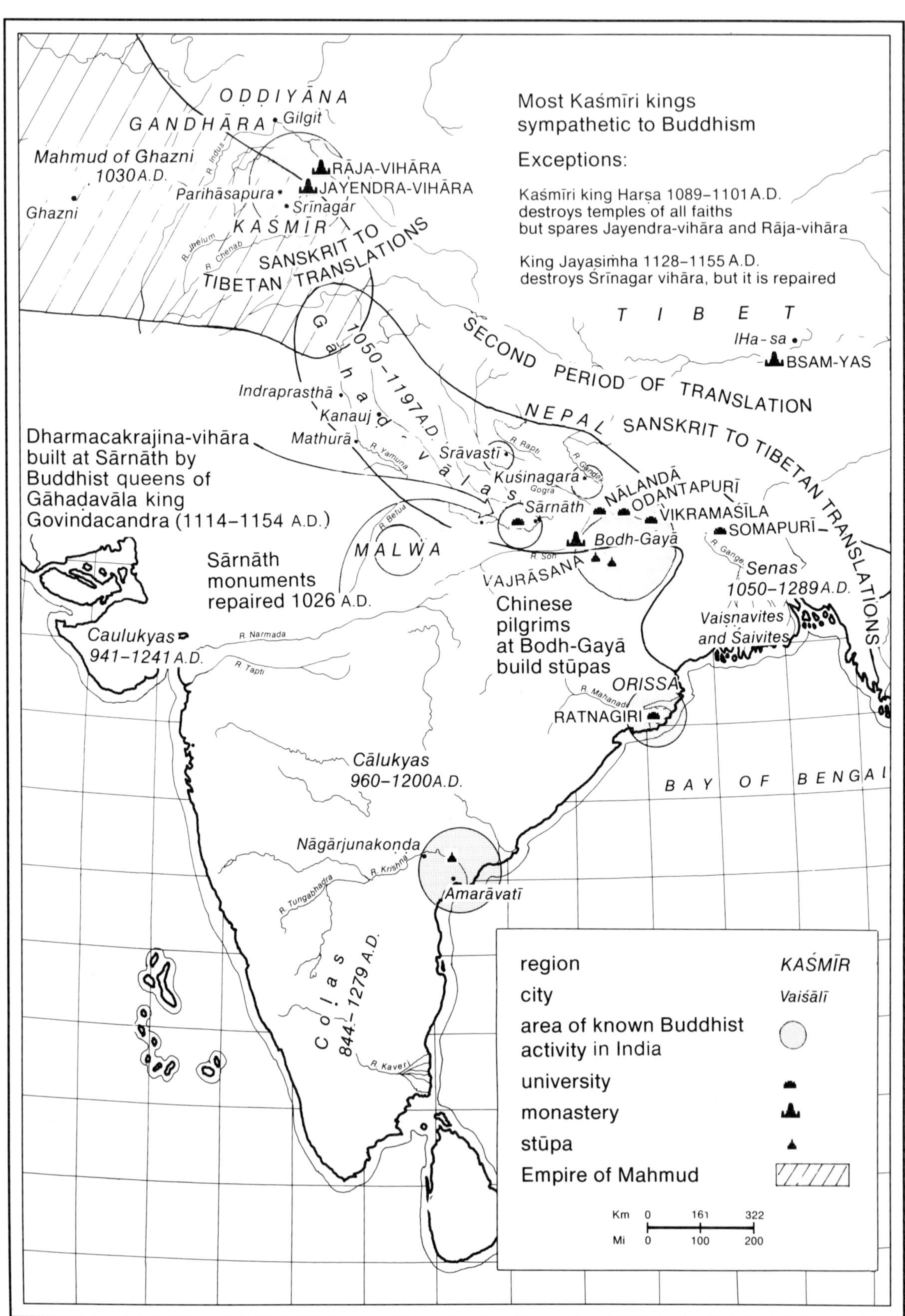

Major sites of Dharma activity during the 10th to 12th centuries

śrīmitra attempted to renovate Somapurī. At Vajrāsana, the king maintained forty Mahāyāna monks and two hundred Śrāvaka bhikṣus, with occasional congregations of ten thousand Śrāvaka monks.

To Rāmapāla is attributed the construction of Jagaddala, one of the last great monasteries built in India. Although Orissa is sometimes cited as its location, Indian scholars place the monastery in Varendra (North Bengal), on the banks of the Ganges and Karotoyā rivers. Jagaddala became a well-known center for Tantra studies. The colophon of the Tarkabhāṣā (NE 4264), a treatise on logic, connects its author, the bhikṣu and great paṇḍita Mokṣākaragupta, with the Jagaddala Monastery. Bengal was the site of two other noted eleventh- and twelfth-century centers of Buddhist learning and culture: Devīkoṭa in North Bengal and Paṇḍita Vihāra in the Chittagong District of East Bengal. The great siddha Advayavajra, also known as Avadhūtapāda and Maitrīpāda, lived in the Devīkoṭa Vihāra; more than fifty of his works were translated into Tibetan and preserved in the Tibetan Canon. The master Prajñābhadra was connected with the Paṇḍita Vihāra; his disciple was the Kashmiri paṇḍita Nāḍapāda (Yaśobhadra).

Abhayākaragupta, regarded as the foremost Mahāyāna master after Atīśa, became Upādhyāya of Vajrāsana during Rāmapāla's reign; later in his life he became Upādhyāya of Vikramaśīla and Nālandā. A prolific author of works on the Guhyasamāja, Kālacakra, and other tantric systems, Abhayā-karagupta was aware of Buddhism's imminent decline in India. He directed his efforts toward preserving texts and translating them into the language of Tibet, where the Dharma was rapidly expanding.

Abhayākaragupta systematically collected all the teachings he could locate, prepared commentaries on them, and worked with his Tibetan disciples to translate more than 130 texts into Tibetan. He wrote down all the knowledge he had accumulated; he compiled the Sādhana-sāgara, or the Ocean of Sādhanas, and prepared the Vajramālā, a text that describes all the maṇḍalas related to the sādhanas. These and more than thirty other works by Abhayākaragupta were also translated into Tibetan and preserved in the bsTan-'gyur. Tāranātha describes Abhayākaragupta as practically the last among the famous great masters to nourish the Dharma with their scholarship, compassion, power, and wealth.

The Sena Kings

The Pālas who succeeded Rāmapāla between 1120 and 1144 were continually besieged by the neighboring rulers. Around 1144, the Sena chief Vijayasena pushed Madanapāla out of his homeland into the Aṅga country, where he died around 1161, ending nearly four centuries of Pāla rule. For a time Pāla leadership persisted in the regions of Nālandā and Gayā; Nālandā's last Pāla patron was Govindapāladeva, who died in 1197.

While the Senas ruled Bihār and Bengal, Śubhākaragupta, Daśabalaśrī, Dharmākaragupta, and other disciples of Abhayākaragupta continued to propagate the Dharma. During the time of King Rāthikasena, a group of scholars led by the Kashmiri paṇḍita Śākyaśrībhadra became known as the Twenty-four Great Ones of Vikramaśīla. The Twenty-four Great Ones included Buddhaśrī of Nepal, who served as the Elder of the Mahāsāṃghikas in Vikramaśīla before returning to teach in Nepal; Ratnarakṣita, Vikramaśīla's master of Tantra and Prajñāpāramitā; Jñānākaragupta, who had a direct vision of Maitreya; Buddhaśrīmitra, renowned for his attainment of siddhi; and Vajraśrī, Daśabala's disciple, who led thousands of disciples to realization.

Tāranātha records that while Vajrāsana was mostly a Śrāvaka center, and other Dharma centers became increasingly rare, the number of Mahāyāna monks at Vikramaśīla and Odantapurī remained undiminished from the time of Abhayākaragupta.

Sena Kings (East Bengal)

Dates	HCIP	Tāranātha
—	Sāmantasena	—
—	Hemantasena	—
1095–1158	Vijayasena	Lavasena
1158–1178	Vallālasena	Kaśasena
1178–1205	Lakṣmaṇasena	Maṇitasena
1205–1220?	Viśvarūpasena	Rāthikasena
—	Keśavasena	

Destruction of the Great Universities

In the mid-eleventh century, shifts of power among the Muslims gathered on India's western border set in motion a chain of events that augured the end of the large universities. The Saljūq Turks under Tughril reunited the Middle East from the Mediterranean Sea to Afghanistan. Their power was broken in 1141 by the non-Muslim Qarā Khitai Turks from eastern Central Asia. Into this void moved the Khvārazm Shāhs and the Ghūrids; it was the Ghūrids who mounted the invasion that led to the conquest of India. To Indian and Tibetan historians, the Ghūrids, as other Persian and Central Asian tribes, were known as Turuṣkas.

The Ghūrids lived between Ghaznī and Herāt; opinion is divided as to whether they were Afghans or Persians. Inspired by earlier Muslim exploits, their leader Mu'izz-ud-dīn Muhammad began raiding India around 1175. In clearing a pathway into India, he first took over Sindh in the south, then the Punjab in the northwest, which were both occupied by other Muslim tribes.

By 1192 Muhammad had conquered Delhi and turned over his army to his general Qutb-ud-dīn Aibak. Aibak prepared the way for further invasions from Ghūr; in 1193 Muhammad again led the Ghūrids into India, where they destroyed all religious centers in Vārāṇasī and Sārnāth and massacred thousands. Muhammad then returned to Ghūr with great caravans of treasure, leaving Aibak in charge. Although the Gujarātis effectively resisted the Ghūrids on the western coast, the Ghūrids increased their hold on Central India.

Historical records suggest the Ghūrid destruction of the Buddhist centers of eastern India was largely due to the exploits of a single Muslim soldier-of-fortune named Muhammad Bakhtyār Khaljī. Muhammad Khaljī put together a small army and in 1196 or 1197 gained Aibak's permission to raid Bihār. From the fortune amassed during these raids, Muhammad Khaljī built up his army, then attacked and destroyed the great monastery of Odantapurī, slaughtering all its inhabitants. Tāranātha writes that the Turuṣkas took over Odantapurī and used it as a camp for their army. From there they mounted raid after raid on the surrounding territory, wreaking great destruction on Nālandā. Concerning the attack on Nālandā or Odantapurī, the Muslim chronicler Tabakāt-i-Nāsirī (c. 1199) recorded:

"The onslaught of Bakhtyār Khaljī was so severe and so thorough that the monks were killed, one and all, so much so, that there was no one left to explain the contents of books that the victor found at the place." (quoted in Elliot, *History of India,* II:306)

The destruction was still continuing in 1235, as reported by the Tibetan monk Dharmasvamin, who traveled to Nālandā and found the temples and vihāras badly damaged and sparsely inhabited. While he was there, three hundred Turuṣka soldiers raided Nālandā from their base at Odantapurī, inflicting even more damage; only two vihāras were spared. Everyone was killed except for Dharmasvamin and the aged abbot, who concealed themselves inside the ruins of the Jñānanātha Temple.

Archaeological evidence verifies that destruction of Nālandā continued over a period of time; Nālandā's walls were six feet thick, and the monasteries were massive. Some areas of Nālandā were occupied for a time after the destruction, but were not well maintained; few images dating from this later period can be found.

From the time of Nālandā's destruction up to the nineteenth century when Nālandā's location was identified, even the name of Nālandā was forgotten in India: the site had became known locally as Baragaon, a corrupt form of Vihāragrāma, Village of the Monastery. The excavations that began in 1915–1916 and continued through 1982–1983 brought into view the impressive remains of this great university.

End of Muhammad Khaljī's Campaign

Lakṣmaṇasena, the Sena king famed for his military prowess, appears to have done nothing to protect Odantapurī or the western part of his empire. Muhammad Khaljī, now at the head of a large army, marched into Bengal unopposed; he took over the Sena's capital city of Nadiyā in 1202 and conquered North Bengal shortly afterward. Somapurī, in the sparsely-inhabited Rājshāhī region, was completely unprotected; even in its decline it was an impressive structure, the largest and highest for miles around. For Muhammad Khaljī's invading army it immediately became a prime target for destruction. Although all of North Bengal was conquered by the Muslims, Lakṣmaṇasena and his descendants Viśvarūpasena and Keśavasena successfully repulsed all attacks from their last remaining stronghold in Vaṅga (South Bengal). Muhammad Khaljī continued to march eastward, then went north along the Brahmaputra River, planning to invade Tibet. But soon after crossing into Tibet, his army was routed by the hill tribes and almost completely destroyed. Devastated and powerless, Muhammad Khaljī died at the hand of one of his own soldiers in 1206. Later Muslim expeditions into easternmost India were

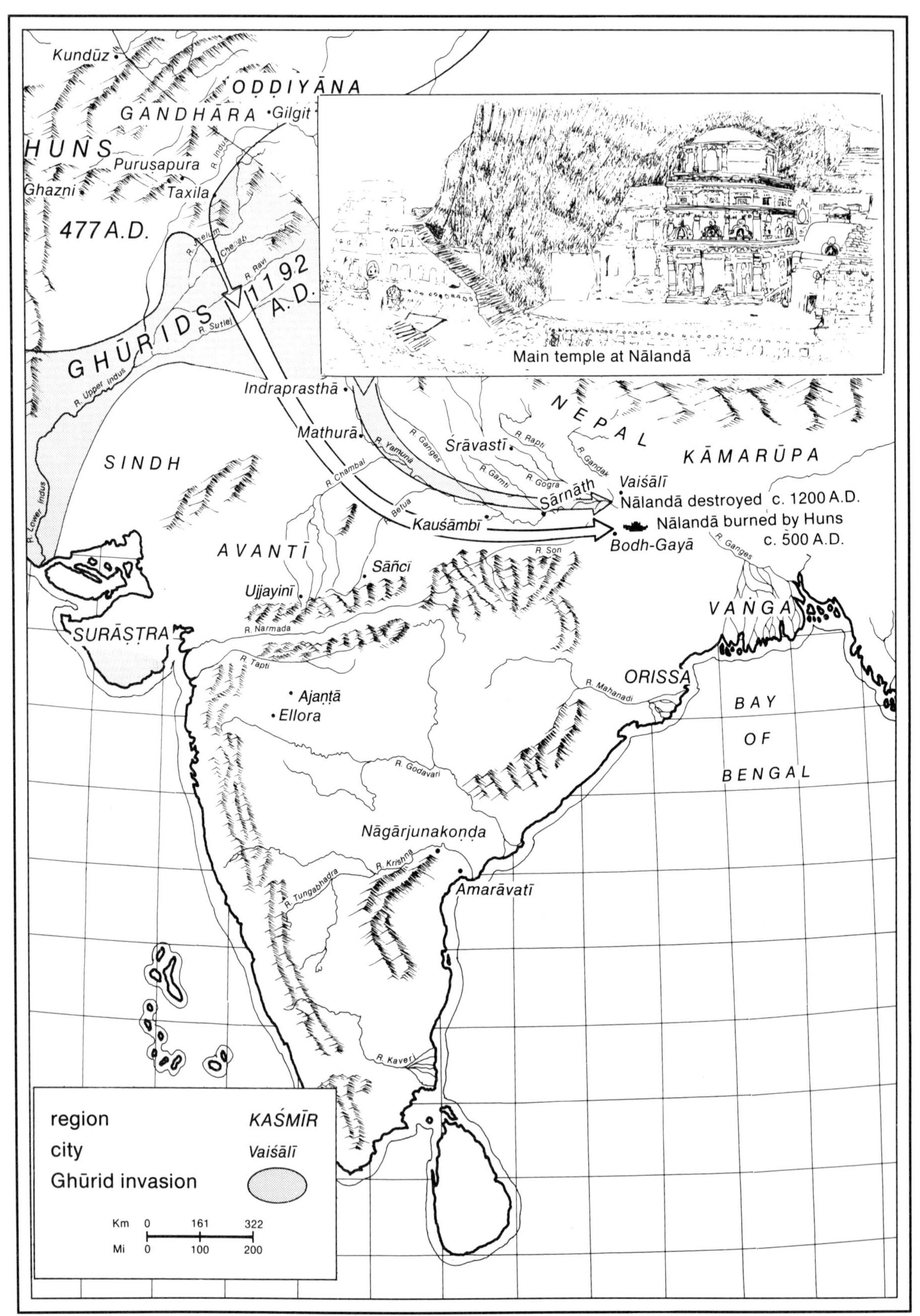

Invasions from the northwest twice destroyed the Nālandā University.

also unsuccessful. The region east and north of the Brahma-putra River remained free from foreign invaders.

Dispersion of Buddhists from India

Many of the paṇḍitas who survived these raids followed Ratnarakṣita to Nepal where they became part of a resurgence of Buddhist studies in that country. Jñānākaragupta, accompanied by a hundred other paṇḍitas, went southwest, and Buddhaśrīmitra and Vajraśrī fled with many other scholars far to the south. Still others went to East Bengal, Kāmarūpa, and Prajyotiṣya (modern Bangladesh and Assam).

In Tāranātha's short summary of Buddhism in Eastern India, he defines the eastern lands as comprising the various sections of Bengal, Kāmarūpa, and parts of Assam. He mentions that there were Sanghas there from the time of Aśoka; all were Śrāvakas until the disciples of Vasubandhu propagated the Mahāyāna in some of these lands. For several centuries after, the number of Buddhist monks there was not very large, but after the time of Dharmapāla, the number of eastern monks rapidly increased.

When the Senas reigned, about half of the monks in Magadha were from Bengal. In Bengal itself, the Śrāvakas merged with the Mahāyāna traditions, while the Mantrayāna tradition, stimulated by the efforts of Abhayākaragupta, continued to gain momentum. Since many Buddhists from the Madhyadeśa sought refuge in the East, the Dharma continued to prosper in that region. King Śobhajāta is said to have established two hundred Dharma centers in the East; King Siṁhajati also supported the Dharma there. For some time, Indian masters from the East continued to visit Tibet, as did the paṇḍita Vanaratna, who came to Tibet in the mid-fifteenth century.

Buddhism may have continued in eastern India for some time. Madhusena, a Buddhist king, ruled in some part of eastern Bengal in 1289, and Buddhism appears to have sur-

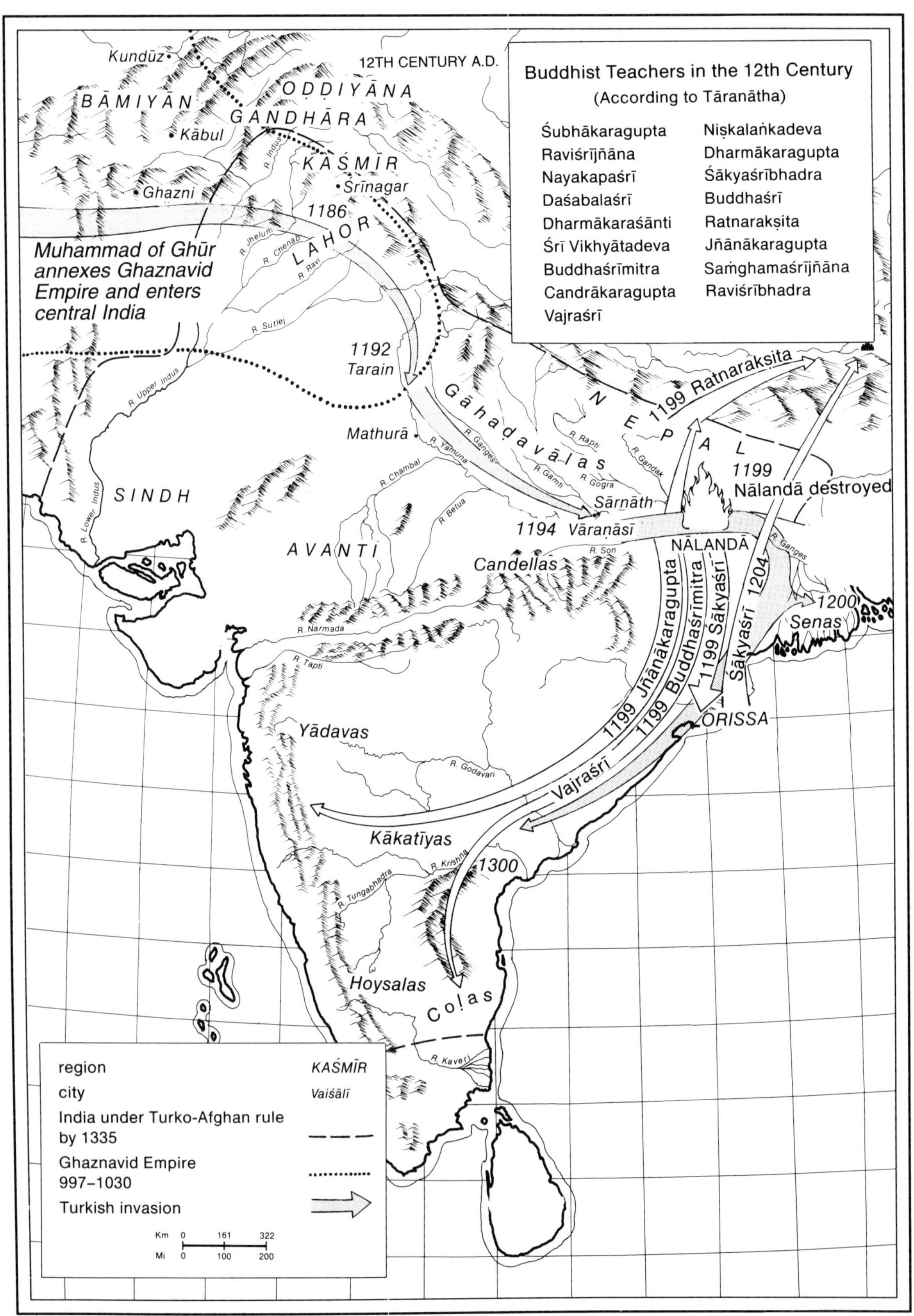

The last great Indian paṇḍitas sought refuge in Tibet and South India.

vived in the kingdom of Paṭṭikerā, which was located east of the Brahmaputra River on the border of Burma. The Paṇḍita Vihāra of Chittagong in Assam appears to have continued Dharma study and practice for centuries, and an ancient Buddhist lineage may have survived there to the present day. In the seventeenth century, the Tibetan pilgrim Buddhagupta Tathāgatanātha visited India and reported Buddhist activity not only in Bengal and Orissa, but also in Triliṅga, Vidyānagara, Karṇāṭaka, and other places in South India.

From Jagaddala to Tibet

The monastery of Jagaddala was the last refuge for paṇḍitas of the great universities. Śākyaśrībhadra, Vikramaśīla's last Upādhyāya, fled just before the Muslim invasion and went east to Jagaddala. There he met Vibhūticandra, master of grammar and Abhidharma, and the logician Dānaśīla, both of whom became his principal disciples. Three years later, in 1204, at the age of seventy-three, Śākyaśrī accepted the invitation of 'Byams-pa'i-dpal to come to Tibet. He left just as North Bengal fell to Muhammad Khaljī. Vibhūticandra and Dānaśīla accompanied him, as did other scholars from Vikramaśīla: Sugataśrī, learned in Mādhyamika and Prajñāpāramitā; Jayadatta, learned in Vinaya; Saṅghaśrī, master grammarian; Jīvagupta, versed in the five texts of Maitreya; Mahābodhi, authority on the Bodhicaryāvatāra; and Kālacandra, holder of the Kālacakra transmission lineage.

Some of these paṇḍitas had studied Tibetan while working with Tibetan disciples in India; now, led by Śākyaśrī, they applied their knowledge to translating all available Sanskrit texts into Tibetan. Dānaśīla, working alone, was able to translate more than fifty works into Tibetan. Most of these paṇḍitas appear to have spent the rest of their lives in Tibet. Śākyaśrī, although advanced in years, returned to Kashmir in 1214. Although the Blue Annals relates that the Dharma was then in full decline in Kashmir, the great paṇḍita converted the king to Buddhism, built monasteries, enlarged the Sangha, and revitalized the Buddhist scholarly traditions there before his death in 1225 at the age of ninety-seven.

Extinguishing the Light

The maelstrom of violence unleashed in India rebounded on the leaders responsible. Mu'izz-ud-dīn (Muhammad of Ghūr) was assassinated in 1206, the same year as Muhammad Khaljī was killed. Mu'izz-ud-din's Ghūrid Empire collapsed soon afterwards; his general, Aibak, consolidated the Ghūrid holdings in India from his control center at Lahore. But fierce struggles for power persisted between competing Muslim interests; the belated uprisings of Hindu princes added to the chaos. With the establishment of the Delhi Sultanate, nearly all of northern India came under Muslim rule, although fighting continued in some regions for generations. Only the areas with well-defined natural boundaries, such as Kashmir, Nepal, Assam, and Orissa, remained autonomous. Buddhist masters and practitioners who had sought refuge in these lands continued to practice and transmit the Dharma.

Late in the thirteenth century, internal dissension broke out in Kashmir; Muslims infiltrated the court, and an army invaded from the west. At this point the historical record concerning Buddhism in Kashmir fades while Śaivite and Muslim struggles for power come to the fore. Kashmiri paṇḍitas continued to enter Tibet and collaborate on translations until the time of Sumanaśrī, who worked with the scholar Bu-ston in the fourteenth century. But when Muslim rule was firmly established in the fifteenth century, Buddhism was completely repressed in Kashmir.

It is difficult to estimate how long Buddhism persisted in Orissa, Assam, and Eastern Bengal, or in what form. With the destruction of the monastic Sangha, the sacred texts, and the philosophical basis of the Bodhisattva lineages, it would have required unusual circumstances for practitioners of Buddhism to remain unaffected by other religions and social customs. There are indications that a Buddhist Sangha continued through the centuries in Chittagong, the southeastern tip of modern Bangladesh. In the eighteenth century, the Thera Saṃgarāja Sāramitta of Arakan came to Cattigrama, a town in the Chittagong district of modern Bangladesh and reformed the Buddhist community there.

The Significance of Loss

For sixteen centuries, the light of the Dharma shone forth from the Holy Land of the Madhyadeśa to illumine the entire South Asian subcontinent: the east, from Assam south to the Godāvarī River; the lands south of the Godāvarī and Narmadā rivers; the west, from Sāñcī to the western coast; north central India, from the Madhyadeśa to the Punjab; and the far northwestern lands of Gandhāra, Oḍḍiyāna, Bāmiyān, and Balkh, deep into modern Afghanistan. The light of the Dharma warmed all of Asia, countering the confusion, greed, and avarice of saṃsāra and easing suffering and conflict in the world. In a steady progression, Sanghas arose to transmit the light of the Buddha's teachings in Śrī Laṅka and Southeast Asia; in China, Korea, and Japan; and in Tibet, Mongolia, and the land of the Manchus.

For a time, Buddhist lands circled India like the outer rims of a great maṇḍala. But after the tenth century, the light of the Dharma dimmed in one after another region of India, flickered for a time, and then vanished. Finally, eighteen centuries after the Buddha walked the routes connecting the great cities of ancient India, the light was extinguished in the heartland of the Dharma. With the central jewel removed from the maṇḍala, the protective power of the Dharma was seriously diminished. Since that time the world has seen the steady acceleration of saṃsāric forces. Confusion, greed, and conflict at all levels of society are poisoning our lives and our environment, and activating a more enlightened view is becoming ever more difficult.

In the last hundred years, archaeologists and historians have brought to light an incredible array of temples, monasteries, and stūpas, together with a treasury of art works concealed or buried for hundreds of years. From the mountains of Afghanistan, honeycombed with meditation caves, to the coast of Andhra, dotted with mounds now revealed as temples and stūpas, monuments of the Dharma are emerging from obscurity to testify to the Dharma's strength and longevity in the land of its origin.

As appreciation of the Buddha, Dharma, and Sangha develops in the West, it is important to deeply consider the question of how and why the Dharma vanished from India, lest we invite the repetition of history and lose what remains of the Dharma in our time. Indian historians, querying the vulnerability of India to the Muslim invasions, have noted an enervating shift in cultural patterns that evolved between the tenth and twelfth centuries. Stratifications of caste were hardening, depriving many of a meaningful social participation; a revival of ancient brahmanic traditions heightened the warrior ethic, glorifying conflict and narrowing vision. Ritual directed to worldly success took a priority over spiritual enrichment and the quest for enlightened knowledge. The society turned inward; injunctions against caste pollution inhibited travel outside the borders of India, and the dangers increasing there went unheeded. Focused on personal glory, distracted by internecine conflicts, India's princes proved unable to protect themselves, their people, or their temples.[2]

These tendencies, diametrically opposed to the Buddha's teachings, created a difficult environment for the Dharma's survival. Constant warfare robbed education and the arts of its strongest supporters, and in time, rulers obsessed with worldly power withdrew their support from the Dharma, which did not glorify them or advance their purposes. As the Dharma declined, India's warrior families became ever more

---

2. *HCIP* V: 125–128.

embroiled. When the Muslim invaders destroyed Buddhist monuments and texts, forced mass conversions to Islam, and killed the monks and all who resisted conversion, Buddhism could not recover. The structure and values of society had changed, closing down the openness and flexibility of society that allows freedom and choice. Centuries later, conditions became more favorable. But by then, memory of the Dharma was lost; in the land of its birth, Buddhism had become a foreign religion.

Perhaps in the future scholars will present and evaluate all the conditions affecting the decline of the Dharma in India. Until a complete examination has been made from all possible perspectives, it is important to keep asking the question, delving ever more deeply into ways to protect against loss and keep open the path to enlightened knowledge.

Further Readings

Tāranātha. *History of Buddhism in India,* pp. 284–331.

Majumdar, R. C., ed. *The History and Culture of the Indian People.* Volume V, *The Struggle for Empire,* pp. 24–41; 398–427.

Chaudhury, Binayendra Nath. *Buddhist Centres in Ancient India,* pp. 194–219.

Mullik, C. C. *Nālandā Sculptures: Their Bearing on Indonesian Sculptures,* pp. 7–35.

Prasad, Ram Chandra. *Archaeology of Champā and Vikramaśīla,* pp. 80–90.

Bibliography

Abhayadatta. *Buddha's Lions: Lives of the Eighty-four Siddhas*, translated by James Robinson. Berkeley, CA: Dharma Publishing, 1979.

Adikaram, E. W. *Early History of Buddhism in Ceylon*. Migoda: Puswella, 1946.

Aśoka. *The Edicts of Aśoka*. Edited and translated by N. A. Nikam and Richard P. McKeon. Chicago: University Press, 1958.

Aśokāvadāna. *The Legend of King Aśoka. A Study and Translation of the Aśokāvadāna*, by J. Strong. Princeton, University Press, 1983.

Banerjee, Anukul Chandra. *Sarvāstivāda Literature*. Calcutta: The World Press Private Limited, 1979.

Barua, B. M. *Gayā and Buddhist Gayā: Early History of the Holy Land*. Calcutta: Chukervertty Chatterjee and Co., 1931.

Basham, A. L. *The Wonder That Was India: A Survey of the Culture of the Indian Sub-continent Before the Coming of the Muslims*. New York: Grove Press, 1959.

Beal, Samuel. *A Catena of Buddhist Scriptures from the Chinese*. London: Trübner & Co., 1871.

Bhadrakalpika-sūtra. *The Fortunate Aeon: How the Thousand Buddhas Become Enlightened.* Berkeley: Dharma Publishing, 1986.

Buddha-Dharma. New English edition. Berkeley: Numata Center for Translation and Research, 1984. Second edition, 1987.

Buddhaghosa. *The Path of Purification (Visuddhimagga)*, translated by Bhikkhu Ñāṇamoli. Second edition. Colombo: A. Semage, 1964.

Burrow, T. *The Sanskrit Language.* London: Faber and Faber, 1955.

Bu-ston Rinpoche. *History of Buddhism,* translated by E. Obermiller. Heidelberg: Institut für Buddhismuskunde, 1931. (Materialien zur Kunde des Buddhismus, 18)

Chaudhury, B. N. *Buddhist Centres in Ancient India.* Calcutta: Sanskrit College, 1969.

Crystal Mirror VI. Berkeley: Dharma Publishing, 1984.

Cunningham, Sir Alexander. *The Ancient Geography of India.* Vol. I: *The Buddhist Period.* London: Trübner, 1871. New enlarged edition; reprinted Varanasi: Indological Book House, 1975.

Cunningham, Sir Alexander. *Four Reports Made During the Years 1862–63–64–65.* Simla: Government Central Press, 1871. (Archaeological Survey of India)

Dagyab, Loden Sherap. "The Sixteen gNas-brtan," in *Tibetan Religious Art.* Part I: Texts. Wiesbaden: Otto Harrassowitz, 1977. (Asiatische Forschungen, 52:1)

Dikshit, Kashinath Narayan. *Excavations at Paharpur, Bengal.* Delhi: Manager of Publications. 1938. (Memoirs of the Archaeological Society of India, 55)

Dīpavaṁsa. *Chronicle of the Island of Ceylon,* translated by B. C. Law. Ceylon: Saman Press, 1959.

Dudjom Rinpoche. *The Nyingma School of Tibetan Buddhism: Its Fundamentals and History.* 2 volumes. Boston: Wisdom Publications, 1991.

Edgerton, Franklin. *Buddhist Hybrid Sanskrit Grammar and Dictionary.* 2 volumes. Reprint edition. Delhi: Motilal Banarsidass, 1972.

Elliot, Sir Henry Miers. *The History of India, As Told By Its Own Historians.* 8 volumes. Allahabad: Kitab, 1963–64.

'Gos lo-tsa-ba. *The Blue Annals,* translated by George N. Roerich. Second edition. Delhi: Motilal Banarsidass, 1976.

Grousset, René. *The Empire of the Steppes: a History of Central Asia,* translated from the French by Naomi Walford. New Brunswick, N.J.: Rutgers University Press, 1970.

Guenther, Herbert V. *Buddhist Philosophy in Theory and Practice.* Shambhala: Boulder, 1976.

HCIP. See Majumdar, R. C., ed. *History and Culture of the Indian People.*

Hirakawa, Akira. *A History of Indian Buddhism From Śākyamuni to Early Mahāyāna,* translated and edited by Paul Groner. Honolulu: University Press, 1990. (Asian Studies at Hawaii, 36).

Hsüan-tsang. *Si-Yu-Ki: Buddhist Records of the Western World,* translated by Samuel Beal. London: Trübner, 1884. Reprint, Delhi: Motilal Banarsidass, 1981.

Huntington, Susan L. and John C. Huntington. *The Art of Ancient India: Buddhist, Jain, Hindu.* New York: Weatherhill, 1985.

Hwui Li. *The Life of Hiuen-tsiang,* translated by Samuel Beal. Second edition. New Delhi: M. Manoharlal Publishers, 1973.

I-tsing. *A Record of the Buddhist Religion as Practised in India and the Malay Archipelago (A.D. 671–695),* translated by J. Takakusu. Delhi: M. Manoharlal, 1966. (first published Oxford, 1896)

Jātakatthavaṇanā. *Buddhist Birth Stories, or Jataka Tales,* translated by T. W. Rhys-Davids. Volume I. London: Trübner, 1880.

Lalitavistara. *The Voice of the Buddha: The Beauty of Compassion,* translated by Gwendolyn Bays. Berkeley: Dharma Publishing, 1983.

Lamotte, Étienne. *History of Buddhism from the Origins to the Śaka Era,* translated from the French by Sara Boin-Webb. Louvain: Peeters Press, 1988.

Law, Bimala Churn. *Kauśāmbī in Ancient Literature.* Delhi: Manager of Publications, 1939. (Memoirs of the Archaeological Survey of India, 60)

————. *The Life and Work of Buddhaghosa.* Delhi: Nag Publishers, 1923.

————. *Rājagṛha in Ancient Literature.* Delhi: Manager of Publications, 1938. (Memoirs of the Archaeological Survey of India, 58)

————. *Śrāvastī in Indian Literature.* Delhi: Manager of Publications, 1935. (Memoirs of the Archaeological Survey of India, 50)

Lineage of Diamond Light. Revised edition. Berkeley: Dharma Publishing, 1991. (Crystal Mirror Series, V)

The Mahāvaṁsa, or The Great Chronicle of Ceylon, translated by Wilhelm Geiger. First published 1912; reprinted Colombo: Ceylon Government Information Department, 1950. New Delhi: Asian Educational Services, 1986.

Mahāvastu, translated by J. J. Jones. London: Luzac, 1948–1956. (Sacred Books of the Buddhists, vols. 16, 18, 19)

The Mahāyāna Mahāparinirvāṇa-Sūtra, translated by Kosho Yamamoto. 3 vols. Ube City, Japan, 1973–1975. (Karin Buddhological Series, 5)

Majumdar, R. C., ed. *History and Culture of the Indian People.* Volume I, *The Vedic Age.* London: George Alwin & Unwin, 1951.

————. Volume II, *The Age of Imperial Unity.* Bombay: Bharatiya Vidya Bhavan, 1951.

————. Volume III, *The Classical Age.* Bombay: Bharatiya Vidya Bhavan, 1954.

————. Volume IV, *The Age of Imperial Kanauj.* Bombay: Bharatiya Vidya Bhavan, 1955.

————. Volume V, *The Struggle for Empire.* Bombay: Bharatiya Vidya Bhavan, 1957.

Marshall, John. *A Guide to Sanchi.* Calcutta: Superintendent Government Printing, 1918. Reprint ed., New Delhi: New Society Publications, 1980.

Marshall, John. *A Guide to Taxila.* Second edition. Calcutta: Superintendent of Government Printing, India, 1921. Reprint edition, Karachi, 1960.

Mizuno Kōgen. *The Beginnings of Buddhism,* translated by Richard L. Gage. Tokyo: Kōsei Publishing Co., 1980.

Mookerji, Radha Kumud. "The University of Nālandā," in *Journal of the Bihar Research Society* 30 (1944), pp. 126–159.

Mukherji, Purna Chandra. *A Report on a Tour of Exploration of the Antiquities of Kapilavastu, Tarai of Nepal, During February and March, 1899.* Delhi: Indological Book House, 1969.

Mullik, C. C. *Nalanda Sculptures: Their Bearing on Indonesian Sculptures.* Delhi: Pratibha Prakashan, 1991.

Nakamura Hajime. *Gotama Buddha.* Los Angeles: Buddhist Books International, 1977

Ñāṇamoli, Bhikkhu. *The Life of the Buddha as it Appears in the Pāli Canon.* Kandy: Buddhist Publication Society, 1972.

Naudou, Jean. *Buddhists of Kaśmīr,* translated by Brereton and Picron. First English edition. Delhi: Agam Kala Prakashan, 1980.

Paramārtha. "The Life of Vasu-bandhu," translated by J. Takakusu, in *T'oung Pao,* Serie II, vol. V (1904), pp. 269–466.

Pischel, Richard. *Comparative Grammar of the Prakrit Languages,* translated from the German by Subhadra Jha. Second edition. Delhi: Motilal Banarsidass, 1965.

Poussin, Louis de la Vallée. *The Buddhist Councils.* Calcutta: K. P. Bagchi, 1976.

Prajñāpāramitā. *The Large Sutra on Perfect Wisdom, with the Divisions of the Abhisamayālaṅkāra,* translated by Edward Conze. Berkeley: University of California Press, 1975.

Prasad, Ram Chandra. *Archaeology of Champā and Vikramaśīla.* Delhi: Ramanand Vidya Bhawan, 1987.

Puri, B.N. "Central Asia and its Peoples' Role in Ancient Indian History," in *Prolegomena to the Sources of the History of Pre-Islamic Central Asia,* edited by J. Harmatta, pp. 181–186. Budapest: Akadémiai Kiado. 1979.

Raychaudhuri, Hemchandra. *Political History of Ancient India from the Accession of Parikshit to the Extinction of the Gupta Dynasty.* Calcutta: University of Calcutta, 1921.

Rockhill, W. Woodville. *The Life of the Buddha and the Early History of His Order, derived from Tibetan works in the bKah-hgyur and bsTan-hgyur.* London: Kegan Paul, Trench, Trübner & Co., 1884.

Saddhamma-saṁgaha. *A Manual of Buddhist Historical Traditions*, translated by Bimala Churn Law. Delhi: Bharatiya Publishing House, 1980.

Santideva. *Entering the Path of Enlightenment (Bodhicaryāvatāra)*, translated by Marion L. Matics. New York: Macmillan, 1970.

————. *A Guide to the Bodhisattva's Way of Life (Bodhicaryāvatāra)*, translated by Stephen Batchelor and Sherpa Tulku. Dharamsala: Library of Tibetan Works and Archives, 1979.

Sankhalia, Hasmukh D. *The University of Nālandā*. Madras: G. Paul and Co., 1934.

Tāranātha. *History of Buddhism in India*, translated by Lama Chimpa and Alaka Chattopadyaya. Simla: Indian Institute of Advanced Study, 1970.

Thomas, E. J. *The Life of Buddha as Legend and History*. London, Routledge & Kegan Paul, 1927. Third edition. (revised) 1949.

Upasak, C. S. *History of Buddhism in Afghanistan*. Sarnath: Central Institute of Higher Tibetan Studies, 1990.

Vasubandhu. *Abhidharmakośabhāṣyam*, translated from the French translation of Louis de la Vallé Poussin by Leo M. Pruden. Berkeley: Asian Humanities Press, 1988–1990.

Vinaya Texts, translated from Pāli by T. W. Rhys-Davids and Hermann Oldenberg. 3 volumes. Oxford: University Press, 1885.

Warder, A. K. *Indian Buddhism*. Second revised edition. Delhi: Motilal Banarsidass, 1980.

Webb, Russell. *An Analysis of the Pāli Canon*. Kandy: Buddhist Publications Society, 1980.

Index

home of the Mahāyāna, 302–303

name and form, 68

Nandā, 80

Nanda, Arhat, 299, 300

Nanda, cousin of the Buddha, 100

Nanda, Yogācāra master, 303

Nandabalā, 80

Nandagarbhāvakrānti-nirdeśa-sūtra, 100

Nandapravrajya-sūtra, 100

Nandin, 177

Nandivardhana, 35

Narada, 373

Naradatta, 48

Narasiṁhagupta, 333

Nārāyanapāla, Pāla king, 392

Narmadā River, 212

Nāropa, 394, 396

Nāsik, 241, 243
    caves, 211. *See also* caves

Naṭa, 170, 173, 183

Naṭabhāṇṭika, monastery, 170

Natika, 104

Neyapāla, 396, 397, 398

nidāna, form of the Buddha's teaching, 142

Nidāna-kathā, 39, 82

nidānas, twelve links of pratītyasamutpada, 66–68

Nigrodha, 96

Nikāyabheda-vibhaṅga-vyākhyāna, 229

Nirmāṇaratis, devas, 12

nirvāṇa, 63, 64, 73, 121, 166

gNubs-chen Sangs-rgyas-ye-shes, 387, 388

Nūpura, 25, 26

Nyagrodha. *See* Banyan Grove Brahmin, 147

vihāra, 106

gNyags Jñānakumāra, 388

Nyāyabindu, 347

Nyāyamukha, 345

rNying-ma, 390

O-rgyan-pa, 390

Odantapurī, 371, 373, 375, 385, 390, 392, 399, 402, 404, 405

Oḍḍiyāna, 136, 203, 204, 237, 322, 368, 385, 387, 390, 396

old age, 68

oral tradition of Buddhism, 165

Orissa, 29, 327, 410

Ou-k'ong, 383

Pacores, 214

Padma, Brahmin, 56

Padmasambhava, Guru, 352, 373, 385, 387, 388

Paiśācī, 249

pairs, miracle of, 105

Paithana, city, 93

Pakṣu River, 126

dPal-brtsegs, 388

Pāla art, 372

Pāla Empire, 368, 392, 397

Pāla kings, 368–370, 371–372, 374, 387, 391, 402

Pālaka, King, 35

Pāli, 246, 249

Pāli Canon, 262, 263–264

Pañcāla
    kingdom of, 28, 33,
    language, 249

Pañcappakaraṇa-aṭṭhakathā, 265

Pañcaskandha-prakaraṇa, 327

Pañcaśṛṅga, King, 313

Pāṇḍava, Mt., 57

Sita-Cintāmaṇi Mahākāla

Tarthang Tulku

*About Tarthang Tulku: A Note from
the Staff of Dharma Publishing*

The general editor for the *Crystal Mirror Series* is Tarthang Tulku, an accomplished Tibetan lama who has made his home in the United States for the past twenty-three years. Since his arrival in India in 1959, Rinpoche has worked with complete dedication for the transmission of the Dharma. As his students, we have learned to find inspiration in his tireless devotion and profound respect for the Dharma.

For seven years while he was living in India, Rinpoche taught at Sanskrit University in Varanasi, establishing an international reputation as a scholar. During this time he founded Dharma Mudranalaya and began publishing texts from the Tibetan Buddhist tradition. He has continued this work in America for over twenty years. Today books by Dharma Publishing, including a number of translations of important Buddhist texts, have been adopted for use in more than five hundred colleges and universities throughout the world.

In addition to his work as a scholar and publisher, Rinpoche has been active as an author and educator. He has written nine books presenting teachings for the modern world, produced two translations, and served as editor of the Nyingma Edition of the Tibetan Buddhist Canon, the Research Catalogue of the Nyingma Edition, and the Guide to the Nyingma Edition. He is founder and president of the Nyingma Institute in Berkeley and its affiliated centers, where several thousand students have come in contact with the Dharma.

In the midst of all these activities, Rinpoche has also found time to serve in the traditional role of teacher for a growing community of Western students. Always willing to experiment, he has established a form of practice for his students in which their work on behalf of the Dharma becomes a path to realization. Many of his students do not have frequent direct contact with Rinpoche, but through the institutions he has established, they are able to grow in wisdom and understanding, while developing practical skills that enable them to make their way in the world. Above all, Rinpoche has devoted much of his energy to the creation of Odiyan, a country center that he hopes will one day change the basis for Dharma practice in the West.

Because of the incredible range of activities in which Rinpoche engages during a single day, it has not been possible for him to verify the accuracy of every element of the books we have produced under his direction. As a result, there may be mistakes in some of the material presented here, for which we take full responsibility. We only hope that on balance we have been successful in transmitting some elements of the Dharma tradition.

Those of us who have had the opportunity to work under Rinpoche in the production of Dharma Publishing books are deeply grateful for the example he has set us. His dedication and reliable knowledge, his steady, untiring efforts, his competence, and his caring allow us to direct our energy with complete confidence that despite our own imperfections, our work can be of benefit to others.